Archaeology of the Solomon Islands

Archaeology of the Solomon Islands

Richard Walter & Peter Sheppard

Otago University Press

Published by Otago University Press
Level 1, 398 Cumberland Street
Dunedin, New Zealand
university.press@otago.ac.nz
www.otago.ac.nz/press

First published 2017

Copyright © Richard Walter and Peter Sheppard

The moral rights of the authors have been asserted

ISBN 978-0-947522-53-7

A catalogue record for this book is available from the National Library of New Zealand. This book is copyright. Except for the purpose of fair review, no part may be stored or transmitted in any form or by any means, electronic or mechanical, including recording or storage in any information retrieval system, without permission in writing from the publishers. No reproduction may be made, whether by photocopying or by any other means, unless a licence has been obtained from the publisher.

Editor: Gillian Tewsley
Design and typesetting: Jane Connor
Index: Diane Lowther

Cover photo: Somboro and Alevangana, Roviana, New Georgia, Solomon Islands (photo by Hamish Macdonald).

Printed in China by Asia Pacific Offset

Contents

Preface 7

Abbreviations 10

1. Background to the study of Solomon Islands archaeology and prehistory 11

2. Cultural geography of the Solomon Islands 16

3. A short history of archaeology in the Solomon Islands 29

4. The Pleistocene and mid-Holocene record 36

5. The Austronesian expansion 53

6. The last 2000 years 90

7. Regional prehistory in the Western Solomons: Process and history 131

8. Conclusion 163

References 168

Index 182

Preface

The two authors of *Archaeology of the Solomon Islands*, Richard Walter and Peter Sheppard, came to work in the Solomon Islands via different routes, but in both cases ultimately through the influence of their colleague and friend Roger Green. In the 1980s Richard was studying archaeology at the University of Auckland where Green was teaching, and his decision to specialise in Pacific archaeology was strongly influenced by Green's lectures and anecdotes on fieldwork in the Reef Islands and Santa Cruz. And in 1988, when Richard was living in the Cook Islands and carrying out his PhD field research on the island of Ma`uke under Green's supervision, Peter was hired by Green as a postdoctoral fellow at the University of Auckland; his role was to conduct lithic analysis and sourcing of material from Green's Reef Island and Santa Cruz Lapita sites. Soon after Peter arrived in Auckland, fresh from fieldwork in Jordan and Portugal and knowing virtually nothing about the Pacific, Green sent him off to the Solomon Islands to look for chert sources on Malaita. That survey along the coastline from Auki to Buma – facilitated by the director of the Solomon Islands National Museum, Lawrence Foana`ota, and Maria Lane, a VSA worker at the museum – quickly demonstrated that chert was ubiquitous in Malaita and the notion of 'a source' was not particularly useful.

Peter later took a quick tour of the Western Solomons during which he met Kenneth Roga, then cultural affairs officer for the Western Solomons and based at Ghizo. Roga showed him a box of potsherds that included material recovered from an intertidal site in Roviana Lagoon, most probably the Panaivili site reported by Reeve (1989); and to Peter's untrained eye these appeared to have some Lapita affinity. In 1995 he returned to the Solomons and toured Roviana Lagoon with Roga, meeting with chiefs and obtaining permission for fieldwork. This resulted in a permit, issued by the Ministry of Education, to conduct archaeological research – possibly the first permit issued by the independent Solomon Islands for such research. In January 1996 Peter returned with a new PhD student, Matthew Felgate; accompanied by Roga and John Keopo, chief archaeologist at the National Museum, they began to survey and map archaeological sites along the barrier islands and to look for intertidal sites. This initiated the New Georgia Archaeological Survey (NGAS) programme, which was proposed to be for three years. Little did they know that the distinctive tidal conditions in Roviana in January (Felgate 2003:279) were especially poor for that task. In frustration with their continued failure to find any ceramics, Roga finally crawled around under their house at Sasavele and, after much searching, discovered the first sherd, an almost microscopic fragment, which suggested the presence of a site nearby. In subsequent fieldwork conducted by Felgate in mid-year, they found an intertidal site (Miho) 100 m from their house at Sasavele Point.

After returning to New Zealand in 1989 and completing his PhD, Richard continued his research in the Cook Islands. He invited Peter to join him in a stone-tool sourcing and exchange programme during which they carried out extensive geological and archaeological sampling throughout the Southern Cook group. This work resulted in a series of papers on East Polynesian exchange and is still generating publications. When Peter commenced the NGAS programme in 1996 he invited Richard to join the programme in order to broaden the available expertise and to benefit from Richard's Pacific experience. In 1997 they were successful in obtaining a two-year Marsden grant (UOA-SOC-0014 Adaptation and Cultural Diversity: The Prehistory of Human Settlement in Roviana Lagoon) from the Royal Society of New Zealand, along with National Geographic funding (3453033 Adaptation and Diversity: The Prehistory and Environmental History of Roviana Lagoon, Western Solomons) in 1998 and additional funding for the project from the University of Auckland and University of Otago. These grants included support for MA and PhD students working on the programme (Takuya Nagaoka MA, PhD; Matthew Felgate PhD; Tim Thomas PhD). In 1997 Peter was also awarded funding for a two-year postdoctoral fellowship to conduct research into oral tradition and material culture in Roviana. This research was carried out by social anthropologist Shankar Aswani, who had obtained his PhD on the study of Roviana marine tenure and was a fluent Roviana speaker. The Marsden grant included funds to study environmental change in Roviana through palynology. John Dodson, then at the University of Western Australia, and his PhD student Sarah Grimes joined the research team in 1998 and collected cores from Roviana and Rendova; the analysis subsequently appeared in Grimes' PhD thesis (Grimes, 2003).

The NGAS survey ended in 1999 and, in 2000, Richard and Peter decided to move operations further west to Ghizo and Ranongga and ultimately to Vella Lavella. Fieldwork at this time was made difficult by the fighting between militias in Guadalcanal, which had essentially isolated the airport and Honiara from the rest of the island. Unfortunately, fear in the Western Solomons of incursions by militia from that fighting had resulted in the development of local armed militias, including one that drew in experienced recruits from South Bougainville. Fighting among the militias of the Western Province resulted in some deaths and displacements in 2000. Despite the tense situation in the capital and regional centres, Richard and Peter carried on with the fieldwork by moving quickly through the capital and townships and basing themselves in remote villages. With a new Marsden grant in 2004 (03-UOA-086 Archaeology and Culture History of Vella Lavella) and with a general cessation of hostilities, they were again able to mount a major research project on Vella Lavella, focused on the regions around the villages of Maravari in southwest Vella and Irigila in the northeast. Once more they were joined by their Solomon Island colleagues Kenneth Roga (by then a member of the Western Province provincial government),

and Lawrence Kiko and Lawrence Foana'ota from the National Museum. The major goal of this research, aside from creating a first culture history for the island, was to develop the means to compare the archaeology and culture history of this island of non-Austronesian speakers with that of the Austronesian speakers of Roviana. This Marsden grant included funding for a social anthropology PhD student, Sarah Krose (2016) – who was based at Maravari and studied 'social entanglements of people, land and ancestors' – as well as funding for more palynology research with John Dodson and a PhD student. Although cores were collected throughout Vella Lavella and Ghizo, they have yet to be analysed. One MA thesis on the late prehistory of Vella was completed by Ann McKenzie (2006).

After the Vella Lavella project ended in 2006 Richard and Peter began to work separately within the Solomons, but always with close communication and mutual support. Peter returned to Roviana in 2007 to survey the relationship of intertidal sites to old beach lines in an effort to understand the history of sea-level change in the lagoon (Sheppard & Walter, 2009). He then shifted his attention to the Eastern Solomons and, with John Keopo, obtained permissions (2009) and a permit to conduct some limited fieldwork on Santa Ana in 2010. Unfortunately, this work was curtailed by land disputes. In 2010 Peter, along with John Keopo and Scarlett Chiu (Academia Sinica, Taiwan), travelled further east to Nanggu village on the south coast of Santa Cruz, to seek permissions to re-excavate at the SE-SZ-8 Lapita site that Green had excavated in the early 1970s. With permissions from the provincial and national government in hand, and after considerable delays and logistical problems, this work went ahead in 2012 when Peter, Richard, Chiu and Keopo were joined by MA student Carly Mailhot. That work has enabled more accurate dating of this site and contributed to a better understanding of the date of initial settlement of Remote Oceania (Sheppard, Chiu & Walter, 2015).

From 2005 Richard has been working on village-based cultural heritage conservation programmes in various parts of the Solomon Islands. In partnership with The Nature Conservancy and local NGOs, he has run heritage workshops with a focus on the weather coast of Guadalcanal, Santa Isabel, Choiseul and the Arnavon Islands in Manning Strait. The work aims to link archaeological site conservation with biodiversity conservation initiatives. It has also supported new research programmes, including site surveys in south and north Santa Isabel and, more recently, excavation work on Sikopo in the Arnavon group. In 2015 Richard was joined by a new PhD student, Charles Radclyffe, who is currently carrying out reconnaissance survey and excavation programmes in northwest Santa Isabel and Choiseul and is continuing Richard's research into early ceramic sites in the Arnavons. Radclyffe is a Solomon Islander – the first to undertake a PhD in archaeology. After 28 years of Solomon Island research, Peter is again returning to his first interest – cherts – in a collaboration with Richard and Radclyffe on the chert sources of northwestern Santa Isabel.

In their various projects in the Solomon Islands Richard and Peter have been supported by many people at central government, provincial government and community levels, including the following individuals. At the Solomon Islands National Museum: Lawrence Foana`ota, Lawrence Kiko, John Keopa, Tony Heorake, Edna Belo and Grinta Ale`eke. In Roviana: chiefs John Roni and Solomon Roni, Joseph Kama, Nathan Kera, Naptili and Sally Tozaka, Gideon Rose, David Kera, Alex Lianga, Arthur Banilinga and Edumali Alepio. The field crew in Roviana included Hickie Riqeo, Joseph Riqeo, Humphry Riqeo, Janice Riqeo, Oswald Alesasa, Gaudry Kama, James Maena, Tona Zere, Kubu Alesasa, Maleie Omese and Bonikera Hickie.

In Vella Lavella the team was supported by chiefs and elders Rimu Baesovaki, James Baesovaki, Walter Semepitu, Milton Putaviri, Franklin Livian and John Menisia. Thompson Gevolo and Lulu Piqe Gevolo and families provided assistance and support.

The team acknowledges the support of Peter Waru, Joseph Warugutaia and Patrick Waura in Santa Ana; Ben Noah, Francis Naida and Ismael Menai Tanan in Santa Cruz; and Chief Leslie Miki, John Pita and the Arnavon Community Marine Conservation Area Management Committee in Santa Isabel.

Throughout the research Rhys Richards has provided advice and assistance to the crew, students and the two principal investigators. In New Zealand, the University of Auckland and University of Otago have supported the research and the work of Hamish Macdonald, Tim Mackrell, Briar Sefton and Rod Wallace. We are particularly indebted to Les O'Neill, who has illustrated our Solomon Island publications for 20 years now and who worked patiently through many revisions of the figures in this volume. Finally, we thank our referees and, in particular, Jim Specht, who generously provided detailed critiques as well as new data and interpretations.

Abbreviations

AMS	accelerator mass spectometry
AMT	Australian Mandated Territory
AN	Austronesian
asl	above sea level
BP	radiocarbon years before 1950
cal BP	calibrated age before 1950 AD
CRA	conventional radiocarbon age
NAN	non-Austronesian
NGAS	New Georgia Archaeological Survey
SESP	Southeast Solomon Island Culture History Project

1

Background to the study of Solomon Islands archaeology and prehistory

Introduction

The Solomon Islands occupy a pivotal position in Oceanic cultural history. Trending west to east between New Guinea and Vanuatu, the island chain lies across the boundary between Near and Remote Oceania, a biogeographic division that has had a profound influence on the course of Pacific exploration and settlement (Green, 1991a) (Figure 1.1). In Near Oceania the islands are mainly intervisible and have relatively diverse and abundant terrestrial and marine resources. Near Oceania was settled as early as 50,000 years ago as hunter–gatherer populations expanded across the deep ocean gap that separates island Southeast Asia from the Pleistocene continent of Sahul (Chapter 4) (O'Connell and Allen; 2013, Summerhayes et al., 2014:214–15) (Figure 1.2). These early arrivals were effective explorers and colonists who spread east along the coastlines and penetrated surprisingly high into the New Guinea highlands by at least 42,000 years ago (Summerhayes et al., 2010). The colonisation of Sahul involved a crossing of the Wallace Line – the biogeographic line that marks the separation between predominantly Asian organisms, including placental mammals, from the predominantly Australian organisms, including the marsupials, of island Southeast Asia and Australia.

Further to the east through New Guinea and into the islands of the Bismarck Archipelago and Northern Solomons there was a gradual decline in terrestrial biodiversity. This required minor responses in human subsistence practices, especially an increased reliance on reef-edge gathering.

It also precipitated the earliest known example of the deliberate human introduction of vertebrate fauna across water barriers – of cuscus or possum (*Phalanger orientalis*) into New Ireland and the bandicoot (*Echymipera kalubu*) into Manus – described as 'forest stocking' (Specht, 2005).

To the east of the main islands of the Solomons chain and across a major water gap of around 350 km, the islands of Remote Oceania are generally smaller, more distant from one another, and there is a marked decline in the abundance and diversity of flora and fauna and, as you move further east, a simplification of geology and associated industrial resources. The settlement of Remote Oceania required new sailing and navigation technologies, and new colonisation and subsistence strategies. The chain of islands making up the Main Solomons represented the limits of Pleistocene settlement of the Oceanic world; new technologies and subsistence practices were needed before further expansion could take place. This is normally associated with the appearance of Lapita groups, with their distinctive ceramic production, in the Solomon Islands sometime around 3000 cal BP.[1]

---

[1]. Conventions for reporting ages based on radiocarbon dates are as follows: cal BP indicates calibrated age before 1950 AD, and BP without cal–uncalibrated radiocarbon years before 1950. All reported calibrated ages are based on use of OxCal version 4.2 (Bronk Ramsey, 2013). Terrestrial dates are calibrated using the SHCal 14 curve unless indicated otherwise; marine shell dates are calibrated using Marine 13 with local reservoir corrections (delta R) as indicated; calibrated date ranges are reported as 95.4% HPD.

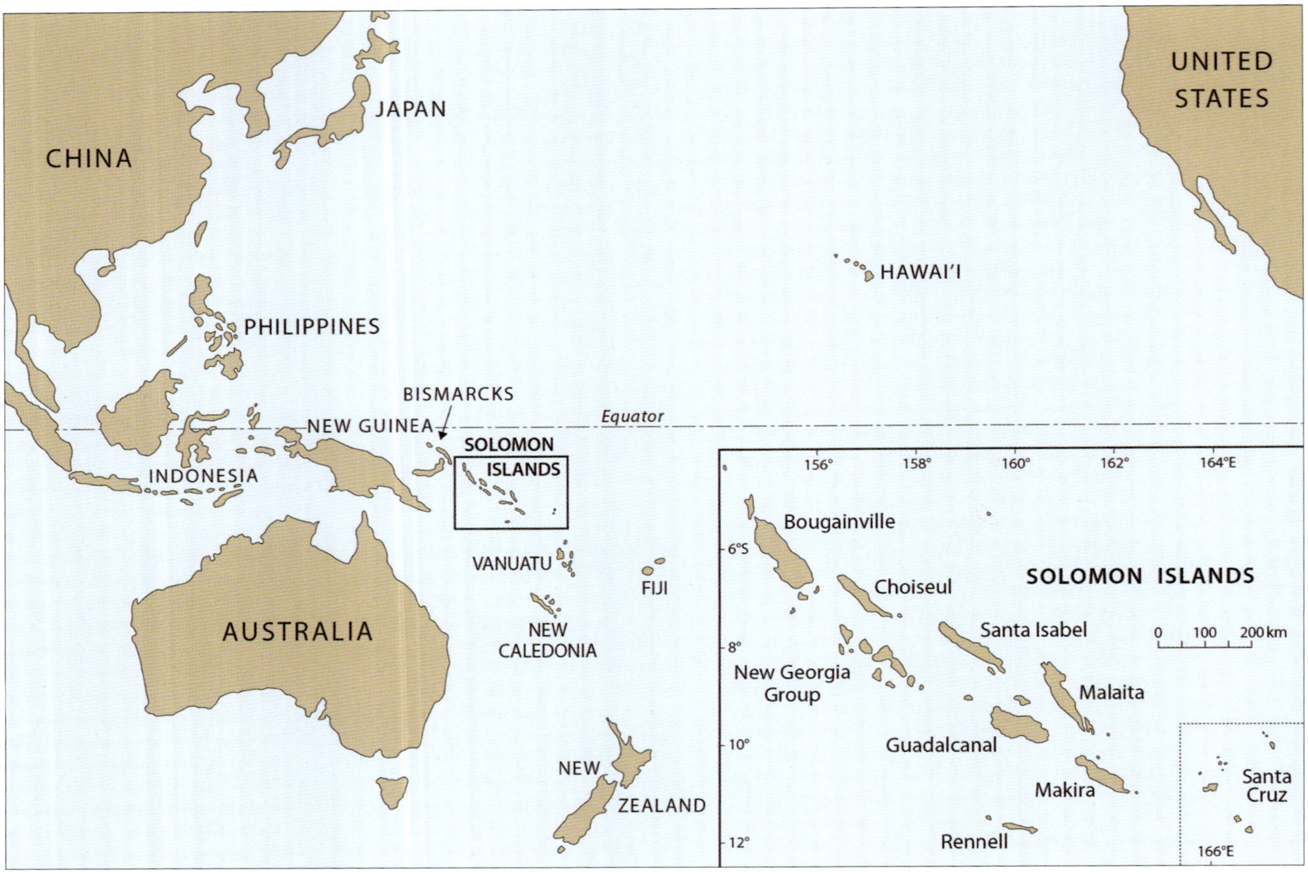

Figure 1.1. Location of the Solomon Islands in relation to the divisions between Near and Remote Oceania.

The major islands of the Solomon group consist of a double chain of intervisible islands stretching from Bougainville in the northwest to Makira (San Cristobal) and Santa Ana in the southeast (Figure 1.3). The northern chain of Choiseul, Santa Isabel, Malaita and Ulawa is separated from the southern chain of New Georgia, Guadalcanal and Makira by the Central Solomons Basin (or 'The Slot' as it was named in World War II). Bougainville is politically part of the Northern Solomons Province of Papua New Guinea but we include it, and adjacent Buka, in this review since the people of Bougainville and the Western Solomons have been interacting continuously for thousands of years and their prehistories are intimately connected. In fact, until late in the Pleistocene many of the larger islands of the Western and Central Solomon groups were joined with Bougainville to form a single landmass known as Greater Bukida or Greater Bougainville (Flannery, 1995).

The large islands of the Solomons chain are separated by relatively sheltered waters. Canoe travel between islands and island groups has always been comparatively easy and nineteenth-century accounts of canoe voyages of over 200 km are common (Bathgate, 1985). Archaeological, oral history and linguistic research clearly shows that

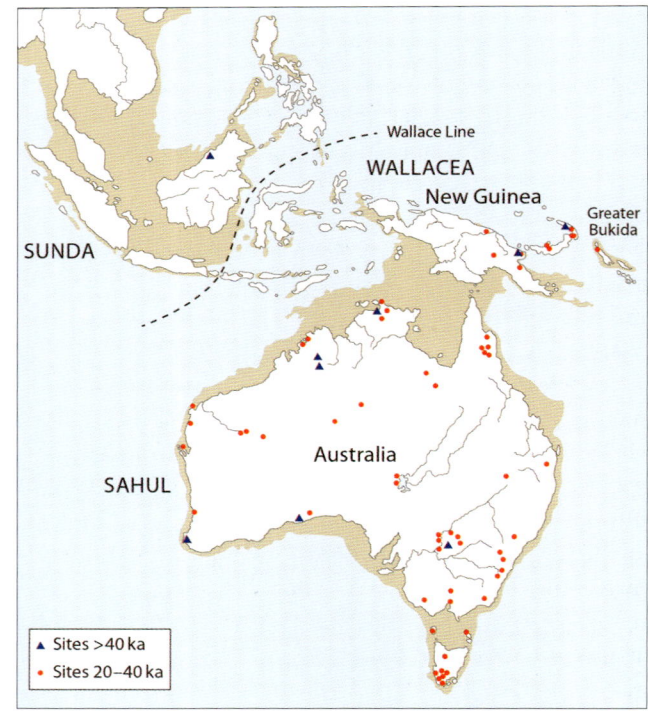

Figure 1.2. The Pleistocene landmasses of Sunda and Sahul (after White & Allen, 2013).

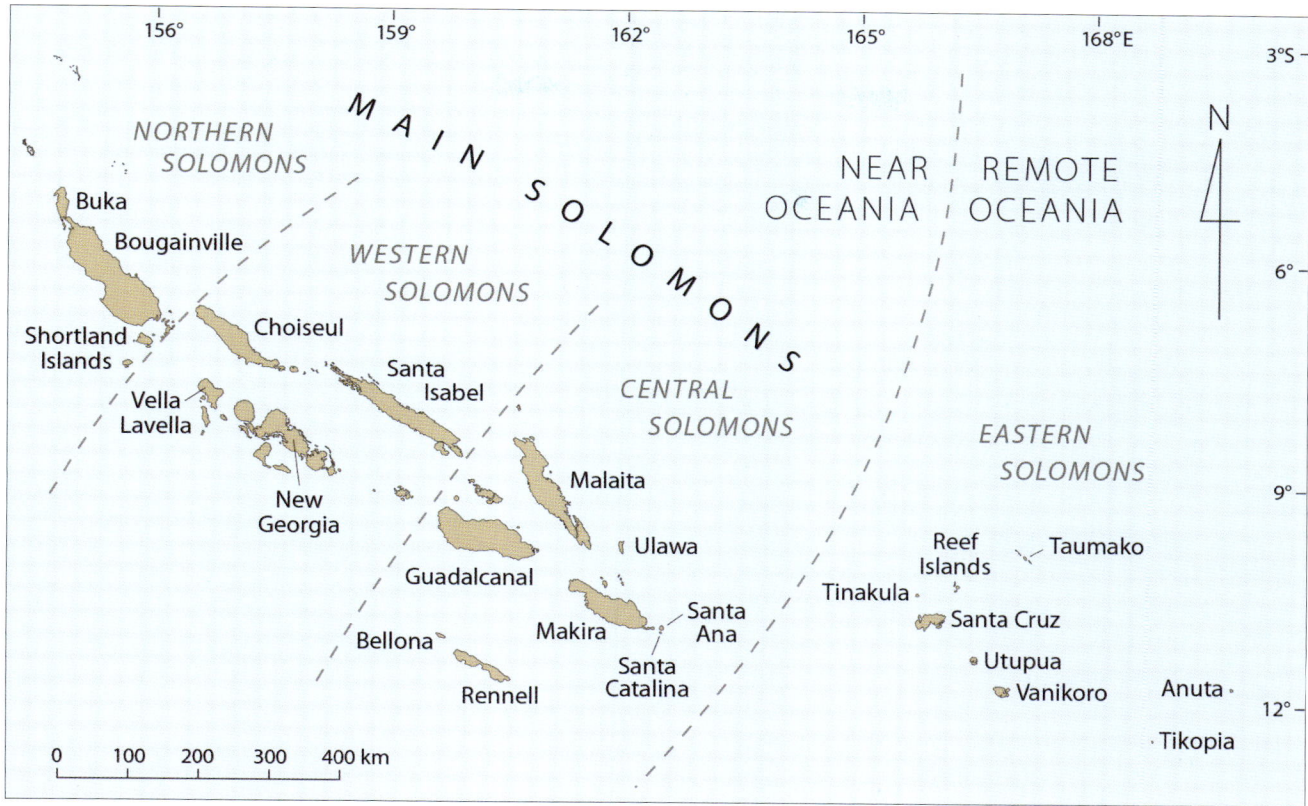

Figure 1.3. The Solomon Islands showing the geographic divisions used in the text.

for millennia Solomon Islanders have enjoyed high levels of interaction and, as a result, complex and often overlapping culture areas have formed. These are defined ethnographically and archaeologically by the patterned distribution of material culture traits, language, religion and other cultural practices. The ethnographic literature provides a rich source of information on the dynamics of social and economic interaction within and between these culture areas. The archaeological study of cultural and economic interaction through time is one of the most important aspects of anthropological research in this area (Walter & Sheppard, 2009).

In this work we have divided the Solomon Islands into regional units. These are not necessarily congruent with modern political provinces; indeed they cut across international boundaries. We first divide the Solomon Islands into two major divisions: the Main Solomons and Eastern Solomons. We further divide the Main Solomons into three divisions: Northern, Western, and Central Solomons. The highest level split is convenient in discussions of general cultural geography (Chapter 2) but for most purposes the archaeology and detailed culture history of the Solomon Islands is discussed in terms of four geographic units – Northern, Western, Central and Eastern Solomons (Figure 1.3) – based largely on spheres of cultural interaction that are ultimately founded on geographical proximity but that also reflect certain historical realities.

The Northern Solomons is made up of Buka, Bougainville and the Shortland Islands. Buka, which marks the northern end of island intervisibility in the Solomons, is separated from the island of Ambitle in the Bismarck Archipelago to the north by 145 km of open sea. The closer island of Nissan is a coral atoll, which was probably not above sea level during the Pleistocene (Spriggs, 1997:29).

The Western Solomons includes the islands of Santa Isabel, Choiseul and the New Georgia Group (New Georgia, Vangunu, Gatokae, Rendova, Kolombangara, Ghizo, Vella Lavella, Ranongga and Simbo). Our research suggests that Western Solomons prehistory has been somewhat distinct from that of neighbouring regions, although the boundary zones to the west (between the Shortlands, east Bougainville and west Choiseul) and the east (between eastern Santa Isabel and west Malaita) are blurred.

The Central Solomon Islands consists of Guadalcanal, Malaita, Ulawa, Makira, Santa Ana and Santa Catalina. These large and diverse islands are separated from the remote Eastern Solomons by a wide water gap which, even during the late Pleistocene low-water period, stretched over 300 km.

The Eastern Solomons is made up of the high volcanic island of Santa Cruz (Nendö) and the small, generally lower islands of the Reef Islands, the Duff (Taumako) Group, Vanikoro, Anuta and Tikopia. Some of the Eastern Solomons are structurally part of the Vanuatu Island arc, which runs on a north–south axis to the southeast (Taylor et al., 2005). This gap between the Main Solomons and the Eastern Solomons is the dividing line between Near and Remote Oceania (Green, 1991a).

The archaeology

Synthesising the Solomon Island archaeological record is a daunting task, given the chronological and geographic scale of the island group, and the diversity of cultures and traditions. The Solomon Islands comprise hundreds of inhabited islands totalling 28,500 square kilometres of land scattered over 1.3 million square kilometres of ocean. Some of these islands have been settled for nearly 30,000 years. Within this space there are a multitude of different ethnic and culture groups and at least 70 languages still spoken.

The purpose of this volume is to review the current state of archaeological knowledge and, building on a recent summary overview (Walter & Sheppard, 2009), develop an updated regional synthesis of Solomon Islands' prehistory. In doing this we focus on the vital role the Solomon Islands plays in addressing key questions on Pacific colonisation and cultural history. We note in particular the following issues.

Pleistocene colonisation of the Pacific

The first settlement of the Solomon Islands occurred around 30,000 years ago, during the Upper Pleistocene, with the establishment of rockshelter habitations on Buka Island in the Northern Solomons. These sites mark the known limit of the first phase of human expansion into the Pacific and provide a picture of subsistence adaptation and technology at the margins of the Pleistocene colonisation range.

Pre-Austronesian (Holocene) expansion and adaptation

The second colonisation event for which there is archaeological evidence in the Solomon Islands is the arrival of the Lapita peoples at around 3000 cal BP. This event occurred relatively late in the Holocene when there were already low-density populations of hunter–gatherers living along much of coastal Near Oceania and into the New Guinea highlands. Unfortunately the early to mid-Holocene record, before the appearance of the Lapita cultural complex, is currently poorly understood by archaeologists. The record from Guadalcanal and New Georgia contains important evidence, including data on palaeoenvironmental change and ephemeral archaeological deposits that attest to expansion along the lagoons and coastal plains of the Solomon Islands during the early to mid-Holocene periods.

The dispersal of early Lapita communities and their interaction with non-Lapita groups

Some of the earliest Lapita sites in Remote Oceania are located in the Eastern Solomon Islands, thousands of kilometres from the so-called Lapita homeland in the Bismarck Archipelago. The current record of Lapita sites in the Solomon Islands suggests an early movement from the Bismarck Archipelago direct to the Reef–Santa Cruz region, with a later eastward expansion from the same source area through the Western Solomons some 300 years later at around 2700 cal BP. This pattern has important implications in terms of Lapita colonisation or migration strategies, and the nature of the interaction between the expanding Lapita populations and earlier resident groups.

The evolution of late period Melanesian diversity

Today the Solomon Islands – indeed all of Near Oceania and much of western Remote Oceania – is characterised by enormous linguistic and cultural diversity. It is often assumed (e.g. Spriggs, 1997) that this diversity is of relatively recent origin; that it postdates Lapita and most likely has its origins in the last 1000 years. Although there is now some evidence that the origins of Melanesian cultural diversity predates Lapita (Gaffney et al., 2015), there was certainly a burst of cultural innovations over the last millennium. This period in Near Oceania has rarely been examined. However, recent work in the Western Province of the Solomon Islands, summarised here, provides insight into the emergence of highly localised material culture complexes, and the ideological structures and exchange systems associated with them.

Despite the strategic importance of the Solomon Islands to the study of the settlement of Remote Oceania, archaeologists have until recently had trouble developing more than a rudimentary account of Solomon Islands' prehistory (Green, 1977), and several authors have lamented the paucity of published material (Kirch, 1997, 2000; Spriggs, 1997, 2000b); indeed, the archipelago has been described as one of the least understood regions of the Pacific (Kirch, 2000:131). Some archaeologists believe there is a serious gap in knowledge due to insufficient archaeological sampling (Spriggs, 2010). We suggest, however, that this claim is misleading (Sheppard & Walter, 2006; Walter & Sheppard, 2009). We argue that a great deal of archaeology has been done over the last 50 years and that many parts of the record are well covered. There is excellent coverage of Lapita in the regions where it is best represented (in the Eastern Solomons) and there is now a substantial and rapidly growing body of data on the ceramic record from the Western Solomons. Long but discontinuous sequences have been proposed for the Shortlands, Buka, parts of the Western Solomons, the Reef–Santa Cruz Islands and some of the Polynesian Outliers. There is abundant primary material available in the form of graduate theses and unpublished reports; although to date there has been no real integration or synthesis of this material. In the following chapters we discuss the current state of archaeological knowledge and directly address some of the current regional research questions in the Solomon Islands.

The following chapter gives context to the archaeological interpretations by providing an overview of the physical and cultural geography and a discussion of the linguistic history of the Solomon Islands. Chapter 3 is a historical review of archaeological work that has been carried out over the last 50 years; it details the scope of regional archaeological coverage and the objectives and outcomes of the various research teams who have worked in the Solomon Islands.

Three chapters are organised around the major chronological divisions in the Solomon Island record: they deal with the archaeological interpretation and, specifically, with the research themes and issues pertinent to each of these phases. Chapter 4 discusses Pleistocene colonisation and the evidence for pre-Lapita occupation in the Holocene period. Chapter 5 looks at the evidence for the Austronesian expansion and, particularly, Lapita: here we defend our own model of Lapita colonisation and migration, based on the Solomon Island data. In Chapter 6 we explore the origins of traditional Solomon Island societies through a study of the archaeological record of the last 1000 years in the Northern and Eastern Solomons.

In Chapter 7 we look at the late prehistory of the Western Solomons and focus on a case study of the emergence of the Roviana Chiefdom, based on our work on the mainland and lagoons of New Georgia in the Western Province. Finally, in Chapter 8 we reflect on the Solomon Island record in relation to wider theoretical issues in Oceanic archaeology and prehistory.

2

Cultural geography of the Solomon Islands

Cultural and geographic background

Although the major islands of the Solomon group form an intervisible island chain and its people were historically highly mobile, easily paddling between islands in their canoes, this ease of interaction has resulted in only a very general level of cultural homogeneity. Indeed, the region is renowned for its extraordinary biological, linguistic and cultural diversity, reflecting geographical propinquity and a complex history of settlement and interaction, both peaceful and violent. What structure there is to the distribution of cultural traits seems to relate largely to how close communities are to one another (Terrell, 1970, 1977a, b). In a series of articles in the 1970s John Terrell developed a model of human geography of the Solomon Islands. Figure 2.1 is a nearest-neighbour analysis (adapted from Terrell, 1977b) that shows relationships among the islands of the Solomons as they exist today. Much of the structure present in this diagram is a result of shared linguistic and other cultural variables in the region.

At the largest scale it is possible to discuss the cultural geography of the Solomon Islands in terms of three zones or island groupings. The Main Solomons (encompassing the Northern, Western and Central Solomons) is one unit; the Eastern Solomons is a second unit (Figure 1.3). The third unit is made up of the Polynesian Outliers — small islands inhabited by Polynesian language speakers that lie at some distance offshore of the larger land masses (Bayard, 1976; Kirch, 1984). These include, along the northern and eastern margin of the Solomon Islands, the islands of Takuu, Nukumanu, Ontong Java, Sikaiana, Nupani, Nukapu, Pileni, Nifiloli, Matema, Taumako, Anuta and Tikopia; and, to the south of Guadalcanal, Rennell and Bellona (Figure 1.3). In fact, Takuu and Nukumanu are administratively part of Papua New Guinea but, as we noted with Bougainville, there are cultural and historical reasons to include them in our discussions of the Polynesian Outliers of the Solomon Islands.

Main Solomons

The Main Solomons includes all islands along the chain from Buka in the north to Santa Ana and Ulawa in the east, a direct distance of 1076 km. Along this band no island is more than 50 km from its closest neighbour – less than a day's paddle (Figure 1.3). Despite this chain of intervisibility, however, the long, linear nature of the group limits interaction between distant areas. Within the chain there are distinct groupings of islands separated by choke points of constrained linkages and increased nearest-neighbour distances, as seen in Figure 2.1.

There are few features that are common to all of the islands of the Main Solomons. Geographically, most of the islands are long and narrow with rugged, often mountainous interiors. The double chain of islands that stretches most of the length of the region was formed by a complex geological history of subduction and uplift along the boundary of the Australian and Pacific plates (Cowley et al., 2004). Although many of the islands are not wide there is a general tendency

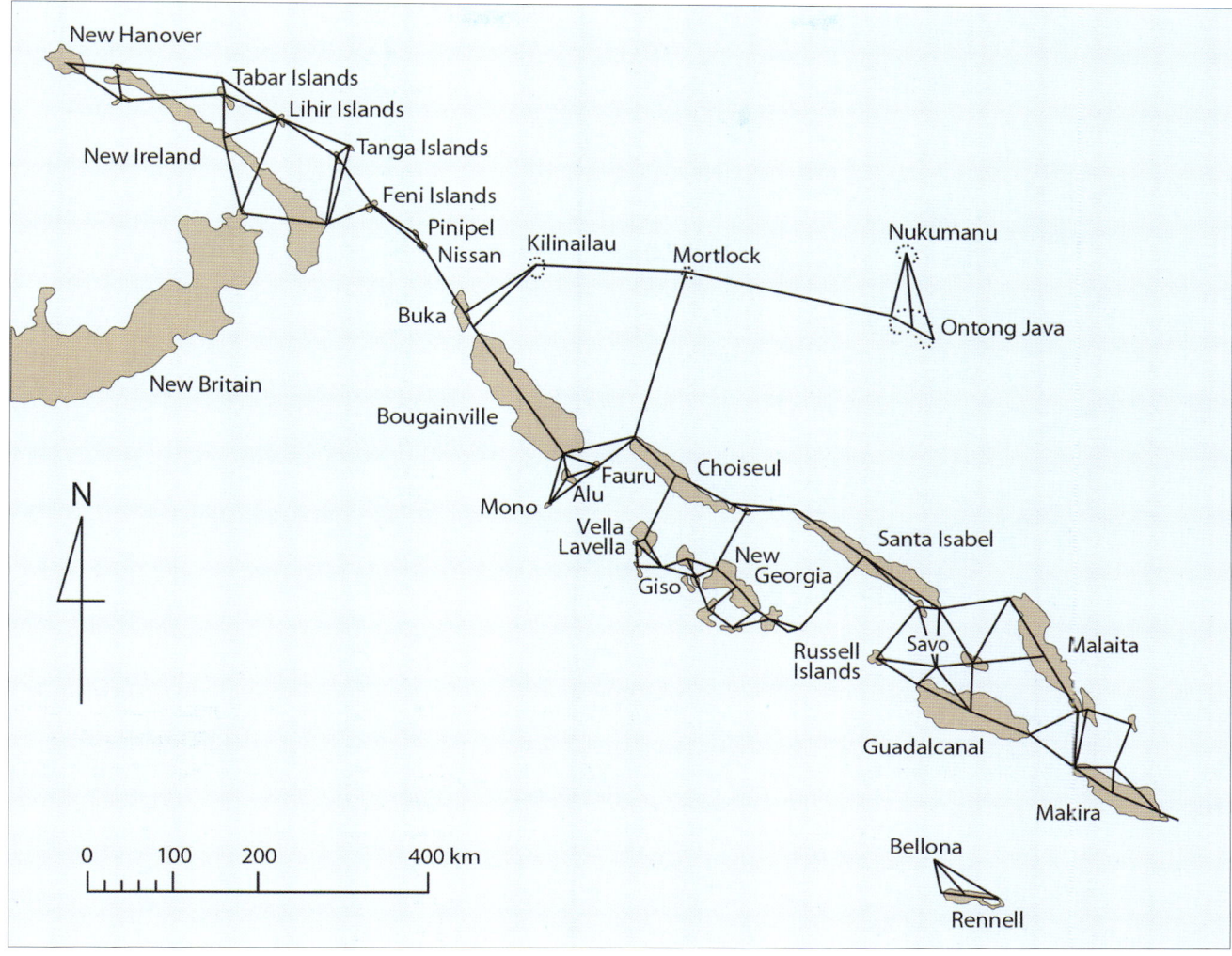

Figure 2.1. A model of connectivity in the Solomon Islands. Nearest-neighbour analysis (adapted from Terrell, 1977).

for a distinction to be made between coastal 'saltwater' and inland or 'bush' people (Roe, 2000). Before 1900 AD, inhabitants relied mainly on taro cultivation, supplemented in some parts of the region by tree crops such as various *Canarium* (Pacific almond) species. For the saltwater people, particularly in the Central and Eastern Solomons, bonito (*Katsuwonis pelamis*) fishing was of major importance (Ivens, 1927) – both for the bounteous returns from trolling through the very large schools that regularly appear off many coasts, and for the association of this activity with male prowess and a variety of ritual and social functions.

Fishing and coastal and interisland travel, of course, required watercraft. The large, light, plank-built paddled canoe with upturned bow and stern, in a variety of styles, was used to travel in the generally sheltered waters throughout the region (Haddon & Hornell, 1936: vol. II, fig. 56), along with a number of small and large canoes designed for specific tasks. Nowhere was the sailing canoe with outrigger common, as it was in much of Polynesia. The distribution of the plank canoe form extended to the north into New Ireland and Tanga; but beyond this in the Bismarck Archipelago, and in the Reef–Santa Cruz region, the outrigger canoe dominated (Haddon & Hornell, 1936: vol. II, 332–33). Although there are similarities in basic economy and fundamental technologies such as canoe design, other aspects of Solomons culture vary significantly. This pattern of geographical variation is best seen in language.

Tryon and Hackman (1983) reported 63 languages from the political Solomon Islands, of which five were languages of the Samoic-Outliers branch of the Polynesian language family, and seven were non-Austronesian (Papuan). The latter included some of the languages of the Reef–Santa Cruz region that are now classified as Austronesian (Ross & Næss, 2007). In the Northern Solomons (Buka and Bougainville) 20 languages are spoken, of which 12 are Austronesian

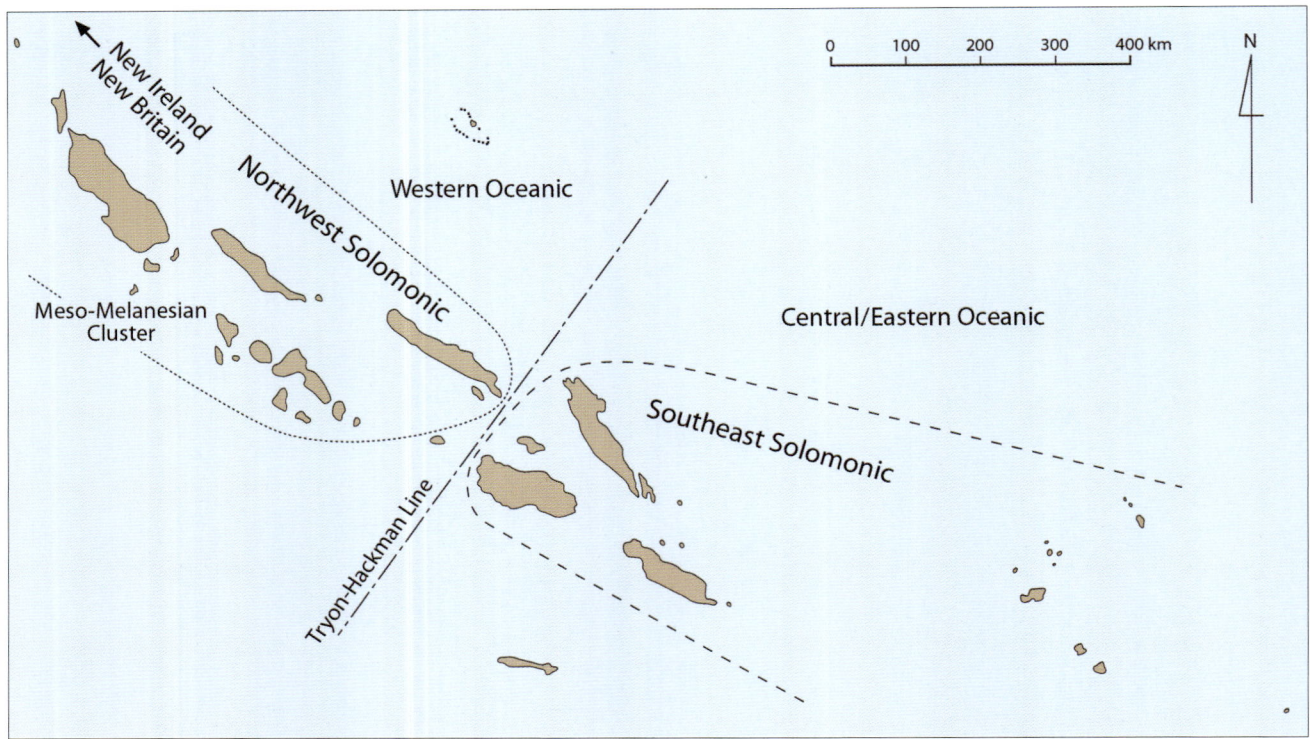

Figure 2.2. Distribution of the main branches of the Austronesian languages of the Solomon Islands showing the Tryon-Hackman Line.

(Terrell, 1977a). Therefore, in the Main Solomons there are at least 57 Austronesian and 14 non-Austronesian languages.

The non-Austronesian (NAN) languages of the Solomons are highly diverse and linguists have found it very difficult to classify them, although they have been loosely described as East Papuan (Ross, 2001). Recently Dunn et al. (2005) have used phylogenetic methods to reconstruct a phylogeny (family tree) that suggests a break-up of linguistic communities some 10,000 years ago. The notion of large-scale population breakup and dispersal at that time is also supported by a recent study of human DNA variation in the region (Delfin et al., 2012). The density of NAN languages decreases from west to east within the Solomons. Most NAN languages are spoken in the interior of Bougainville, three (or possibly two; Dunn and Ross (2007) have suggested only two of these are actually NAN) in the Western Solomons, and one each on the isolated islands of the Russell Group and on tiny Savo off the coast of Guadalcanal. Whether this fall-off reflects the original distribution of NAN languages in the Solomons is unknown. Pawley (2009) has argued that differences between Austronesian languages in the Western and Eastern Solomons may indicate considerably more interaction between Austronesian and NAN speakers in the west, which in turn implies differences in the distribution of NAN speakers.

All of the Austronesian languages of the Solomon Islands belong to the Oceanic family. Within the Main Solomons they are further subdivided into two major subgroups: Northwest Solomonic and Southeast Solomonic (Pawley, 2009; Ross, 1988) (Figures 2.2–2.4). The boundary between these two groups runs roughly north–south between Santa Isabel and Malaita; only Bugotu at the eastern tip of Santa Isabel belongs to Southeast Solomonic and represents an intrusion from the east in the last 1000 years (Pawley, 2009) (Figure 2.4).

The Southeast Solomonic group includes languages of Nggela, Guadalcanal, Malaita, Makira, Ulawa and Santa Ana–Santa Catalina. The Northwest Solomonic group includes all languages of the Western and Northern Solomons, including Nissan, which lies midway between Buka and New Ireland (but excluding Bugotu). This linguistic boundary, known as the Tryon-Hackman Line, marks a very real and practical division in the Solomon Islands (Figure 2.2). Today, people on either side of this line see much similarity in neighbouring language groups but very real differences across the boundary, and this inhibits communication. Pawley (2009) has also described the languages of Southeast Solomonic as very conservative, with low rates of divergence compared to the much more variable languages of the Northwest Solomonic type.

Further subdivision of these major linguistic groups appears to reflect geographical proximity and long-term

CULTURAL GEOGRAPHY OF THE SOLOMON ISLANDS

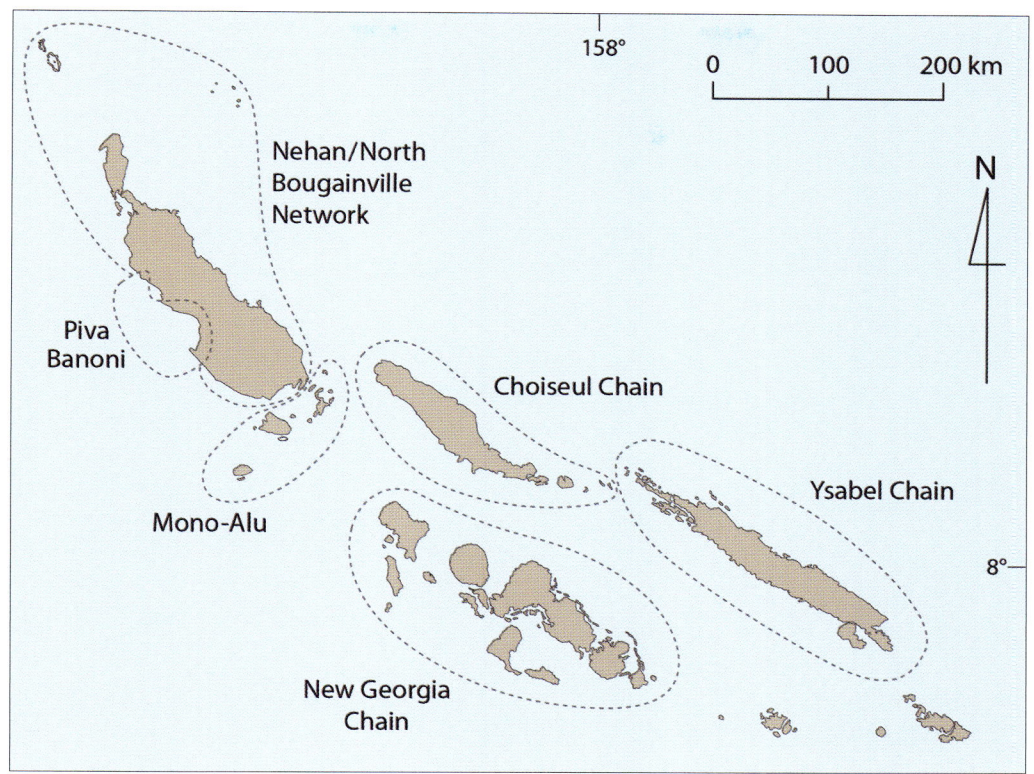

Figure 2.3. Distribution of the main language groups of Northwest Solomonic (after Ross, 1988).

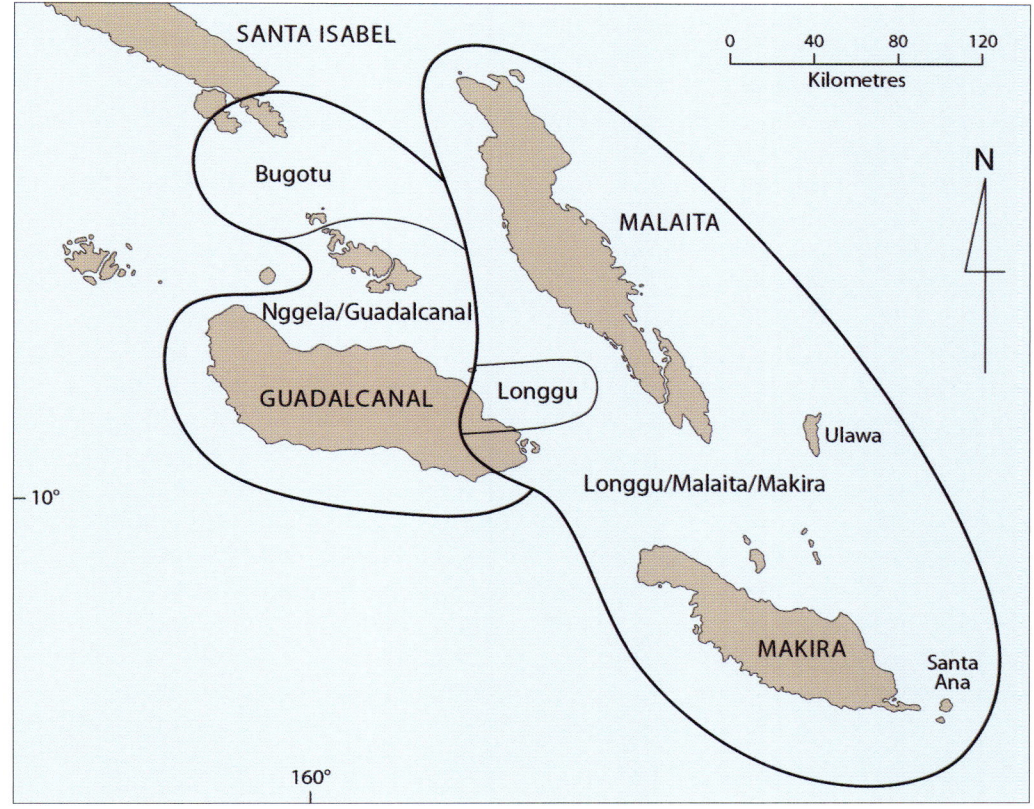

Figure 2.4. Distribution of the main language groups of Southeast Solomonic (after Lynch et al., 2002).

patterns of interaction. Southeast Solomonic languages can be divided into Makira–Malaitan, which includes the western end of Guadalcanal, and Guadalcanal–Nggelic, which includes Bugotu on Santa Isabel, Nggela and central and eastern Guadalcanal. Ross (1988) divides the Northwest Solomonic into five primary subgroups: Nissan–Buka–North Bougainville, west Bougainville (Piva–Banoni), South Bougainville–Shortlands, Choiseul and Santa Isabel–New Georgia Group. Pawley (2009) further separates Santa Isabel and the New Georgia Group: he argues that there is little evidence to unite them and any period of common development must have been brief. Scholars debate the origins of the major groupings. Ross (1988) argues that Northwest Solomonic was part of a Meso-Melanesian linkage or dialect chain that originated in the region centred on South New Ireland and stretched into the Bismarck Archipelago. Pawley (2009:524) suggests that the ancestral Northwest Solomonic languages arrived in the Western Solomons 'some centuries after the Proto-Oceanic break-up'. This is assumed to correlate with the initial spread of the Lapita culture. Recent studies of modern Solomon Island DNA conducted by Delfin et al. (2012: fig. 7) show strong associations between New Ireland and New Britain on the one hand, and between the Northern and Western Solomons on the other. The Tryon-Hackman division is not clearly marked in their data but there does appear to be a division, supported by study of HV1 sequences and YSTR haplotypes, that suggests limited movement of males across that boundary (Delfin et al., 2012:557). Pawley (2009:537 and n. 15) states that the origins of the Southeast Solomonic linguistic group are unclear but that they are separate from those of the Northwest Solomonic, and 'scraps of evidence' may reflect some tentative relationship to the languages of Remote Oceania.

The pattern of relationships proposed for languages largely matches the pattern of interaction as generated by Terrell's nearest-neighbour analysis (Figure 2.1). The network is most constricted at the eastern end of Santa Isabel and it is there that we might predict a break in the chain of interaction. In fact the separation between Isabel and Malaita/Nggela fits the Tryon-Hackman division and the subdivision of Southeast Solomonic from Northwest Solomonic.

Other cultural items, although they are not nearly as well studied or as easily comparable as languages, repeat the linguistic pattern. Deborah Waite (1969) has studied variation in sculpture and art styles across the Solomons and observed substantial patterning, particularly across the Tryon-Hackman Line.

This study has revealed the existence of sharp local distinctions and overriding continuities in the function and iconography of Solomons sculpture. Sculpture from the Eastern islands is distinguished from that of the Central [New Georgia Group, Santa Isabel, Choiseul] and Western [Bougainville, Buka] islands by a wealth of animal carvings, post sculpture, and decorated bowls. Much of the carving appeared in architectural contexts. The impulses governing the production of these objects stemmed largely from the cult of the shark and bonito and the related ceremonial rites.

The attention given to architectural and animal sculpture in the islands southeast of Ysabel was supplanted by canoe sculpture in the Central Solomons. At the same time, aquatic imagery was overshadowed by symbolism inspired by local headhunting practices and accompanying mortuary concepts. The use of shell-inlay ornament is a definite link between Eastern and Central Solomons sculpture. This black-and-white ornamental tradition did not extend west of the New Georgia islands and Choiseul.

The Western Solomon Islands, art-historically speaking, were a divided area. Carvings from Southern Bougainville and the Bougainville Straits Islands shared features with carving from the Central and Eastern Solomons (e.g. hocker figures and post sculpture, respectively), while carvings from central and northern Bougainville, Buka and off-shore islands such as Pororan belonged to another sphere. (Waite, 1969:171–72)

Another systematic study of Solomons material culture is that of compound fishhooks by Cummings (1973). These trolling hooks, used in bonito fishing throughout the Solomons, share a basic design, but individual attributes vary considerably. Although Cummings had a limited sample (N=61) based on the collections of the Chicago Field Museum and published descriptions, he was able to define a number of types that show geographical variations. Looking at specimens that were definitely attributed to an island (Cummings, 1973: Table 3), a specific form (Type A) was associated with the Buka Strait region; another (Type B) to the South Bougainville, Shortlands, New Georgia Group and Santa Isabel region (and a single sample attributed to Makira). Another two types (C and D) were attributed to the Santa Isabel, Nggela, Makira, Santa Ana–Santa Catalina region. One distinctive form (E) was confined to Malaita; and another (F), based on published examples, was confined to Ulawa and Makira. With the exception of the single B sample attributed to Makira and a few problematic Isabel samples there is once again a good split along the Tryon-Hackman Line and hints of the structure provided by linguistics.

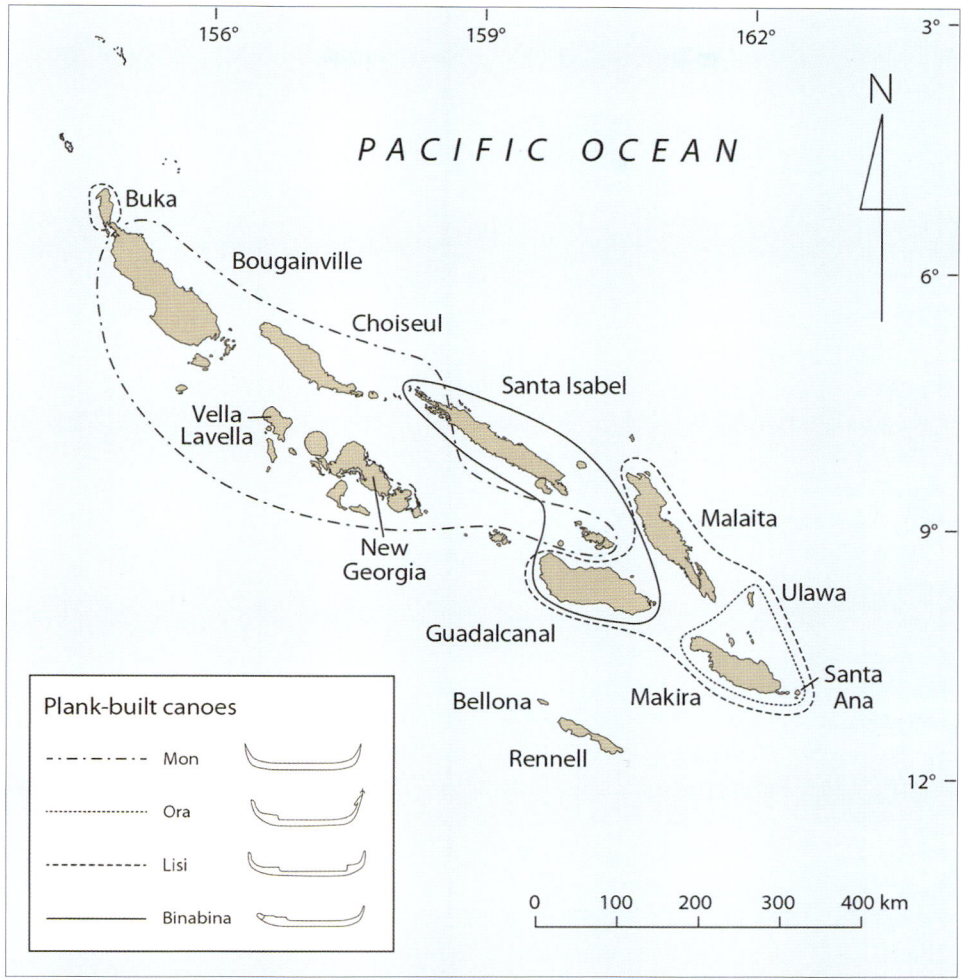

Figure 2.5. The distribution of plank-built canoes styles in the Solomon Islands (from Haddon & Hornell, 1936).

Perhaps one of the most distinctive items of material culture to show regional patterning is the plank-built canoe (see above). The basic form of these craft is found throughout the length of the Main Solomons and up into the fringes of New Ireland, but there are distinctive regional styles that once again mirror fairly closely the pattern of linguistic relationships. Charles Woodford, the early British administrator in the Solomon Islands, observed in his very thorough study of Solomons canoes that:

> This particular type of built-up canoe appears to be peculiar altogether to the Melanesian inhabitants of the British Solomons. In the German Islands of Bougainville and Bouka [sic] to the north-west, the type of dug-out canoe with the outrigger is observed, and the same type of canoe occurs in the Santa Cruz Group and in the New Hebrides to the south-east. It is comparatively easy to determine at a glance the place of origin of one of these Solomon Island canoes, since the shape and scheme of ornamentation differ on the various islands. (Woodford, 1909:508)

The early Spanish explorer Alvaro de Mendaña gave a basic description of this canoe form in 1568 while he was on the east coast of Santa Isabel in the vicinity of Estrella Bay.

> Their canoes are very well made and very light; they are shaped like a crescent, the largest holding about thirty persons. They are so swift that, although our ships under sail started two leagues ahead of them, with a good wind and all the sails set, they caught us up within the hour. Their speed in rowing is marvelous; they row in the fashion of the people of Cartagena. (Amherst and Thomson, 1901:109)

Figure 2.5 (reproduced from Haddon and Hornell, 1936: fig. 56) shows the distribution of plank-built canoe styles. The mon style, characteristic of the Western Solomons, extends from there into the Northern Solomons and, with decreasing frequency, as far as Nissan. The lisi form is most characteristic of the Eastern Solomons, although in the Makira–Ulawa region there is a local ora style. Within the Central Solomons, Haddon and Hornell's data shows what appears to be a region of overlapping styles across Santa Isabel (Ysabel), Nggela (Florida) and Guadalcanal. Although there is very likely a true region of overlap, some of it may be a function of poor-quality data. Most of the data used for description of Santa Isabel is derived from Woodford (1909), who travelled through the region after intensified headhunting activity in the late nineteenth century had decimated the population (White, 1991) and driven people either to the Kia region of northeast Santa Isabel in the west or to Bugotu in the east. Most of Woodford's discussion is based on his study of the Bugotu region. The extension of the mon style to the Kia region is understandable, as the Kia people had strong ties to Roviana and elsewhere in New Georgia; however Woodford does not explicitly report the binabina form extending beyond Bugotu.

The other anomaly, from a geographical point of view, is the extension of the mon form into Nggela, based on the brief report by Codrington (1891:295). With the exception of this anomaly the distribution of the mon canoe matches that of the Northwest Solomonic language group, while the distribution of the lisi form matches (apart from the exclusion of the Nggela group) the distribution of Southeast Solomonic. However, if we revise the binabina distribution to Bugotu, Nggela and Guadalcanal, it matches the Guadalcanal–Nggelic language subgroup of Southeast Solomonic. The Makira–Malaitan subgroup is not directly matched by a distinctive canoe form, however the ora form unites the far eastern islands into a Makira–Ulawa grouping.

This review of the geographical distribution of language, art styles, fishhooks and canoes shows considerable similarity among the patterns. Although we have not looked closely at the NAN language speakers it appears that other than language, they share many cultural features with their nearest, generally Austronesian neighbours. Our work in the NAN island of Vella Lavella has revealed considerable borrowing of culture and language from near Austronesian neighbours, including aspects of political organisation, exchange, ritual, and the headhunting complex that dominated the Western Solomons (Sheppard et al., 2010b; see also Terrill, 2011). So although culture does not simply reflect language in the Solomons, variation in cultural features, including Austronesian language, does appear to map onto geography. From these observations we might hypothesise that based on items such as plank-built canoes and general art styles, the Main Solomons forms a distinctive cultural unit, and that the linguistic boundary formed by the Tryon-Hackman Line also marks a major boundary for other aspects of culture. Development of this pattern would appear to fit most closely with a model of in situ differentiation structured by geographical propinquity of a founding Austronesian population. Linguistic data does not, however, suggest a common recent ancestor for Northwest and Southeast Solomonic followed by a later divergence in languages (Pawley, 2009). Alternative explanations might involve separate Austronesian settlement of the Eastern Solomons, either from the east or west, with gradual expansion out to the geographical choke point at the eastern end of Santa Isabel. Such a settlement must have involved people with cultural forms that were not too different from those in the Western Solomons; or else it occurred long enough ago for a widespread development and sharing of a base of such useful innovations as the plank-built canoe and compound fishhook. Genetic data does not at present provide much evidence for separate origins of Northwest and Southeast Solomonic: the Bismarcks are seen as the major source of both NRY and mtDNA haplogroups in the Solomon Islands (Delfin et al., 2012:560).

Other core differences between the Western and Central Solomons are not so easily explained in simple functional or evolutionary terms. The differences in art style noted by Waite are marked, and speak of distinctive heritages that are related to major differences in patterns of ritual and political economy. In the Western Solomons the headhunting complex and its associated ritual and shell valuables economy that underpinned chiefly polities was a powerful force for the promotion of the associated art styles throughout the region (Chapter 7). Although the roots of this headhunting complex are prehistoric (Sheppard et al., 2000; Walter and Sheppard, 2001), it intensified greatly in the nineteenth century (Zelenietz, 1979). It is most probable that the Roviana (New Georgia) links with the Kia region of Santa Isabel date to this time of increased trading and raiding, stimulated in part by the European demand for turtleshell and the Roviana demand for heads. Recent history, then, might account for the cultural similarity between New Georgia and western Santa Isabel and perhaps for the spread of this tradition further west.

The elaborate headhunting complex does not appear to have existed in the Central Solomons, and Codrington (1891:345) states that people east of Santa Isabel did not make expeditions for the sole purpose of procuring heads, although heads were sometimes preserved as trophies. The British administration clearly did not view head-taking in the east as the essential administrative problem it posed in the west (Woodford, 1909). In the Central Solomons, raiding and trading were common and, although violent, these acts were more often related to vendetta actions and the work of assassins rather than large-scale raids designed to take heads and captives. Whereas in the west canoe houses were associated with war canoes, in the east they were associated

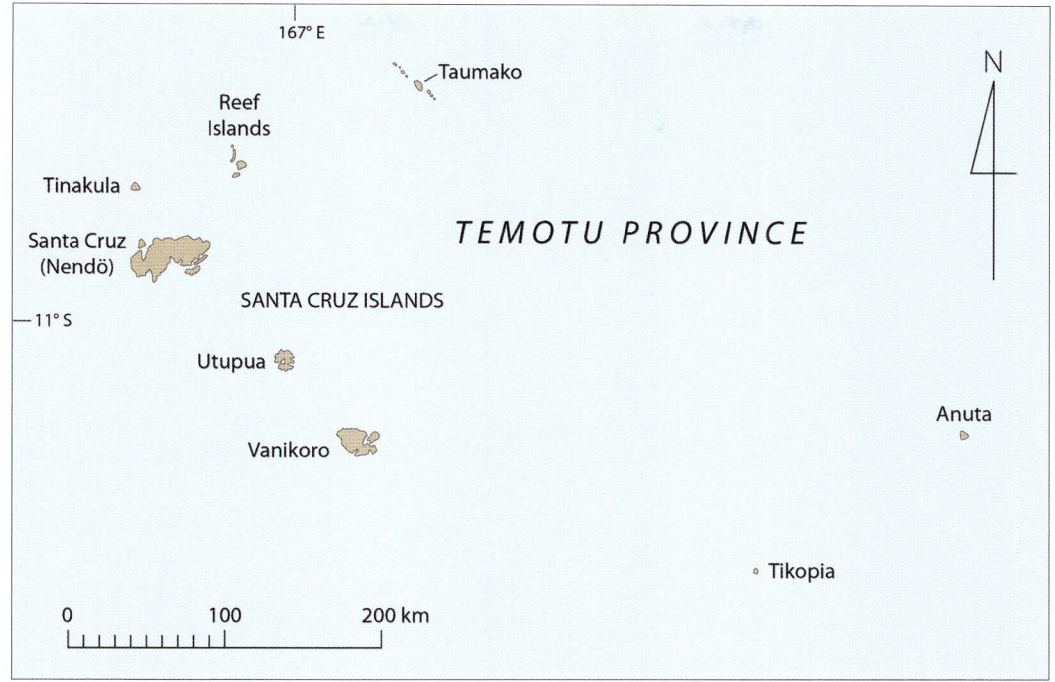

Figure 2.6. The Temotu region of the Solomon Islands including the Reef–Santa Cruz group.

with bonito fishing canoes and, often, with the seclusion of young boys and the elaborate ritual around their initiation into the bonito cults (Davenport, 1981; Ivens, 1927:130–31, 294–304; Walter & Green, 2011). Like headhunting in the Western Solomons, bonito fishing served in the Central Solomons as a key focus around which art styles developed and spread. How old this difference is, or whether the headhunting complex is a development out of the bonito cult, is unknown – although the Western Solomon view of headhunting as a type of fishing suggests there may be a connection (Barraud, 1972).

Eastern Solomons

As a culture area the Eastern Solomons encompasses most of Temotu Province (Figure 2.6). It consists of a core group of islands that have maintained continuous interaction from the time of their settlement by people of the Lapita archaeological tradition, as well as a number of more isolated islands less frequently visited by their distant neighbours, of which many are Polynesian Outliers. The Reef–Santa Cruz group (Figure 2.6), located more than 350 km southeast of Ulawa and Santa Ana in the Main Solomons, forms the core of the Eastern Solomons culture area as defined here. Although Taumako (including Pileni) is technically one of the outliers and linguistically Polynesian, it has had continuous, strong connections with the Reef–Santa Cruz group. This water gap between the Main Solomons and the Eastern Solomons represents the first major open sea crossing for populations settling Oceania. Previously people had moved down a chain of intervisible islands, separated by short distances (<150 km), that extends almost unbroken back from the Main Solomons into Indonesia and mainland Southeast Asia.

The Reef–Santa Cruz group includes Santa Cruz (Nendö), the Reef Islands, Tinakula, Utupua and Vanikoro. These islands form a southeast-trending chain of intervisibility: the largest interisland distance is 63 km from Santa Cruz to Utupua. The next closest island is the Polynesian Outlier Tikopia, which lies 213 km to the southwest of Vanikoro and was only infrequently visited by sailors from the Reef–Santa Cruz Islands or Utupua (Davenport, 1964a). The Reef Islands are a set of atolls and sand cays 45 km northwest of Santa Cruz; all the other islands are higher volcanic islands. The small island of Tinakula is an active volcano which has periodically showered its neighbours in the Reef Islands and Santa Cruz with ash (Green et al., 2008). Santa Cruz is the largest island (505 km^2) at the centre of the group, and contains the administrative centre at Lata. The other islands in the group are much smaller; Vanikoro is the largest at 173 km^2.

Despite the small size of these islands they support considerable cultural diversity. The island of Santa Cruz has, according to Ross and Næss (2007), a chain of Austronesian dialects that include Nanggu and Natügu, while on the Reef Islands Äiwoo is spoken by the Main Reef Islanders and Polynesian languages (Pileni/Vaeakau) by Outer

Reef islanders. The small island of Utupua supports three languages, and it is possible more were spoken there in the past (Green, 1976b:55); and three additional languages are spoken on Vanikoro. There has been considerable debate on the languages of Santa Cruz and the Main Reef Islands. Some early research concluded that, although they formed a subgroup, they were 'mixed' languages with Austronesian admixture into a non-Austronesian (Papuan) base. Recent research (Næss & Boerger, 2008; Ross & Næss, 2007), however, has shown that Äiwoo and the other languages of Santa Cruz are Oceanic Austronesian languages with no evidence of Papuan influence. This work has also concluded that, leaving aside the Polynesian Outliers, the languages of Reef–Santa Cruz, Utupua and Vanikoro form a subgroup of Oceanic, which Ross and Næss (2007) label Temotu. Those authors suggest the group is most probably a first-order subgroup of Oceanic, distinct from the other Austronesian languages of Remote Oceania or the Main Solomons and apparently most closely related to languages of the St Matthias group (Mussau) in the Bismarck Archipelago. Recent phylogenetic analysis of Austronesian languages has also supported the identification of Temotu as a first-order subgroup (Gray et al., 2009). Similarly the DNA work of Delfin et al. (2012:554) reveals that the Santa Cruz sample is totally unlike the Main Solomon Islands, which they have extensively sampled; in their data Santa Cruz is most closely related to samples from the Bismarck Archipelago and sits (in their fig. 7a) close to the sample from Mussau. Together this would indicate that the peoples of the Santa Cruz group have shared a distinctive common history, dating back to the time of the earliest breakup of the Oceanic and the first settlement of Remote Oceania – a point we return to in Chapter 5 when we discuss the spread of Lapita.

The coherence of the Temotu language group was maintained historically in part by a complex web of economic and social interaction among the islands. This is epitomised by the well-known red-feather money exchange system described by the ethnographer William Davenport (1962; see also Chapter 6). Belts made of red feathers from a species of honeyeater (*Myzomela cardinalis*) were used as exchange valuables on Santa Cruz, the Reef Islands and Taumako for social transactions such as marriage, as well as to purchase commodities, yet the belts were only made on Santa Cruz from feathers obtained both locally and on Utupua and Vanikoro. Sailors from the Reef Islands moved feathers and finished currency between islands using te puke voyaging canoes built on Taumako. Reef Islanders in turn obtained currency through the exchange of women with Santa Cruz. Although the people of Utupua and Vanikoro did not use red-feather currency, they obtained the shell discs and woven cloth that were used in their exchange system from Santa Cruz and the Reefs. Beneath the formal exchange-valuable networks lay the movement of people and other commodities, including food, and this evened out disparities among these small islands (Davenport, 1975b). The large island of Santa Cruz could provide food to the atolls, raised coral islands and sand cays of the Reef Islands, while women moved from the Reefs to Santa Cruz as concubines and wives. Similarly, population imbalances could be evened out by people shifting from one island to another in the event of disease or overpopulation. As a result of this long-term process of interaction and interdependence the people of this extended archipelago have formed a self-sufficient cultural pattern that mirrors in large part the extent of the Temotu language subgroup.

Although there was no regular travel outside of the Reef–Santa Cruz region, there was occasional contact with islands to the southeast and northwest. Islanders made infrequent, often accidental voyages to Tikopia in the historic period (i.e. after the period of written records), and the islands were well known to one another. Strong easterly winds often drove canoes west toward the Main Solomons into what the Santa Cruz people called 'The Seas Without Return' (Davenport, 1964a). Malaita was feared, as castaways often faced a hostile reception there, but they maintained friendly relations with Santa Ana and Makira, where castaways were cared for. The island of Tinakula figures in the mythology of Santa Ana, and Santa Ana is mentioned in the mythology of Santa Cruz. Davenport suggested that the carved wooden dukna figures (deity images) of Santa Cruz may be related to the distinctive carving tradition of Santa Ana (Davenport, 1990).

Polynesian Outliers

The Polynesian Outliers are isolated islands or small clusters of islands in Melanesia or Micronesia that are inhabited by Polynesian-speaking peoples. The existence of the Polynesian Outliers has been known since the early nineteenth century, but until the 1970s it was unclear how Polynesian speakers came to be distributed on islands far outside the Polynesian triangle. One possibility (e.g. Churchill, 1911) is that they were 'stay behinds' – groups of Polynesians who remained behind during the eastward migration of the Polynesian ancestors. Pawley (1967) demonstrated that all Polynesian Outlier communities spoke languages in the Nuclear Polynesian subgroup of the Polynesian language family, which developed subsequent to the colonisation of Fiji and West Polynesia (Figure 2.7). This invalidated the 'stay behind' model, and it is now generally understood that the Outlier communities derive from back

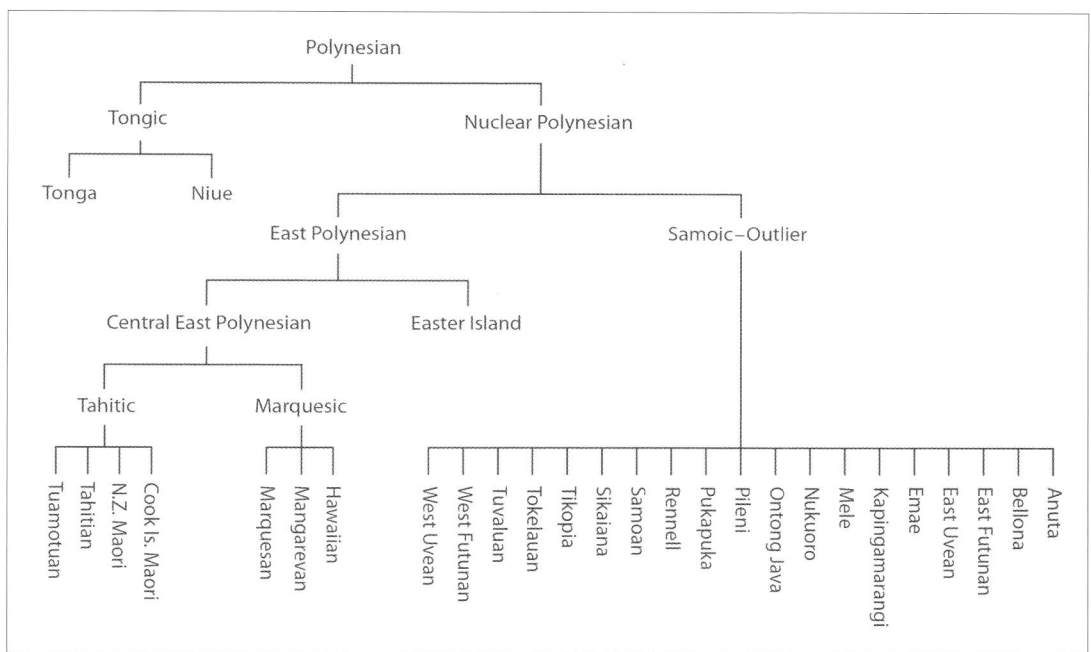

Figure 2.7. Phylogenetic relationships among the Polynesian languages showing the Polynesian Outliers falling into the Samoic branch of the language tree.

migration events out of Polynesia, although the individual island histories involve multiple influences (Bayard, 1976). Seven Polynesian Outlier languages are found spread across a number of islands in the Solomons: Sikaiana, Luangiua (Ontong Java), Vaeakau–Taumako (previously Pileni) and including dialects Aua, Matema, Nifiloli, Nukapu, Nupani), Rennell, Bellona, Anuta and Tikopia (Figure 2.8).

All of the Polynesian Outliers of the Solomon Islands are very small atolls or low volcanic islands and are located between 50 and 160 km from their nearest large neighbour. Irwin has plotted island accessibility (angle of target against distance to the nearest inhabited neighbour) and has shown that all of these Outlier islands form distinct clusters at the apparent limits of permanent settlement (Irwin, 1992: figs 70 and 71). Isolation has meant that the occupants of these islands are generally good sailors who make use of outrigger voyaging canoes such as the te puke of Taumako, which were employed in the red-feather trading system (Davenport, 1962) that linked Taumako, the Reef–Santa Cruz group and Vanikoro. Isolation has also meant that, although there has always been some interaction with distant neighbours in the Main Solomons, the Outliers have retained distinctive identities – most obviously so in terms of language (Pawley, 1967). Ancient connections with Western Polynesia are evidenced in archaeology by the presence on the Solomon Islands Outliers of adzes that have been sourced to Samoa by geochemistry (Best et al., 1992) and petrography (Campbell, 2008). Although the culture history of these islands is often complex it is generally believed that this screen of small, remote islands has, over the millennia since Western Polynesia was settled, had a steady influx of canoes from the east, driven westward by the prevailing winds. This need not deny the sailing capability of Polynesians; it simply reflects the outcome of centuries of accidental drift voyages (Ward et al., 1973) – as are historically well documented (Davenport, 1964a) – and the potential founder effects of small numbers of Polynesians on the very small populations of these islands. It seems probable that, over the years, many more Polynesians landed on the Main Solomon Islands and were absorbed without trace.

The Northern Outliers along the eastern edge of the Solomons also show considerable evidence of ongoing interaction with Micronesia to the north: this is seen in material culture, oral tradition and biology. The backstrap loom (Figure 2.9), which is found in the Solomons Outliers (Nuguria, Taku, Nukumanu, Ontong Java, Sikaiana, Taumako and Tikopia – but also on Santa Cruz, Banks Islands, Northern Vanuatu and Mussau) (Riesenberg & Gayton, 1952), is distributed north along the chain of Polynesian Outliers into the Caroline Islands. In the Solomon Islands the loom's presence is a result of contacts through Micronesia, although its ultimate origins lie in Southeast Asia. Similarly, the distinctive shell adzes made from *Terebra* and *Mitra* shell are viewed as evidence of interaction with Micronesia (Doherty, 2009; Intoh, 1999). Oral history from Ontong Java speaks of considerable interaction with people

ARCHAEOLOGY OF THE SOLOMON ISLANDS

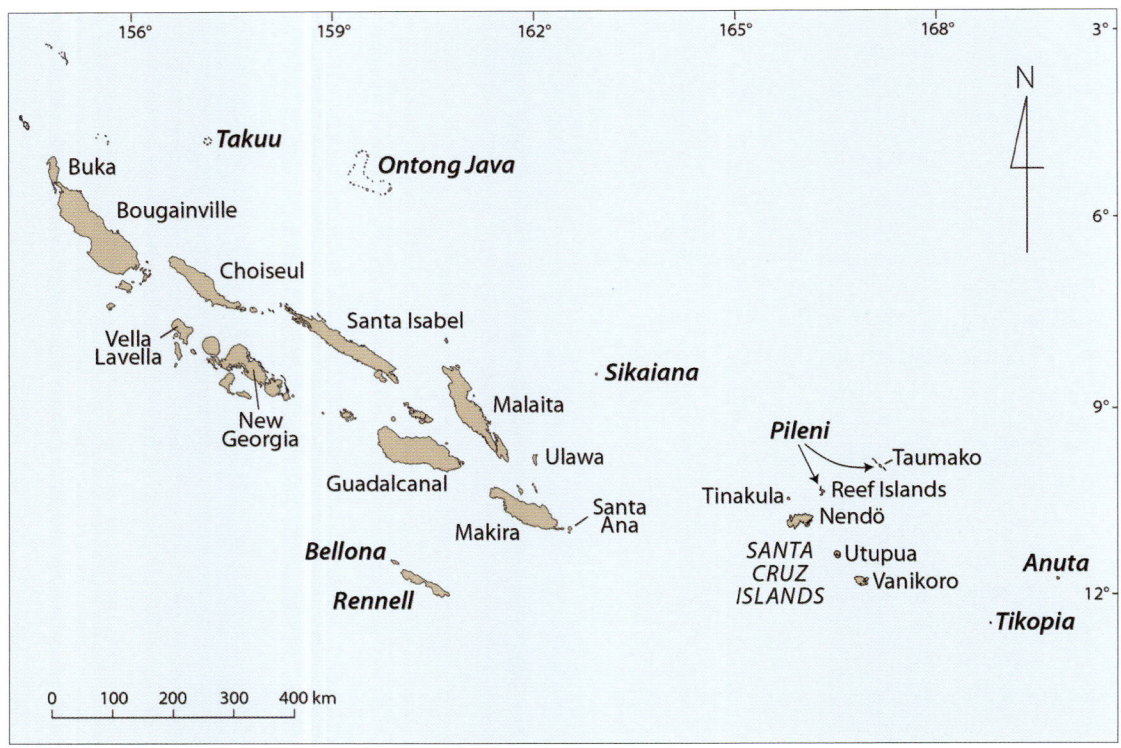

Figure 2.8. Location of the Polynesian Outlier islands in the Solomon Islands.

Figure 2.9. Backstrap loom in use in Ontong Java in the 1960s (photo by William Davenport) (copyright 2005 University of Pennsylvania Museum of Archaeology and Anthropology).

described as Micronesian (John Keopo, pers. comm., 2008), and distinctive mitochondrial DNA sequences from Ontong Java have recently been identified as Micronesian (Gentz, 2005:462), which supports earlier studies (Shapiro, 1933). As Leach and Davidson note for Taumako (2008:322–23), although people of the Outliers speak languages that are clearly related to Samoic, there has doubtless been contact and influence from many sources and directions since people first set foot there.

Most recently, Wilson (2012) has proposed that the Outliers of the Solomon Islands have not simply been the recipient of external contacts, but have figured prominently in the expansion into East Polynesia. In a radical reinterpretation of Polynesian linguistic subgrouping, Wilson (2012) has cited 73 grammatical and lexical innovations that define nested groupings of the Northern Solomon Island Outliers (Sikaiana, Takuu, Luangiua) as well as Kapingamarangi and Nukuoro in the Caroline Islands. These innovations are all shared with East Polynesian languages, thus providing strong support for a Proto-Northern-Outlier–East-Polynesian subgroup lying below the higher-order Nuclear Polynesian language subgroup (Figure 2.10). The historical implication is that East Polynesia may have been settled from a northern route out of the Northern Solomon Island Outliers. Other interpretations are possible, but this is the most parsimonious and it is attractive since it solves one of the big problems in East Polynesian cultural history – that of deriving the East Polynesian cultural traditions directly out of Samoa.

In discussing the relationships among the Solomon Island Outliers, Wilson (2012) draws on Bayard's (1976) review of the cultural relationships of the Outliers. Bayard documented evidence from oral tradition that suggests the Northern Outliers were not only in contact with one another but may have had some knowledge of islands further to the east in Tuvalu. Wilson also cites Moyle's (2007) account of the atu lou – an annual voyage from the northern atolls into the Eastern Solomons. These Takuu traditions may even allude to connections further east into Samoa and Fiji. Indeed, Wilson suggests that a practice of regular voyaging from the Northern Solomons through to Samoa, based on an ancient precursor of the atu lou, may have been the mechanism for the settlement of East Polynesia. While the linguistic evidence strongly supports a connection between the Northern Outliers and East Polynesia, we believe the actual processes and nature of the interaction needs a great deal more consideration, and that the models proposed by Wilson (2012) are not necessarily the best options. The larger point, however, is that the Northern Outliers participated in a voyaging tradition that exposed them not only to one another, but to influences from the Main Solomon Islands and probably also to other Outlier communities lying some distance to the east and west. The nature of the voyaging tradition is an area that needs some further study, especially if it has implications for the colonisation of East Polynesia.

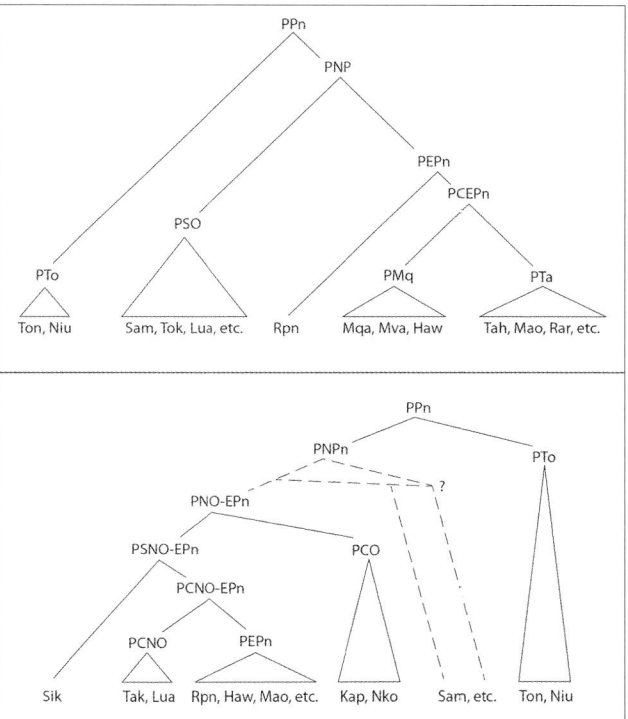

Figure 2.10. Polynesian language relationships showing the standard (e.g. Ross, 1979) model (above) compared with the Wilson (2012) model below. In all abbreviations the leading 'P' represents a proto language: Pn Polynesian, NP/NPn Nuclear Polynesian, EPn East Polynesian, SO Samoic–Outlier, To Tongic, Mq Marquesic, Ta Tahitian, NP-EPn Northern Outlier–East Polynesian, SNO-EPn Solomons Northern Outlier–East Polynesian, CNO-EPn Central Northern Outlier–East Polynesian, CNO Central Northern Outlier, Ton Tonga, Niu Niue, Sam Samoa, Tok Tokelau, Lua Luanguia, Rpn Rapa Nui, Mqa Marquesas, Mva Mangareva, Haw Hawaii, Tah Tahiti, Mao Maori, Rar Rarotonga, Tak Takuu, Kap Kapingamarangi, Nko Nukuoro.

Wilson's hypothesis is not contradicted by the recent genetic study of Delfin et al. (2012:555), which included data from Ontong Java, Tikopia, Rennell and Bellona. Their study indicates that although these islands have some variability that indicates separate founder effects or distinctive histories, together they share a common basic genetic profile that is distinctively Polynesian and that would not appear to rule out an origin of East Polynesia speakers in the Northern Outliers. Additional comparison of the Solomons genetic data with that from Remote Oceania including Vanuatu, New Caledonia and Micronesia is needed in order to clarify the relationship of the Outliers to patterns of interaction and settlement in Remote Oceania.

The formation of Solomon Islands cultural geography

The cultural geography of the Solomon Islands is structured by geographical distance and isolation, origins and timing of founding settlements, and the development of local innovations and histories, including the differential impact of Western economies. The culture and history of the Outliers are shaped most strongly by the fact that their isolation and size place them on the margins of viable settlement, and that they are downwind of large population centres to the east. Once Western Polynesia and Micronesia were settled and population levels had risen they would have provided a continual source of drift and purposeful voyages that would have had a strong impact on the very small Outlier founding populations. Not all Outliers are geographically isolated; however, like the Polynesian speakers of the Outer Reef Islands, they seem to occupy marginal habitats that are suitable only for small populations, within which they are able to maintain at least their linguistic identity. In these situations Outlier populations tend to integrate and share the cultural features of their neighbours (e.g. Leach & Davidson, 2008).

The Reef–Santa Cruz group is the most isolated cluster of islands in the Solomon Islands, located over 350 km southeast of the Main Solomons and over 200 km north of Tikopia and the margins of Vanuatu. This isolated position, across the Near Oceania boundary, of a group that includes some moderately sized high islands, has facilitated the development and maintenance of a distinctive cultural system that has grown from the founding population and which, based on linguistic evidence, originated in the Bismarck group. Although subsequent population arrivals from the east and north have brought them into the sphere of influences that have impacted the Outliers, neither that force, nor occasional contacts with the Main Solomons, appears to have had a marked impact on the culture of the region.

Nowhere in the Main Solomons is isolated, and distances between islands are short enough, and the waters sufficiently sheltered, for paddle canoes to have become the main mode of transport. However, the distance along this chain of narrow islands is such that one might expect the development of clines of cultural similarity. Despite this there is a major cultural and linguistic distinction found at the end of Santa Isabel in the Central Solomons. Although linguistic history might predict that this difference is based on separate founding populations, nearest-neighbour analysis suggests that any east–west division in the Main Solomons would develop at this point. The difference might have arisen through cultural drift and differential levels of interaction. Conversely any differences in founding populations or regional histories would have been maintained at the Malaita–Santa Isabel division. Such a process is shown historically by the intensification of headhunting in the Western Solomons in the nineteenth century, driven by the impact of Western traders' desire for turtleshell from the rich turtle-hunting grounds of the region, and the economic and sociopolitical opportunities the trade in turtle shells provided. Although Western Solomon Island headhunters raided as far east as Nggela and the western end of Guadalcanal, the elaborate headhunting complex that spread throughout the Western Solomons did not move east of Santa Isabel. For an explanation of this phenomenon we need to consider the history of founding populations, the geography, resource distribution and the expanding activities of both the regional and world systems.

3

A short history of archaeology in the Solomon Islands

Early history

Many of the first European clergy, traders and ethnographers to visit the Solomon Islands made reference to material culture and culture history (e.g. Guppy, 1887; MacLachlan, 1938; O'Reilly, 1940, 1948; Thurnwald, 1934). In addition, troops stationed in the Solomon Islands during World War II made some observations and collections of archaeological materials, particularly in the Northern Solomons (Kraus, 194; Shutler & Shutler, 1964). The first dedicated archaeological research work we are aware of, however, was a reconnaissance survey carried out in the Western Solomons in 1964 by Masashi Chikamori of Keio University, Tokyo (Figure 3.1). On Vella Lavella the Keio team carried out coastal and inland surveys, and excavated several terraces and house platforms dating to the late prehistoric and early historic period. On Simbo, Choiseul, New Georgia and Vella Lavella they recorded shrines and other stone monument sites, and described a range of artefacts from those sites that we now recognise as characteristic Western Solomons shell ornament types, such as *Tridacna* rings and *Conus* discs. On north New Georgia they surveyed an irrigated taro system, and on Choiseul they excavated a cave deposit containing a ceramic record that they recognised as comparable to that of Bougainville and the Shortland Islands to the north (Chikamori, 1965).

In 1966 Ron Lampert from the Australian National University (ANU) carried out reconnaissance survey and small-scale excavation on the mainland of Buka, and on the island of Sohano in the straits between Buka and Bougainville. On Sohano, Lampert located a rockshelter site (DAA) and carried out test excavations there (Lampert, 1966) (Figure 3.2). The DAA site was revisited by Specht (1969), who showed that the rockshelter material was part of a large, low-density deposit of around 25,000 m^2 that extended from the limestone cliff onto the beach and reef flat. The deposit spanned around 2500 years and contained pottery in a range of different decorative styles. Stephen Wickler also worked at DAA during his PhD research of the late 1980s (see below). On Buka, Lampert recorded surface deposits of pottery in the Malasang area where much of the later archaeology work has been concentrated, and raised the possibility of pre-ceramic horizons (Wickler, 2001:5). The important outcome of Lampert's work was that it alerted archaeologists to the presence of a number of rich, pottery-bearing deposits on Buka, and the possibility of constructing a regional ceramic sequence. Following on from Lampert's survey, Jim Specht – also from ANU – spent seven months working on Buka the following year as part of his PhD research. Specht collected pottery from surface deposits and from excavated horizons and used these to define a six-phase ceramic sequence, starting at 2500 cal BP with late-Lapita ceramics (Specht, 1969, 1972; see also Chapter 5). This was the first ceramic sequence reported from the Solomon Islands.

Wickler built on Lampert's and Specht's early work on Buka when he carried out a survey and excavation programme there in 1987 as part of his PhD research from

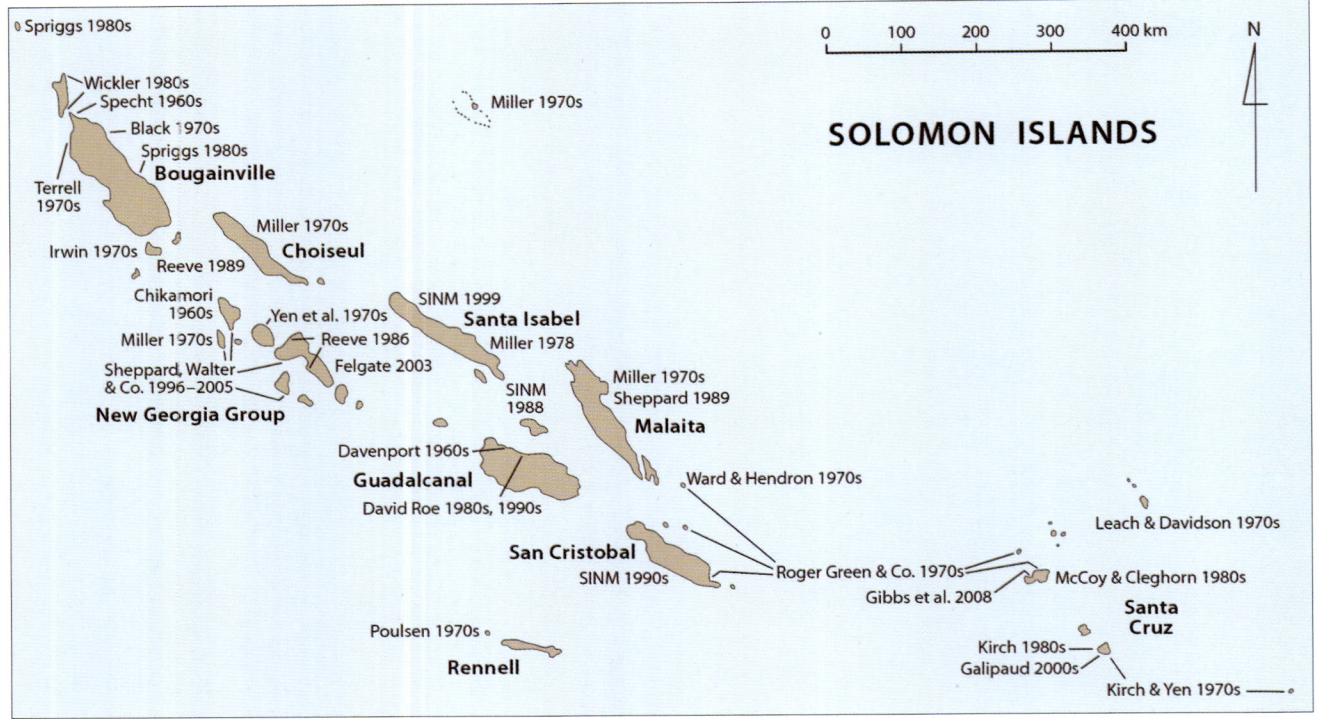

Figure 3.1. Location of archaeological fieldwork activities (after Walter & Sheppard, 2009).

the University of Hawai`i. He extended Specht's survey coverage and increased the ceramic sample through both surface collecting and excavation. Wickler's work confirmed the basic structure of Specht's ceramic sequence, but he made some minor alterations to the dating (Chapter 5). Importantly, he also extended the spatial range of the sequence: he argued that it applied also to north Bougainville (2001:168). The other major contribution of Wickler's work on Buka was the discovery of Pleistocene levels in the Kilu Cave (DJA) deposits (Chapter 4).

In the early 1960s Shutler and Shutler (1964) described some surface-collected ceramic sherds from Teop in north Bougainville. These were later placed into context when John Terrell took up research on Bougainville as part of his PhD fieldwork from Harvard in 1969 (Terrell, 1970). Terrell's work built on the earlier efforts of Specht and Lampert to the west by carrying out ceramic surveys along the north coast and eventually down as far as the Buin region in the south. Terrell (1976) and Black (1977) excavated at Teop, a traditional trading centre and the source of the sherds reported by Shutler and Shutler (1964). Buka pottery of Specht's post-Lapita Sohano to Recent phases was found in surface contexts at Teop, and excavations confirmed occupation in the area from at least Specht's Malasang Phase (assigned by Wickler (2001) to 800–500 cal BP; see also Chapter 5). Terrell showed that pottery was reaching Teop from Buka as well as from the Kieta region, 100 km down the northeast coast of Bougainville. Terrell also documented a southern pottery sequence on the basis of fieldwork in Buin that had connections with the Shortland sequence described around the same time by Irwin (1972).

Geoff Irwin's work in the Shortland Islands was carried out from 1970 as part of his MA research from the University of Auckland (Irwin, 1972, 1973). He described a three-phase pottery sequence starting at 1500 cal BP. By the Middle Phase (1000–200 cal BP) the Shortland pottery showed strong affinities with the earliest Buin ceramics. This suggested an exchange link, and this assumption was supported by the discovery of Buin-manufactured sherds in the Shortland assemblages and vice versa. Spriggs (1992, 1997:171) later reported a three-phase sequence from the Kieta Peninsula that was very similar to the Shortland sequence (Spriggs, 1993b:197). He also pointed to similarities and possible connections between the pottery traditions of south Bougainville and the Shortland Islands on the one hand, and those represented by surface-collected material reported by Miller (1979) from Choiseul on the other.

Further to the east, the anthropologist William Davenport undertook excavations (1964–66) at a number of locations on Santa Ana Island in the Central Solomon Islands (Davenport, 1972a). These included a major excavation at Feru, where he investigated a series of small

A SHORT HISTORY OF ARCHAEOLOGY IN THE SOLOMON ISLANDS

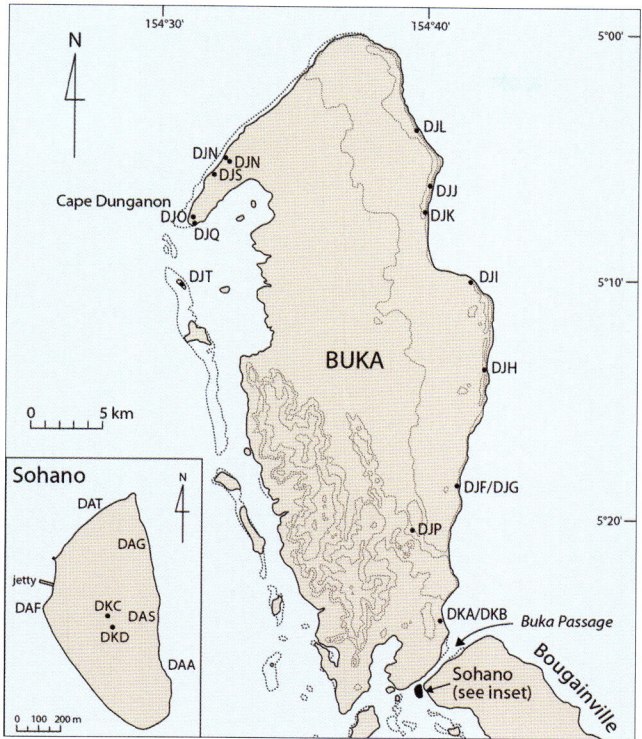

Figure 3.2 Location of archaeological sites in Bougainville located during the surveys of Lambert, Specht and Wickler.

later investigation of Feru I and II (Black & Green, 1975; Swadling, 2000) in which they re-examined the context from which the ceramics were obtained. Sheppard carried out the reconnaissance phase for a further planned investigation there in 2010 (see below).

Extending his archaeological interests to Guadalcanal, Davenport identified the Vatuluma Posovi (Foha Cave) site, just west of Honiara, as a potential source of information on the early occupation period, and he excavated some test pits towards the back of the cave (Davenport, 1968, n.d.; Davenport et al., n.d.). Tom Russell and James Tedder, who were expat government officers, carried out subsequent work there in the late 1960s (Russell, 2003). These excavations showed that the site had potential significance, but they also emptied the cave of nearly all the archaeological deposit while producing very little stratigraphically reliable archaeological information. It was this situation that prompted David Roe to return to the site in 1987–88 to clarify the position of Vatuluma Posovi in the Guadalcanal sequence (Roe, 1993:39) (see below). The site is now generally considered the only possible representative of a pre-Austronesian expansion to the east of Buka.

rockshelters (Feru I and II) along a cliff line on the western side of the island, and excavations further to the east at Rate, and at the inland cave of Kanope. Observation of the open excavations at Feru I in 2009 indicated that over 52 cubic metres of deposit was excavated in that area. A small amount of plain undecorated pottery was recovered from Feru and Rate. Roger Green and Gil Hendren undertook a

In 1968 Jens Poulsen from the University of Aarhus in Denmark carried out a survey and excavation programme on the Polynesian Outlier of Bellona (Figure 3.3). The work involved reconnaissance survey and mapping, small-scale excavation and surface sampling of sites in order to build up a first culture history sequence. Poulsen used oral history and ethnographic data to place his sites in a broad chronological framework. He described a range of monumental features, including house mounds and similar ceremonial structures. Excavations at one of these sites

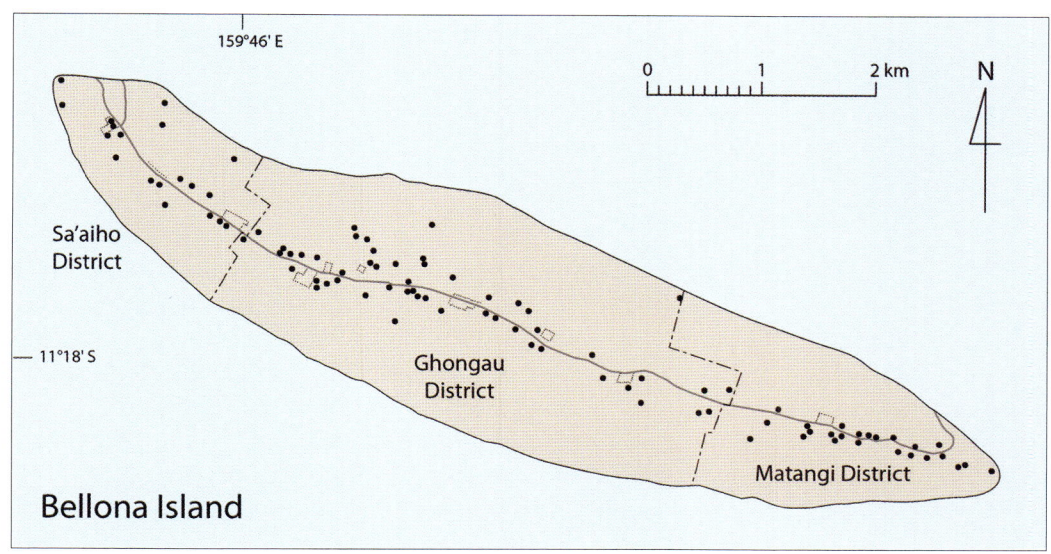

Figure 3.3. Location of archaeological sites on Bellona recorded by Poulsen (after Poulsen, 1972).

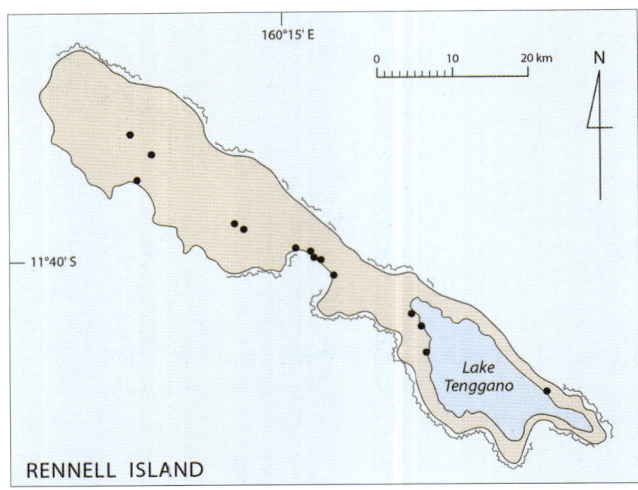

Figure 3.4. Location of archaeological sites on Rennell recorded by Chikamori and Takasugi (after Chikamori & Takasugi, 1985).

recovered shell adzes, scrapers and tooth ornaments as well as six sherds of pottery from the earliest levels. Although Poulsen described the pottery as Lapita, it is undecorated and not definitively attributable to Lapita; it is generally similar to the type of post-Lapita plainware found widely in Remote Oceania. The earliest horizons date to around 2000 cal BP (Poulsen & Polach, 1972:197).

Poulsen's investigation was the first archaeological study of a Polynesian Outlier in the Solomon Islands. Further Outlier work continued in 1973 and 1975 when Masashi Chikamori and Hiroaki Takasugi from Keio University carried out survey and excavation programmes on the adjacent island of Rennell (Chikamori, 1975; Chikamori & Takasugi, 1985). They recorded sites and surface features broadly similar to those found by Poulsen's team on Bellona, including house and grave mounds with dressed-stone slabs, rockshelter sites and open settlements (Figure 3.4). They proposed a four-phase sequence, with first settlement occurring, as on Bellona, at around 2000 cal BP. The material culture included a range of shell adzes, fishhooks, pumice and coral grinders and abraders. No pottery was reported.

Southeast Solomon Island Culture History Project

In 1970 Roger Green (University of Auckland) and Doug Yen (Bernice P. Bishop Museum, Hawai`i) set up the Southeast Solomon Island Culture History Project (SESP) (Green, 1973b; Green & Yen, 2009; Yen, 1982). This was a programme made up of a number of autonomous but conceptually and logistically linked research projects, and was designed to establish cultural sequences for this part of Melanesia. It was the first large multi-institutional, multidisciplinary archaeology programme ever carried out in Near Oceania. The SESP was set up at a time when Lapita was just being recognised as a pan-Oceanic phenomenon (Golson, 1968, 1971) and some of the established notions of Polynesian origins were being challenged, along with many traditional ideas about the relationship between Melanesian and Polynesian cultural history. The idea was to map out an archaeological baseline on the eastern fringes of Melanesia (or, in today's terms, on the western border of Near Oceania) from where the early ancestors of Polynesia were thought likely to have originated. Under the umbrella of the SESP, site surveys and excavations were carried out widely in the Reef–Santa Cruz Islands, Makira, Santa Ana, Uki, Ulawa and Vanikoro (Green & Cresswell, 1976; Kirch, 1983a) (Figure 3.5). It also involved work in the eastern Polynesian Outliers, with major and influential publications dealing with the Tikopia (Kirch & Yen, 1982) and Anuta (Yen & Gordon, 1973) sequences.

The SESP generated data from the Reef–Santa Cruz region that is critical to the modern synthesis of Lapita, and established basic sequences for islands and island groups that set the directions for the next four decades of research. It also supported a generation of students and early-career archaeologists who have gone on to make major contributions to Oceanic archaeology. Many of the projects under the SESP generated large data sets that were worked on sporadically for decades in various laboratories and have only recently reached publication stage. For example, in 2008 Leach and Davidson published the results of their SESP research on Taumako (Leach & Davidson, 2008) and in 2011 Walter and Green published the results of the SESP excavations at Su`ena, on Uki Island (Walter & Green, 2011). Other SESP projects have been reopened recently with new fieldwork initiatives. Martin Gibbs (University of Sydney) returned to Pamua on Makira in 2011 and extended the survey and inventory of features at Mwanihuki begun by Green, Allen and Kaschko (Green, 1976e) in 1972. In 2010 Peter Sheppard carried out preparatory work on Santa Ana with a view to re-excavating Feru II, and in 2012 the authors, together with Scarlett Chiu (Academia Sinica, Taiwan) and in collaboration with the Solomon Islands National Museum carried out an excavation at SZ-8, the Lapita site at Nanggu on the south coast of Santa Cruz that was first excavated by Green in 1971 (Chapter 5).

So far the SESP teams have published more than 100 papers, monographs and books in a range of fields including archaeology, linguistics, ethnobotany, material culture and ethnography (Foana`ota, 1996; Yen, 1982). A paper by Green and Yen outlines the 'current research and the documentation efforts that have been or are being undertaken for the whole

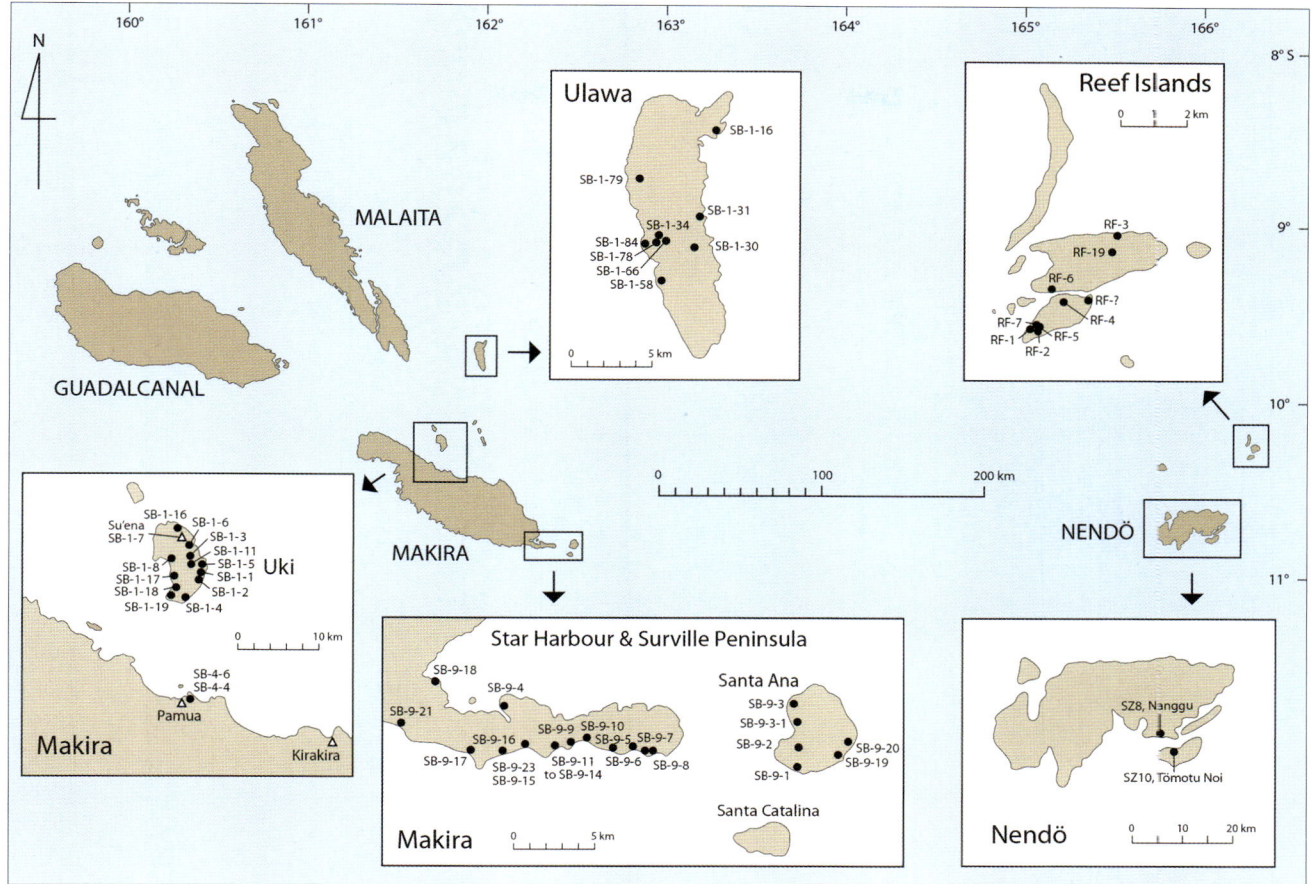

Figure 3.5. Eastern Solomons sites investigated during SESP work (based on maps in Green & Cresswell, 1976 and Doherty, 2007).

body of data that was initially gathered by the participants in the … SESP' (Green & Yen, 2009:147). This updates the Foana'ota (1996) summary of SESP work, lists ongoing projects, and provides information on the current location of excavated material and archived texts.

One of the unexpected outcomes of the SESP was the development of one of the first historical archaeology projects to be carried out in tropical Oceania. This was the investigation of Spanish settlement sites at Graciosa Bay, Santa Cruz (Allen, 1976; Allen & Green, 1972) and at Pamua on Makira (Green, 1973a). These sites relate to Alvaro de Mendaña y Neyra's attempted colonisation in 1595 after his discovery and exploration of the Solomon Islands (1567–68) (Amherst & Thomson, 1901; Gibbs, 2011). Rev. Charles Elliot Fox had collected ceramic sherds of European manufacture at Pamua in the 1930s (White, 2002), and this led members of the SESP to investigate the site. Typological analysis of sherds (Allen & Green, 1972) from both locations showed that they contained a range of domestic and utilitarian ware, with a greater diversity at the Pamua site, which was the second of the two settlements (Kelloway et al., 2013:57). Petrological studies indicated that the ceramics had origins in both the New (South America) and Old Worlds (Dickinson & Green, 1973; Kelloway et al., 2013). Gibbs has recently commenced a new phase of investigation of the Spanish sites reported by the SESP teams at Pamua and Graciosa Bay (Santa Cruz) (Blake & Gibbs, 2013; Gibbs, 2011; Kelloway et al., 2013). Teams from New Caledonia and France have also conducted research on Vanikoro on early European exploration: they have recovered evidence of the expedition led by the French explorer La Pérouse, who disappeared in the southwest Pacific in 1789 (Galipaud & de Biran, 2006).

Most recently, a team led by Johannes Moser of the German Archaeological Institute, in cooperation with the National Museum of the Solomon Islands, has undertaken research on the little-studied (Miller, 1980a) island of Malaita. Excavations in 2012 at Maniaha in east `Are`are (Moser, pers. comm., 2013) have begun to investigate the long flint knapping tradition, which has been described previously by anthropologists (Ivens, 1931; Ross, 1970) from historic materials, but not yet studied by archaeologists.

Solomon Islands National Museum

The Solomon Islands National Museum was established in 1969 under the British Protectorate. Its early history was strongly influenced by the Southeast Solomon Island Culture History Project, which provided opportunities for training and fieldwork for Solomon Islands staff and for expatriates associated with the museum. The SESP work raised the profile of archaeology considerably and, after the major phases of fieldwork were completed, the museum became the focus for archaeological research in Solomon Islands and began a series of its own research initiatives.

During the early 1970s a number of surveys were carried out by Solomon Islands-based groups associated with the museum under the leadership of the first directors, Anna Craven and Henry Isa (Miller, 1980a); these included work on Vella Lavella by Wall in 1972 and Foana`ota in 1973, and on New Georgia by Tedder in 1973 (Foana`ota, 1974, 1996). Regional survey work continued when the National Museum and Cultural Centre in Honiara established the National Site Survey Project in 1976 (Foana`ota, 1979). Daniel Miller, a British volunteer attached to the museum in 1975, set up the scheme with the assistance of Roger Green (1972) using a New Zealand model, and directed the early surveys until 1978, when his contract expired. This included work on all the islands of the New Georgia Group as well as Choiseul, Santa Isabel, Malaita, Makira and Ontong Java (Miller, 1978, 1979; Miller & Roe, 1982). In the Western Solomons the surveys reported a considerable number of ceramic deposits, mostly scatters of plainware; however, they also recorded a coastal site at Nuatambu on Choiseul that contained deposits that extended below the water table. Between 1978 and 1981 the Site Survey Project continued under the direction of another volunteer from Britain, David Roe, until he left to take over the directorship of the Guadalcanal Cultural Centre (Rukia, 1989a). In 1983 Lawrence Foana`ota, who was the first Solomon Islander trained in archaeology (he graduated from the University of Auckland in 1982), took up the directorship of the National Museum; he held the position until he retired in 2010, when Tony Heorake became director.

From the 1980s archaeological survey work seems to have been concentrated on Guadalcanal, and the results of Roe's work there are contained in his 1993 PhD thesis and subsequent publications (Roe, 1989, 1993, 2000). Although the National Museum has limited resources for fieldwork it has continued to conduct small surveys, primarily directed toward cultural resource management in threatened areas. This has included work on Nggela (Rukia, 1989b), Santa Isabel (Keopo & Kawamura, 1999) and Makira. Museum staff, especially John Keopo and Lawrence Kiko, also work with international projects, including those of the current authors.

Western Province archaeology

The largest and longest running archaeological research programme in the Solomon Islands of recent times has involved the various projects we have directed in the Western Province. In 1996 we commenced the New Georgia Archaeological Survey (NGAS), which focused on the Roviana Lagoon region of New Georgia and ran until 1999. The work involved extensive survey and excavation and resulted in our recording and mapping over 700 shrines and other monumental features, plus a series of intertidal ceramic sites. As well as establishing a baseline archaeological sequence for the region, the archaeological work studied the emergence of the Roviana Chiefdom system and associated headhunter complexes and ancestor cults of late prehistory (Sheppard et al., 2004; Sheppard et al., 2000; Walter & Sheppard, 2001; Walter et al., 2004; see also Chapter 6).

The NGAS project included a number of student research programmes that culminated in MA or PhD theses. Matthew Felgate developed a comprehensive ceramic sequence for the New Georgia region for his PhD (University of Auckland); this was based mainly on ceramics recovered from intertidal sites, and covered the period from late Lapita at around 2800 cal BP to recent times (Felgate, 2003; Felgate & Dickinson, 1998). Takuya Nagaoka carried out a survey and classification of shrine types in Roviana as a master's programme (University of Auckland) (Nagaoka, 1999) and has recently completed a PhD on the archaeology of households and settlement on Nusa Roviana (Nagaoka, 2011). Tim Thomas (University of Otago) carried out a PhD study of material culture and exchange systems in Roviana Lagoon; focusing especially on the shrines, exchange valuables and votive offerings, he studied the manner in which material culture was used to negotiate social relationships in nineteenth-century Roviana society (Thomas, 2003). Sarah Grimes (University of Western Australia) joined the NGAS project to carry out a PhD study of environmental change and human impact on environments in Roviana Lagoon (Grimes, 2003).

From 2003 we moved the focus of our work northwest to Vella Lavella where we carried out a similar field programme to the New Georgia study: the Bilua Bifoa project. The aim of the project was to extend the study of late prehistoric sociopolitical development in the Western Province by comparing a non-Austronesian region (Vella Lavella) with the Austronesian sequence from New Georgia (Sheppard et al., 2010b). In this project we addressed the question of how powerful cultural traditions, such as those associated with the headhunting and ancestor cults, are able to cut across major cultural and linguistic boundaries. This project also included graduate student research: Anne McKenzie (University of Auckland) has completed a master's study of monumental architecture on Vella Lavella that provides a valuable comparison with Nagaoka's study from Roviana (McKenzie, 2007), and Sarah Krose (University of Auckland) has completed her PhD research on traditional kinship and tenure practices in Maravari village (Krose, 2016).

Following on from the NGAS work, Thomas continued his research in the Western Province with projects on Rendova and Tetepare (Thomas, 2009). On both these islands there is a rich record of late-period shrine and platform construction not dissimilar to that of New Georgia. There are local variations in architecture, material culture and burial practice, but enough similarity in the implied underlying traditions to suggest that the communities there were involved in a shared 'community of practice' that also encompassed New Georgia (Thomas, 2009). Thomas's work on Rendova and Tetepare is ongoing.

New initiatives in the Western Solomons are adding to the ceramic record and building up a picture of the late-period archaeological landscape – including the work of Melissa Carter (University of Sydney), who has been carrying out projects on Santa Isabel with a focus on the Kia region, where she has found a record very like that from Roviana and Vella Lavella (Carter et al., 2012).

Summary

There have been two major foci for the archaeological work in the Northern and Western Solomons. The first focus has been on the ceramic record: this has involved detailed and extensive surface survey and excavation programmes over a period of 50 years, with follow-up motif and fabric analyses. These have resulted in sound, reasonably well-dated sequences from Buka, various parts of Bougainville (North Bougainville, Teop, Buin, Kieta), the Shortland Islands and parts of the New Georgia Group, and these can be compared with some confidence. The ceramic record of the rest of the New Georgia Group, Santa Isabel and Choiseul is growing slowly, but still needs attention.

The other focus has been on the post-Lapita record, particularly of the last 1000 years. This work has been spearheaded by the NGAS and Bilua Bifoa projects and the various projects of Thomas (e.g. 2003, 2009), which aim at understanding the historical development of the traditional societies of the Western Solomon Islands (Chapter 6).

In the Central Solomon Islands the Poha Valley work on Guadalcanal stands out. It is the only archaeological sequence from that region that has been developed to date, although it is still patchy. More survey and excavation work would be useful in Guadalcanal, especially to clarify the nature of the early to mid-Holocene record. There has been only limited archaeological research on Malaita, and survey work that builds on the work of Moser in East `Are`are should be a high priority for the future.

In the Eastern Solomon Islands the focus has been on the Lapita record, and the work carried out on the Reef–Santa Cruz sites has played a central role in the development of Lapita archaeology. A thesis by Moira Doherty (University of Auckland) has built on the Lapita base to provide an overview of post-Lapita developments in the Reef–Santa Cruz Islands (Doherty, 2007).

In the following chapters we draw on the results of these projects to develop a synthesis of Solomon Islands prehistory. Deficiencies in the current record determine that this will be a working model, open to revision as the state of our archaeological knowledge improves.

4

The Pleistocene and mid-Holocene record

Pleistocene settlement of Oceania

For much of the Pleistocene, New Guinea, mainland Australia and Tasmania were linked into a single continental landmass, known as Sahul, that covered nearly 11 million square kilometres during the lowest sea stands of the last glacial maximum (20–22,000 BP) (Allen & O'Connell, 1995:395). During the same period much of island Southeast Asia was similarly joined and formed the region known as Sunda (Voris, 2000) (Figure 1.2). Sea levels fluctuated throughout the Upper Pleistocene, exposing and then recovering extensive areas of the continental shelf, but Sahul was always separated from Southeast Asia along a sea gap corresponding to the biogeographic boundary zone of Wallacea (Dickerson et al., 1928) (Figure 4.1). There are several potential island-hopping routes across Wallacea but all potential routes available to humans would have required at least one crossing of at least 90 km, and several of more than 30 km (Birdsell, 1977). How humans made the crossing is still unclear (Allen & O'Connell, 2007) but it probably involved the use of bamboo rafts or bark canoes capable of carrying a minimum viable colonising group of five or more people. The early colonisation of Sahul by humans probably involved many trips across Wallacea over several thousand years, including return voyaging back to Sunda (Allen & O'Connell, 2007; Spriggs, 1997:27). There have been several claims that these first crossings to Sahul occurred before 50,000 BP and perhaps beyond 100,000 BP (Roberts et al., 1990, 1994) but these claims are contested on various grounds (O'Connell & Allen, 2004); the earliest reliable dates lie in the range 42–45,000 BP (Summerhayes et al., 2009; Summerhayes et al., 2010). Sites of this age are dispersed between the Huon Peninsula of Papua New Guinea in the

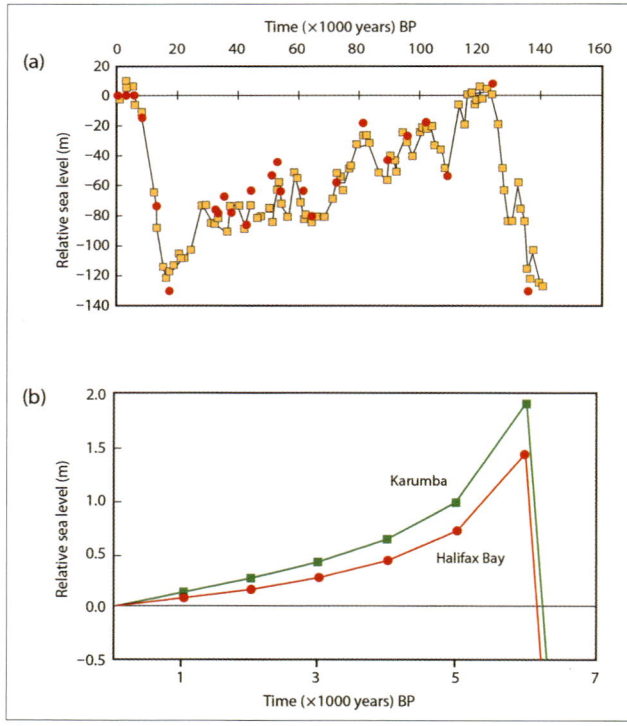

Figure 4.1. Pleistocene fluctuations in sea levels affecting western Melanesia. Upper figure from Chappell et al. (1996, fig. 1); lower figure after Nakada & Lambek (1989, fig. 10).

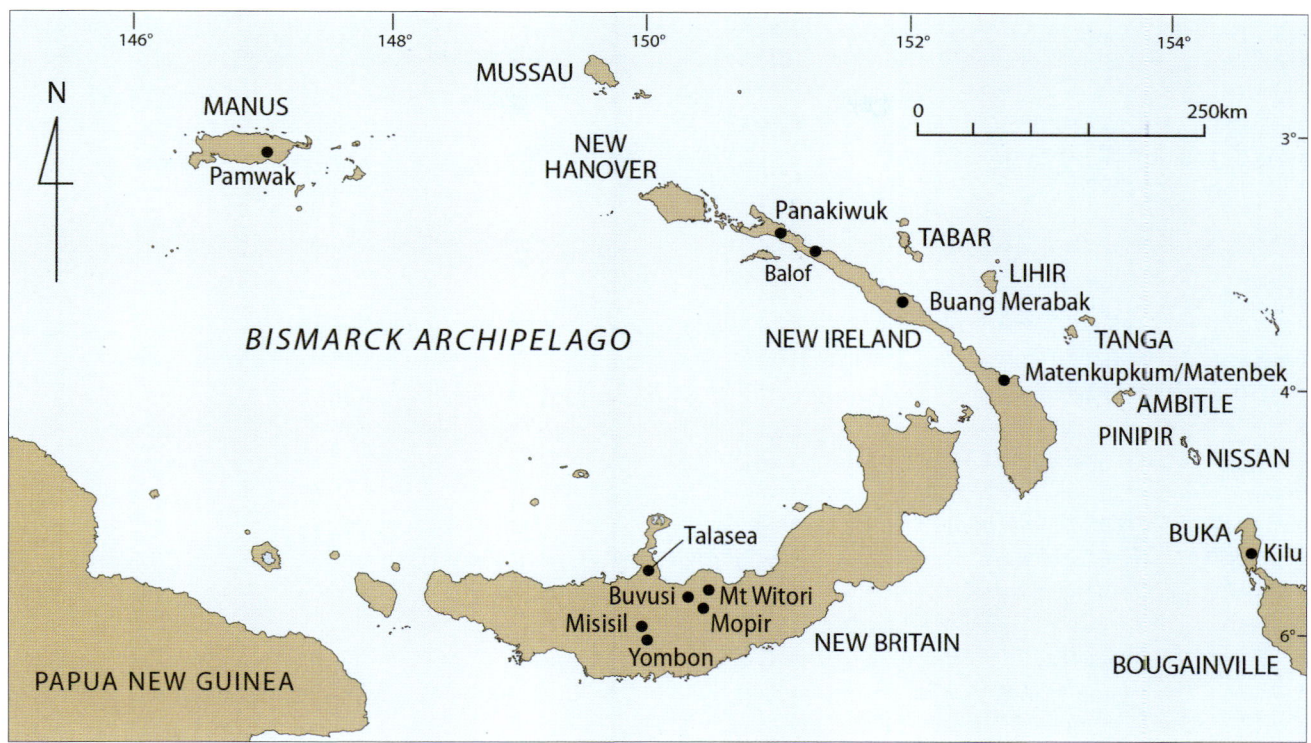

Figure 4.2. Location of Pleistocene archaeological sites in the Papua New Guinea–Solomon Islands region.

north and the southwest tip of Western Australia, which suggests efficient and rapid dispersal along coastlines.

Who these colonising people were is as important as when they arrived, although the two are clearly related. The ability to make the sea crossings, rapidly traverse the continent of Sahul and adapt to a wide range of environments implies an organisational ability normally associated with modern humans (Leavesley, 2007:309). This is consistent with the archaeological record of human skeletal remains from Sahul, which all are anatomically modern, although few, if any, specimens are reliably dated to the early colonisation period. The date of 45,000 BP also coincides roughly with the first appearance of anatomically modern humans in the wider Sunda–Sahul region (Barker et al., 2002), and the colonisation of Sahul appears to have been part of the first spread of modern humans far beyond Africa (Allen & O'Connell, 1995:396). By 40,000 BP the colonisation of Sahul was well advanced and the first sites were appearing in the islands of the Bismarck Archipelago, which had remained separated from the mainland of Sahul at all times during the Pleistocene (Torrence et al., 2004) (Figure 4.2). The earliest dated site in the Bismarck Archipelago is Buang Merabak on New Ireland, which dates to 39,500 BP (Leavesley et al., 2002; Leavesley & Chappell, 2004) and represents the first phase of human expansion eastward into the true Oceanic world.

There are a handful of sites now known from the Bismarck Archipelago that date to the first colonisation phase of about 39–35,000 BP, and they appear to represent the activities of small, highly mobile groups of hunter–gatherers exploiting both coastal and inland resource zones. At 29,000 BP the

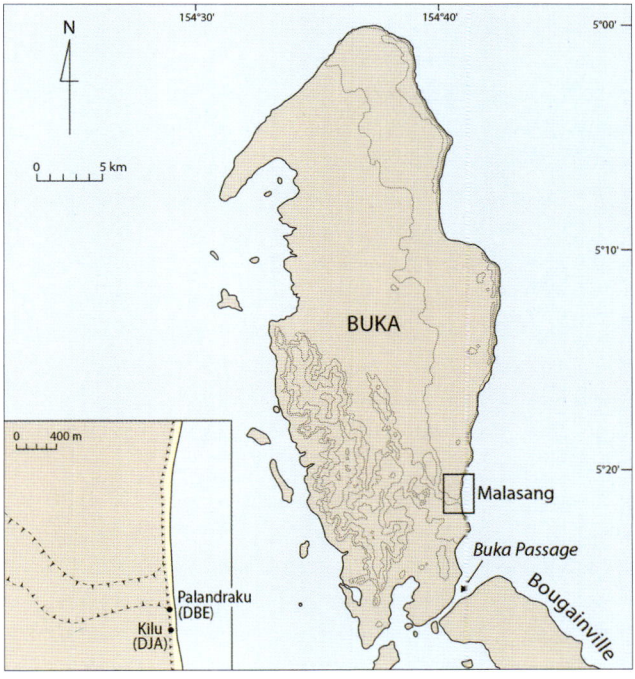

Figure 4.3. Buka and Buka Passage, showing Kilu Cave (DJA site).

next major push to the east occurs with the occupation of the Solomon Islands chain. This is represented by a single site, Kilu Cave, located in the raised limestone formations of Sohano in southeast Buka (Wickler, 2001; Wickler & Spriggs, 1988) (Figure 4.3).

Pleistocene occupation of the Solomon Islands

The colonisation of Buka represents a landmark event in the settlement history of the Pacific, from three different angles. At 180 km from New Ireland or 150 km from Ambitle, the settlement of Buka from the Bismarck Archipelago involved a longer ocean trip than any previous voyage into Oceania; indeed, it was probably the longest ocean voyage ever undertaken in the world at the time. The voyage was on the extreme margins of island intervisibility and probably marked the threshold of technological capabilities for Pleistocene seafaring. Today the Green Islands (Nissan and Pinipir) lie en route, at around 65 km north of Buka. Whether these uplifted coral atolls of Pleistocene age were above sea level at the time Buka was first settled is currently unknown. If not, the voyagers would have had to travel about 50 km out of New Ireland, or from Ambitle Island, before they spotted the coast of Buka. At this point, in favourable atmospheric conditions, both New Ireland and Buka would have been visible on the horizon, but any changes in conditions could easily have put the travellers out of sight of land for hours or even days. The second factor is that this appears to have been the first one-way colonisation event in Pacific history; there is no evidence in the Kilu Cave record of subsequent contact with the Bismarck Archipelago until many thousands of years after first settlement. And third, the crossing from mainland New Guinea to the Solomon Islands was accompanied by a general decline in terrestrial and marine biodiversity that had important economic implications for the first settlers.

The Bismarck Archipelago contains 52 mammal species, but this drops to 45 in the Solomons and then falls sharply to 12 in Vanuatu (Alejandra & Gregory, 2005). Among the vertebrate taxa that were not found in natural distribution in the Solomons chain is cuscus, which was an important hunting prey in the Pleistocene Bismarcks. Current archaeological evidence suggests that the cuscus did not arrive in the Solomons until about 3300 BP: this left a few species of bats, reptiles and rats (including two now extinct species) as the only terrestrial vertebrates available to the first hunters (White et al., 2000). The reefs, too, had a lower biodiversity than those of the Bismarcks (Leavesley, 2006:198). The result of this biogeographic decline was that the Pleistocene forests of the Solomon Islands were probably marginal for a terrestrial hunting and gathering economy (Bailey & Headland, 1991). Indeed, until the excavation of Kilu Cave it was generally supposed that the settlement of the Solomons chain would have been delayed until the development of food-production systems in the mid-Holocene. The discovery of early cultural levels in the Kilu Cave deposit suggests either that this assumption is unfounded, or that these first arrivals employed some other economic strategies. The excavations at Kilu Cave were modest in scope but the results have greatly influenced our understanding of the critical early phase of island Melanesian colonisation.

Kilu Cave (DJA site) – Buka Island

Buka is a large island about 55 km long and 15 km wide, separated from Bougainville by an 800-metre-wide strait known as Buka Passage (Figure 4.3). The north and east coasts of the island are formed by tectonic uplift and contain extensive areas of limestone cliffs and raised terraces. The Kilu Cave site is located on one of the uplifted regions of the southeast coast, at Malasang, about 8 km north of Buka Passage. Kilu is one of a number of solution caves at the base of a limestone cliff, and the cave mouth currently stands at about 8 m above sea level (asl), 65 m from the coast. Based on models in Chappell and Shackleton (1986), Wickler (2001:37) estimates that the cave was approximately 46 m asl at the time of first settlement and as much as 130 m asl at the end of the Pleistocene occupation.

The main chamber of Kilu Cave is about 33 m wide at the mouth and extends back 17 m. It has a dry floor sloping gently down (east) to a steep talus slope (Figures 4.4 and 4.5). In 1987 Stephen Wickler excavated a 3 x 1 m trench near the back wall of the main chamber at an area where he considered that the sediments were likely to be deepest and least disturbed (Wickler, 2001:33) (Figure 4.6). The excavations reached a depth of 2.25 m onto a flowstone floor. The sediments were largely homogeneous and were comprised mainly of weathering products from the cave roof. Detailed stratigraphic divisions were difficult to define; Wickler interpreted the excavation units as comprising two main layers, each containing several sublayers or lenses (Figure 4.7). The lower layer (Layer II) was laid down during a Pleistocene occupation spanning the period c. 29,000 to 20,000 BP. Layer II was deposited in the early Holocene, following a period of abandonment that spanned approximately 10,000 years.

Wickler used three shell samples to date Layer II. These were collected at a depth of 200 cm and the results are presented (uncalibrated) in Table 4.1.

THE PLEISTOCENE AND MID-HOLOCENE RECORD

The midden from Layer II included a wide range of terrestrial and marine species broadly similar in content to the Pleistocene sites of New Ireland (Leavesley, 2006; Leavesley et al., 2002). A total of 1148 bones of terrestrial vertebrates were identified to seven major classes (rodent, bat, snake, varanid, skink, agamid, unidentified reptile). The assemblage was dominated by rat, including two now extinct species (*Solomys spriggsarum* and *Melomys spechti*). No Polynesian rat (*Rattus exulans*) was identified, although it appears high up in the Layer I deposit. Only three bird bones (representing a hawk, a rail and a pigeon) were identified from Layer II. There were seven taxa in the fishbone assemblage ranking at 5% or higher (accounting for 90% of the total fishbone assemblage). These were Labridae (wrasses), Serranidae (groupers and cods), Balistidae (triggerfish), Elasmobranchii (sharks and rays), Scombridae (mackerels and tunas), Coryphaenidae (dolphinfish) and Scaridae (parrotfish). The dominant molluscan fauna in the assemblage were *Nerita* spp. and *Turbo* spp.

Based on the midden data, Wickler (2001) interpreted the major terrestrial component of the subsistence system in the Pleistocene levels as comprising a generalised forest hunting strategy targeting small mammals, reptiles and birds. There is less evidence for the hunting of colonial seabirds and flightless forest species than might be expected

Figures 4.4 and 4.5. Kilu Cave (photos by Stephen Wickler, used with permission).

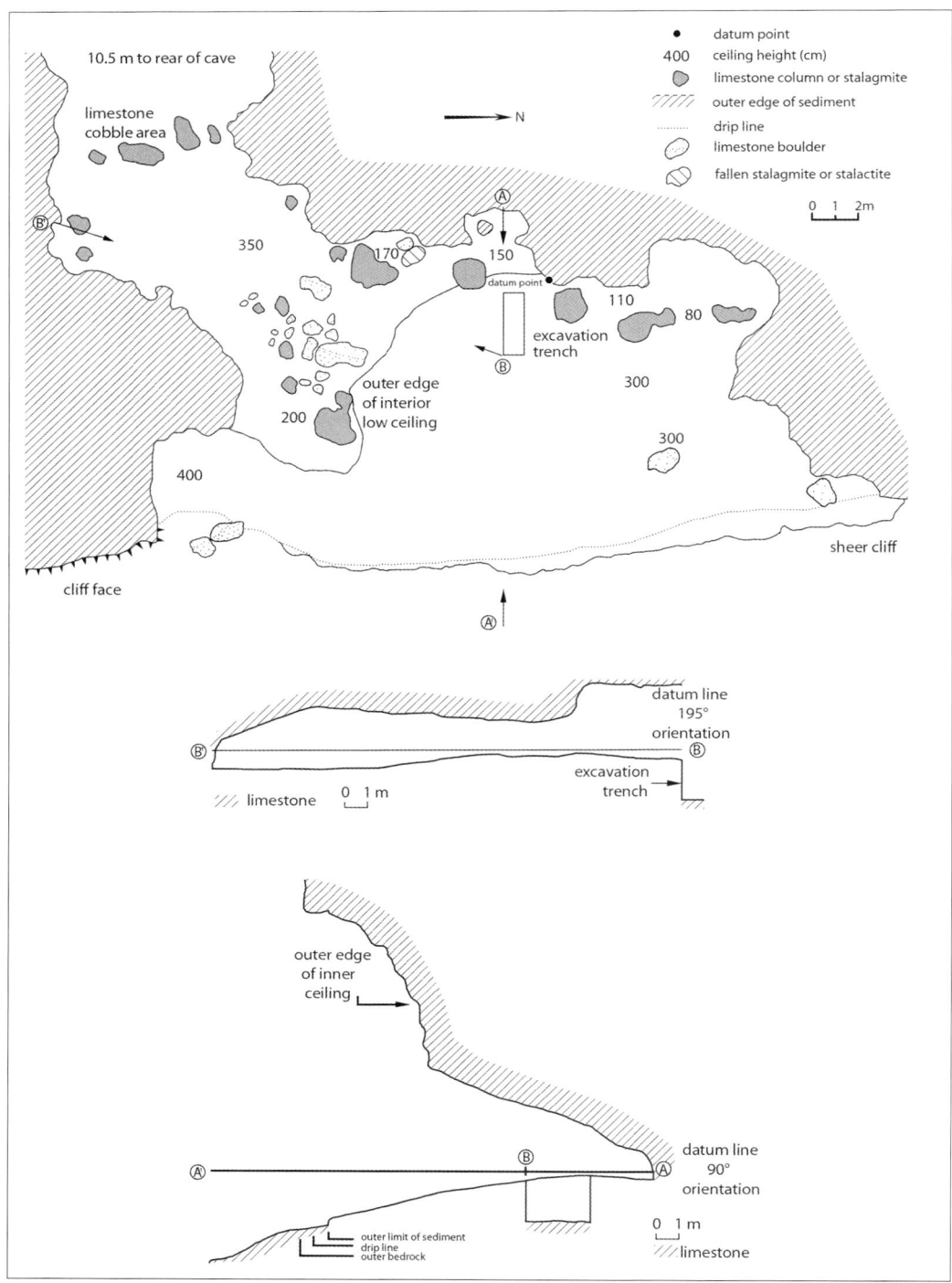

Figure 4.6. Plan of Kilu Cave excavation units (from Wickler, 2001).

in a colonisation-phase Pacific site (Steadman, 1995). This may be a sampling or taphonomic issue, although the earliest sites from New Ireland also contain scant evidence for the targeting of such species (Steadman, 1999; Summerhayes et al., 2009). The shellfish being eaten at Kilu were mainly rocky shore taxa, and there is a remarkable similarity in taxonomic representation – and changes through the sequence – with shellfish found at Matenkupkum, the Pleistocene site on New Ireland (Wickler 2001:233). The fishbone assemblage, however, is quite unusual.

Most Pacific fishbone assemblages are strongly weighted in favour of four or five families and these are usually restricted

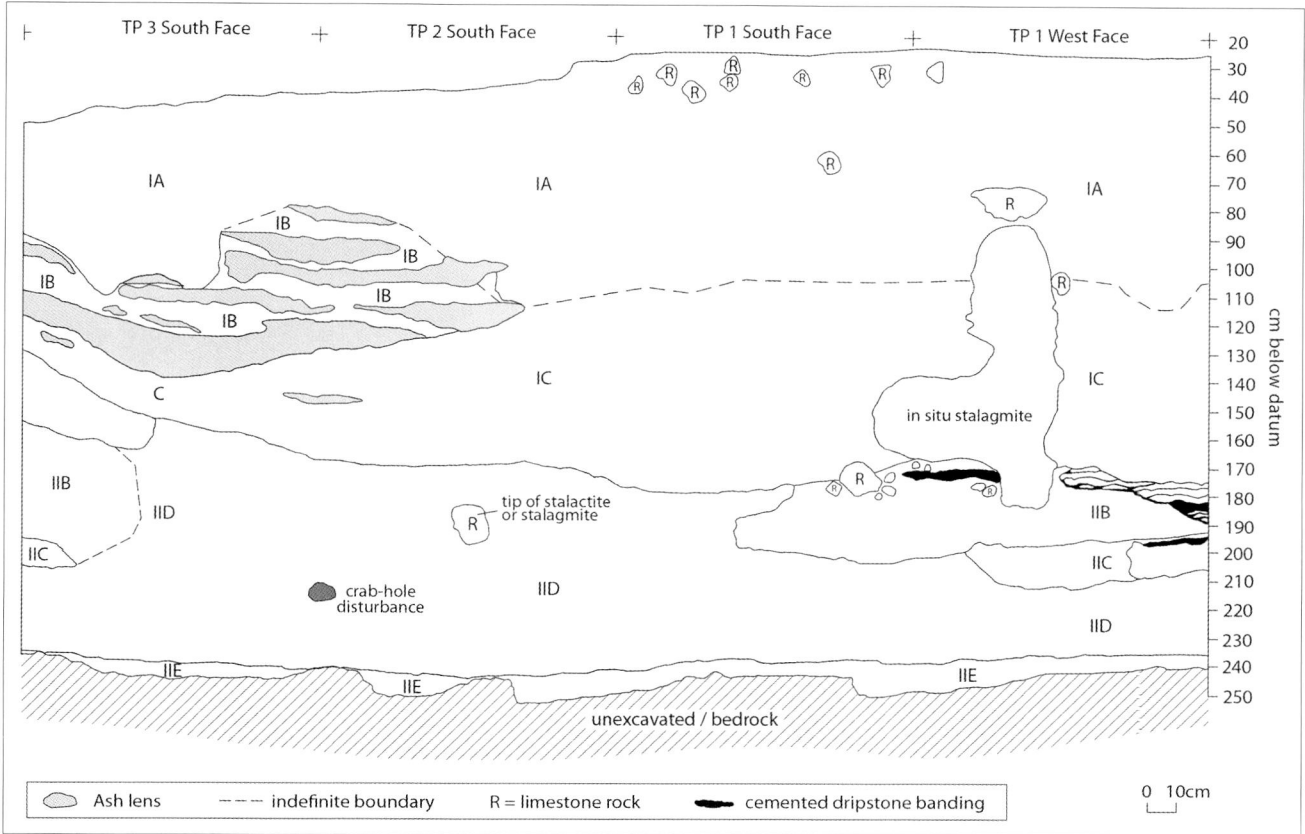

Figure 4.7. Stratigraphy of the Kilu Cave excavations (after Wickler, 2001).

to a small number of ecological zones (Butler, 1988; Walter, 1989, 1998). In contrast the dominant taxa at Kilu inhabit a range of different zones – inshore benthic (Serranidae, Balistidae, Labridae), inshore pelagic (Elasmobranchi), reef edge, coral zone (Scaridae) and offshore pelagic (Scombridae) – and include both carnivorous and herbivorous species. Allen (1993:141) has argued against inferring a complex technology to account for the Pleistocene fishbone assemblages from New Ireland sites. Yet the diversity of ecological niches and feeding behaviours of the fish represented at Kilu Cave certainly suggests an advanced technology. In most parts of the Pacific these taxa would be caught using baited hooks (Labridae, Balistidae, Serranidae, Elasmobranchi), traps (Balistidae), nets (Balistidae, Scaridae), spears (Scaridae) or lures (Scombridae). There is no one-to-one correlation between taxa and fishing method, but it seems very unlikely that the fish families represented in the lower Kilu Cave assemblage were caught using generalised foraging methods. The absence of any material culture evidence for fishing behaviour is unfortunate.

The stone toolkit from Kilu Cave includes mainly coarse-grained volcanic stone flakes, along with specimens in quartz, calcite, chert and limestone. The assemblage consists mainly of unretouched waste flakes. The volcanic stone was probably locally sourced in the form of river cobbles, as indicated by the presence of cortex on many of the larger flakes. The only non-lithic artefacts from Pleistocene levels at Kilu Cave are worked fragments of *Turbo marmoratus*, which were also found in later Holocene levels at the site.

Although the stone tools are relatively simple they have proved extremely informative. Microscopic analysis undertaken by Tom Loy has revealed traces of plant residues adhering to some of the flake edges, and these contain identifiable starch grains and raphides (crystals of calcium oxalate)(Loy et al., 1992). From the earliest levels of Layer II these include starches of *Colocasia esculenta* (taro) and *Alocasia* sp. Studies of use-wear suggest that

Sample	Provenance	CRA
ANU-5990	TP1, IID/21	28,340 ± 280
Beta-26150	TP3, IID/18	23,820 ± 290
Beta-26149	TP3, IIB/15	20,140 ± 300

Table 4.1. Radiocarbon dates from Kilu Cave (DJA) Layer II. All samples are marine shell (from Wickler, 2001: Table 3.27).

the tools may have been used for processing raw taro corms (Wickler, 2001:234). This raises the stakes in the study of subsistence adaptations in Pleistocene Oceania considerably.

One of the most intriguing questions that emerges from these residue identifications is the possibility that the early Pleistocene settlers may have developed some form of wild plant management systems, involving an intensive exploitation of pre-domesticated taro. Wild stands of *Colocasia* would have been present in the Buka region. But given the low returns for plant gathering in the Pleistocene forests of island Melanesia, the big question is whether the Kilu people were simply harvesting wild taro or whether they engaged in other types of management activities. Domesticated taro has larger and more edible corms than the wild varieties, and these only developed as a result of long-term human selection. Spriggs (1997:38) suggests that the amount of residue present on the Layer II tools is an indication that this selection process had already started early on in the Kilu Cave occupation. This implies that one of the keys to early survival in the Solomon Islands may have been the active management of natural stands of *Colocasia* and other pre-domesticates through activities such as expanding and improving optimal growing zones. This could have been achieved by removing competitive plant species and increasing available light by clearing bush around swamps and river edges. These types of activities have been described as a form of 'cultivation without domestication', a possible precursor to indigenous Melanesian plant domestication (Spriggs, 1997:32; but see also Spriggs, 2000a). Wickler has gone further to suggest that charcoal remains of coconut and *Canarium* – the latter most probably an introduction from mainland New Guinea (Yen, 1996) – supports the possibility that, by terminal Pleistocene levels, tree cropping was also being practised. However, the charcoal remains he cites appear to be from basal levels of Layer I (Wickler, 2001:234, 240, Table 8.11) and thus of Holocene age; it is unclear if any charcoals of coconut and *Canarium* were well provenanced to Pleistocene levels.

Beyond Buka – Pleistocene expansion into the Solomon Islands

Kilu Cave contains the only archaeological record of Pleistocene expansion into the Solomon Islands. It is, however, a very strong record and begs the question of how far down the Solomons chain Pleistocene settlement advanced. There is nothing obviously different about the environment of Buka, so eastward settlement is unlikely to have been restricted by geographical or economic factors (Spriggs, 2000b:116). Nor is there any major technological barrier to overcome; when Kilu Cave was first occupied many of the larger islands of the Solomons chain were still part of Greater Bukida (Greater Bougainville), so Pleistocene settlers should have been able to push down the coasts as far to the southeast as modern Nggela in the Florida Group and across a very narrow channel to Guadalcanal.

There is an archaeological visibility and survival problem, however. Population densities for much of the Pleistocene would have been extremely low and likely concentrated around coastlines. With the rising sea levels of the Holocene period most of the coastal sites would have been submerged; indeed, the places where sites are most likely to survive are precisely in locations, like the Sohano formations of Buka, where there are raised limestone terraces abutting steep marine shelves. Such places have produced the earliest archaeological sites of coastal New Guinea, on the Huon Peninsula and in the Bismarck Archipelago. Such locations have not as yet been targeted for intensive archaeological survey, but we have identified several key regions of the Western Solomons as suitable candidates for systematic investigation. The most promising area lies along the northeast coast of Rendova, where there is a series of raised limestone terraces between about 280 and 400 metres above sea level, adjacent to the deep waters of the passage between New Georgia and Rendova islands. In 1999 we carried out a reconnaissance survey above Busana Bay on Rendova and located several shallow rockshelters; in one of these we excavated a volcanic oven stone at a depth of 1.1 m in a highly degraded limestone clay. Datable materials have yet to be recovered from sites along the Rendova terrace series, but further survey work there would be desirable.

Terminal Pleistocene changes

Kilu Cave was abandoned about 20,000 BP, at the same time as a number of other Pleistocene sites were abandoned in the Bismarck Archipelago to the west. In fact, this date appears to mark a major period of change in settlement patterns throughout island Melanesia. A number of reasons have been canvassed for this, including a drop in sea levels towards the glacial maximum, although in the case of Kilu Cave falling sea levels did not dramatically affect access to the coast (Specht, 2005:248; Wickler, 2001:37) Whatever the immediate cause, there is evidence that changes in settlement patterns were just part of a larger reorientation of subsistence systems and technologies throughout the region at this time. Gosden (1995) has argued that these changes can be characterised as a tendency away from a strategy whereby people moved between scarce resources, to one in which resources were moved to people.

One of the more dramatic elements in support of this argument is the appearance of introduced animal species in the midden record of the New Ireland sites (Flannery & White, 1991:108). The earliest of these new arrivals was the cuscus, which was introduced from the New Guinea mainland and which rapidly became one of the prime targets of forest hunting activities in island Melanesia. Other arrivals from New Guinea include a species of wallaby (*Thylogale browni*) and a commensal rat species (*Rattus praetor*), both of which appear in terminal Pleistocene deposits (Allen et al., 1989; Flannery & White, 1991; White et al., 2000). The transport of raw materials for manufacturing stone tools also increased from this time: in the New Ireland sites, obsidians have been identified that derived from the New Britain sources of Talasea and Mopir (Summerhayes, 2009), more than 350 km away.

Allen et al. (1989) argue that these changes in resource relationships demonstrate a level of human mobility and interaction that is not evidenced in the first 10,000 years of occupation, although Torrence et al. (2004) suggest that, at least in New Britain, the movement of raw materials over longer distances was a feature of settlement patterns from first settlement. Tree crops, including *Canarium* and coconut, were used by the end of the late Pleistocene, and Spriggs (1997:61) following Gosden (1995) has suggested that by 20,000 BP the economies of island Melanesia might have shifted into a hunting–horticulture regime that foreshadows the emergence of true production systems in the early Holocene. More recently, Matthew Spriggs (2000a) has moderated this position: he has suggested that a foraging lifestyle that also involved movement of species to replicate the diversity of the forests of mainland New Guinea may have been a long-term strategy in island Melanesia. Specht (2005) likewise provides a note of caution on overinterpreting the patchy late Pleistocene archaeological dataset. It does seem clear, however, that the independent development of domesticates in Highland New Guinea occurred in the mid-Holocene (Denham & Haberle, 2008), and mobile coastal populations may at that time have been involved in complex interaction both with the Highlands and with horticultural populations to the west in island Southeast Asia (Donohue & Denham, 2010).

Other than the abandonment of Kilu Cave after nearly 10,000 years of intermittent and low-density occupation, with the implication of a shift to new patterns of resource use, there is no direct evidence for any of these purported changes in the Solomon Island record. The New Ireland obsidians and the commensal animals do not appear in the Solomon Islands until the mid-Holocene. The only hint of continued contact with the west is the appearance of *Canarium* charcoals at 10,400 BP at Kilu, which suggests an introduction from New Guinea sometime in the terminal Pleistocene. Overall, however, the evidence points to the Solomon Islands having been largely isolated from developments in the west during most of the Pleistocene.

The early to mid-Holocene record

Towards the end of the Pleistocene the geomorphology of the Solomon Islands underwent changes that brought about new opportunities for human exploitation. The general model of coastal development is that sea levels rose with the retreat of the northern ice sheets from a low of around 170 m below current levels at 17,000 BP (Voris, 2000), to reach their highest stands between 5500 and 6000 BP. This was followed by a period of sea-level decline as a result of hydrostatic adjustment (or bounce-back). The specific history of coastal change in the Solomon Islands, however, varied greatly from region to region and was the result of both sea-level changes and geotectonic processes (Mann et al., 1998:273, fig. 15).

The first and most dramatic outcome of rising sea levels was the separation of Greater Bukida into a dispersed island chain. The loss of landmass was offset by the creation of hundreds of kilometres of new coastal reefs and, eventually, extensive coastal lagoon systems. Initially sea levels rose steadily and coral reefs struggled to keep pace. Narrow fringing reefs built up in concert with the rising seas, but they dropped directly into deep water and so offered little protection from the elements. In most places there was insufficient time for low coastal benches to develop, and much of the coastline would have been quite unattractive to human settlement (Nunn, 1998:247; Terrell, 2002). There are not many archaeological sites known from early to mid-Holocene period in the Solomon Islands, but there are three areas where we can catch enough of a glimpse to reconstruct a broad outline of events.

Buka and the Northern Solomons

The earliest known Holocene horizons in the Solomons are in Kilu Cave (Layer I, especially levels IB and IC) dated between the period 10,000 to 5000 cal BP (Figure 4.7). The site was more intensively occupied at this time than during the Pleistocene: the density of midden increased, as did the deposition rate; a number of fireplaces were recorded and there were changes in site use, technology and economic practices. Much of the activity represented in this period is related to cooking and food preparation (Wickler 2001:40).

Artefacts from the early Holocene levels at Kilu Cave include perforated shark teeth and vertebrae and a *Terebralia* shell chisel or abrader. Stone-tool production fell off from about 8000 cal BP, and only four flaked-stone tools were recovered from Upper Holocene levels. Other tools from this level include an anvil stone, a ground-stone implement and a fragment of a *Tridacna* shell adze (Wickler 2001:39).

A cuscus bone was first reported in Layer IC at a date of around 9000 cal BP, although Wickler took a conservative approach and considered the possibility that the bone was intrusive (i.e. had found its way into that layer from an upper horizon), since it was a single specimen (Wickler, 2001:221). Later, direct dating of the bone using accelerator mass spectrometry (AMS) techniques confirmed it to be intrusive at early Holocene levels (Spriggs, 2000:353), which is consistent with the evidence from the Lebang Takoroi site on Nissan Island where cuscus appears from about 5000 cal BP (Spriggs, 1991). Charcoal remains of coconut (*Cocos nucifera*) and *Canarium* (both *C. indicum* and *C. salomonense*) have been confidently identified from early Holocene horizons at Kilu (Wickler, 2001:234). Coconut could be a natural colonist of these islands but *Canarium* was most probably a human introduction from the New Guinea mainland. It is likely that harvesting nuts and tree fruits was an integral part of island Melanesian subsistence throughout the Holocene.

The tail end of the Holocene sequence from Kilu overlaps the earliest lenses at Palandraku Cave (Site DBE), located 250 m to the north. The DBE site was first excavated by Specht in 1967 and again 20 years later by Wickler. The pre-ceramic horizons date to about 5000 BP and contain a low density of cultural material that is interpreted as representing a temporary and non-intensive occupation (Wickler, 2001:42). The artefact assemblage includes unretouched stone flakes similar to those found in Kilu Cave, but at Palandraku these flakes are mainly chert, along with some examples of quartz, calcite and fine-grained volcanic stone. The faunal remains point to continued forest hunting of small game, including endemic reptiles, bats and rats. *Phalanger*, the introduced rat species and the domesticates do not appear until the later Lapita horizons. An earth oven was also found in the pre-ceramic levels.

The length of occupation of the Palandraku Cave site is unclear. The radiocarbon dates bracket a period of about 500 years but on stratigraphic grounds the actual occupation appears likely to have been no more than a century or two, so Palandraku does not extend the Buka pre-ceramic sequence much beyond that provided by the Kilu Cave deposits. Nevertheless we see, in Buka, a pattern that is repeated elsewhere in Bougainville and the Main Solomon Islands of a dearth of sites that fall within the mid-Holocene to Lapita period. This formative period just before the arrival of Austronesian settlers is represented only by the Guadalcanal rockshelter sites in the Poha Valley (see below).

Archaeologists have commented on the poor visibility of sites in the pre-ceramic Holocene record elsewhere in Near Oceania (Kirch, 2000:83; Sheppard, 2009; Specht, 2009), although they have made some progress in pulling the Holocene record together in West New Britain (Torrence, 2002). Recently archaeologists have argued that the distribution patterns of stemmed obsidian tools and of mortars and pestles in Papua New Guinea can be used to define sets of overlapping social networks that existed in the period 8000–3300 cal BP (Torrence & Swadling, 2008). These items are best known from mainland Papua and the Bismarck Archipelago, but they are found as far east as Bougainville: 'Like the mortars and pestles, the astoundingly large spread of stemmed tools … must be the product of social interaction that operated across a vast area, stretching from Biak Island in the west to Bougainville in the east (a distance of c. 2200km)' (Torrence & Swadling, 2008:609). These artefacts are not yet dated in Bougainville as they have not been found in secure contexts in association with suitable organic dating materials, but their existence raises the possibility that the Northern Solomons were participating in social networks stretching into the Bismarcks and beyond from the early Holocene. In fact, the Solomon Islands record of the early Holocene, while it is poorly resolved at present, does suggest some changes in mobility, economic systems and settlement patterns. The Kilu Cave data, for example, could support Torrence and Swadling's (2008) argument that beginning early in the Holocene, the Solomon Islands were once again in contact with the Oceanic world to the west (but see also Specht, 2005).

By the mid-Holocene, a few thousand years before the appearance of the first ceramic horizons, there were also changes in coastal dynamics. The coastal plains were reflooding to form shallow inshore lagoons, and as sea levels started to stabilise, local tectonic processes overtook rising sea levels as the major influence on coastal environments. Highly varied coastlines developed throughout the Solomon Islands and in many places, as sea-level rise tapered off, coral growth caught up and wide coral platforms grew out from the shorelines, creating zones of increasing potential for coastal foragers. Lateral erosion also increased and shore platforms started to cut deeply into the islands at the low-tide level. In areas where tectonic uplift was taking place this created raised beach terraces which later became prime habitation zones. The modern Solomon Island environment was unfolding, including the extensive coastal lagoon systems that support so many modern populations. It is possible that many of the coastal sites from this period may be buried under deep erosion deposits caused by a combination of natural changes in coastal morphology and increased sedimentation from expanding coastal bush clearance.

Population movement into and through the Solomon Islands and eventually out into Remote Oceania was a process that may well have been either triggered or supported by the creation of the new coastal environment (Terrell, 2002). Thus the history and timing of lagoon formation in the Solomon Islands could be a key factor in explaining early settlement and adaptation in the region. Below we examine the situation in New Georgia as a case study of the types of coastal processes that were occurring in the Holocene before the appearance of new cultural horizons associated with the arrival of Austronesian-speaking populations.

The Western Solomons

New Georgia, in the Western Solomons, contains some of the most extensive lagoon systems in the Solomon Islands, where they typically consist of long, shallow inshore lagoons lying between a string of barrier islands and a mangrove-lined mainland shoreline (Figure 4.8). The formation of the New Georgia Group was initiated in the Pliocene with a subduction reversal in which the Australian plate began to be subducted under the Pacific plate, creating an arc of Plio-Pleistocene volcanism in the New Georgia region (Mann et al., 1998; Stoddart, 1969). The increasing weight of this volcanic mass resulted in net subsidence of the islands. The normal sequence of barrier-reef formation around a central volcanic core involves coral building keeping pace with subsidence and resulting in shallow lagoons forming behind a barrier reef. This process was interrupted in New Georgia around 150,000 BP by tectonic uplift created by eastward movement of the Australian Plate and the Coleman Seamount, which raised the lagoon floors (Mann et al., 1998) (Figure 4.9) to form low, coastal plains behind a chain of raised barrier islands. Rivers flowed across the plains, cutting deep channels between the modern barrier islands. As sea levels rose at the end of the Pleistocene the plains started to flood once more, forming shallow lagoons. Along the barrier islands of the larger lagoon systems of New Georgia, wave notches in the exposed limestone cliffs record a complex sequence of geotectonic uplift and subsidence overprinted by variation in relative sea levels in the Holocene period.

In 1998 the authors, in partnership with John Dodson and Sarah Grimes from the Department of Geography at the University of Western Australia, obtained swamp cores from a number of locations in Roviana Lagoon with the aim of gaining insight into patterns of vegetation history associated with these coastal changes (Grimes, 2003). We selected core

Figure 4.8. The inshore lagoons of the Western Solomon Islands (Roviana Lagoon) (photo by authors).

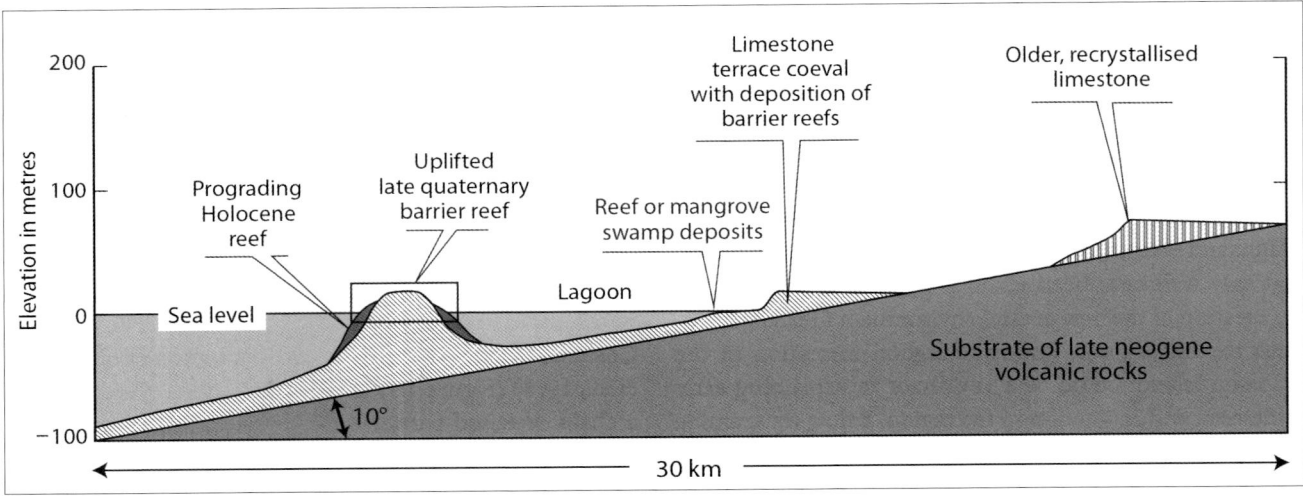

Figure 4.9. A model of late quaternary reef limestone in the New Georgia Group after Mann et al. (1998).

sites along the mangrove shores of the barrier islands, in the swampy river valleys on the mainland coast, lake beds on islands along the edges of both Roviana and Vonavona lagoons and on the northeastern side of Rendova (Figure 4.10). The results of the palynological and sedimentological analysis refer mainly to the later part of the Holocene, but before the appearance of definite archaeological signals. With the previously published geomorphological results a simple but useful palaeoenvironmental sequence for Roviana Lagoon can be developed (see Grimes, 2003: Table 5.1).

1. 10,000 BP. Sea-level rise at the end of the Pleistocene caused a gradual flooding of the coastal plains formed initially by the tectonic uplift of tertiary lagoon systems.
2. 6000 BP. Sea levels reached their highest stand. Sea-level notches, some of which record the mid-Holocene high stand, are commonly present at variable elevations resulting from geotectonic movement of 1–10 m above living coral in Roviana Lagoon. Some of these have been dated, using marine shells in growth position, to between 6500 and 5500 BP by Mann et al. (1998), who assume a +2 m mid-Holocene high stand (Sheppard & Walter, 2009).
3. 4000 BP. Roviana Lagoon reached approximately its current form but with slightly higher than modern-day water levels.
4. 3700–2600 BP. First appearance in the Roviana and Vonavona pollen cores of evidence of small firing events (Kolomateana site) dated to around 3500 BP. These may have been caused by humans clearing land for horticulture. Evidence of increased charcoal influx after 3500 BP (UWA 29 2980 ± 240 BP, 3698–2489 95.4% HPD) at the Kolomateana site is followed by a sharp decline and then a marked increase in charcoal deposition after c. 2000 BP (Grimes, 2003). This pattern is similar to that seen at the Tamberamakoto site, which has a large charcoal signal at levels dated to 3220 ± 60 BP (UWA-13, 3561–3242 95.4% HPD) followed by a metre of low to no charcoal influx until after 2660 ± 40 BP (ANSTO OZF 135, 2849–2520 95.4% HPD) (Grimes, 2003, fig. 4.11). Deposition of two distinct clay layers after 3100 BP at Tamberamakoto are inferred to result from erosion of a landscape disturbed and opened by burning (Grimes, 2003:171). Pollen of *Artocarpus altilis* (breadfruit) has been identified at levels dated to c. 3100 BP.
5. 2600 BP. Sea levels reached approximately their current level. Evidence for burning intensified at all sites, and the vegetation patterns indicate the presence of an anthropogenically modified landscape. This pattern very closely matches that seen from pollen cores on Guadalcanal (Haberle, 1996).
6. 800 BP. From about 800 BP there is a noticeable increase in charcoal concentrations in combination with evidence for the expansion of fernlands and a decline in forest trees. An abundance of nut and fruit trees, seeds and microfossils suggests a period of coastal forest clearance and conversion to garden land.

It is likely that the other lagoon systems of the Solomon Islands, not only in the Western Province but also to the east in Malaita and the Marau Sound area of Guadalcanal, followed a similar pattern of change during the Holocene. Thus, shortly after 6000 BP conditions in much of the Solomon Islands would have been increasingly favourable for human expansion. No actual sites of this age have been recorded in the Western Solomons but ephemeral signs of human activity of mid-Holocene age have been identified in Guadalcanal.

THE PLEISTOCENE AND MID-HOLOCENE RECORD

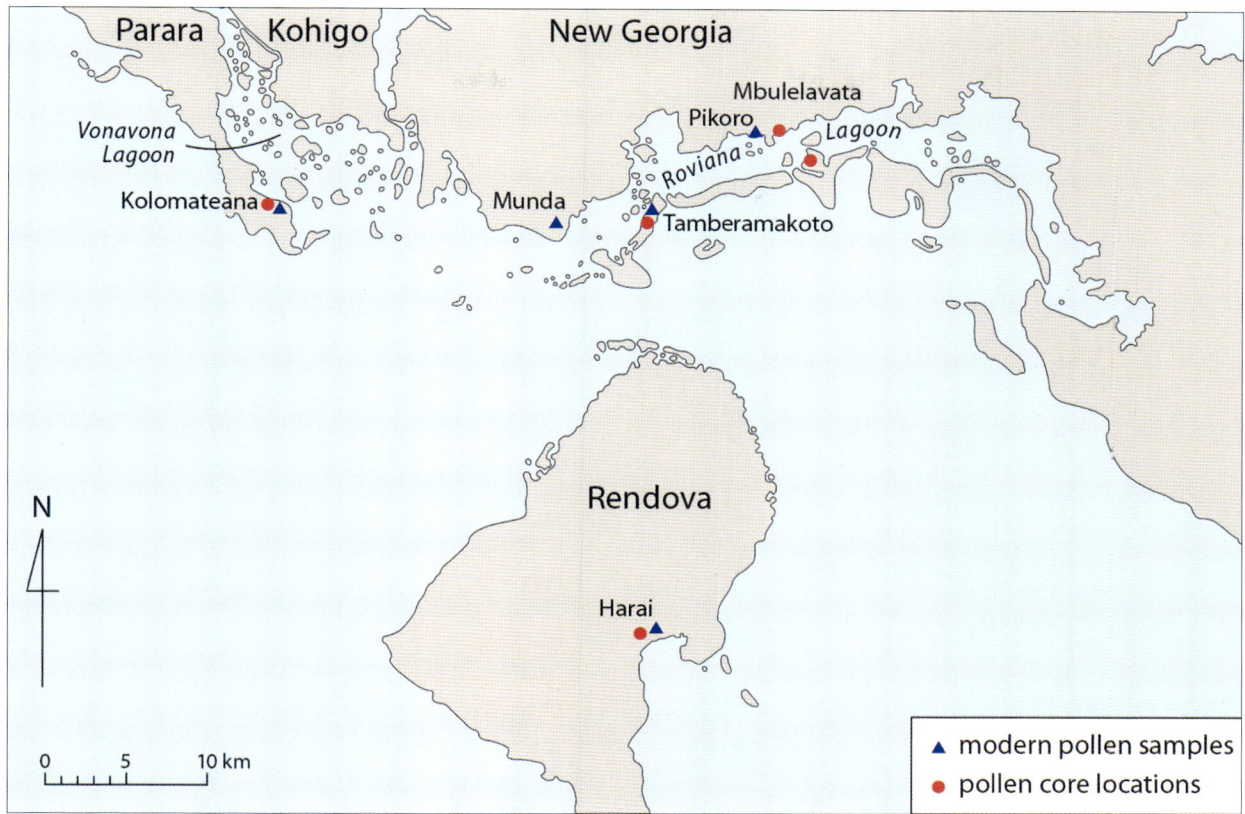

Figure 4.10. Locations of pollen core sites (from Grimes, 2003, fig. 3.1).

The Guadalcanal sequence

The Guadalcanal sequence reported by David Roe (1993) is the longest archaeological sequence reported so far from the Solomon Islands east of Buka. The sequence is based on only a small number of sites and on limited excavation data from the northwest of the island (Figure 4.11). The Guadalcanal work provides a useful, although patchy, record of mid-Holocene cultural change and environmental interactions just prior to the Lapita expansion out of the Bismarcks. Roe's Guadalcanal sequence is described below with special reference to the mid-Holocene levels. Some issues arising from Roe's interpretation of the Guadalcanal record, particularly in reference to Austronesian and Lapita expansion, are addressed in later chapters.

The Guadalcanal sequence is based on excavations of cave and rockshelter deposits in the Poha and Vura valleys, and on a single open settlement in the Visale area of northwest Guadalcanal. It also draws on palaeoenvironmental data, especially the palynological work of Simon Haberle (1996). The earliest cultural horizons are from Vatuluma Posovi (SG-2-1) (also known in the literature as Poha Cave or Fotoruma Cave), located 3 km west of Honiara and about 2 km inland up the Poha Valley (Figures 4.11 and 4.12).

Vatuluma Posovi (Poha) Cave

The site (SG-2-1) was located in the 1960s and was first excavated by William Davenport in 1966 and then by amateur archaeologists Tom Russell and James Tedder. These excavators recovered a variety of shell and chert artefacts but no obsidian, shell adzes or ceramics. Their excavations removed over 150 cubic metres of deposit from the cave, which in its maximum dimensions measured 11.7 by 6.7 m with deposits over 3 m deep (Davenport, 1968, Davenport et al., n.d., Roe, 1993:44, Russell, 2003). Russell and Tedder recovered samples from the basal deposits, which they dated to about 3330–2770 cal BP. The results of these investigations indicated the potential early age of the site, and Green (1977) accepted the possibility that it might represent a pre-ceramic occupation of the region. Unfortunately their excavations removed nearly all the intact deposits from the cave (Davenport, 1968) and, for years after the first excavations, Poha Cave remained very difficult to evaluate. The position of the site datum was uncertain and this meant the reconstructed stratigraphy could not be properly assessed. The artefacts, too, needed to be properly studied and all the archaeological data correlated with the radiocarbon dates.

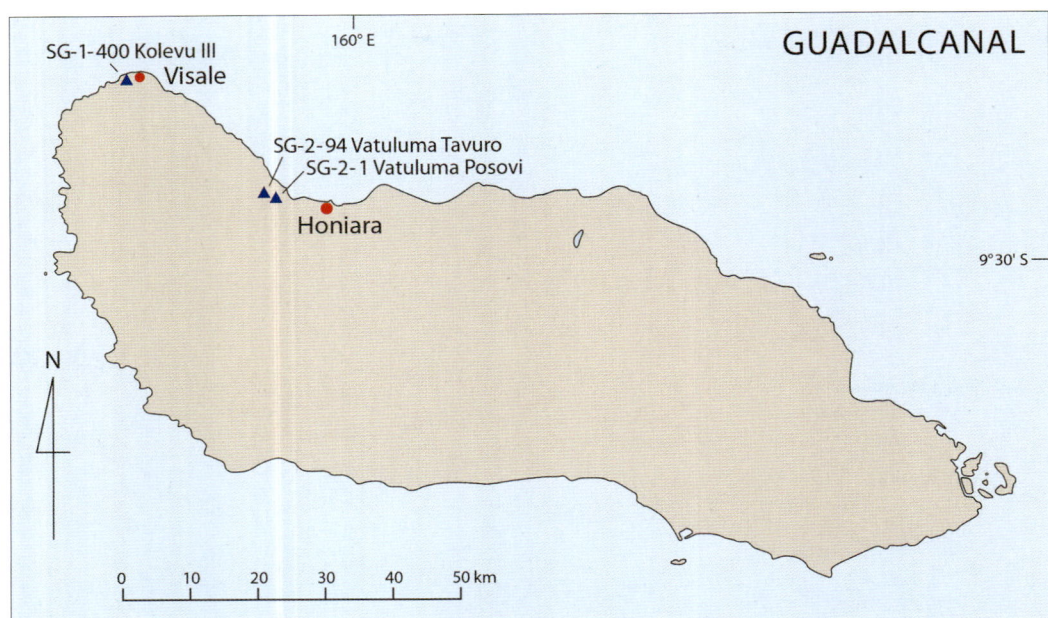

Figure 4.11. Location of archaeological sites in Guadalcanal (after Roe, 1993).

Figure 4.12. Detail of reconstruction of community at Poha Cave (painting by Briar Sefton, used with permission).

Davenport's collections were returned to the Solomon Islands Museum in the 1980s and David Roe took on the task of integrating the Vatuluma Posovi site into the regional sequence. Roe worked on the archival and artefactual material and then returned to the site in 1987–88, where he succeeded in locating a small remnant portion of cultural deposit near the front of the cave. Despite Roe's valiant efforts to resolve the earlier excavation data, the task was only partially successful. We now rely, for stratigraphic information, on Roe's excavation of the small remaining portion of the site. According to Roe the site contained five occupation phases which he defined on the basis of the previous unpublished reports, correlated against his own excavation data and field observations (Figures 4.13 and 4.14). Phase 1 is relevant to the current discussion and the full sequence is reviewed in Chapter 6.

Phase 1 (6000 to 4000 cal BP)

Phase 1 is the earliest, mid-Holocene phase and was defined by two dates (ANU-6733 and ANU-6744) which bracketed a deposit containing 'small quantities of artefacts – chert flakes and chips, a single *Trochus* armband fragment and *Trochus* fishhook blanks – and quantities of terrestrial animals and marine fish and shell midden of predominantly freshwater species …' (Roe, 1993:66). In fact, the artefacts appear to be more closely associated with the stratigraphically higher sample (ANU-6734 from Layer 3(I), 3940 ± 220 BP on *Canarium* charcoal), which calibrates to 4876–3699 (95.4% HPD) cal BP. No artefacts or other cultural materials were

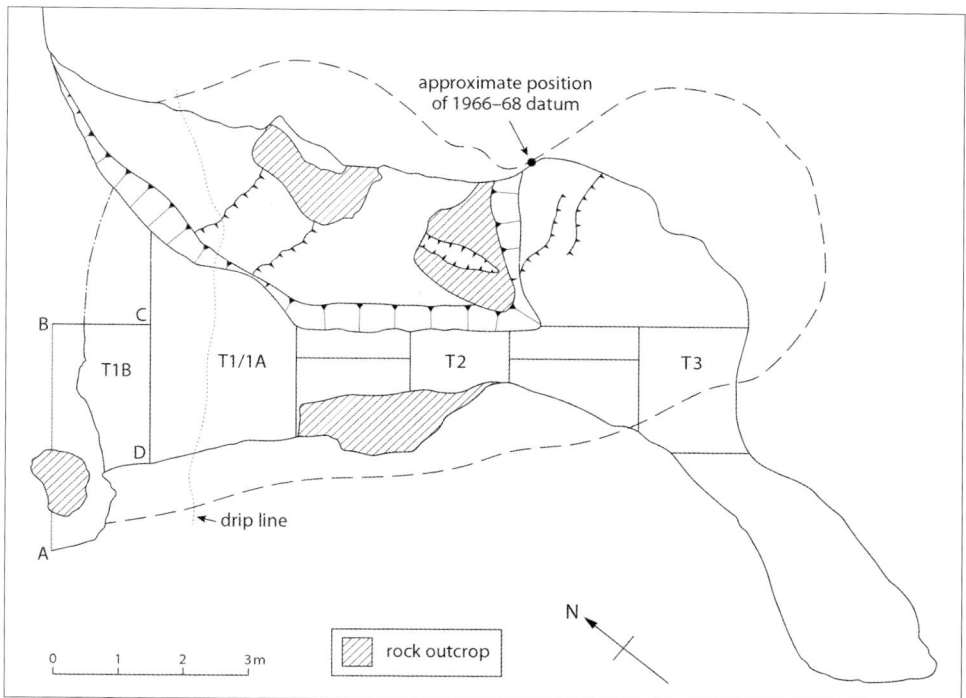

Figure 4.13. Plan of Vatuluma Posovi Cave excavations (after Roe, 1993).

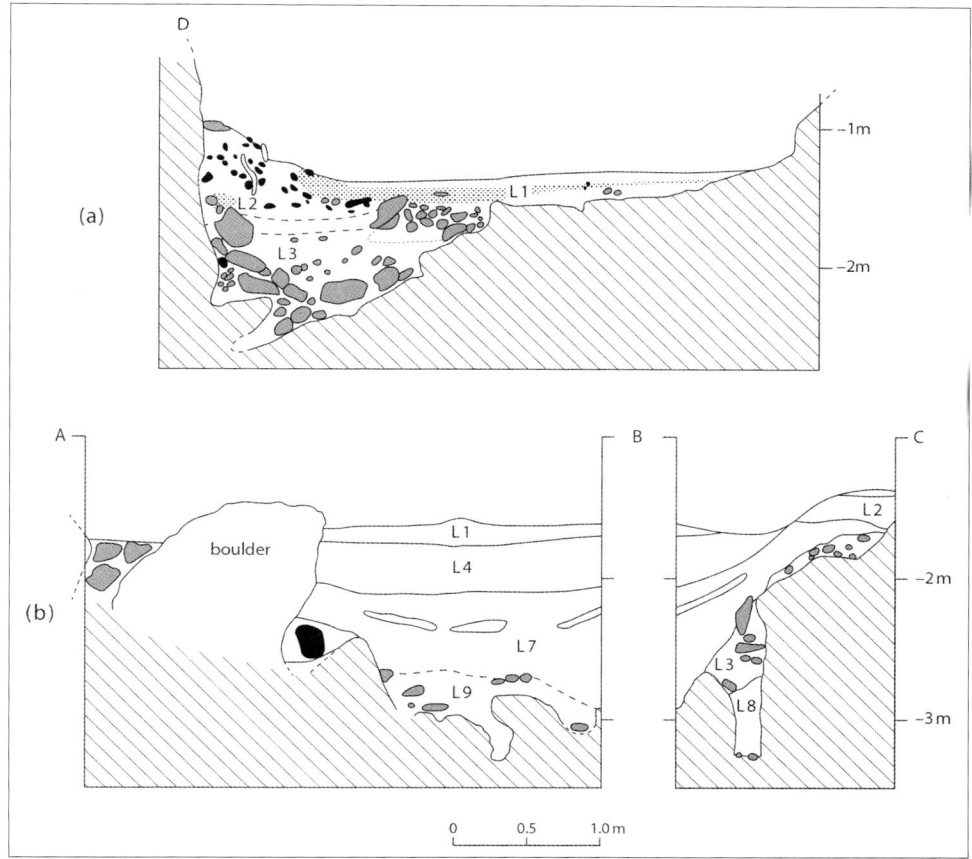

Figure 4.14. Stratigraphy of Vatuluma Posovi Cave excavations (after Roe, 1993). See Figure 4.13 for location of excavations.

recovered from Layer 3(III) (Roe, 1993:64), which is dated by ANU-6733 (5430 ± 220 BP on *Canarium* charcoal) and which we calibrate to 6652–5709 cal BP (95.4% HPD) (Roe, 1993:63). Thus a conservative interpretation of Phase 1 might place occupation at Vatuluma Posovi closer to the upper end of the band (perhaps around 4500 cal BP) than the lower (Figure 4.15). The vertebrate faunal assemblage from Phase 1 was extremely fragmentary and much was unable to be identified. Identified specimens included a single bone from an unidentified megapode plus some fragments of bone from terrestrial mammals – murids (rats) and bats – and reptiles. Marine and terrestrial fishbone was present. The molluscan assemblage was dominated by shellfish from fresh and brackish water habitats, although marine specimens of *Turbo* sp., *Trochus* sp., *Gafarium* and *Anadara* were present. *Canarium* nutshell was also found.

Vatuluma Tavuro Cave

Unlike Vatuluma Posovi, Tavuro Cave (SG-2-94) had not been badly disturbed and the stratigraphy was relatively easy to define. Although the observed layers were not present in all the excavation units, Roe was able to define a two-phase occupation sequence that described the site as a whole. The authors have ascribed the dates for the two occupations on the basis of discussions in Roe (1993:114–15). Occupation 1 dates between approximately 4400 and 2150 cal BP and Occupation 2 from around 1000 cal BP to recent. The artefacts from Occupation 1 include a *Trochus* sp. ring fragment, and chips and flakes of chert that are similar to source materials located in Eastern Guadalcanal and Malaita (Roe, 1993:116). In Occupation 2 the use of chert continues but the size of individual pieces declines, as does the range of sources used. The molluscan assemblages provide an indication of changing environmental exploitation strategies. The Occupation 1 material is dominated (80% by weight) by freshwater species; this decreases to 52% in the later occupation. Mangrove species (e.g. Veneridae spp.) are present in Occupation 1 but not in Occupation 2, which Roe (1993:116) suggests is indicative of a decline in mangrove-fringed coastlines in favour of muddy–sandy shore environments. This could be attributed to siltation effects, perhaps associated with the clearance of coastal forest and conversion to grasslands. The faunal assemblages also suggest a similar environmental change. Occupation 1 layers contained taxa associated with undisturbed forests, such as the endemic murids of the *Uromys* genus. These disappear from Occupation 2 layers and there is a general decline in the use of terrestrial vertebrates as a food source. *Canarium* nutshell was found throughout the deposit but increased greatly in relative abundance in the Occupation 2 deposits.

Roe (1993, 2000) has developed a three-phase sequence for northwestern Guadalcanal in which each of the phases is named in the local Nginia language and refers to associated environmental zones. The Hoana Phase is summarised below, and the Hamosa and Moru phases are discussed in Chapter 6.

Hoana (Forest) Phase (6400–2200 cal BP)

The Hoana Phase is represented archaeologically by the earliest levels at Vatuluma Posovi and Vatuluma Tavuro. The economic system points to the exploitation of 'relatively undisturbed and undeveloped forest and the collection of molluscan foods from fresh and brackish water environments' (Roe, 1993:95). The faunal assemblage includes endemic rats and reptiles and, together with the molluscan faunas, this is indicative of a generalised forest edge and riverine hunting and gathering system. *Canarium* nuts were harvested, but nut-processing stones have not been identified. At present the full extent of coastal exploitation is not known but marine species are represented at Vatuluma Posovi, and the Buka results suggest that inland economic practices would have been complemented by a fishing component. The artefact assemblage from the Hoana Phase includes chert flakes, *Trochus* shell arm rings whose appearance is dated by ANU 6734 (3940 ± 140 BP) in Layer 3(I) at Vatuluma Posovi, and a few *Trochus* shell items that might be fishhook blanks in Layer 3(II) (Roe, 1993:63–64). These occur from at least 4500 cal BP, while polished stone adzes and shell beads appear sometime well after 3000 cal BP in Phase 3 of the Vatuluma Posovi sequence (Roe, 1993:71). In the early levels of the Hoana Phase, chert was sourced from a number of locations in Guadalcanal: this suggests population mobility; perhaps even the presence of coastal exchange systems. By late in the Hoana Phase, cherts considered to be from Malaita were also being used.

Summary

Climate changes at the end of the Pleistocene brought the development of new coastal environments throughout much of the Solomon Islands that may well have triggered a movement of people eastward to take advantage of new economic opportunities. Beginning around 10,000 BP gradual flooding of the coastal plains started to open up the lagoon systems; within a few thousand years they would have supported a rich and diverse marine biota. Today these environments are among the richest in Melanesia and support some of the densest human populations. By at least 6000 BP, when sea levels were at their highest, the lagoons of the Western Province must have been strong attractors

THE PLEISTOCENE AND MID-HOLOCENE RECORD

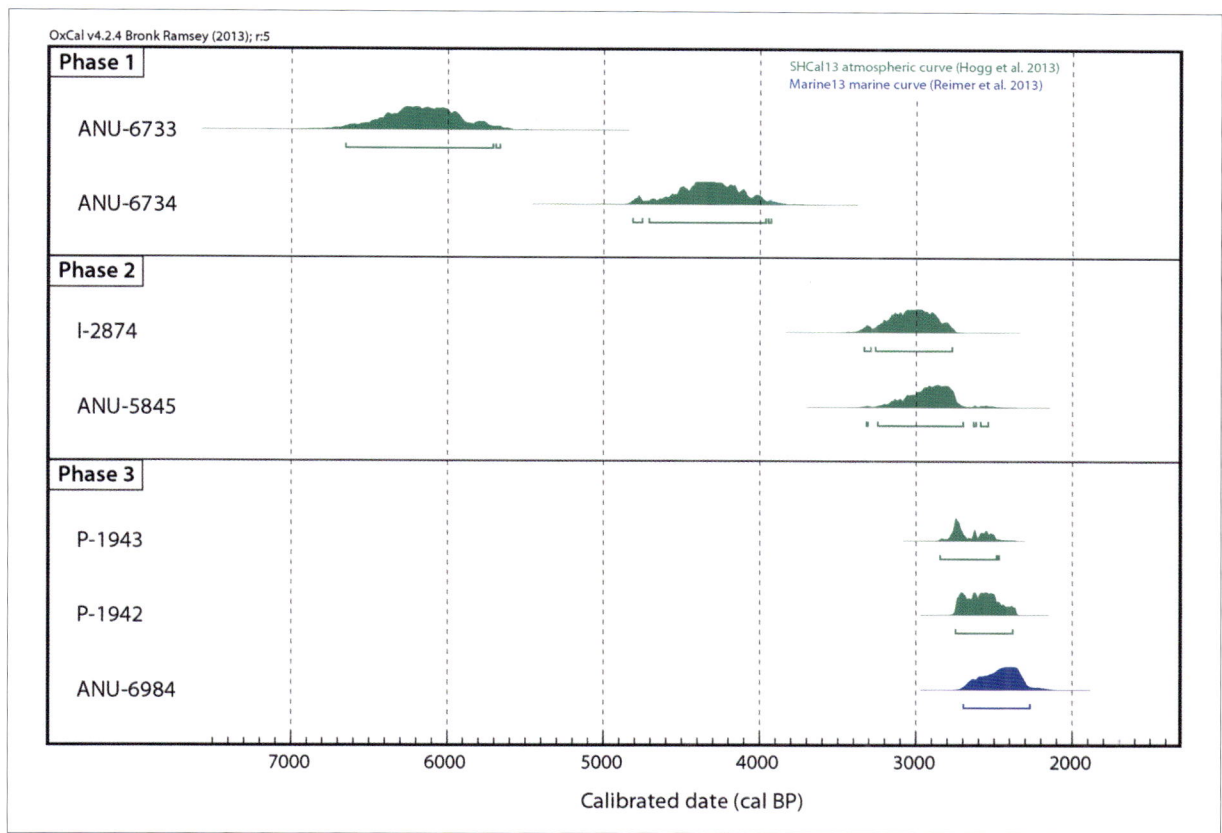

Figure 4.15. Plot of radiocarbon dates from Vatuluma Posovi Cave from Roe (1993) (OxCal v.4.15).

to human settlement, given that there were populations residing in the Northern Solomons, no more than a few days' travel away by coastal canoe. Yet, so far, there is only a faint hint of pre-Lapita eastward expansion into the Solomon Islands chain out of the zones of Pleistocene settlement in the Northern Solomon Islands or further to the west.

East of Buka, the lower deposits of Vatuluma Posovi and Vatuluma Tavuro contain the only direct record of human activity dating prior to the Lapita expansion. There are indirect hints of human activities of approximately the same age in the palaeoenvironmental evidence from the Western Province and Guadalcanal. These are mainly in the form of charcoal concentrations that could be interpreted as indications of landscape firing, and pollen signals of forest clearance. But we need to be cautious in interpreting both these records. Dating the Guadalcanal cave sites is problematic because of the complexity of the stratigraphy and the difficulty of relating the artefactual material directly to well-provenanced and well-dated radiocarbon samples. Indeed, we see little strong evidence linking cultural material to the earliest radiocarbon dates at Vatuluma Posovi; we suggest, instead, that the earliest levels at both Vatuluma

Posovi and Vatuluma Tavuro date no earlier than the later end of the suggested age range, to around 4200–4000 cal BP. The pollen record from New Georgia also presents problems. Most of the sample cores come from sediments dating to the period when the lagoons and lakes were first forming. They are shallow and do not typically contain long sequences against which an anthropogenic record stands out. Because they are shallow, there is also the problem of deriving narrow date ranges for any putative human events. Thus there are hints in both the landscape and the archaeological record of movement into the Western and Central Solomons from the mid-Holocene, but so far the signals are somewhat weak and equivocal.

In fact, the immediate pre-Lapita period is seriously underrepresented archaeologically in Melanesia (Sheppard, 2009) – but is one of a number of crucial periods in Oceanic prehistory. The absence of pottery does not help and it is quite possible that the sites may be difficult to identify; they look very like Lapita sites or even immediately post-Lapita sites, but without the ceramics. On Nissan Island, Spriggs (1991a, b) initially described the aceramic Halika Phase, dating to around 3650 cal BP, as 'Lapita without pots' because, bar pottery, the material culture is very similar to that found in

Lapita sites. This includes such items as pearlshell 'knives', shell fishhooks and Talasea obsidian (Spriggs, 2000b:454). As Roe suggests, the later Vatuluma Posovi layers may be another candidate for this designation. Until further work is done in surveying potential early to mid-Holocene deposits, the Lapita expansion from 3500 cal BP represents the strongest Holocene signal of human expansion. This expansion is the topic of the following chapter.

5

The Austronesian expansion

Lapita and Austronesians in Oceania

The middle of the second millennium BC marked a turning point in Oceanic prehistory. During this period there was increased interaction and movement throughout western Oceania and island Southeast Asia. Indigenous populations in New Guinea and the Solomon Islands found themselves dealing with a stream of cultural, genetic and Austronesian linguistic influences that had been moving through island Southeast Asia from an origin zone somewhere in the vicinity of Taiwan (although recent research suggests a more important role for development and interaction in central island Southeast Asia) (Donohue & Denham, 2010; Soares et al., 2011)). The speed and nature of this movement is unclear but it seems to have started by at least 4000 cal BP with movement south out of Taiwan (Anderson, 2005; Bellwood, 2006). This stream of interaction, which brought with it new lifestyles and languages, also brought the means not only to move into the vast oceanic world of Remote Oceania with its far-flung and relatively depauperate islands, but also to establish viable economies on arrival. These new sailing technologies and economic strategies were spread throughout island Melanesia and out into Remote Oceania by peoples carrying the Lapita culture who, from the Bismarck Archipelago, soon established settlements across the Near/Remote Oceania boundary in the Reef–Santa Cruz Islands, Vanuatu, New Caledonia, Fiji and West Polynesia. Descendant communities some generations later pushed further east, opening up East Polynesia and settling New Zealand in the early second millennium AD as the final phase of the Austronesian expansion.

Not surprisingly, much of the archaeology of island Melanesia in both Near and Remote Oceania has been concerned with tracing the arrival and spread of Lapita. The most obvious archaeological signal of Lapita is the appearance in the archaeological record of the distinctive Lapita ceramics – including, in the earliest phases, a finely made toothed or 'dentate' stamped component (Figure 5.4). Dentate stamped Lapita ceramics make their first appearance in the Bismarck Archipelago in the range 3450–3350 cal BP (Specht, 2007). In Vanuatu, Lapita sites date from around 3000 cal BP, and they are present in Fiji by 2900 cal BP (Bedford et al., 2006; Galipaud & Swete-Kelly, 2007; Nunn et al., 2006; Sand, 2007a; Sheppard et al., 2015a) (Figure 5.1). The first Lapita sites with dentate stamped pottery in the Solomon Islands were reported from beyond the Near/Remote Oceania boundary in the Eastern Solomons, where the SESP team located a number of Lapita sites in the Reef–Santa Cruz Islands in the 1970s (Green, 1976c). Initial dating of these sites indicated the earliest was Nanggu (SE-SZ-8) on Santa Cruz, which Green et al. (2008) dated, using marine shell, between 3150 and 3000 cal BP at a 68% confidence interval. Most recently, our new work at that site indicates, based on dating of charcoal, a younger age of c. 2900 cal BP, which more closely aligns it with all of the other initial Lapita settlement dates in Remote Oceania (Sheppard et al., 2015a). Given the early date of the Reef–Santa Cruz sites and the large distance between there and the Bismarck Archipelago (>1500 km), archaeologists anticipated filling in the gap by finding Lapita sites of in-between age in the Central, Western and Northern Solomons (Green, 1979). In fact the anticipated evidence has failed to

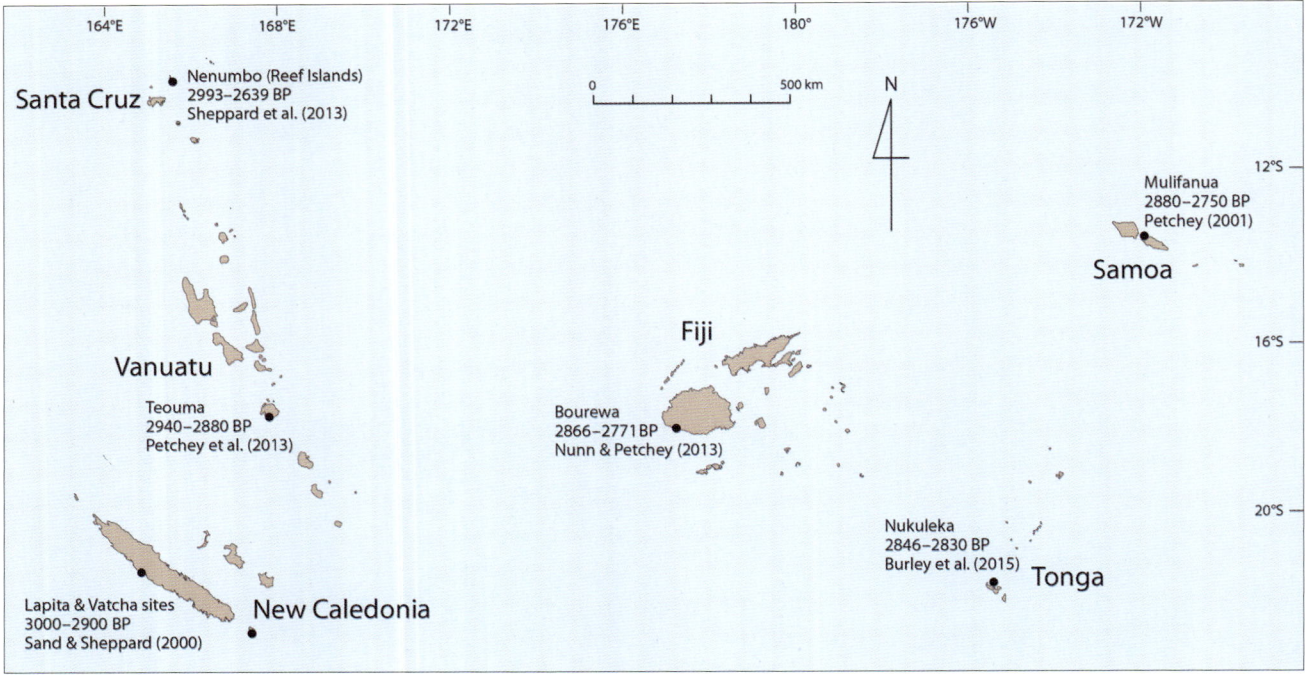

Figure 5.1. The location of earliest known archaeological sites in eastern Remote Oceania.

materialise despite substantial archaeological work over the last 30 years. We review the current record of Lapita sites in the Solomon Islands below and show how the distribution and dating support a discontinuous or 'leapfrog' model for the Lapita colonisation of the Solomon Islands (Sheppard & Walter, 2006). This has broader implications for interpreting the Lapita colonisation of the southwest Pacific (Sheppard, 2011).

Northern Solomons

The Northern Solomons has long been known to have a lengthy, if somewhat complex ceramic history (Specht, 1972; Spriggs, 1992; Summerhayes, 1987; Terrell, 1976; Wickler, 2001). As described in Chapter 3, Specht developed a six-phase pottery sequence for Buka, based largely on surface collections and small-scale excavation (Specht, 1969) (see also Table 5.1). Specht designated the earliest phase as the Buka phase – which he considered to represent a late Lapita occupation, and which he assigned to the period 2500 to 2220 cal BP (Specht, 1969:214, 306; Wickler 2001:6). The Buka style was characterised by the use of a paste that was heavily tempered with finely crushed shell. The ceramic vessels were made using paddle and anvil construction methods and, unlike later styles, slab-building was also practised. The dominant vessel form was an open bowl; less common forms included restricted bowls and necked vessels with flaring rims (Wickler, 2001:131). Decoration included rim notching and body sherds with rectilinear incised and relief motifs. Specht also reported a few excavated sherds with dentate stamping (Specht, 1969:194).

Stephen Wickler worked on Buka from 1987: he revisited many of the sites recorded by Specht, and vastly increased the surface collections of ceramics (Figure 3.2). Wickler paid particular attention to intertidal reef sites, and on three of these he found deposits that contained dentate ceramics. Two of these sites (DAA and DAF) were on Sohano Island in Buka Passage and had previously been recorded by Specht. The third, DJQ, was located on the southern end of Cape Dunganon on the northwest coast of Buka (Figure 3.2). Wickler was unable to date these sites directly but considered, on stylistic grounds, that they likely predated the Buka-style assemblages. To resolve the issue of chronology he carried out a seriation exercise, in which he included the Nissan Island Lapita assemblages reported by Spriggs (1991b) as a control. The seriation, based primarily on the percentage of dentate stamping, resulted in a revised sequence. The most significant element of this was the addition of a pre-Buka style Lapita phase, which Wickler assigned the date range 3200–2500 cal BP (Wickler, 2001: Table 1.1). In developing the revised sequence Wickler chose not to follow the earlier convention of naming the phase using a local type-site name; instead he called the pre-Buka phase 'Lapita'. He also defined a cultural sequence to run parallel to the ceramic sequence. In the cultural sequence

Specht (1969) Buka Ceramic Sequence		Revised (Wickler, 2001) Buka Ceramic Sequence		Buka Cultural Sequence (Wickler, 2001: Table 1.1)	
Style	Dates BP	Style	Dates BP	Phase	Dates BP
				Pleistocene	29,000–10,000
				Early to Mid-Holocene	10,000–3200
		Lapita	3200–2500	Early Lapita	3200–2500
Buka	2500–2200	Buka	2500–2200	Late Lapita	2500–2200
Sohano	2200–1500	Sohano	2200–1400	Sohano	2200–1400
Hangan	1500–1300	Hangan	1400–800	Hangan	1400–800
Malasang	1300–800	Malasang	800–500	Malasang	800–500
Mararing	800–300	Mararing	c. 500–300	Mararing/Recent	500–0
Recent	c. 300–0	Recent	c. 300–0		

Table 5.1. Buka Ceramic and cultural sequences proposed by Specht (1969) and Wickler (2001: Table 1.1).

the 'early Lapita' phase is equivalent to the 'Lapita' ceramic phase, and the 'late Lapita' phase is equivalent to the 'Buka' ceramic phase (Table 5.1)

Wickler placed the DJQ site at the start of the early Lapita phase and assigned it the date range 3000–2800 cal BP to align with the Lapita phase of the Nissan sequence (Wickler, 2001:241). The outer-reef component of DAF he considered equivalent to the Nissan DES site, dating to around 2800–2500 cal BP. The central reef section of DAF he proposed to date at 2500–2300 cal BP, and the inner reef section 2300–2100 cal BP (Wickler, 2001:241). The DJQ site had over 56% (n=188) of decorated sherds with dentate stamping; this declined sharply to 1.9% (n=77) at DAF, and dentate stamping was replaced by increasing proportions of unbounded incision punctation and appliqué relief (Wickler, 2001:108–12). Although dentate stamping seems to virtually disappear on Buka at this point, many of the characteristics of Lapita ceramic technology and design lasted into the Buka ceramic style.

In addition to changes in pottery style and form, Wickler infers changes in settlement patterns during the Lapita phases from changes in the distribution of ceramics. He suggests that the concentrations of pottery on the central and outer portions of the intertidal reef flats at DJQ and DAF are indicative of refuse dumping from stilt-house occupation, and that this may reflect a pattern in which Lapita settlements were spatially segregated from non-pottery-using indigenous populations (Wickler, 2001:241). These sites also produced a small number of stone adzes in oval to lenticular, plano-convex and plano-lateral cross-sections that are typical Lapita forms (Wickler, 2001: Table 7.8). Other artefacts that are also generically of Lapita style (e.g. Kirch, 1988a) included various chert and volcanic stone flakes and a small number of shell chisels and ornament fragments.

Wickler's (2001) comparative study of ceramic pastes and decoration has greatly improved Specht's (1969) already sound sequence for Buka. It provides an early link into the Nissan sequence to the west, and the post-Lapita phases have some continuity with ceramic phases in Bougainville through to the Shortlands and Western Province (see Chapter 6). But some caution is needed in interpreting the absolute ages assigned to the Lapita-phase sites. We note that the relative quantities of obsidian sources in Lapita sites have been shown in various places to be related to chronology (Sheppard, 1993, White & Harris, 1997). If this is so, we would expect a similar ratio of Admiralties to New Britain obsidians in Solomon Island Lapita sites of about the same age. Instead, the Lapita sites in Buka and the Reef–Santa Cruz Islands differ dramatically. Talasea obsidian represents less than 2% of the sample in Buka – the remaining sourced pieces (87%) originate from Lou in the Admiralties Group (Wickler, 2001:178) – whereas it represents over 90% of the sample in the three earliest Reef–Santa Cruz sites. If obsidian source ratios are any indication of age, the earliest Lapita horizons on Buka may not be quite as early as current models suggest.

Western Solomons

Ceramic-bearing sites have been reported nearly everywhere in the Western Solomons where archaeological surveys have been carried out (Figure 5.2). Chikamori (1965) first reported ceramics in the Sirebangara Cave site near Vurango village in Choiseul, and Yen later reported sherds on Kolombangara (Miller, 1979:148). During the National Site Survey programme, Miller recorded four ceramic-find

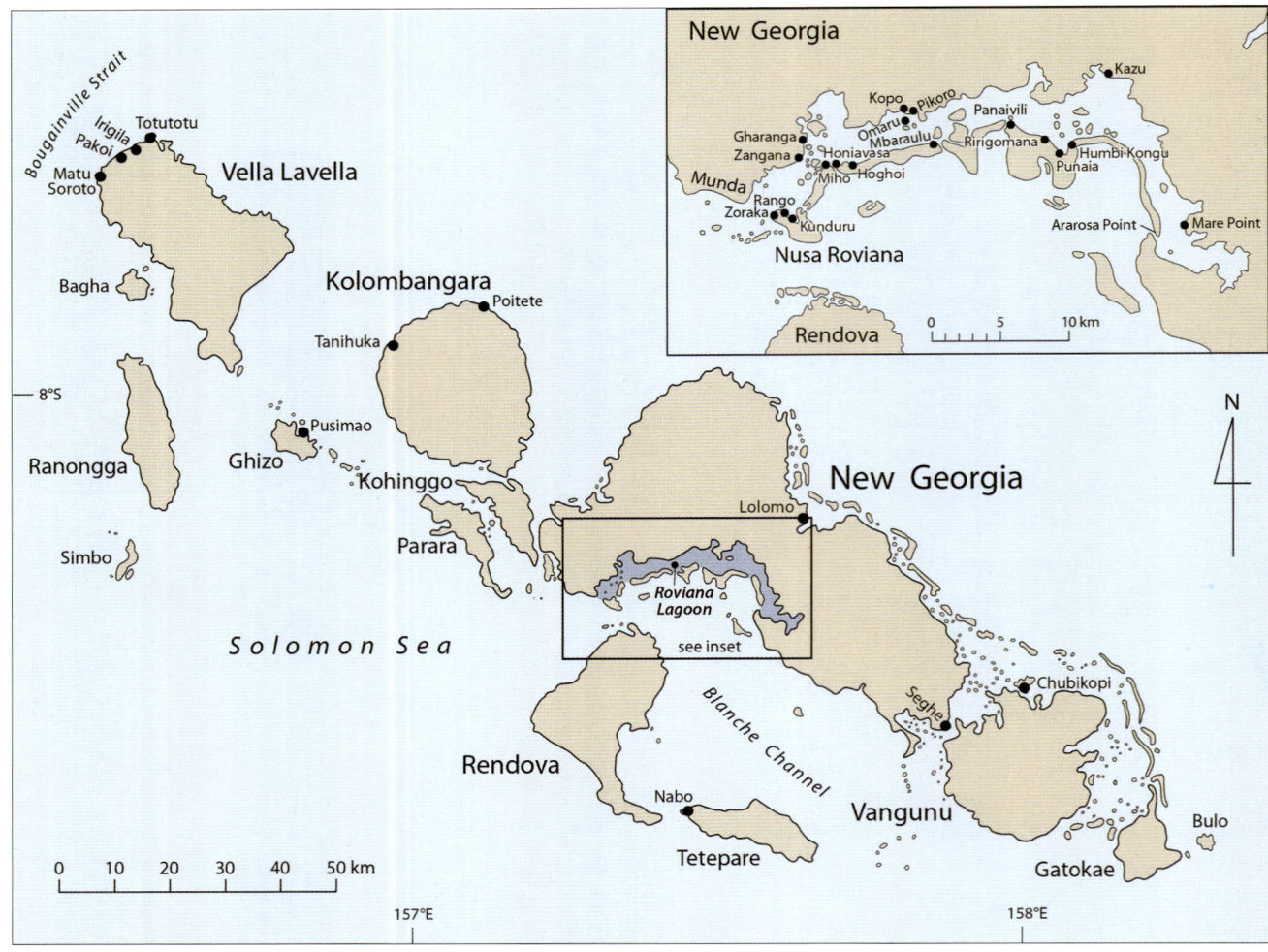

Figure 5.2. The location of ceramic-bearing archaeological sites in the New Georgia Group, with Roviana Lagoon as inset.

spots on Simbo, five on Kolombangara and four on Choiseul, of which two were on the small island of Vaghena off the eastern tip of the main island. The most common decorative technique reported was shallow incising on a thin ware, although appliqué, punctation and notched rims are also mentioned. Unfortunately there are no radiocarbon dates associated with this material, although the test excavation in a deep beach deposit at Nuatambu Island (SC-7-6) off southeast Choiseul suggested some stratigraphic control was possible.

Nuatambu Island is a small double islet made up of three basalt hills. Two are joined by a strip of sand, which is under water during high tides. Historically the location is important for the manufacture of shell valuables (kesa) (Scheffler, 1965), and pottery was found on the surface in association with the debris from shell-ring manufacture. A total of 13 layers were excavated using natural stratigraphy to a depth of 1.8 m, with one metre of deposit lying below the water table in a one-metre square located on the flat at the foot of the slope, where slope wash has accumulated. Miller (1979:71) interpreted the site as having been formed through rapid subsidence of the islet. This is consistent with the geomorphology of Choiseul, which is rapidly subsiding (Mann et al., 1998), but it is also possible that the site was originally a stilt-house settlement in an intertidal zone. The one metre of deposit below sea level seemed particularly rich in ceramics. A variety of notched lip rims were found throughout the deposit, as well as curvilinear incised ware (Richards, 2011); however, brushed body sherds were found only in the bottom levels, where they seemed to replace the shallow incised decorative style. Miller noted (1979:78) that although the sample was small the sequence seemed to replicate that observed by Irwin (1972) in the Shortland Islands. To date this is the longest excavated ceramic sequence in the Western Solomons; however, since Miller's work it has become clear that much older ceramic deposits can be found at intertidal sites throughout the Western Solomons.

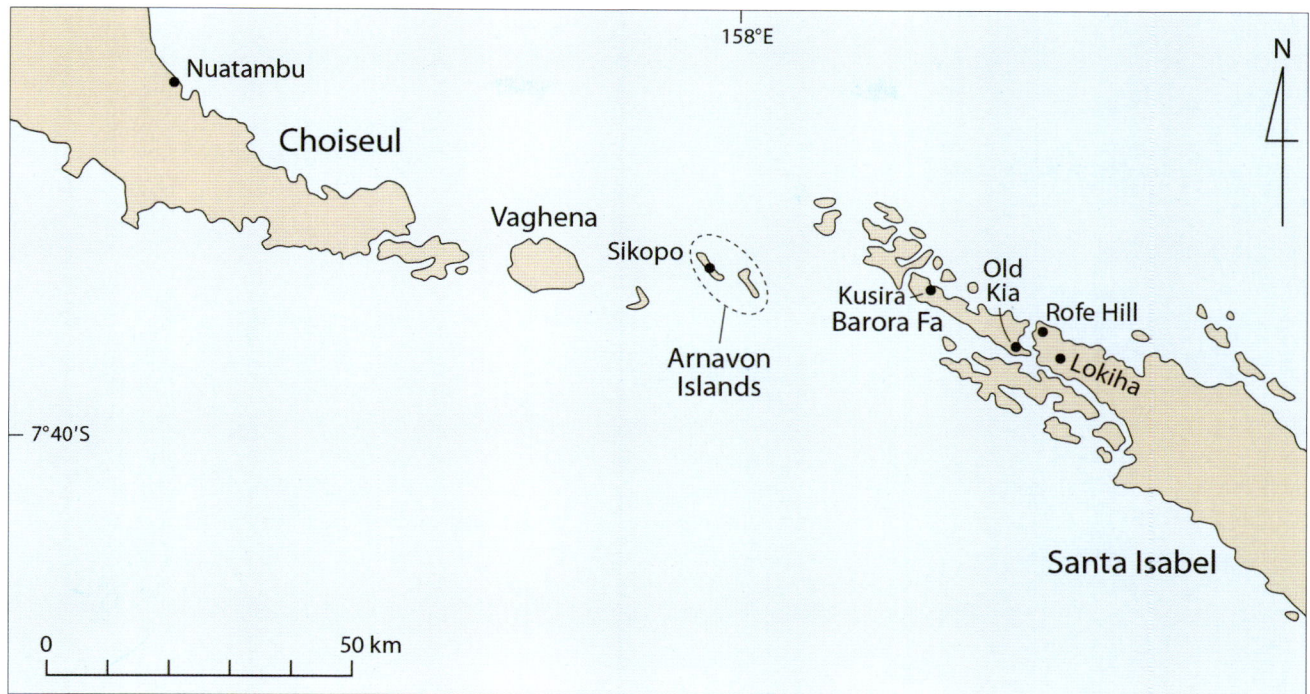

Figure 5.3. The location of archaeological sites on Santa Isabel and Arnavon Islands.

Continuing the National Site Survey programme, Reeve (1989) reported intertidal ceramic sites on Vella Lavella and New Georgia, including on north New Georgia. In the 1990s the New Georgia Archaeological Survey work expanded the ceramic survey in New Georgia and reported a range of assemblages from Roviana Lagoon, north New Georgia and Marovo (see below). This left Santa Isabel as the only major island where pottery had not been found, although this situation has recently changed with reports of ceramic-bearing sites from several regions (Carter et al., 2012) (Figure 5.3). In the southwest, on the offshore island of Vitori, a few dozen plain orange-brown sherds were recovered from surface deposits; and in the northwest of Santa Isabel, plainware ceramics were recovered from three stratigraphic layers at Rofe Hill that span an age range from about 1750 cal BP to the historic period (Carter et al., 2012:64). About 10 km to the southeast of Rofe Hill, an assemblage of several hundred sherds was recovered from a hillfort site at Lokiha. This was also a plainware assemblage but it included some sherds with rim impressions. At Kusira a ceramic assemblage recovered from an intertidal site included at least one sherd with a crenulated rim and punctation. The authors have compared the Kusira material with the intertidal assemblages from Roviana Lagoon and Kolombangara (Felgate, 2003:128; Summerhayes & Scales, 2005; and see below). In 2011 Walter observed surface ceramics on the island of Sikopo in the Arnavon Island group, between northwest Santa Isabel and Choiseul (Figure 5.3). The sherds included examples with incised, punctate and fingernail impressions which, in hand specimen, looked very similar to the late Lapita Roviana Lagoon intertidal assemblages. In fact, the Arnavons were a major source of turtleshell for the Roviana headhunters, and the islands contain shrines that are similar in form to those we have recorded along the Roviana coasts. It is possible, then, that the sites and surface assemblages on Sikopo have a direct connection with Roviana.

Most discussion of Solomon Island ceramics has focused on the decorated wares that mark the early end of the ceramic sequence. The most common decorative techniques in the Western Solomons is shallow incising; and appliqué, punctation and rim notching have also been reported. Plainware assemblages have been found in low densities in Choiseul, Isabel and in a number of our surveys in Roviana Lagoon and Ranongga. These clearly date to the more recent past, suggesting a plainware tradition generally followed the loss of decorated ware. Ceramic production continued in Choiseul until recent times and we believe that pottery from the Choiseul production centres was finding its way into New Georgia and probably Santa Isabel and elsewhere in the Western Province into the early twentieth century (Buhring et al., 2015; Dickinson, 2006; Findlater et al., 2009; Nagaoka, 2011). Although the ceramic sequence from the Western Solomons is still not fully defined, over the last few decades there has been a concentrated effort in the Roviana region of New Georgia and a chronology of the ceramic phase there has slowly emerged.

Unravelling the decorated ceramic sequence from Roviana Lagoon

Although Miller's limited survey in the Roviana district of New Georgia did not locate any ceramic deposits, subsequent research has found numerous intertidal sites throughout Roviana Lagoon (Figure 5.3). The first site located was reported by Reeve (1989) after he and Spriggs visited Roviana Lagoon. Reeve reported ceramics at the Panaivili location in the village of Patmos, located on the western end of the barrier island of Ndora. The ceramics were discovered in the intertidal zone just around the corner from a passage between barrier islands, on the sheltered, mainland-facing lagoon edge. At Panaivili ceramics and fire-cracked rock occur in some abundance in a band about 30 m wide, just offshore and extending through the shallow water towards the point at the edge of the passage. Although ceramics and other artefacts are continually accumulating as lag deposits in this active canoe landing and anchorage area, collections by Reeves and Spriggs and excavations by local villagers included ceramics and artefacts that led Reeve (1989) and Spriggs (1997) to suggest that much of the deposit dated to a late Lapita or immediately post-Lapita time period. These included a range of plainware sherds as well as some incised, pinched, fingernail-impression, punctate and applied-relief wares. *Tridacna* adzes, a *Cassis* shell chisel, a *Tridacna* arm ring and a range of *Conus* shell rings and bracelets were also found, but these are not necessarily contemporary with the ceramics. A polished adze from the site, however, was of a characteristic Lapita form, and a blade made of obsidian that was most probably imported from the Bismarck Archipelago was also recovered (Reeve, 1989:55). Although the Panaivili deposit was undated, Reeve suggested an age of c. 2500 cal BP, and he contrasted the Panaivili thick ware with the thin incised ware containing both shell and mineral temper that Miller noted in his surveys in the Western Province. In this model of ceramic variation both decoration and pot form simplified: the later pots were limited to globular and subglobular forms as opposed to the carinated complex forms noted at Panaivili (Reeve, 1989:61). In his report Reeve also noted that he had recovered pottery similar to the Panaivili assemblage from a coastal terrestrial site on northwest New Georgia (Koqu Orovoro) and on the northwest coast of Vella Lavella (Irigila).

During the NGAS programme directed by the authors, we revisited the Panaivili site and conducted surveys of the intertidal zone and coastal flats throughout the length of Roviana Lagoon (Sheppard et al., 1999). This resulted in the location of some 20 similar sites from Araroso Point in the east to Nusa Roviana at the western end of the lagoon. Subsequently we have located similar sites in the intertidal zone in Marovo Lagoon (Seghe Channel, Chea, Marovo Island), off the northern end of Ghizo Island where we also recovered an obsidian flake (Sheppard and Walter, 2013), and at a number of sites in northern Vella Lavella (Irigila region). Recently, Summerhayes and Scales (2005) have reported similar assemblages from Kolombangara that included a small number of dentate stamped sherds (see also Terrill & Keith, 2006), and Felgate (2007) has found additional intertidal sites on north New Georgia.

As part of the NGAS programme, Matthew Felgate carried out research at the western end of Roviana Lagoon that focused on the intertidal ceramic-bearing sites (Felgate, 2001, 2003). His surveys produced the first few dentate stamped ceramics from two sites (Honiavasa and Nusa Roviana) in Roviana Lagoon, and provided the first radiocarbon-based chronology for the New Georgia ceramic sequence. Charcoal from a sherd from Panaivili was dated to 2130 ± 90 BP (AA-33504), and a smoke-derived carbon deposit on a sherd from the Hoghoi site was dated to 2619 ± 45 BP (2782–2489 95.4% HPD) (NZA-12353) (Felgate, 2001:48). The sherds from these sites contain rectilinear incised, punctate and pinched decoration as well as a variety of lip treatments, including crenulated or horizontally deformed lips (Felgate, 2003). Felgate reports a shift from complex carinated pot forms in the earlier Honiavasa site to simpler forms and often thinner wares in the post-Lapita sites (Felgate, 2001:53), dating to the mid to late first millennium BC (Figure 5.4).

At present the earliest assemblages of pottery from the Western Province seem to be from the tail end of the dentate stamped Lapita pottery tradition. Most of the ceramics fall within the incised and appliqué decorative tradition, which is very closely related to late and immediately post-Lapita assemblages from the Bismarck Archipelago. These include the assemblages reported by Garling (2003) from the Tanga group, and from Lasigi (Golson, 1991) and Fissoa (White & Murray-Wallace, 1996), both on mainland New Ireland. However, all of the sites recovered to date – and the number is now considerable – have only limited amounts of dentate stamped ceramics. So far, none of the Western Solomons sites have more than two or three dentate stamped sherds and none are like the earliest intertidal sites from Buka (DJQ) and Nissan (DES), which have high percentages of dentate pottery. If we assume the amount of dentate stamping in an assemblage relates to age – following, for example, the

Figure 5.4. Some decorated Western Solomons ceramics collected by Matthew Felgate and the authors in Roviana Lagoon.

dentate-to-incised chronology from the Mussau (ECA) site (Kirch, 2001:208) – then these sites would be at the earliest from the end of the Lapita sequence, and most would date to a period after the complex Lapita pot forms have been replaced.

The apparent absence, in the Western Solomons, of sites with high proportions of dentate ceramics like those found in the Northern Solomons and Bismarck Archipelago needs to be explained. It is of course possible that the dentate-to-incised chronology of the Bismarck Archipelago is not mirrored in the Western Province; the two regions may simply differ in the relative importance of dentate stamping over incised and appliqué within the decorated ceramic inventory. It could also be argued that the absence of dentate stamped ceramic horizons simply reflects the lack of survey and, in particular, intertidal survey (Felgate, 2001:55, 2003:190–92, 2007; Spriggs, 2010). However, the amount of survey and archaeological research time expended in the region is now considerable, and it is our view that the absence of rich dentate stamped Lapita deposits in the Western Solomons is real, not an artefact of sampling, and that it relates to chronology (Sheppard & Walter, 2009). Put simply, the Lapita ceramics appear later in the Western Solomons than in Buka, and the earliest sites in Roviana Lagoon date later than the earlier sites in the Buka sequence of DAA, DAF and DJQ. We discuss this issue further below.

During his analysis of the intertidal sites of western Roviana Lagoon, Felgate studied aspects of sherd taphonomy and distribution and concluded that the sites of the early ceramic period were stilt-house settlements (Felgate, 2003; Felgate et al., 2012). This is a similar conclusion to that reached by Wickler in regard to the early ceramic sites in Buka (Wickler, 2001). Further to the west, Spriggs interpreted the Lapita phase at Nissan to involve stilt houses constructed over the reef flat (Spriggs, 2000b:455), and Kirch (1991) reported a similar architecture at the Lapita settlement of Talepakemalai on Mussau. Stilt houses have also been tentatively identified in the archaeological record of the Arawe Islands (Gosden & Webb, 1994), Kreslo (Specht, 1991) and Emirau (Summerhayes et al., 2010). So, on current evidence it appears that a stilt-house tradition originating with Lapita spread from the Bismarcks though the Solomons chain at least as far southeast as New Georgia. Stilt-house construction occurred earlier in Buka, but in the New Georgia region it was introduced by people who were making an incised and appliqué decorated pottery and carrying small amounts of obsidian, who moved out of the New Ireland region and through the Solomons chain at least as far as New Georgia in the very late Lapita period (around 2600 cal BP).

Although the archaeological record suggests very strongly that early Lapita colonisation did not extend into the Western Solomon Islands, it is worth considering what we can learn from the palaeoenvironmental record. According to Grimes (2003:237) the sedimentary record of Roviana Lagoon indicates a period of vegetation and sedimentary changes starting after 4000 cal BP. The pollen record shows a number of periods of burning from about 3750 cal BP, followed, around 3400 cal BP, by increases in ferns and a decline in woody vegetation. Between 3200 and 2750 cal BP there are records of further burning and erosion events. It is difficult to distinguish these early signals from natural events, and it is really only from 2700 cal BP, coincident with the first appearance of pottery, that the vegetation and sediment data can be said to clearly represent 'an anthropogenically-modified landscape' (Grimes, 2003:231). But the Roviana record, when compared with that from Guadalcanal (below), does leave open the possibility of gardening some hundreds of years before the influx of pottery-bearing groups or influence in the late-Lapita period. The newly emerged lagoons with abundant and easily won fisheries from 4000 cal BP must have been a major attractor for human settlers.

In many respects the late Lapita movement out of the Bismarck Archipelago into the Solomons is mirrored by similar movements into the south Papuan coast (Sheppard et al., 2015b). Both represent late Lapita-period expansion of a ceramic tradition with some dentate stamped ceramics in the earliest assemblages followed by fall-out of the dentate component and local development of a simplified ceramic sequence. The south Papuan sequence appears to date a little earlier and, in its development, is stylistically unrelated to the Western Solomons; however, it is indicative of movement throughout the Solomon Sea post-Lapita expansion into Remote Oceania. Such activity is also very directly shown by the transport of small amounts of ceramics containing a very distinctive quartz-hybrid temper from Woodlark Island in the Massim region of PNG (Tochilin et al., 2012) into many of the intertidal sites in the Western Solomons (Sheppard et al., 2015b). This pattern of considerable interaction over more than 400 km is unusual in the Lapita period, where most pottery is locally made and only transported from the nearest-neighbouring clay-bearing islands.

Central Solomons

The most striking characteristic of the Lapita period in the Central Solomon Islands is the lack of decorated Lapita-style pottery (dentate stamped or incised) – or, for that matter, the almost complete lack of pottery from any time period. Although this could be a consequence of limited investigation (Spriggs, 2010), the type and amount of survey in a series of areas in this region is comparable to or even exceeds that employed in the Reef–Santa Cruz region by the SESP teams. In the Reef–Santa Cruz Islands the surveys had little apparent problem locating a considerable number of ceramic sites, including a high density of Lapita sites. When their attention was turned to the Central Solomons, however, similar survey methods and test excavations found no Lapita sites and only one ceramic site. The areas covered by the teams included survey and excavation by Whitney, Green, Ward and Hendren on Ulawa (Hendren, 1976; Ward, 1976), survey and excavation on the small isolated island of Uki by Green (Green, 1976d), survey and excavation on Santa Ana by Swadling, Green and Hendren (Swadling, 1976) and survey and excavation on the Star Harbour Peninsula of Makira (Green, 1976e). Subsequent

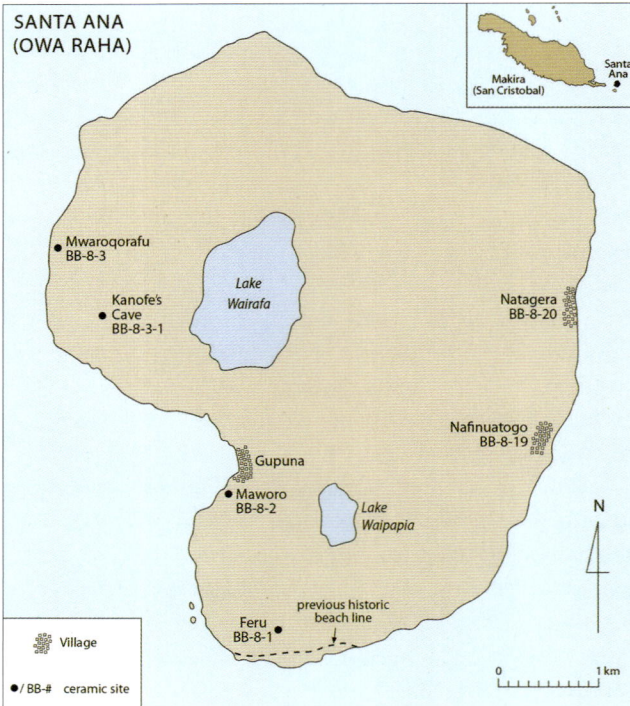

Figure 5.5. The location of archaeological sites on Santa Ana in the Central Solomons (after Swadling, 1976).

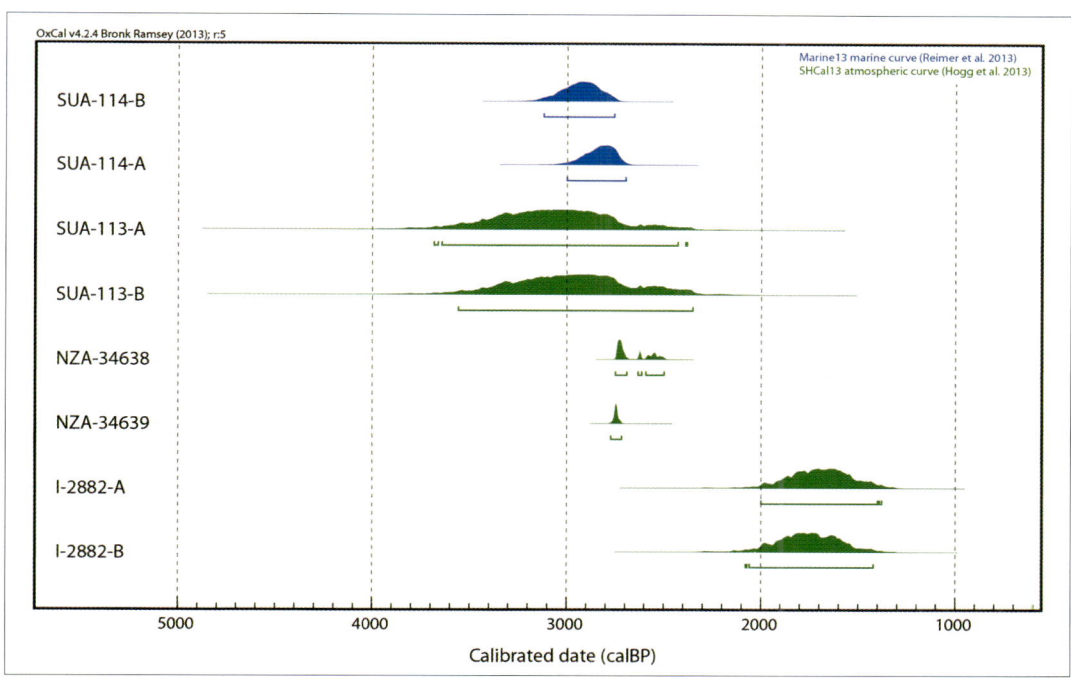

Figure 5.6. Plot of radiocarbon dates from archaeological sites on Santa Ana (OxCal v.4.17).

to this research, members of the Solomon Islands National Site Survey spent several weeks surveying and excavating sites in the Arosi district of Makira (Miller, 1979:87–109), and there have been a few additional surveys over the last few decades by members of the National Museum (John Keopo, pers. comm., 1999). Most recently a team from the University of Sydney led by Martin Gibbs (Blake et al., 2015) has reported on a number of seasons of fieldwork near Pamua on Makira where, despite finding sites dating back to c. 3000 cal BP, they have found no ceramics, beyond those related to the Spanish settlement associated with the explorer Mendaña in 1596 AD. Similarly, a number of field seasons of work in the East `Are`are region on Malaita by the German archaeologist Johannes Moser (pers. comm., 2015) has failed to find any ceramic record. Taken together, this represents a considerable amount of archaeological research in the area which, if expended in the Reef–Santa Cruz region, would certainly have resulted in the discovery of at least one Lapita site.

Although ceramic sites of Lapita age have not been identified, other archaeological deposits dating to the relevant time period have been reported. William Davenport excavated the Feru II cave on Santa Ana (1972a) (Figure 5.5): in the middle (70–130 cm) of a deposit that contained cultural material to a depth of 216 cm he recovered a small sample of poor-quality very friable plainware pottery, including a rim sherd with a serially incised lip (1972a:177). This was dated to 1275 ± 105 BP by a radiocarbon sample (I-2878) made up of dispersed charcoals found within the 70–130 cm zone. Green revisited Feru II and reinterpreted the stratigraphy. He divided the deposit into upper and lower units, separated by a sterile sand (Black & Green, 1975:30). Dates from a hearth in the base of the deposit suggested that the pottery-bearing layer was created during the early to mid third millennium BP (Figure 5.6). These dates were derived from a combined *Tridacna* shell sample (SUA-114, two dates A 3050 ± 70, B 3142 ± 70 BP) and a small charcoal sample (SUA-113, two dates: A 2860 ± 250; B 2946 ± 250 BP). Unfortunately, the charcoal date has a very large associated error, and an appropriate marine reservoir correction for the shell date is unknown. The shell dates in Figure 5.6 were calibrated using a delta-R of 0. Recent AMS dating by Sheppard (2013), of small charcoal samples recovered by Green from Feru II in association with the ceramics, has provided two new dates on charcoal (NZA-34638 2595 ± 20; NZA-34639 2653 ± 20) that calibrate in the range 2752–2500 (95.4% HPD) cal BP (Sheppard, 2011:833). The sherd sample from the site is very small, but Green recovered additional sherds and the total sample size is about 20 (Swadling, 1976:127), and Davenport recovered an additional rim sherd (undecorated but missing the lip) at the Rate site, located in a shallow cave some 4 km along the shore from Feru II. The Rate sherd was recovered from a depth of 106 cm and is undated, but a charcoal date from 85 cm (I-2882) suggests it potentially dates to a post-Lapita period (two dates: A 1810 ± 135; B 1864 ± 135 BP) (Black &

Green, 1975). This ceramic assemblage is unlike that found elsewhere in the Solomons, although it is tempting to suggest that it is the result of sporadic contact with Santa Cruz, 400 km due east. Oral tradition in Santa Cruz describes drift voyaging to Santa Ana, which is known as the 'island of women' (Davenport, 1990). There is no subsequent ceramic tradition in Santa Ana and – as noted above – on nearby Makira, sites of the Lapita time period contain no ceramics (Blake et al., 2015).

There has been only limited archaeological survey and excavation on Malaita. This work was conducted by Daniel Miller (1979, 1980b) in the Kwaio district as part of the National Site Survey programme. Sheppard conducted a brief reconnaissance survey along the coast between Auki and Buma while looking for chert sources in 1989, and noted large amounts of chert debitage (drill points and cores) on islands in the Langalanga Lagoon. Most recently, Johannes Moser has recovered dense lithic workshop deposits after a few field seasons working in East `Are`are. These are very like the assemblages recovered by the Southeast Solomon Island Culture History Project on Ulawa. A considerable number of anthropologists have also conducted long-term research on Malaita and, although some have paid attention to stone artefacts (e.g. Ross, 1970), none have reported finding any ceramics. Some archaeological survey and excavation has been conducted on the islands of the Florida Group by Alex Rukia, a trained archaeologist who was formerly associated with the National Museum. Excavation of caves on Nggela Pile revealed a very shallow cultural deposit absent of any ceramics (Rukia, 1989b).

Although the large island of Guadalcanal is for the most part unexplored by archaeologists, the area in proximity to the capital Honiara and the area along the plains and ridges to the west, which is easily accessible by road, have received some of the most prolonged and intensive survey of any region in the Solomons. The Guadalcanal sequence developed by David Roe (1993), discussed in the previous chapter, shows that the island was probably occupied before the Lapita period and most likely had resident populations during the early Lapita movements into the Eastern Solomon Islands around 3000 cal BP. So far, however, no ceramic deposits have been located. Layer 3(I) at Vatuluma Posovi dates just earlier (ANU-6745 3940 ± 140 BP on *Canarium* nutshell) than Lapita and contains a very limited non-ceramic assemblage that includes two chert flakes and a *Trochus* armband fragment. Additional finds of three pieces of cut *Trochus*, interpreted as fishhook blanks, were recovered from Layer 3(II), but Roe notes (1993:63) that this deposit may be disturbed and may include material from more recent levels. Lapita-age occupation is represented in upper horizons at Vatuluma Posovi (1993:67) and the artefact assemblages include *Trochus* fishhook blanks, a *Trochus* armlet fragment, chert chips and a ground shell bead. This pattern is replicated at the cave site of Vatuluma Tavuro, where the basal spit in Layer 4 returned dates of early Lapita age with chert flakes and a *Trochus* arm-ring fragment but no pottery (Roe, 1993:110).

Although the excavated material culture at Vatuluma Posovi is limited in quantity and variety, it is augmented by the abundant rock art visible on the rockshelter walls (Figure 5.7), which makes this the largest known gallery of rock art in the Solomon Islands, and among the largest in island Melanesia (Roe, 1992). The art covered by cultural deposits at Vatuluma Posovi indicates an age greater than 3100–2900 cal BP (Roe, 1992:111) – the oldest well-dated rock art in island Melanesia. As documented by Roe (1993: 121, app. 7), rock art is commonly found throughout the Solomon Islands, often on boulders distributed across the landscape (Figure 5.8), along with boulders bearing the cupule marks created when they are used as *Canarium* nut-cracking anvils.

Although the Lapita-age cave sites on Guadalcanal contain items that are in a very limited sense 'Lapita-like', there is a notable absence of ceramics. Decorated Lapita pottery is often not abundant in cave deposits in the Bismarcks or Santa Cruz, but the complete absence of pottery from deposits of this age – when we know the Central Solomons was in contact with the Lapita populations in the Reef–Santa Cruz region – is extraordinary. At this point we should once again consider Roe's Hoana Phase, which dates to 6400–2200 cal BP (although we have argued that it might commence as late as between 4000 cal BP, see Chapter 4). In our view the Hoana Phase might be better described as a two-phase unit with a dividing line, based on the dated pollen record, at about 2600 cal BP. A shell bead and polished stone adzes, excavated by Russell and Tedder, appear well after 3000 cal BP in Phase 3 of the Vatuluma Posovi sequence, dated on charcoal at 2550 ± 60 BP (P-1942) (2746–2379 95.4% HPD) (Roe, 1993:70, 176). And we also see a change in the types of chert from an opaque grey-brown porphyroid chert, which Roe (1993:178) suggests could be either from eastern Guadalcanal or Malaita, to the inclusion of more translucent orange-brown Malaitan and Ulawan material like that recovered from the Reef–Santa Cruz Lapita sites. It also coincides with evidence for considerable environmental change, which Haberle (1996) dates as occurring after the deposition of a volcanic ash (tephra) in Mela Swamp in the range 3158–2322 (95.4% HPD) cal BP. Together this might signal the arrival, at a time that coincides with developments in the Western Solomons,

Figure 5.7. Rock art at Vatuluma Posovi with David Roe indicating the original height of the cultural deposits which covered much of the art (photo by Tim Thomas, 2007).

Figure 5.8. Rock art on an igneous boulder called Sikeura Tamana Lado on the south bank of the Timbala River northeast of Irigila on Vella Lavella ((h) 1.6 m, (w) 2.1 m, (l) 2.8 m). Oral tradition states that 'Seven giant brothers came down from the interior to this point and made the engravings on the stone. They then turned into dolphins and swam down the river. They can still be seen today in the reef passage at Irigila village.' (Photo by authors)

of new settlers or ideas that include new economic practices and technologies. Roe's hesitation in defining a Lapita phase from the Hoana data sets is well founded, given the absence of obsidian and Lapita ceramics and the apparent continuity in artefact forms – particularly in the use of *Trochus* arm rings and fishhooks – from the earliest levels in Guadalcanal (Roe, 1993:184–86). However, the presence of significant changes in material culture and the palaeoenvironmental record in the mid third millennium BP – especially the appearance of stone adzes, which are strongly associated in Melanesia with Lapita – is indicative of an important cultural shift which, as in the Western Solomons, is likely associated with the movement of Austronesian-speaking populations into the region.

The palaeoenvironmental data from Guadalcanal supplements the archaeological record of first human arrival. The northern plains of Guadalcanal today support a vegetation that is maintained by regular human firing. But by as early as the beginnings of the pollen record at c. 3200 cal BP, grasslands and fire were already an integral part of the environment (Haberle, 1996; Roe, 1993:95). Although there is no direct evidence in Roe's Hoana Phase for agricultural activities (including animal husbandry), there were 'massive' human impacts on the environment in the form of increased forest clearance and erosion, beginning within the period bracketed from 2750 to 2150 cal BP (Roe, 1993:119). Haberle (1996) reported two pollen cores from the northern alluvial plains of Guadalcanal. Radiocarbon dates derived from 'woody organic layers' in the Laukutu Swamp core provided an estimated age, for the base of the swamp, of 3690 to 3080 BP (95.4% HPD) (ANU-6462) (Haberle, 1996:335). Both cores contained a tephra layer that was dated to immediately after 3158–2322 cal BP (95.4% HPD) (ANU-6464) in the Mela Swamp sequence (Haberle, 1996:335). The tephra is probably from an eruption on nearby Savo Island. Both the Laukutu and Mela cores show continuous low-level charcoal influx, but the Laukutu Swamp core shows appreciable fluctuation after c. 3200 and before 2100 cal BP, and dramatic and sustained charcoal influx after 2100 cal BP. This coincides with the dramatic rise in charcoal influx at c. 2700 cal BP that is noted in the Roviana cores where, in general, intense burning would appear to have developed in the later part of the third millennium BP. In Roviana this correlates to the oldest date available for the intertidal sites, at Hoghoi. If we accept the sustained rise in the charcoal influx as a proxy for slash-and-burn horticulture and the radical transformation of the economy based on a Lapita horticultural complex, then sustained Lapita influence does not occur in Roviana until c. 2700 cal BP, or late Lapita times. In Guadalcanal it might start then, too, although it could also commence about 2200 cal BP when the Lapita ceramic sequence of the Eastern Solomons had ended with the loss of pottery production (see below).

The current evidence from both the archaeology and the palaeoenvironmental record is that Guadalcanal might have experienced an influx of people and ideas in the mid third millennium cal BP. But there is no evidence to suggest that it was colonised by bearers of a dentate stamped (or any other) pottery tradition. Although evidence is limited, the appearance of the high-quality Malaitan or Ulawan chert on Guadalcanal at this time suggests increasing mobility, like that evidenced by the movement of similar material across the Near Oceania boundary into the Lapita sites of the Reef–Santa Cruz region. The archaeological and palaeoenvironmental evidence could also support the argument that the next major influx of settlers was around 2200 cal BP, towards the end of the ceramic phase in the Reef–Santa Cruz Islands.

Eastern Solomons

The SESP work in the Eastern Solomon Islands was the first detailed regional survey of Lapita in Remote Oceania, and the results played a formative role in the development of Lapita archaeology. In a sense, the work was fortuitous. We now know how difficult it is to locate Lapita horizons anywhere between Buka and the eastern edge of Makira, and so far none have been found there above the high-tide line. Surprisingly, the SESP team found a high level of Lapita visibility in the Reef–Santa Cruz region: using relatively low-intensity survey methods they located 10 terrestrial sites with classic dentate stamped and incised Lapita pottery and a number of plainware sites (Figure 5.9). They did not search systematically in the intertidal zone. Six open sites with dentate stamped pottery were reported on the Main Reef Islands and four on Santa Cruz (Green, 1976c). Two of the Santa Cruz sites were located on the small offshore island of Tömotu Neo. Another rockshelter excavation on Tömotu Neo (Növlaö SZ-47) failed to produce any dentate stamped ceramics but did contain a stratified sequence with plainware ceramics. One of the basal layers produced a radiocarbon date that overlapped the decorated Lapita-ware horizons (McCoy & Cleghorn, 1988:107).

The density of early Lapita sites in this relatively small zone now seems extraordinary. At the time there was some expectation that similar site densities might also be found in the Central and Western Solomon Islands, although SESP had failed to find any in the Eastern Solomons. This was a sensible expectation given the low levels of regional survey

THE AUSTRONESIAN EXPANSION

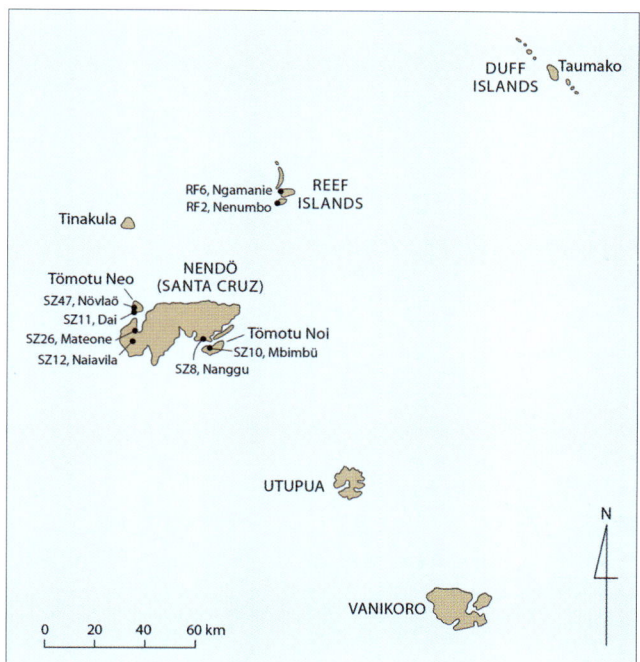

Figure 5.9. Locations of archaeological sites in the Reef–Santa Cruz Islands (after Green, 1976c).

in those places, and the relatively impoverished nature of the Reef–Santa Cruz ecosystems compared with those of the larger and more diverse landmasses to the west. But it now seems that the Reef–Santa Cruz Islands are unusual in the density of the Lapita presence. One factor in this might be preferential site preservation in the Reef–Santa Cruz Islands as a result of the deposition of ash from the active volcanic island of Tinakula, some 50 km west of the Reef Islands. Tinakula was active at some point in the first millennium AD (Green et al., 2008) and deposited up to 30 cm of ash over the Nenumbo (SE-RF-2) site on the islet of Te Motu Taiba. Sporadic ash showers also appear to have sealed a number of deposits on the low coralline islands where normal soil accumulation would have been limited, as well as covering sites on Santa Cruz, although there is only limited evidence for it at the Nanggu (SE-SZ-8) site on Santa Cruz. Another factor relating to local volcanism is that the ash showers would enhance soil fertility and so attract and support higher densities of settlement, particularly of horticultural communities, as Lapita undoubtedly were (Green, 1978:32). For reasons given below, however, we argue that the density of sites in the Reef–Santa Cruz Islands is an actual reflection of Lapita settlement.

Patrick Kirch (1983a) carried out additional research in the greater Reef–Santa Cruz group as part of the SESP programme: he directed four weeks of fieldwork on the small, high, volcanic double island (Banie and the much smaller Teanu) of Vanikoro, located 125 km southeast of Santa Cruz. Test pits in the Emo Dune site on Teanu (SE-VK-10) showed up to 1.9 m of disturbed unstratified deposit. A charcoal date (UCR-967, 1750 ± 85) from near the bottom of this deposit calibrated to 1825–1418 cal BP (95.4% HPD). No Lapita-period ceramics were recovered, although a small collection of excavated and surface sherds are described as having rectilinear incised and applied relief decoration like those found on Tikopean ceramics of the same period and attributed to the Mangaasi tradition of Vanuatu. Examination of temper in these sherds by Dickinson showed a high probability of a source on Espiritu Santo (Kirch, 1983b). As the islands appear to be actively subsiding, Kirch (1983a:75) suggested that Lapita sites may have been submerged under reef or mangroves. Recently Jean-Christophe Galipaud has reported finding Lapita ceramics on Vanikoro in a submerged situation, however this material has yet to be described. If this is in fact an intertidal site and not simply the result of rapid subsidence, it is of interest, as such sites are not reported in Remote Oceania – with the possible exception of the Bourewa site in Fiji (Nunn & Heorake, 2009) and a deposit exposed in a riverbank (SE-SZ-45) on Santa Cruz that Green suggested (Green et al., 2008) might have been an uplifted intertidal situation.

Lapita sites of the Reef–Santa Cruz Islands

Green excavated three of the Reef–Santa Cruz Lapita sites: Nenumbo (SE-RF-2) and Ngamanie (SE-RF-6) in the Reef Islands and Nanggu (SE-SZ-8), which is located 60 km to the southwest on the larger high island of Nendö (Santa Cruz). The rich assemblages from these sites formed an important data set for the early development of Lapita models, but the potential value of the data has been undermined to some extent by recent controversies over dating. Archaeologists have proposed two alternative interpretations of the relative ages and ordering of the sites – referred to as the '8, 2, 6' versus the '6, 2, 8' sequence, based on the site numbers. Although the three sites span a relatively short time period, the alternative interpretations imply different patterns of cultural change, including in the development of the ceramic motifs, so resolving the relative chronology is important. Our recent work at SZ-8, discussed below, sheds new light on this debate.

In the first reports of the Lapita investigations, Green used a combination of relative and absolute dating methods to argue for the '8, 2, 6' sequence (Green, 1978:32). Initially, radiocarbon ages were only available on two of the sites (RF-2 and RF-6), and Green used a seriation exercise to determine the relative position of SZ-8 (Green, 1978).

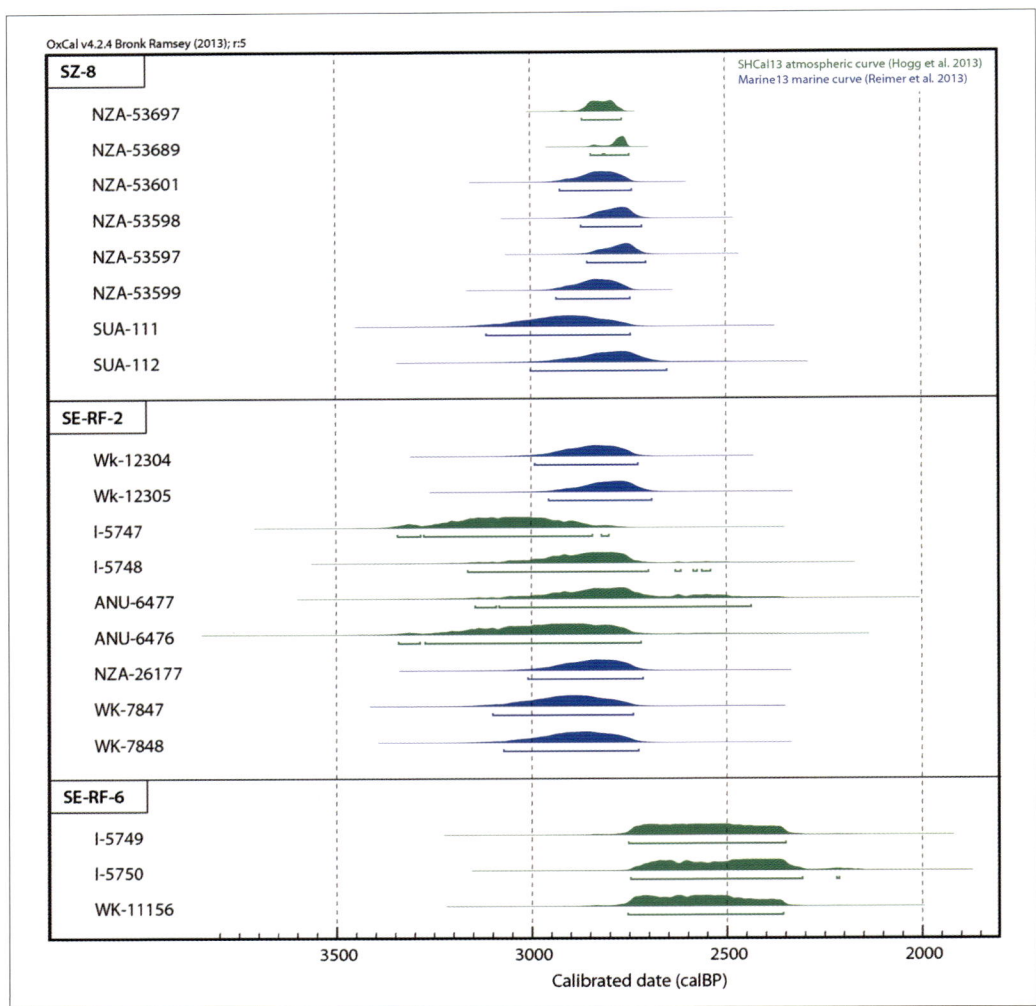

Figure 5.10. Plot of radiocarbon dates from archaeological sites in the Reef–Santa Cruz Islands (OxCal v.4.15).

The original order for the three Lapita sites, SZ-8, RF-2 and RF-6, derived from the design study done by Donovan (1973) using all the decorative material for body-sherds in a rather general way. Subsequently, Green (1978) assembled a more formal set of 54 Lapita design motifs useful in establishing linkages between a number of regions with Lapita sites of which all but the Watom site were located in Remote Oceania. (Green, 1991b:198)

The design study was supplemented by some obsidian hydration age estimates that were undertaken by Ambrose (1996). A radiocarbon date was later obtained on marine shell from SZ-8; this was calibrated in the range of 3048–2876 cal BP (1 sigma) (Figure 5.10), which appeared to support the 8, 2, 6 sequence (Green, 1991b: Table 3). Green (1991b) noted that the trajectory of ceramic design change implied by the 8, 2, 6 sequence followed a simplification over time – a fall-off in the cultural forces maintaining the elaborate decorative system of the horizon style. This follows a common culture historical model whereby an initial coherent and widespread horizon style, such as Lapita, breaks down into more simplified regional style zones. A similar pattern was independently discovered in the changes over time in proportions of obsidian and chert: the 8, 2, 6, sequence mapped declining amounts of obsidian coming from the Bismarck Archipelago, over 2000 km to the northwest (Sheppard, 1993: Table 5.2). Change in the sources of stone used to manufacture tools indicated a process of regionalisation, with distant sources of obsidian gradually replaced by chert from Ulawa and Malaita 400 km to the north, and small amounts of chalcedony from nearby Taumako.

Best (2002:89–92) and later Felgate (2003) have challenged the 8, 2, 6, sequence based on alternative models of ceramic change. Best, for example, argued that the original Donovan (1973) study of ceramic motifs showed that the execution of designs is simplest or crudest in the

	Obsidian		Chert	
	Weight	Weight/m2	Weight	Weight/m2
SZ-8	245.0	34.6	161.0	23.4
RF-2	9.5	17.36	12.6	23.1
RF-6	26.4	6.12	45.4	10.5

Table 5.2. Proportions of obsidian to chert in the Reef–Santa Cruz Lapita sites.

SZ-8 site, and the pattern that Green observed was related to problems of sample size. Best concluded by placing SZ-8 at the recent end of the sequence and RF-6 at the earliest end. If Best were correct, the charcoal dates from RF-6 would have to be unrelated to the occupation, and the lithic data pattern as a whole would imply an increase in long-distance transport over time – although again, the arguments about sample size could be raised. Green and colleagues have addressed the concerns of Best (2002) and Felgate (2003) by refining the dating model using a combination of new dates, newly determined delta-R values and Bayesian calibration models. Green et al. (2008) gave a new calibrated age estimate for SZ-8 of 3300–3000 cal BP (1 sigma), but they suggested the site was actually occupied for about 100 years.

This placed SZ-8 firmly at the beginning of the Reef–Santa Cruz sequence and as early as any other site of the Lapita colonisation phase of Oceania (Green et al., 2008:49). For RF-2, Jones et al. (2007) report an occupation duration of about 50 years within a span of 3145–2825 cal BP (1 sigma), which leaves an overlap with SZ-8. Most recently a chicken bone from RF-2 has been dated (NZA 26177) at 3047 ± 25 BP (Beavan Athfield et al., 2008: Table 5A) Isotopic data indicates that this chicken had a high marine contribution to its diet (δ^{13}C -15.9 δ^{15}N 12.9), which indicated it was considerably younger than a comparable charcoal sample. RF-6 is the youngest of the three sites, and Green and Jones (2008:16) estimate a 50–100 year occupation in the period 2800–2300 cal BP (1 sigma). Although the original Green sequence seemed, in 2008, to be well supported, it was and still is possible – and in fact probable – that sample size and variation in the nature of the samples from sites of very different size and, possibly, function need to be taken into consideration when comparing these assemblages. Sheppard and Green (2007; see also Green, 2009) conducted sampling experiments to assess potential sample size effects and concluded that variation in the frequency of ceramic decorative motifs among these sites cannot be accounted for by sampling size alone.

Material	Context	Lab Code	δ13C[‰]	CRA[1]	Error
Charcoal	Layer 1 oven	I-5752		910	95
Two Tridacna sp.	Square VV-50, Level 4, 40–60 cm dbs towards base of Grey Sand layer, Layer 2	SUA-112	0.02[2]	3140	70
Turbo astrea (?)	Square HH-61, Level 5, first lens 60 cm dbs Grey Sand layer, Layer 2	WK-12305	2.8	3149	57
Trochus niloticus	Square PP54, Level 4, 45–60 cm dbs Brown Sand layer, Layer 2	WK-12304	1.6	3192	51
Misc. clam + 1 Tridacna	Square DD-64, Level 4, 45–60 cm dbs at base of coralline grey brown sandy layer, Layer 2	SUA-111	0.02[2]	3250	70
Charcoal	Square A3, Layer 2, NW Quadrant Sieve	NZA-53716	-29.2	1327	18
Charcoal	Square B2, Layer 2/3 interface – 70 dbs, beside rock in linear feature, east face of square	NZA-53689	-24.9	2710	15
Charcoal from inside shell (NZA-53598)	Square A2, Layer 2	NZA-53697	-26.6	2768	15
Trochus sp.	Square A2, Layer 2	NZA-53598	4.06	3137	24
Atactodia striata (?)	Square B3, bottom of Layer 2, SE Quadrant, side of rock, Bag 72	NZA-53597	-12	3121	24
Tridacna sp.	Square A2, SE Quadrant, Layer 2/3 interface. Associated with oven stones, Bag 32	NZA-53601	3.43	3180	24
Cerithium egenum (?)	Square A2, Layer 2/3 interface	NZA-53599	-6.7	3189	24

1. Conventional radiocarbon age   2. Assumed value see Green et al. (2008: Table 2)

Table 5.3. Radiocarbon dates from Nanggu (SE-SZ-8) (from Sheppard et al., 2015a: Table 1).

In December 2012 we returned to the Nanggu (SZ-8) site, along with Scarlett Chiu, in an attempt to improve the dating of that site and to collect a better faunal sample (Sheppard et al., 2015a). Excavation of 12 square meters adjacent to the grid established by Green revealed that preservation of organics was, as found by Green, extremely poor at the site. No fauna other than marine shell was recovered. Charcoal was very rare in the Lapita deposit and was limited to two very small samples (NZA-53697 and 53689); however, one of these (NZA-53697) was recovered from within a marine shell (NZA-53598 Trochus) (Table 5.3). We obtained a total of four marine shell dates, all of which provided a conventional radiocarbon age equivalent to those obtained earlier on marine shell by Green et al. (2008). The charcoal samples, however, clearly date to the same period as the RF-2 site. This indicates that the delta-R value for the south central coast of Nendö needs to be re-evaluated and not assumed based on values from the Reef Islands. These results indicate that the earliest Lapita dates in the Reef–Santa Cruz region date after 3000 BP and most probably not earlier than 2900 BP. Our new AMS dates have very small errors; this is a considerable improvement on the earlier dates from the Reef–Santa Cruz site, which have large errors for the charcoal samples. What is now needed is to redate the other Reef–Santa Cruz sites with improved precision.

Ceramics

As noted above, the ceramic series from the excavated Reef–Santa Cruz Lapita sites have engendered much debate, primarily over how changes in decorative motifs might be used to seriate these sites and whether the samples are biased by various factors (e.g. sample size, breakage, site structure and function). These questions are explored in some detail in Green (2009). Here we will step back from the details of that debate and consider some of the more general characteristics of the assemblages.

Today the sherds recovered are generally a buff-red colour and fairly friable. The Reef–Santa Cruz sites often have very high pH, and that combined with the tropical climate makes for an extreme weathering environment. Even the chert artefacts have a thick weathering patina (Sheppard & Pavlish, 1992), therefore the current state of the ceramics may not closely reflect their original state. However, casual examination of sherds suggests that although the elaborate decorative designs are generally well executed, the often slab-built pottery body on which the design is placed frequently seems to be poorly executed. Donovan (1973, vol. 2:72) has noted that this is particularly evident at site SZ-8 where, although fine pieces exist, the remainder seem 'clumsy and unfinished'. The paste is tempered with both shell and sand, and it is probable that the clay itself is derived from the high basaltic island of Nendö. Examination of the temper by Dickinson (Dickinson, 2006; Dickinson & Shutler, 2000) indicates that most, if not all of the temper could have been sourced locally – which suggests local manufacture. In the calcareous Reef Islands a large volume of mineral temper has been transported, along with the clay (Parker, 1981), from Nendö as either raw material or finished pots. There are also a small number of tan-coloured sherds with an unusual volcanic sand temper, which are from an as yet unknown region (Dickinson & Shutler, 2000:243). Burley and Dickinson (2010) report a similar tan sherd from the Nukuleka site on Tongatapu, which contains an identical temper to those from SZ-8. Dickinson has hypothesised that the 'most probable source would be a dacitic high island along the New Hebrides island arc of Vanuatu and the eastern Solomon island outliers (Santa Cruz group)' (Burley & Dickinson, 2010:1024).

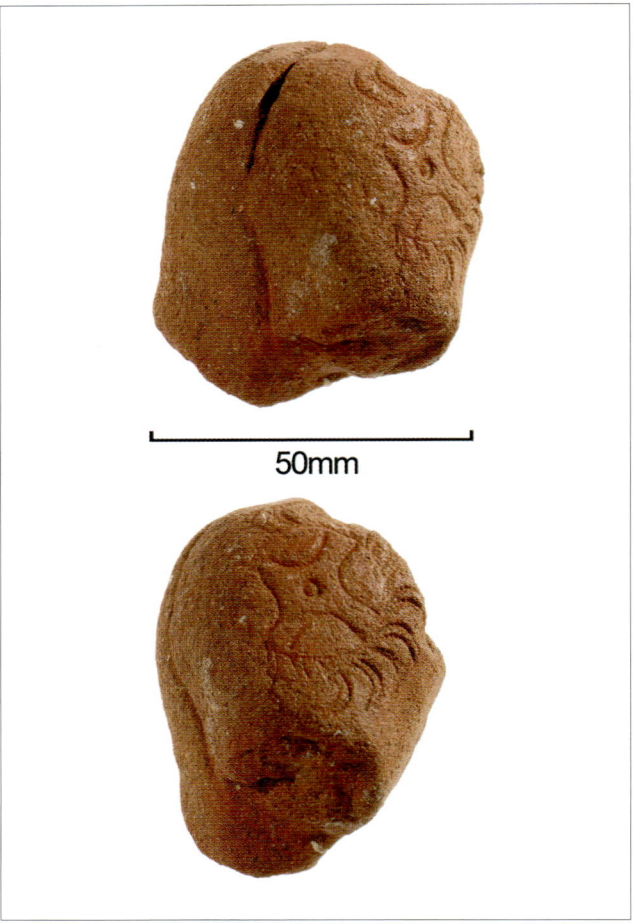

Figure 5.11. Anthropomorphic ceramic piece from the RF-6 Reef–Santa Cruz Lapita site.

THE AUSTRONESIAN EXPANSION

Figure 5.12. Zoomorphic ceramic piece from the SE-SZ-8 Reef–Santa Cruz Lapita site.

A considerable range of pot forms are reported from the Reef–Santa Cruz sites, including flat-based dishes, open bowls, restricted-mouth pots (Donovan, 1973), cylinder pot stands (Best, 2002; Parker, 1981) and a number of modelled clay pieces including a fragment of a dentate stamped human torso, and a bird that may have originally perched on the rim of a pot (Figures 5.11 and 5.12). Examination of the distribution of pot forms at RF-2 (see below) indicates an association of the flat-based plates or bowls with a probable house, and the globular restricted-mouth pots with a cooking area (Sheppard & Green, 1991).

Lapita is recognised most readily by the very distinctive dentate stamped decoration, but as in most ceramic assemblages, most sherds are undecorated. A large portion of these are likely to be from the undecorated bases of pots; however, the presence of undecorated rims indicates a considerable number of plain vessels. Of the 8082 decorated sherds from the Reef–Santa Cruz Lapita sites, 68% are dentate stamped and the remainder are incised (Felgate, 2003: Table 4). Although dentate stamped decoration varies from 65% (SZ-8) to 76% (RF-2) of decorated ceramics at these sites, it is unwise to use the differences in percentage of dentate stamping as a simple measure of time. As Felgate has pointed out (2003; also Felgate et al., 2012), different amounts of breakage at each site may bias samples and will probably result in variation in the reporting of dentate versus incised decoration in the assemblages. Differential breakage will also bias the recognition of motifs, since smaller decorated pieces may not be able to be assigned to a specific motif class.

Using the analysis of Donovan (1973, based on Mead et al., 1973), Green (2009) reports 79 general decorative motifs in his SZ-8, RF-2 and RF-6 ceramic database – based on the 1694 sherds for which a motif was recordable. Although there has been plenty of focus on differences between the motif inventories of these sites, what is most striking is the similarities. Nearly all motifs are represented in all three sites, although a considerable number of motifs are represented at very low frequency in each site. The most common motif (14%) reported for all sites is Motif 69 – a small circle or oval, either in a band on its own or bordered by parallel bands of dentate stamped cross-hatched pattern (the RZ3 restricted zone marker) (Donovan, 1973, vol. 2:87) (Figure 5.13). The most common sets of motifs are all variants on combinations and arrangements of larger half-circles or ovals. Thus Motif 1 (4.2%) is a lineal arrangement of contiguous half ovals, either as a single line or as double or multiple lines of this basic wave-like pattern. Motif 2 (5.1%) takes this basic M1 pattern and shifts every other line one half of an oval to make an overlapping wave pattern. This motif has 16 variants or 'alloforms', described by Donovan (1973:89). This basic set of motifs is closely related to Motif 5 (8.7%) and Motif 6 (5.5%). Here, chains of ovals or half ovals are created using Motif 2, offset as per M2 but reflected along a central axis to build a symmetrical complex pattern. The most complex form of Motif 5 has a

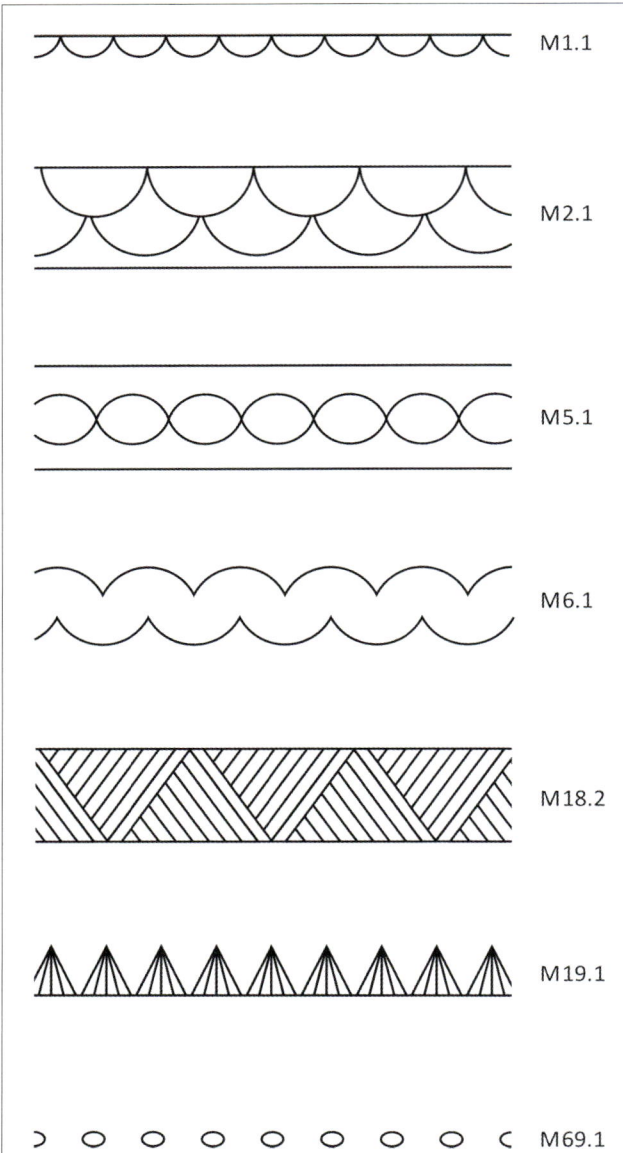

Figure 5.13. Motifs from the Reef–Santa Cruz ceramics discussed in text (after Donovan, 1973, fig. 4).

Figure 5.14. Lapita face design from the SE-RF-2 Reef Island Lapita site.

small circle (Motif 69) placed at the centre of the central row of ovals in this symmetrical pattern. Motif 6 differs from Motif 5 in that the central line of ovals are offset a half position, whereas in Motif 5 the central row is of matched half-circles that form a complete oval. Together these motifs make up 23.5% of all motifs. They illustrate how Lapita design systems are composed mostly of a small set of design elements and rules of reflection and symmetry which, together, play (in this case) on a wave-like theme. The other most common theme is the use of straight lines to fill triangles, either as sets of parallel lines set on an oblique angle to create a basket-weave-like pattern (Motif 18, 5.3%) or as sets of straight lines radiating from the apex of a triangle (Motif 19, 6.6%). Variants of these motifs make use of the simple circle (Motif 69) or the basic half-oval (Motif 1). As Donovan noted (1973:68), much of the precision and similarity of designs built on a small set of design elements must relate to the use of a common but restricted tool set consisting of a dentate straight line, a dentate crescent or half-oval, and a small circle. Best (2002) has suggested that the inventory of tools used may have included a roulette which, he argues, is required to make the detailed zone marker bands and the famous anthropomorphic images (see below) – although Ambrose (2007) questions this proposition.

Perhaps one of the most widely recognised Lapita designs from the Reef–Santa Cruz region is the face design from RF-2 (Figure 5.14). Anthropomorphic designs were reported on and illustrated from the Reef–Santa Cruz sites by Donovan (1973: vol. 2:1301–03), including the one shown in Figure 5.11. Terrell and Schechter (2007, 2009) introduced a dissenting voice with their suggestion that the so-called anthropomorphic design is actually a reference to sea turtles; but most archaeologists seem to accept that these designs represent a human face (e.g. Best, 2002; Chiu, 2007; Kirch, 1997; Noury, 2007; Sand, 2007b). If this is indeed the case, the face motif is part of an important Lapita theme: perhaps the faces represent ancestors whose significance to the living communities was part of a widespread social tradition. Spriggs' examination of these designs (1990, 1993a; see also Best, 2002) has shown how many of the individual motifs can be seen as abstractions or simplifications of these 'face' designs or portions of them.

THE AUSTRONESIAN EXPANSION

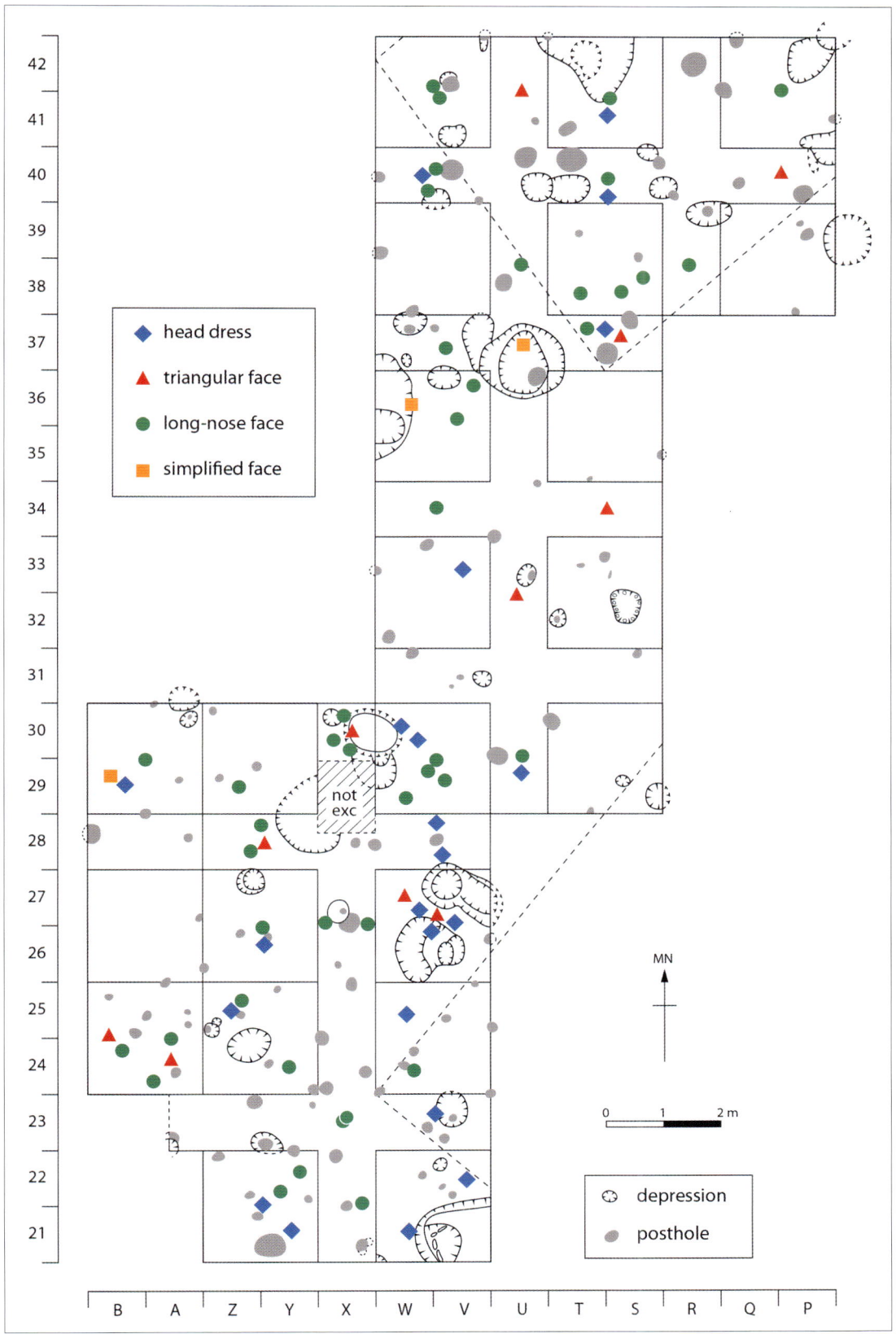

Figure 5.15. Distribution of the face motif in the SE-RF-2 Reef Island Lapita site (from Chiu, 2007).

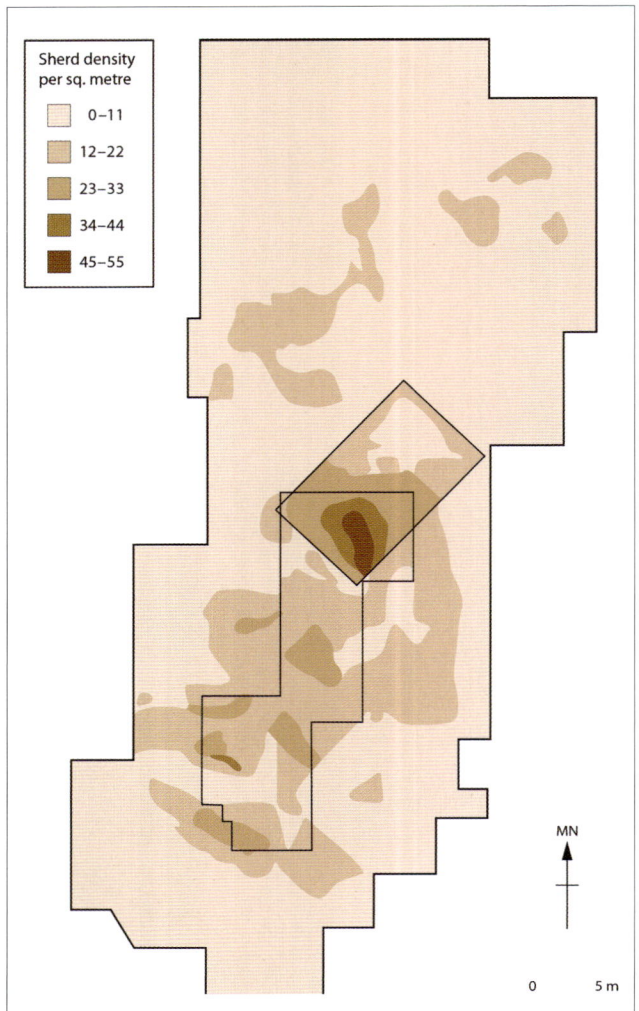

Figure 5.16. Density of pot sherds at the RF-2 Reef Island Lapita site (from Sheppard & Green, 1991).

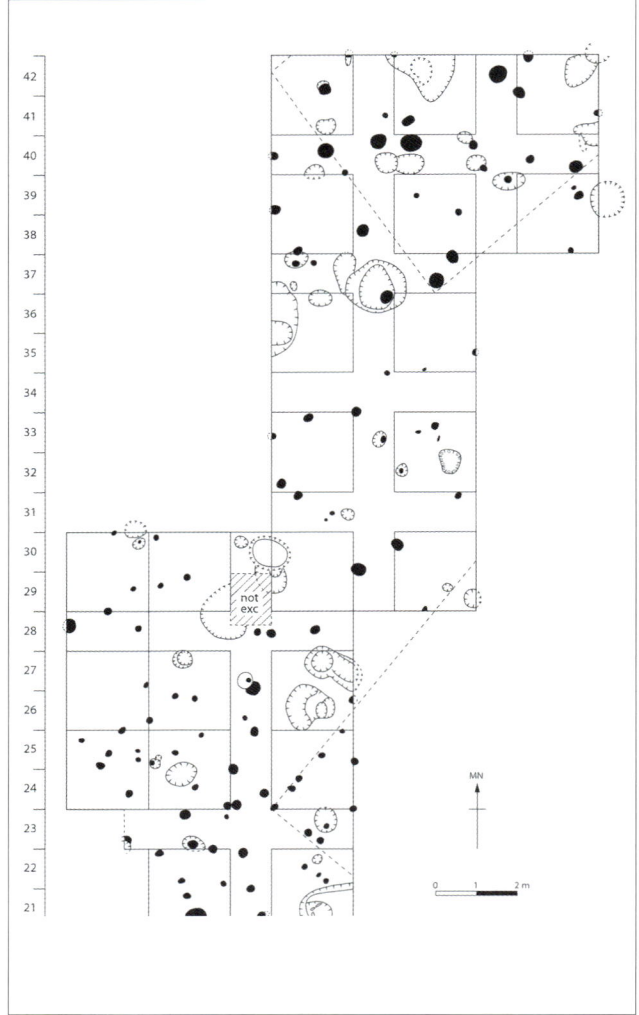

Figure 5.17. Spatial distribution of postholes at the RF-2 Reef Island Lapita site (from Sheppard & Green, 1991).

Clear examples are the 'nose' motifs M8 to M10. Scarlett Chiu has taken up Spriggs' suggestion to examine in closer detail the form, distribution and associations of these 'face' designs. She has recorded 105 examples of this motif in the Reef–Santa Cruz sites (Chiu, 2007) and provided a detailed study of their distribution at RF-2 (Figure 5.15). The presence of such a wide variety of face motifs and no clear pattern of spatial segregation indicates little support for any simple pattern of face design change over time, or association with distinct social groups.

The Lapita ceramic tradition in the Reef–Santa Cruz Islands, like Lapita in most regions, at some point lost its decorated component along with its complex pot forms and modelled clay items. Ultimately, ceramic production is dropped from the record entirely. Although this does not seem to be a long, gradual process in the Reef–Santa Cruz Islands, it is not clear exactly when the decorated to plainware transition occurred or when pottery production ceased, because many of the dated assemblages have large, overlapping error ranges. The RF-6 assemblage, for example, has a high proportion of dentate stamped ware dating to the period 2755–2357 (WK-11156, 95.4% HPD) – something that suggested to Best (2002) that it must be older than the associated radiocarbon dates. However, the error of 88 years on the conventional radiocarbon age (CRA) creates a large calibrated range, and this is exacerbated by the presence of a distinct plateau in the curve at this time range. The predominantly plainware assemblage of RF-19 – which has only six dentate and incised sherds out of a total of 785 pieces – overlaps RF-6 with dates in the range 2738–2430 cal BP (WK-7852, 95.4% HPD). This suggests that the transition to plainware

Figure 5.18. Artist's impression of the small Lapita settlement at SE-RF-2 (painting by Briar Sefton, used with permission).

probably occurred sometime after 2700 and before 2500 cal BP. The end of ceramic production would appear, based on the I-10810 (2157–1720, 94.2% HPD) radiocarbon sample from SZ-47 (Növlaö), to be sometime after 2000 cal BP (McCoy & Cleghorn, 1988).

Excavation of Nenumbo (RF-2)

At the Nenumbo (RF-2) site, Green carried out a large areal excavation of 153.5 m² which has provided one of the most complete descriptions to date of an early Lapita settlement. Before commencing excavation, he made a surface collection of pottery sherds. The resulting distribution patterns suggested the effects of three discard processes:

1. a background scatter of sherds across the living area of the site and grading out towards the apparent limits of regular site use, resulting from everyday breakage and loss
2. a dense rectilinear concentration of sherds towards the centre of the site, resulting from intensive discard in the vicinity of focused work areas
3. a number of small, scattered patches of higher sherd density, resulting from discard around a sequence of low-intensity, probably overlapping work zones (Sheppard & Green, 1991:91).

When the excavation data was added, the dense rectilinear sherd scatter could be seen to fit over an area of postholes, suggesting the presence of a structure that measured around 7 m x 10 m (Figures 5.16 and 5.17). On the evidence of the initial sherd distribution and posthole patterns, the site was interpreted as a small hamlet of around 1100 m², comprising 'one large central structure which has to the

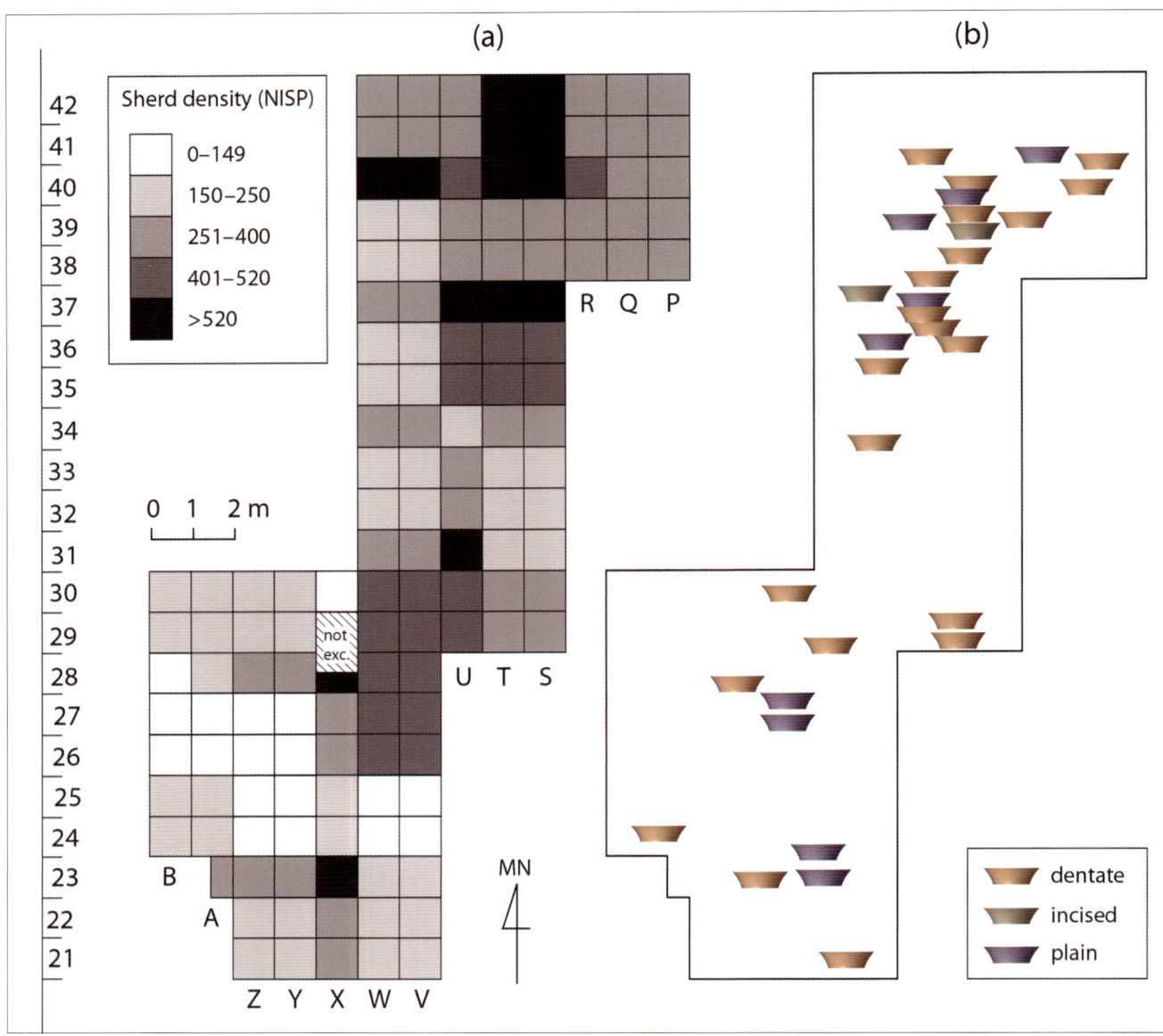

Figure 5.19. Spatial distribution of pot forms at the RF-2 Reef Island Lapita site. 5.19a shows density of sherds across the site; 5.19b shows the distribution of dentate, incised and plain specimens of flat-bottom bowls probably associated with food preparation and consumption (after Parker, 1981) (from Sheppard & Green, 1991).

south an area of smaller structures which, based on the frequency and lack of coherent pattern, may represent a number of building episodes over time' (Sheppard & Green, 1991:92). The structure has been interpreted as a house, and the abrupt edges of the sherd distributions suggest that it had closed walls, at least at floor level (Green & Pawley, 1999). The low-density presence of midden indicates that limited food consumption and preparation took place inside the structure, but the distribution of stone artefacts and debitage suggests that its primary role was as a base for stone-tool use and manufacture including, especially, the preparation of chert points (Sheppard & Green, 1991:100).

Adjacent to the southern end of this structure was an area of ovens, pits and small post and stake holes, which was interpreted as defining a cooking area. On the whole, the distribution pattern of features and artefacts gives the impression of a short-term occupation, or at least one not muddied by episodes of rebuilding and replacement or by changes in site function (Figure 5.18).

A range of pot forms were reconstructed based on the work of Parker (1981), and their distribution was plotted against the other excavated data. Restricted and large, open-mouth pot forms were found to be strongly associated with the cooking area in the south of the site, while flat-bottomed

THE AUSTRONESIAN EXPANSION

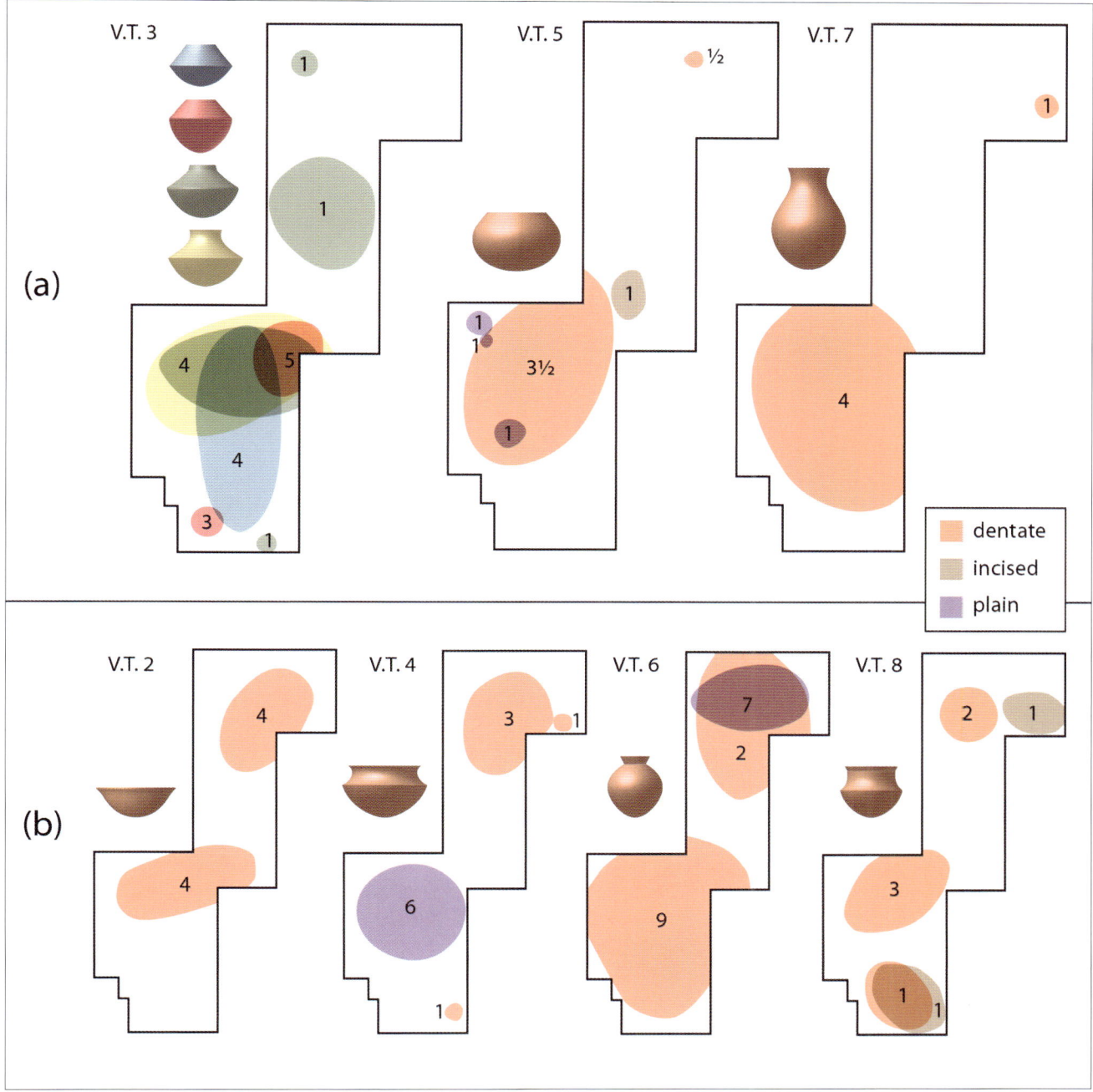

Figure 5.20. Spatial distribution of pot forms at the RF-2 Reef Island Lapita site: (a) shows the distribution (MNV values) of dentate, incised and plain specimens of globular, restricted-mouth forms probably associated with food preparation and consumption; (b) shows the distribution (MNV values) of various vessel forms argued to be of more specialist function (after Parker, 1981), (from Sheppard & Green, 1991).

bowls were found in higher relative proportions in the vicinity of the structure. More specialised pot forms were found clustered in various parts of the site, including the cooking area and the structure (Figures 5.19 and 5.20). This provides hints on pot function and social practice, although care that must be taken in comparing small ceramic samples from limited excavation contexts (Green, 1976c:255).

Long-distance movement of stone

The Reef–Santa Cruz Islands are impoverished in raw materials compared to the Bismarcks and the majority of larger islands in the Main Solomons, yet the Lapita sites there contain an abundance of exotic lithic materials, including high-quality obsidians and chert (Figure 5.21). The obsidian in the Reef–Santa Cruz Lapita sites originated from four different sources. Talasea obsidians from West New Britain, 2000 km to the west, dominate the assemblages at 97.5% by weight. Admiralties (Lou Island) sources are the next most abundant, followed by a very small quantity from the comparatively close Banks Island sources on Vanua Lava and Gaua, 400 km to the south. In addition, a single piece of obsidian has been sourced to Fergusson Island in the Milne Bay Province of eastern Papua New Guinea (Green, 1987; Green & Bird, 1989; Sheppard et al., 2010a). The obsidian assemblages contain a relatively low proportion of retouched pieces, and the only specialist forms are gravers – an enigmatic tool form that has also been found in Lapita sites in New Caledonia and in the Bismarck Archipelago, including Mussau (Sand & Sheppard, 2000; Sheppard, 1993, 2010).

The chert in the Reef–Santa Cruz Lapita sites most likely originated from sources on Ulawa or Malaita, at least 400 km away to the west, where foraminifera-rich, high-quality microquartz cherts are plentiful (Sheppard, 1996). A small amount of chalcedony was also recovered; this probably originated from the Duff Islands, a Polynesian Outlier 100 km to the east, which formed part of the historic Reef–Santa Cruz trading system. Other samples of exotic stone have also been identified, including pieces of quartz-muscovite-garnet schist which could be from Guadalcanal or from metamorphic formations further to the northwest (Papua New Guinea, D'Entrecasteaux Islands or Louisiade Archipelago). Green metasediments and volcanics are represented by adzes and adze-reworking flakes (Green, 1978; Sheppard, 2010). Some of this material could conceivably be from volcanic sources on Santa Cruz, but it is certainly exotic to the Reef Islands.

As Green and Kirch (1997) note, the exchange system that the Reef–Santa Cruz Lapita communities were engaged with is so far unique: nowhere in the Lapita 'homeland' of the Bismarck Archipelago can we see such source complexity and transport distance. In the Bismarck Lapita world most of the obsidian originated from 'close' sources (Specht, 2002), and although Green and Kirch (1997:29) describe the Mussau system as highly complex, the large number of long-distance relationships clearly evident in the Reef–Santa Cruz region constitute a much higher degree of social complexity and technical proficiency. In many respects the Reef–Santa Cruz resource procurement systems and associated social networks look like an expanded version of the Mussau system where the linkages have been stretched to their limit.

The transport of Talasea obsidian into the Reef–Santa Cruz Islands provides particularly useful insights into the nature of Lapita exchange systems and their role in the colonisation process. Sheppard (1993) makes a strong case that the obsidian from Talasea was obtained through direct procurement and that this involved a number of voyages over a few generations after the establishment of the first settlements. An estimate of the total quantity of raw material and the weight per cubic metre for each of the three sites is shown in Table 5.2. Core reduction relied on relatively wasteful freehand, hard-percussion methods; there is scant evidence for core preparation, or for the adoption of standardised core forms or reduction strategies (Sheppard, 1993:129). There was also a low level of flake utilisation, and in all three sites 30% of the obsidian cores were discarded before they were exhausted. In short, the obsidian assemblages provided no evidence for the type of economising behaviour one would expect with declining access to a valuable raw material. There was a decline in the density of obsidian through time, and an increase in the relative importance of chert obtained from much closer sources. This change was accompanied by a reduction through time in the sizes of obsidian cores and debitage, perhaps indicating more careful use or curation. We discuss the changing patterns of obsidian use in the Lapita communities of the Reef–Santa Cruz Islands in the review of Lapita colonisation models for the Solomon Islands below.

Before examining the Lapita period record in the Polynesian Outliers, we note another feature of the Reef–Santa Cruz sequence which distinguishes it from its neighbours to the west and east. So far, and despite the comparatively large number of sites that have been located through survey, surface collections and excavation, there have been no post-Lapita decorated ceramics recovered. The ceramic sequence in the region grades into a plainware tradition of a much reduced range of simpler pot forms with, at most, a few examples of impressed and notched rims (Doherty, 2009). The ceramic tradition seems to end entirely, based on the Növalaö Rockshelter sequence, between 2100 and 1900 cal BP. No ceramics have been found of the post-Lapita incised and applied-relief body decoration, like that associated with the Mangaasi ceramic tradition in Vanuatu (McCoy & Cleghorn, 1988:114), or the New Caledonia incised Puen tradition, or the paddle-impressed decoration style called Podtanean (Sand, 1996). In this, the Reef–Santa Cruz region differs from its close neighbours to the south (Vanikoro, Tikopia, Anuta), which have all produced pottery assemblages that have been regularly compared to the Vanuatu-like post-Lapita tradition (Kirch, 1983b; Kirch & Yen, 1982; McCoy & Cleghorn, 1988). It could be that the Reef–Santa Cruz area fell outside the Vanuatu exchange network, or sphere of influence, in the post-Lapita period. This interpretation needs to be tempered with

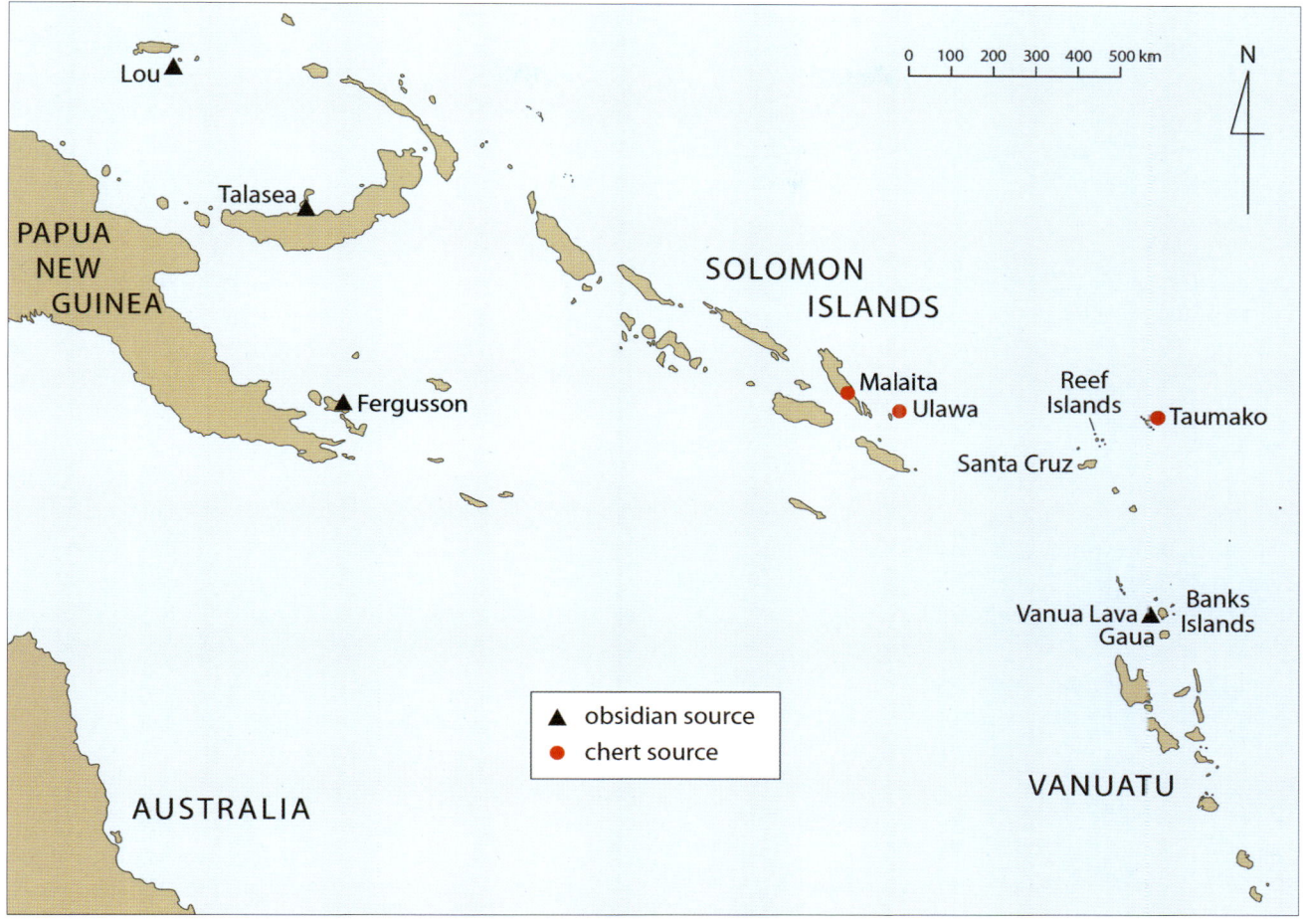

Figure 5.21. The location of sources of exotic stones found in Eastern Solomon Island Lapita sites.

caution, however, as Bedford (2000:172–74) has argued that the Tikopia sample is possibly too small to permit close comparison to the Vanuatu material, and the plain applied decorative bands seen on at least one Vanikoro sherd are quite unlike banding found in the Central Vanuatu sequence. More recently, Bedford (2006:174–92) has argued that there is in fact little resemblance among the post-Lapita incised and appliqué traditions to Mangaasi. In fact, most areas in island Melanesia seem to take separate developmental paths, creating regional tradition. Yet it is interesting to note that in the Bismarck Archipelago also, the Lapita dentate and incised tradition was gradually replaced by, or finished with, an incised, applied-relief and punctate decorative repertoire that is technically reminiscent of Vanuatu wares (Garling, 2003; Spriggs, 1997:124–25; White & Murray-Wallace, 1996), although it seems probable that they are slightly older than Mangaasi (Bedford, 2006:173). The failure of the Reef–Santa Cruz ceramics to transform in a similar way to those of the Bismarcks could be explained by the loss of the long-distance relationships signalled by the early obsidian movement and, therefore, a severing of long-distance ties before the late Lapita developments in the Bismarcks. This cannot be the entire explanation, however, as we see a similar simplification in design and form ending with a plainware and then the cessation of pottery production around 2000 cal BP in the Banks Islands and various parts of Vanuatu, and most definitely on the southern island of Erromango (Bedford, 2006:173). It seems that after 2000 cal BP we see much reduced evidence for interaction throughout the area, and increased regionalisation. This still leaves the larger question of why post-Lapita ceramic series should transform in similar ways in widely dispersed regions, separated by a zone of sharply reduced interaction.

Subsistence

Although innovations in sailing technology allowed people to reliably move out across the Near/Remote Oceania boundary, the colonists' ability to establish permanent settlements in the relatively resource-poor islands to the east depended on their being able to transport and successfully establish domesticated plants and animals. The Reef–Santa Cruz region would have been the most resource-poor environment encountered by Lapita settlers to date, and provided the first test of island domestication technology – the process of introducing and establishing a viable subsistence system based on wholly introduced products. The sheer abundance of Lapita sites in the Reef–Santa Cruz region attests to the success of this venture, although the direct evidence for food production (horticulture and animal husbandry) is not particularly strong. A series of pits and ovens, including what might have been a breadfruit storage pit, was found at RF-2 (Green & Pawley, 1999): this suggested that the production, storage and cooking of tubers or breadfruit in earth ovens was important. Alison Crowther's (2009:199–206) study of starch residues on ceramics from RF-2 clearly indicates cooking of taro (*Colocasia esculenta*), and analysis of sediment samples from the Lapita deposits identified banana starch and phytoliths – although care needs to be taken with this association, given potential disturbance in these layers (Sheppard & Green, 1991).

All the Lapita sites have produced a small number of pig bones, including teeth and a worked tusk (Green, 1976c) – although Anderson (2009:1508) has questioned the stratigraphic integrity of these samples. He points out that rat bones originally described as European (Green, 1976c) were found in the same layers as pig remains, which suggests disturbance and the possibility of intrusion of the pig. Our work at SZ-8 failed to produce bone of any kind in the Lapita deposits, and it seems possible that the pig bone from that site dates to the later occupation period associated with the charcoal date (I-5752 910 ± 95 BP) obtained by Green from an oven in the base of the brown layer (Layer 1) (Green & Jones, 2008). We obtained a similar age (NZA-53716 1327 ± 18 BP) on charcoal recovered from Layer 2 in 2012. However, not all the faunal remains are necessarily intrusive into the Lapita deposits at the other Lapita sites, as White et al. (2000) have shown that at least some of these 'European' rat bones are actually from the New Guinea species *Rattus praetor* – which casts doubt on the argument for stratigraphic disturbance. Chicken (*Gallus gallus*) is reported from Layer V of SZ-33 (Mdailu) on Santa Cruz and from RF-2, where a direct date on one chicken bone (Beavan Athfield et al., 2008; see also above) confirms the Lapita age of this faunal introduction. Other larger bird bones identified at RF-2 are from a species of megapode that has since been extirpated in the Reef–Santa Cruz Islands. It is noteworthy that no other subsequently extirpated species were found in the Reef–Santa Cruz sites, which contrasts with most settlement-period sites in the Pacific (Steadman, 2006). Along with pig, several species of rat appear to have been introduced with the Lapita settlers: *Rattus praetor* and *Rattus exulans* are both reported from RF-2 (Green, 1976c; White et al., 2000).

Marine resources represented in the Lapita midden assemblages include a range of reef and lagoon shellfish and inshore reef fish. The latter include sharks, which were likely taken along the inshore reefs and shoals, but there is no evidence for pelagic fishing – such as for bonito or tuna, which are such important catch components in recent times (Green, 1986). On the whole, as Green (1976c) pointed out, the faunal assemblages from the Lapita sites were quite insubstantial in comparison to the assemblages from later sites sampled by the SESP teams. One point of interest is that the most common bones by weight and frequency are those of sea turtles, which suggests that in the Reef–Santa Cruz region, as in Tikopia and Anuta (below) and other parts of Remote Oceania, the Lapita settlers made considerable use of the easily obtained turtles in previously untouched island waters.

Lapita sites of the Polynesian Outliers in the Eastern Solomons

There are at least nine Polynesian Outlier communities in the Eastern Solomon Islands, located on the islands of Pileni, Aua, Nupani, Nukapu, Nifiloli, Matema, Taumako, Anuta and Tikopia (Figure 2.6). Seven of the outlier islands in the Eastern Solomons share the Vaeakau–Taumako language. Six of these islands are located in the Reef Islands and the seventh, Taumako, is the largest island in the Duff group of islands located to the northeast. Anuta and Tikopia have their own, mutually intelligible languages (Anutan and Tikopian). Taumako, Anuta and Tikopia have all been the subject of archaeological research efforts and full sequences have been published. We summarise the early Austronesian settlement of these islands below, and in the following chapter we review the more recent phases of the island sequences, including the arrival of the Polynesian populations.

Taumako

The first archaeological work on Taumako was a site survey carried out by Roger Green in 1970 as part of the SESP. Green recorded a small number of sites in 1970 then returned in 1972 to carry out an excavation at the Kahula site, where a surface collection of shell adzes had been recovered (Leach & Davidson, 2008:27). Leach and Davidson continued the work there for a single field season in 1977, during which time they carried out a comprehensive site survey and excavation programme that has resulted in the publication of a full sequence for the island (Leach & Davidson, 2008).

The site with the earliest dated horizons was Te Ana Tavatava (Site 19), located on the Tavatava land unit on Lakao Island, approximately 9 km northwest of Taumako Island

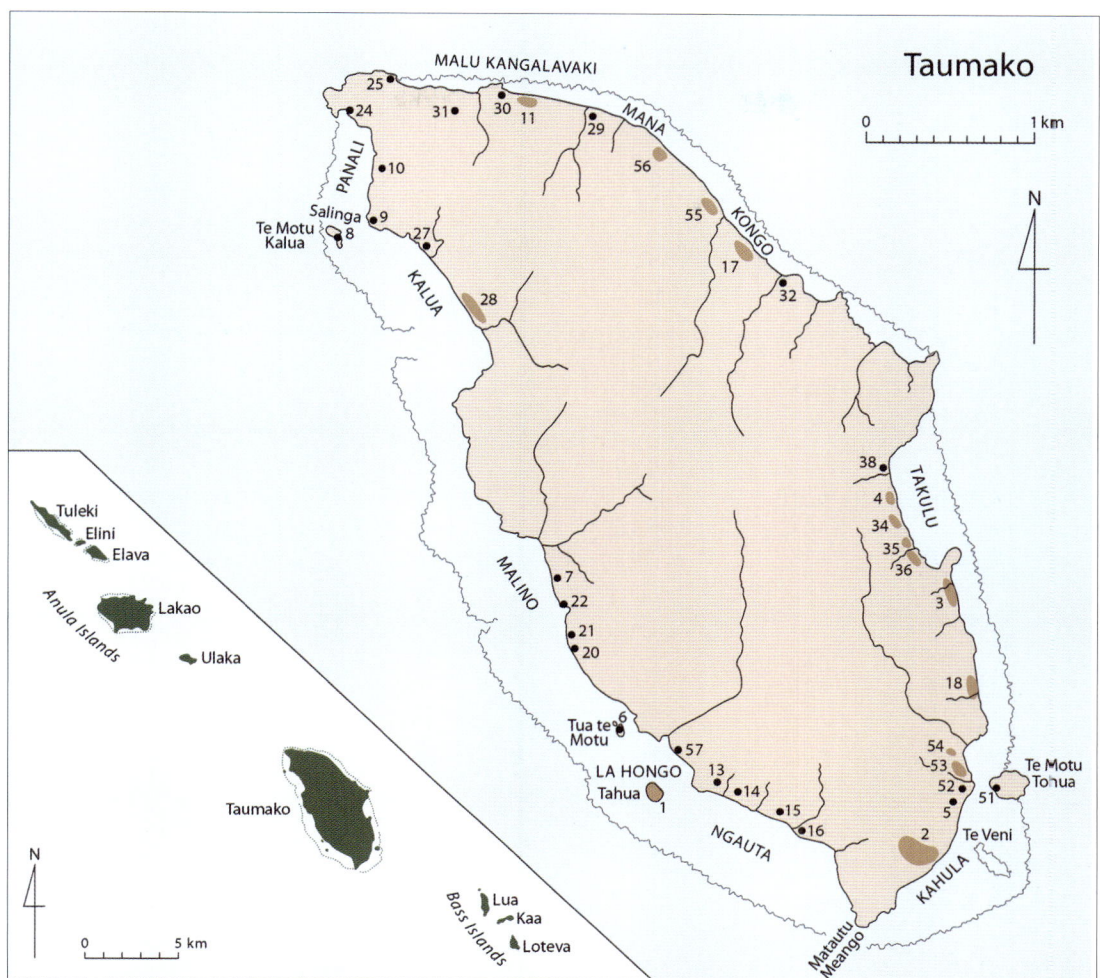

Figure 5.22. The location of archaeological sites on Taumako in the Eastern Solomons (after Leach & Davidson, 2008).

(Figure 5.22). Site 19 consists of a large coral gravel (kilikili) mound that is interpreted as a 'village mound', located in front of a small cave ('ana' means cave in Vaeakau–Taumako and many other Polynesian languages) (Figure 5.23). A total of 94 potsherds were found on the mound surface, of which 92 were plain and two were 'semi-punctured without nubbins' (Leach & Davidson, 2008: Table 4.9). Another 346 sherds were recovered from excavations carried out both within the cave itself and outside on the main mound.

Tavatava contains the only identified horizon from the Tavatava period, which is the earliest period in the Taumako sequence, dated to 3000–2400 cal BP (Leach & Davidson, 2008:296). The Tavatava period is represented by the first phase of occupation at Site 19, which Leach and Davidson (2008:296) refer to as the 'Level I' or 'cave occupation' phase. The Level I phase is contained within Layer 4 and Layer 5 of excavation units within the cave and is dated by two radiocarbon samples on charcoal soil from Layer 4 (NZ 4638 and NZ 4641) (Leach & Davidson, 2008: Table A12.1) that we calibrate to 2701–2325 and 2783–2380 cal BP respectively (95.4% HPD). Pottery was found in situ in Layer 4, and the excavators believe that all the pottery on the site derives from that layer. Outside the cave, the pottery was found in Layer 3, where it is considered intrusive. The largest ceramic assemblage, however, was recovered not from intact stratigraphy but from within the fill of two unusual pit features located within the cave. These coral slab-lined features extended to depths of more than 2.5 m. Their function is completely unknown, although Leach and Davidson suggested that they could be wells. The pit fill contained 200 sherds, including four dentate stamped specimens (Leach & Davidson, 2008:94–95, Table 4.9).

Other artefacts from the Tavatava period include *Tridacna* adzes, and personal ornaments in the form of *Conus* rings and discs and a possible *Tridacna* shell breastplate (Leach & Davidson, 2008:296, fig. 4.21-J). The small flaked-stone assemblage consists mainly of chert flakes made of a local silicified coral (n=511), although six obsidian flakes

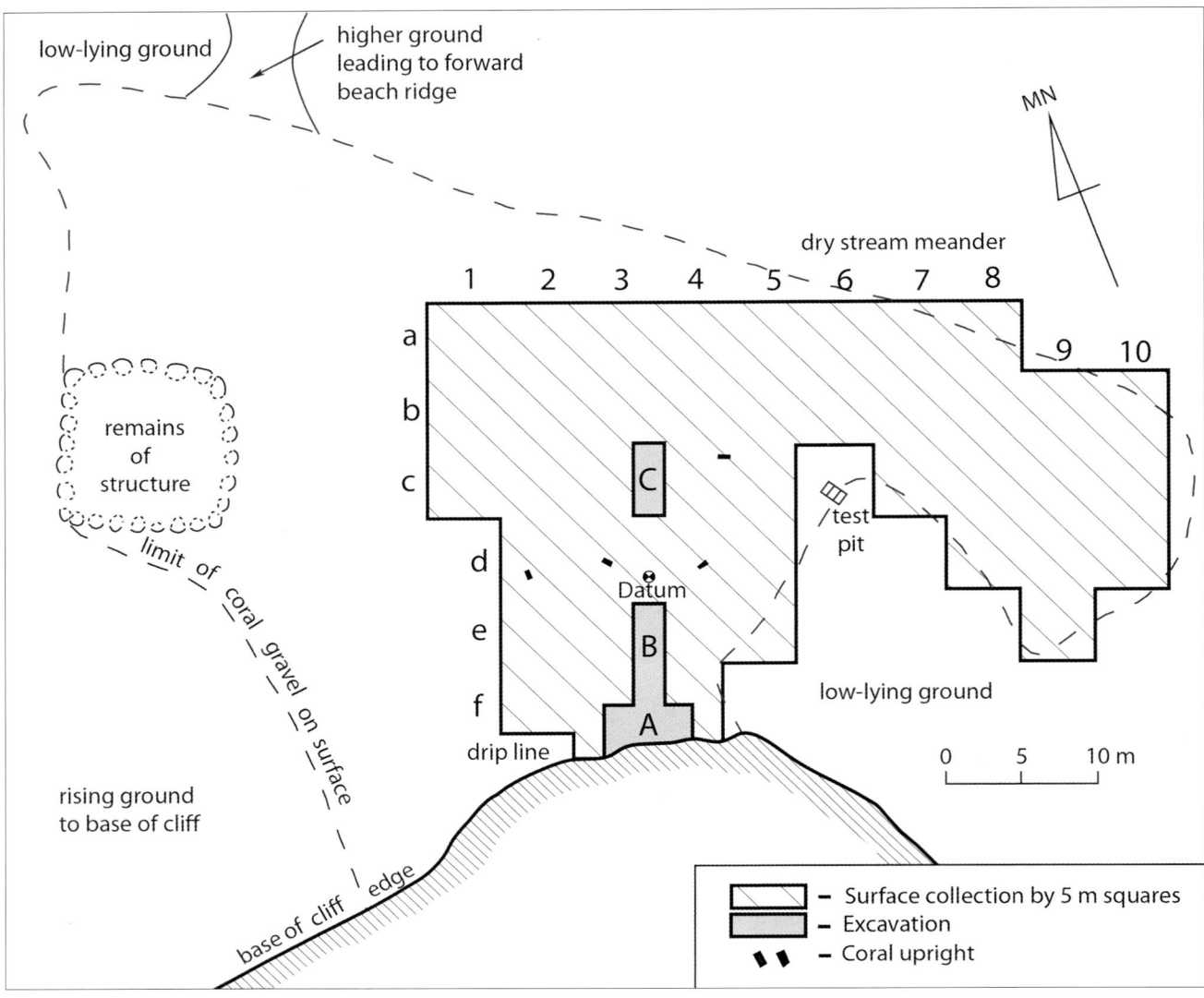

Figure 5.23. Plan of Tavatava (Site 19) excavation (after Leach & Davidson, 2008).

were also recovered, one of which was from Layer 4. The obsidian is thought most likely to derive from sources on Banks Island (Vanuatu), 450 km to the south (Leach & Davidson, 2008:125). The fishhook assemblage consisted of about 50 hooks, hook fragments and tabs (Figure 5.24). These comprised one-piece hooks made of *Trochus* and *Turbo marmoratus*, the point of a large composite hook and a fragment of a *Trochus* shell lure (Leach & Davidson, 2008:309, Table 4.25). The one-piece hooks were similar in form, style, material and size to Tikopian and Anutan assemblages (Leach & Davidson, 2008:309; see also Kirch & Rosendahl, 1973; Kirch & Yen, 1982:238–43).

Considerable quantities of fauna (especially of shellfish) were recovered from the Te Ana Tavatava excavations; these include, in the earliest levels, a wide range of shellfish taxa and a small quantity of fish. Pig was present in small amounts throughout the sequence, which tends to support the claim for pig in the early Lapita phase in the Reef–Santa Cruz Islands (Green, 1976c). A dog bone from Layer 5 is particularly significant. Most archaeologists assume dog accompanied the Lapita settlement east of the Main Solomons, although some claim the evidence for dog prior to 2000 cal BP in Remote Oceania is 'weak to non-existent' (Matisoo-Smith, 2007:160). Although some turtle bone was recovered from the site, Leach and Davidson (2008:93) saw no evidence for intensive exploitation of marine resources; they suggest the assemblage is more typical of a settled horticultural population.

Does the Tavatava period represent the arrival of early Lapita settlers in the Taumako group? The age range (3000–2400 cal BP) assigned by Leach and Davidson to the Tavatava period overlaps the dentate Lapita phase in the

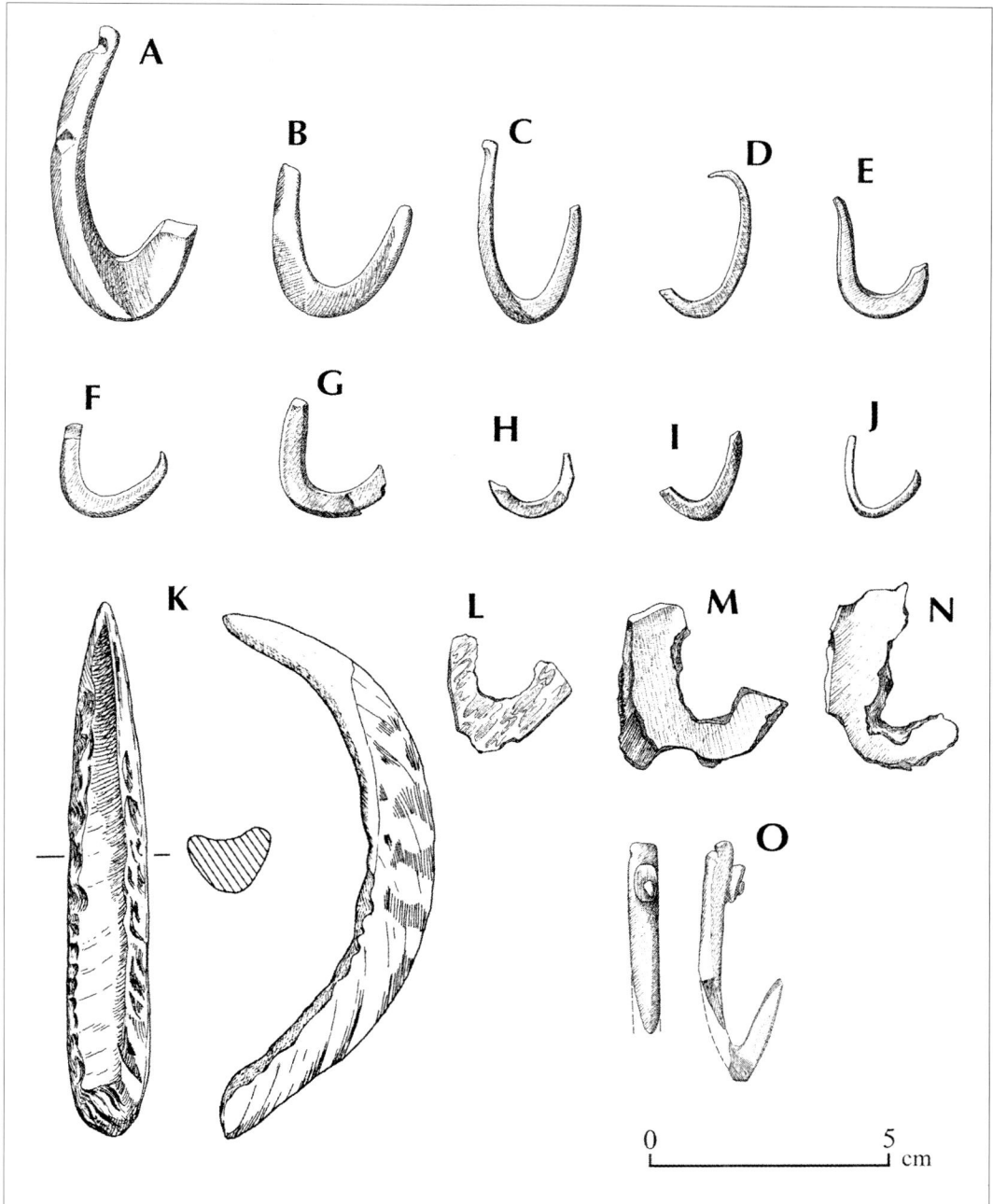

Figure 5.24. Fishhooks from Tavatava Phase sites (from Leach & Davidson, 2008, with permission).

Reef–Santa Cruz Islands, so that is a possibility. But there is some question as to whether a colonisation date of 3000 cal BP is justified by the radiocarbon evidence.

The actual calibrated age range of the two samples from Layer 4 at Te Ana Tavatava reported by Leach and Davidson is 2855–2348 cal BP (2 sigma) (Leach & Davidson, 2008: Table A12.1). However this was calculated using the northern hemisphere calibration curve from IntCal04 (Leach & Davidson, 2008; Reimer et al., 2004). Although we recognise that the shifting intertropical convergence zone can bring northern hemisphere systems south to the end of the Solomons for at least part of the year, we choose to use the southern hemisphere curve for all Solomons dates, as simply replacing the southern curve with the northern one will only replace one unknown error term with another. Using the southern hemisphere curve, the calibrated age range for the oldest sample (NZ 4641) is 2783–2380 BP (95.4% HPD). This is fundamentally the same age range as the plainware assemblages in the Reef–Santa Cruz Islands, which also display a very similar range of plain pot forms. The chert in Layer 4 is petrographically and chemically similar to source material from Aua Bay on the other side of Lakao Island from the Te Ana Tavatava site (Leach & Davidson, 2008:295). A small amount of identical material is reported by Sheppard (1996) from the RF-2 Lapita site in the Reef Islands – which means that Lakao Island must have been visited prior to the deposition of Layer 4 at Ana Tavatava. This has led Leach and Davidson (2008:295) to the view that 'it is reasonable to suggest occupation of the Taumako group as a whole by about 1000 BC'. In fact, there is no archaeological support for this in Taumako and, although it would appear that highly mobile Lapita explorers knew of and visited the region, there is currently no evidence that the islands were settled at that time. In fact it is rather surprising that the Malaitan and Ulawan chert sources remained important, albeit declining through time, in the Lapita and post-Lapita assemblages in the Reef–Santa Cruz region when a source of chalcedonic chert was much closer.

The ceramic assemblage that is most similar to that of Tavatava outside of the Reef–Santa Cruz region is Kiki ware from Tikopia (see below), which dates from about 2900 cal BP (or 2800 cal BP, below) and, like the Tavatava material, is predominantly undecorated. The shell ornaments from the Tavatava period are generally similar to Lapita forms (e.g. Kirch, 1988a; Szabo & Summerhayes, 2002), although some of these forms predate Lapita and last well into post-Lapita periods.

In summary, we consider the Tavatava Phase to represent settlement by people of the Lapita tradition, but not as part of the original movement into the Reef–Santa Cruz region. Instead, Taumako was likely colonised around 500 years later, which falls within the calibration range of the NZ 4641 radiocarbon sample. Perhaps colonists arrived from the Reef–Santa Cruz Islands – although we would also leave open the possibility that they came from the south, from Vanuatu.

Tikopia

Archaeological investigations on Tikopia were carried out by Pat Kirch in 1977–78 as part of a joint project with Doug Yen on the prehistory and historical ecology of the island under the umbrella of the SESP. Extensive surface survey and excavation resulted in the development of a full prehistoric sequence, which was matched against a model of environmental change. The resulting 1982 publication *Tikopia: The prehistory and ecology of a Polynesian Outlier* mapped the long-term interplay between Polynesian subsistence practices and landscape response, and became a foundation work in Polynesian historical ecology (Kirch & Yen, 1982). The excavation data from Tikopia was used to construct a four-phase cultural sequence, the earliest phase of which, the Kiki Phase, contained a Lapita component. We concentrate here on the Kiki Phase data; the cultural sequence is discussed in more detail in Chapter 6.

The Kiki Phase is represented by the Zone C layers in the Sinapupu depositional sequence (TP-47 to TP-53 and Site TK-36) at Sinapupu, and Layer II at the TK4 site at Kiki (Kirch & Yen, 1982:312, Table 7) (Figure 5.25). The earliest dated deposit on Tikopia is Layer IV at TP-52, which is a calcareous dune sand containing scattered charcoal and a few sherds that were interpreted by the excavators as intrusive from Layer III. The charcoal sample from Layer IV (UCR-965) returned an age range of 3970–3272 cal BP (95.4% HPD). If UCR-965 actually dates a cultural horizon, it would be the earliest such horizon in Remote Oceania. However, the excavators interpreted two radiocarbon samples (UCR-964 and 966) from Kiki Phase deposits as supporting a more likely colonisation date of around 2900 BP. The faunal assemblage associated with these samples included unusually large shellfish specimens, such as might be expected to have grown on a previously unharvested reef system (Kirch & Yen, 1982:312–14, Table 50). Thus Kirch and Yen concluded that the early date (UCR-965) represented, at most, a brief visitation to the island, followed by full settlement during the Kiki Phase some four to eight centuries later. Given that UCR-965 did not derive from a cultural horizon and has not been supported by similar findings over the subsequent 35 years of research in Remote Oceania, it would be sensible now to place this date to one side. This leaves the two Kiki Phase dates (UCR-964 and 966) which calibrate, at the earliest, to around 2900 cal BP (UCR 964 2961–2437 95.4% HPD) using the latest calibration data as providing the best estimate for first Tikopian settlement. This date is slightly earlier than the earliest dates from Taumako and contemporaneous with those from Anuta (below).

From the two Kiki Phase layers more than 3000 generally small sherds were recovered and used to define the Kiki Phase pottery. It is described as a slab-built, paddle- and anvil-finished pottery with two temper variants (volcanic or calcareous sand) and two general forms (jars and bowls) (Kirch & Yen, 1982:192–97). Only 27 decorated sherds were recovered (0.8%); the predominant decoration was notching and incising of the lip of the pot rim, along with one pinched crenulated rim. Almost all of the body sherds were plain, although five sherds carried dentate stamp designs and a further two had simple appliqué decoration. Other material found in the Kiki Phase assemblages included a

THE AUSTRONESIAN EXPANSION

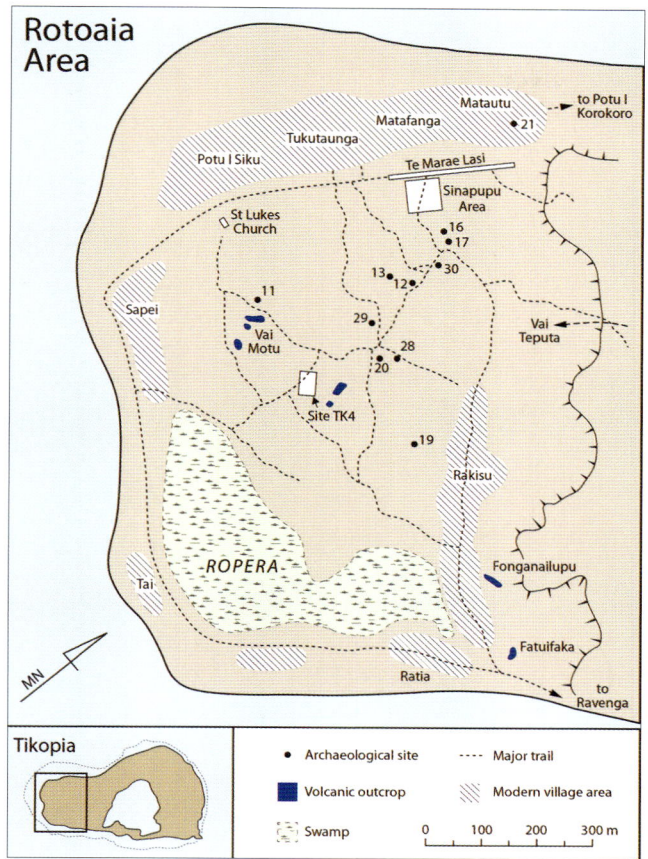

Figure 5.25. The location of archaeological sites on Tikopia (after Kirch & Yen, 1982).

large and morphologically diverse *Tridacna* shell adze kit and various shell, coral and echinoderm spine abraders and scrapers. Personal ornaments included *Conus* beads and *Trochus* armbands; but the diagnostic ornament type of the Kiki Phase was a *Spondylus* shell bracelet unit (Kirch & Yen, 1982:245) similar to those found in the Tavatava Phase sites in Taumako (Leach & Davidson, 2008:107, fig. 4.21-H). Four stone adzes were assigned to the Kiki Phase – three from the surface of TK-4 and one excavated from Layer C of the Sinapupu sequence. The three surface adzes are made of exotic material. One adze made of amphibolite must be derived from one of the more geologically complex areas in Melanesia. Kirch and Yen (1982:236) suggest a source in the Central or Western Solomons; however, sources further to the north or to the south in New Caledonia are not precluded. Although this set of adzes are surface finds, their forms are similar to other Lapita-period adzes and quite unlike the assemblage of ethnographic quadrangular adzes which Kirch and Yen relate to Polynesian settlement and to sources in Western Polynesia. The flaked-stone tool assemblage was made up of various siliceous stones that were mainly referred to as cherts and chalcedonies. Sourcing these materials is difficult, but Kirch and Yen (1982:260) following Ward (1976) suggest Ulawa as a possible source for cherts, while the chalcedonies were thought likely to have come from Vanuatu. Sheppard (1996) in his examination of the assemblages was unable to examine any of the cream-coloured cherts that were believed to be from Ulawa; however, he did concur with the general attribution of the chalcedonies to Vanuatu as most probable. In addition, 14 pieces of obsidian were recovered from Kiki Phase layers. Again, these were not sourced using modern methods but were thought, on hand specimen analysis and specific gravity measures, to have originated from western sources (Fergusson Island or New Britain), although a Banks Island origin cannot be ruled out (Kirch & Yen, 1982:260). Recent reanalysis (Spriggs et al., 2010) of 13 of these pieces has shown that 10 are from the Banks Islands and three from sources in the Admiralty Islands. The fishhook assemblage was made up of a range of one-piece shell hooks in both jabbing and rotating forms. The predominant shell used was *Turbo marmoratus*, with at least one specimen of *Turbo petholatus*. Three specimens of a distinctive *Trochus* shell lure were found at TK4. Similar forms had been reported from the early Reef Island sites (Kirch & Yen, 1982:243, fig. 97), and one recovered from Tavatava-period contexts on Taumako (Leach & Davidson, 2008: fig. 4.25-O) is also similar.

The Kiki Phase is interpreted as a period of initial human arrival on a pristine island. The pristine nature of the environment is reflected in the large size of the molluscan fauna in the midden, as well as the high relative abundance of turtle (TK-4, 1349 bones or 50.5% of the assemblage) and various terrestrial avifauna, including megapode. The colonists brought pig, dog, fowl and rat and practised a mixed hunting, fishing and horticultural economy (although the latter is inferred from indirect evidence (Kirch & Yen, 1982:326)). Pig is reported from the earliest deposits, with a small number of bones reported from Layer 2 at Site TK-4 and Zone C2 at Sinapupu; while dog is reported only from Zone C2 at Sinapupu. Chicken was reported from the TK-4 site where 19 of the 29 chicken bones recovered from all Tikopian assemblages were found. TK-4 also contained 13 megapode bones. Megapode bones are absent from later deposits, and Kirch and Yen (1982:282) interpreted this as indicating that extirpation of megapode occurred at the end of the Kiki Phase. The Polynesian rat (*Rattus exulans*) is also very common in the earliest deposits.

The Kiki Phase assemblage can be described as late Lapita: 'Kiki Phase material culture falls within the range described by Green (1979) for the Lapita Cultural Complex,

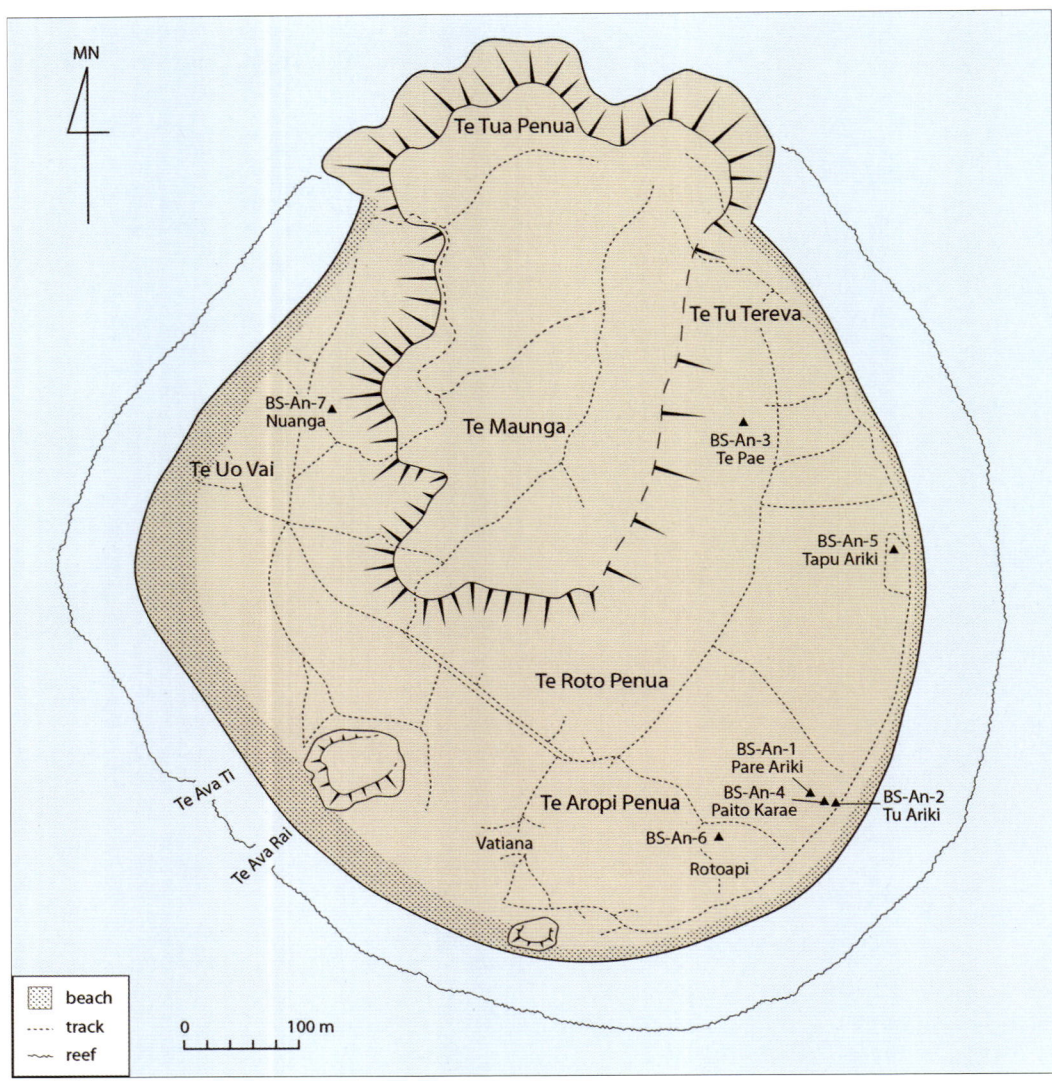

Figure 5.26. The location of archaeological sites on Anuta (after Yen & Gordon, 1973).

and Kiki Ware ceramics in particular represent a late phase of the Lapitoid Series' (Kirch & Yen, 1982:327). Kirch and Yen (1982:327) were unable to decide on the likely origin of the Kiki Phase colonists; they point out that there are some parallels with both western (Reef–Santa Cruz) and eastern (Vanuatu, Fiji) material culture, and that contact with both areas during the Kiki Phase seems likely.

Anuta

Anuta was first visited by Roger Green and Doug Yen during the SESP programme in 1970, and an archaeological team made up of Pat Kirch and Paul Rosendahl joined Yen when he returned to the island in 1971 to study Anutan agricultural systems under the programme (Yen, 1973a). The team carried out a wide-scale survey programme with test excavations in a number of locations (Figure 5.26).

Their aim was to develop a basic cultural sequence for the island to supplement that inferred from the traditional histories and linguistic information (Yen & Gordon, 1973). The site of AN-6, located inland of Rotoapi Village, was the major site for the excavations because it had the deepest, least disturbed stratigraphy, and this spanned a large part, if not all, of the Anutan sequence. The sequence at this site was first reported by Kirch and Rosendahl (1973a, 1973b) and then subsequently revised by Kirch (1982).

AN-6 produced more than 1000 portable artefacts, including 707 pottery sherds and a sizeable assemblage of shell fishhooks from the lowest level, Layer III (Zone E of Kirch, 1982). The sherds were generally small and in fair to poorly preserved condition. The pottery was a slab-constructed ware finished using paddle and anvil methods and was made with both volcanic and calcareous sands, sometimes

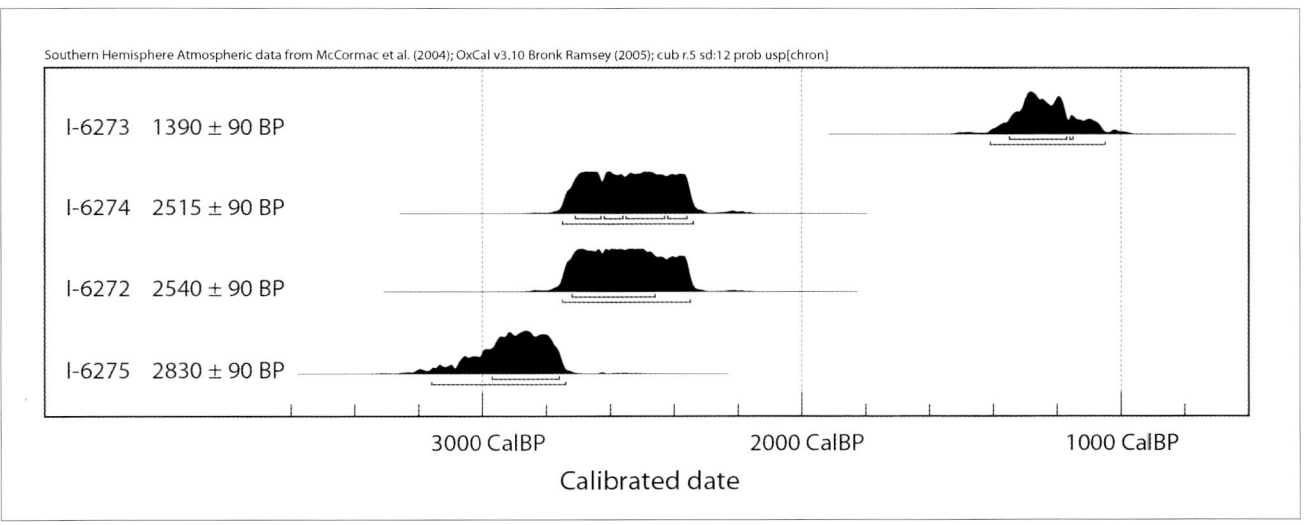

Figure 5.27. Dates from sites on Anuta (Kirch and Rosendahl, 1973a, b) recalibrated by the authors.

mixed. The Anutan ware is essentially a plainware pottery but 13 sherds (five of which are from the same vessels) had linear incisions or grooves. The tempers were described by Dickinson (1973), who attributed all but two sherds to a local origin; the tempers of the remaining two were presumed exotic. The forms were difficult to identify but included a predominance of jars. The AN-6 Layer III assemblage was the first large assemblage of fishhooks ever recovered in association with Lapita-age pottery. The hooks were of one-piece form in both jabbing and rotating varieties. Unlike Tikopia, where *Turbo marmoratus* was the main shell used for hook manufacture, the predominant shell used on Anuta was *Turbo petholatus*. *T. marmoratus* does not occur on the Anutan reefs, but worked fragments of *T. marmoratus* were found in TK-6 and may attest to some contact with Tikopia. The AN-6 assemblage also produced about 20 *Tridacna* and three *Cassis* shell adzes from Layer III.

Subsistence data from AN-6 included a wide variety of reef shellfish and fish. The earliest, Layer III, assemblage included a large amount of turtle, fish and bird. The very similar pattern of early exploitation of turtle mirrors the situation in Tikopia and argues for the importance of this easily captured resource for settler communities. Whether the bird bone from the earliest levels includes chicken has yet to be confirmed.

Layer III at AN-6 was dated by three radiocarbon samples (I-6272, I-6274 and I-6275, reported using a 5568 half-life) which Kirch and Rosendahl (1973b) interpret as indicating first occupation around 2800 cal BP, although they leave open the possibility that the island was settled somewhat earlier than 3000 BP (Figure 5.27). We have recalibrated these dates to 3156–2745 cal BP (1 sigma). All of these samples are reported to be on small carbonised wood specimens (2–6 mm) and coconut (Kirch & Rosendahl, 1973a:96). Given what we now know of Lapita settlement in the Eastern Solomon Islands and Northern Vanuatu and of the ceramic sequences there, the AN-6 wares would appear to date no earlier than 2800 BP and perhaps some centuries later, in agreement with dates for the plainware sequences in the Reef–Santa Cruz Islands, Tikopia and Taumako. The first settlers utilised a plainware pottery, one-piece fishhooks and a variety of shell adzes. Comparing the ceramic assemblages in 1973, Kirch and Rosendahl (1973a:102) pointed to the general similarities with other Solomon Island assemblages (Santa Ana, Bellona) and more generally to the plainware component of Lapita in its fullest distribution (Bismarcks to Samoa). By the time of the Tikopian analysis more was known of Melanesian ceramic traditions and it is probably more useful to identify the Anutan ware as a pottery derived from the Lapita tradition with close parallels to the Tikopian Kiki Phase ware and to the other plainwares of the Eastern Solomons and Vanuatu. In the early phases of settlement on Tikopia and Anuta there are also similarities in the non-ceramic components, notably the shell adzes and one-piece fishhooks, that suggest either that there was contact between the two islands or that they were settled as part of the same general migration episode. Kiki Phase ceramics were replaced on Tikopia by wares that are in general terms like Vanuatu Mangaasi-type wares although, as noted above, Bedford (2006:183) argues that these associations are now much less secure. Since these wares do not appear in the Anutan sequence it seems that contact between the islands was suspended from at least around 2100 cal BP, but probably much earlier.

A model for Lapita settlement of the Solomon Islands

It has generally been assumed that Lapita settlers would have followed an essentially west-to-east route, settling the Northern and Western Solomons before moving through the Central and Eastern Solomons (Green, 1979: fig. 2.12). Following from this, the apparent lack of a dentate stamped Lapita record between Buka and the Reef–Santa Cruz Islands has been assumed to be an artefact of incomplete sampling, or the concealment or destruction of sites as a result of geotectonic processes. Contra to this view, we have argued that the current distribution pattern of Lapita ceramic sites is approximately correct; that there is nothing much missing (Sheppard & Walter, 2009; Walter & Sheppard, 2006). While it is very difficult to argue from negative evidence, it is also difficult to evaluate and compare survey methods and to determine how much more, and of what sort, is required before we can agree that the negative evidence is conclusive. Attempting to address this question, Felgate (2003) compared the extent of archaeological reconnaissance work and concluded that there may not have been, at that date, enough coastal survey in the Western and Central Solomons to find early Lapita sites. He also suggested that geological processes may have buried or destroyed much of the record (Felgate, 2003:503, 2007). At a general level this is reasonable, at least in relation to old ceramic sites. However, in the Western Solomons, intertidal sites with stylistically similar late-Lapita to post-Lapita ceramics have been found in a number of islands with widely varying geologies and histories (e.g. Mann et al., 1998). This indicates that geological processes may not be as much of a problem as earlier feared. In fact, the arguments about geological processes and site taphonomy that some archaeologists raise to explain divergences from expected site distributions in the Solomon Islands (e.g. Felgate, 2003, 2007) are based on quite simple models of geotectonics. A recent review of tectonic history in the Western Solomon Islands, designed to evaluate claims for missing sites, shows that there has been a considerable variety of coastline types, from steep, exposed coasts with villages often perched up on coastal cliffs, to lagoons fringed by mangroves, coastal swamps and raised-reef barrier islands (Sheppard & Walter, 2009). This diversity reflects considerable variation in geotectonic processes and rates throughout the region. A schematic representation of rates of Holocene uplift in the Western Solomons, based on Mann et al. (1998: fig. 8B), is shown in Figure 5.28. This shows that rates of uplift are greatest around Tetepare and Ranongga. Uplift is effectively zero in northern Vella Lavella and across Kolombangara. Further north and across the New Georgia Sound, the drowned coastline and mangrove swamps of northwestern Santa Isabel and eastern Choiseul indicate substantial subsidence (Mann et al., 1998:264). At a smaller scale the pattern can be even more variable: the earthquake of Easter 2007 demonstrated that both sudden and significant uplift and subsidence could occur within the region over comparatively short distances, such as along the length of Roviana Lagoon (Sheppard & Walter, 2009). All this shows that models based on gradual geotectonic movement may be too simplistic – and confirms our view that the current distribution of ceramic sites in the Solomon Islands is approximately representative and is certainly adequate for the construction of a model for Lapita settlement. Before we discuss such a model it is worth briefly reviewing the current distribution patterns of dentate stamped or other ceramic assemblages that could be assigned to the early Lapita period commencing around 3000 cal BP or slightly later.

A leapfrog model

Taking as the starting point the argument that the Solomon Islands archaeological record is substantially representative, we have proposed a four-stage model for Lapita colonisation which we have referred to as a 'leapfrog' model (Sheppard, 2011; Sheppard & Walter, 2006; see also Figure 2.2).

1. The first Lapita colonisation of the Solomon Islands occurred via direct migration of Lapita peoples into the Reef–Santa Cruz Islands from the Bismarck Archipelago, leapfrogging the main islands of the Solomon group.

According to this scenario the Reef–Santa Cruz Islands represent the zone of first settlement of Remote Oceania, although this may have to be extended into Vanuatu in light of the rich sites being uncovered there (Bedford, 2003). In support of the leapfrog (or direct colonisation) model we have already shown that there are no early Lapita-age (3300–3000 cal BP) sites anywhere in the Solomon Islands east of the Reef–Santa Cruz Islands that could be part of a wave of advance. In addition, there is some direct support for this elsewhere in the archaeological, linguistic and biological record.

Lapita people are often characterised as being long-distance traders but this is not generally true, and the Reef–Santa Cruz Lapita evidence for the long-distance movement of substantial amounts of obsidian from the Bismarck Archipelago, more than 2000 km distant, is a unique case. While Bismarcks obsidian is found in sites as far away as Fiji and New Caledonia, the total amount recovered in sites beyond the Reef–Santa Cruz group is very small and could be explained as heirloom material. Based on the excavated sample, a total of 275 kg of Bismarck Archipelago obsidian

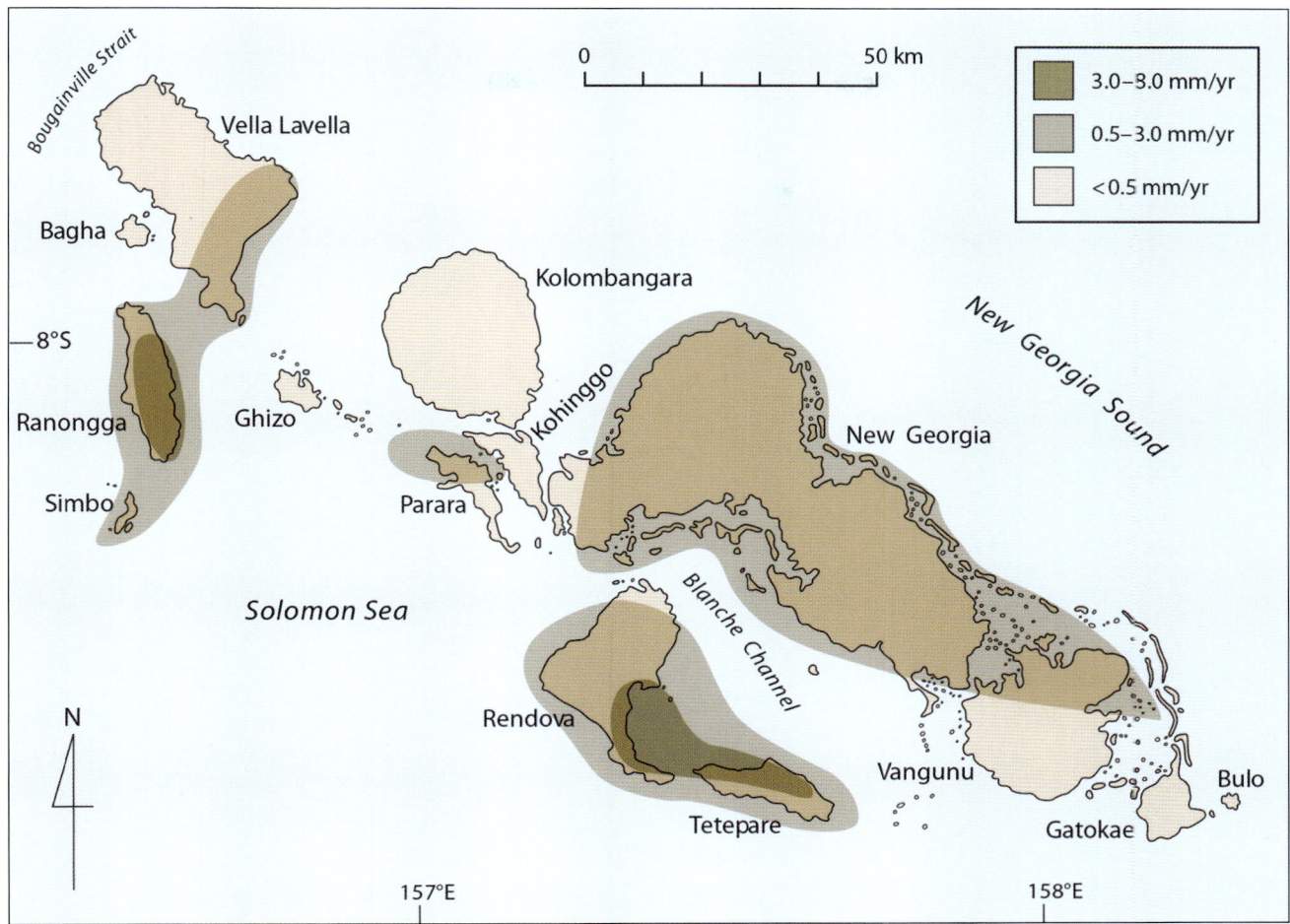

Figure 5.28. A schematic representation of rates of Holocene uplift in the Western Solomons (after Mann et al., 1998, fig. 8B).

is estimated to be present in the three Reef–Santa Cruz sites excavated by Green, and the actual amount transported to all Lapita sites in the region is likely to have been many canoe-loads (Sheppard, 1993:129). Specht (2002:45) has more recently estimated a total amount of obsidian transported to all the Reef–Santa Cruz sites as ranging between 845 and 1125 kg. The dating models suggest this importation involved repeat voyages and ongoing interaction between the Reef–Santa Cruz Islands and the Bismarck Archipelago over some hundreds of years. The nature of this unique long-distance relationship cannot have been based on the technological necessity of procuring flakable stone, since plenty of alternative solutions were available. The obsidian was more likely an incidental byproduct of important social relationships that were maintained between the homeland and colonies (Sheppard, 1993). A number of possible explanations have been canvassed as to what these relationships might have been. Kirch (1988a), for example, raises the idea of long-distance exchange as providing a 'lifeline' to vulnerable colonies, and Green (1996) has talked of the drive by colonial groups to 'reproduce' homeland environments, including technological resources. Perhaps, as Specht (2002:44) suggests, long-distance exchange between colony and homelands in the early colonisation phase may have been a conscious attempt to replicate the homelands, including 'the social and ideological contexts within which obsidian and other goods were essential and valuable components'. Developing the theme of homeland connections, Sheppard (1993) has suggested that Talasea obsidian may have had a symbolic association such that, over the course of a complex commodity value history, the process of acquisition from the homelands, rather than its actual use, imbued the material with its highest value. Or obsidian may have been a prestige good, perhaps because of its homeland associations, where conspicuous consumption overrode economical use (Specht, 2002:44).

Whatever the social, cultural or technological imperative, there is now a very good record in Oceania of colonising groups engaging in long-distance exchange relationships between homeland and colony for several generations following first settlement. Building first on work in the Mailu region of coastal Papua New Guinea, Irwin and Holdaway (Irwin, 1987; Irwin & Holdaway, 1996) have described this behaviour as 'coloniser mode exchange' where 'the importing of raw materials appears to be integral with colonisation and changes subsequently in a generally similar way' (Irwin & Holdaway, 1996:228). Specht (2002) reviewed the evidence for coloniser-mode exchange in Lapita and found, despite the often poor quality of available data, some support for the concept; he noted that 'a distinction between sites with large or small pieces of obsidian might then allow recognition of some sites as part of a colonisation front' (Specht, 2002:39). Most recently, Walter et al. (2010) have argued that the Austronesian colonisation of New Zealand involved the implementation of similar coloniser-mode exchange practices, again involving the distribution of high-quality obsidians. The essential elements of colonisation-mode exchange as described by these authors are well represented in the Reef–Santa Cruz case and strongly support the conclusion that this region was colonised directly from the Bismarck Archipelago. They can be summarised as follows:

a   An early pulse in initial high-volume and long-distance movement of raw material, usually obsidian, that is procured directly from a source in the 'homeland' zone.
b   A lack of economising behaviour in the use of obsidian, suggesting that its value 'was not that of a scarce utilitarian commodity' (Sheppard, 1993:135).
c   A fall-off through time in the use of material from distant sources relative to local stone supplies, accompanied by an increasing efficiency in the use of the distant source material.

There is additional genetic and linguistic support for a model of direct settlement of the Reef–Santa Cruz Islands from the Bismarck Archipelago. Mitochondrial DNA evidence summarised in Sheppard and Walter (2006:61–62) and in detail in Sheppard (2011) shows that the modern genetic make-up of populations in the Reef and Santa Cruz region is more similar to those of New Britain and Vanuatu and New Caledonia to the south than to Solomon Islands populations directly to the west. This has been confirmed most recently by the first detailed genetic study of modern Solomon Island populations by Delfin et al. (2012:554), which shows the genetic make-up of Santa Cruz to be unlike any populations in the Main Solomon Islands and closest (2012: fig. 7a) to the sample from Mussau in the St Matthias group north of New Ireland.

This is in full agreement with the linguistic research of Ross and Næss (2007), who have recently re-evaluated the Reef–Santa Cruz Austronesian languages: they suggest that these languages form a first-order subdivision of Oceanic and that their closest relationships are also to be found in the St Matthias group, not with the languages of the Eastern Solomons. Phylogenetic analysis of Austronesian languages also supports this argument (Gray et al., 2009). We would note that Delfin et al. (2012:561) see their results for Santa Cruz as posing something of a 'conundrum'; however, this is simply because they make the common assumption that Lapita DNA should look like that of East Polynesia or have a high 'Asian' component. This is clearly not necessarily a safe assumption, and we look forward to more detailed genetic study of the Lapita-descendent populations of Vanuatu and New Caledonia and of Lapita human remains.

2. The Northern and Western Solomon Islands were settled shortly after 2700 cal BP by an Austronesian expansion from the west during the late Lapita period. This established an intertidal settlement pattern – based on stilt houses plus the use of a ceramic suite including incised and appliqué ceramics – that spanned Near Oceania from New Ireland to New Georgia.

The archaeological evidence for this movement has been summarised above and is well supported by the palaeoenvironmental data, which shows increased forest clearance in the Western and Central Solomons around 2600 cal BP – indicating the arrival in the region of new technologies and economic practices (Grimes, 2003; Haberle, 1996).

3. The eastern outliers of Tikopia, Anuta and Taumako were settled after 2800 cal BP from within a sphere of interaction that included the Reef–Santa Cruz Islands and Northern Vanuatu.

It is unclear where exactly the outliers were settled from, but the archaeological record shows that there was interaction within this zone, and this is reflected in the movements of materials from Banks Island, Taumako and Eastern Solomons. If the outliers were settled from the Reef–Santa Cruz Islands, this likely occurred just before, or at the time of, the transition to plainwares – although the modern genetic data does not support settlement from Santa Cruz. There has been only very limited archaeological reconnaissance on the other Solomons Polynesian Outliers of Rennell and Bellona to the south of Guadalcanal, or Sikaiana and Ontong Java to the north of Malaita and Santa Isabel, and it is yet unclear when they were first settled (Chikamori, 1975; Miller, 1979). The genetic research of Delfin et al. (2012:556) has looked at modern populations from Rennell, Bellona, Tikopia and Ontong Java and concluded that they were settled by small populations from Remote Oceania in separate founder events, although the neighbouring islands of Rennell and Bellona share a genetic history.

4. The Central Solomons were colonised by Austronesian-speaking populations independently of the late Lapita movement into the Western Solomons.

Sheppard and Walter (2006) tentatively suggested a settlement based on a back movement from the region of the Reef–Santa Cruz Islands after the loss of ceramics in that region; however that is not well supported on linguistic (Pawley, 2009) or genetic grounds. An alternative scenario would, following Ross (1988), have a movement of Austronesian speakers out of the Bismarck Archipelago, but before the development of the Lapita cultural complex.

6

The last 2000 years

Late period transitions

The period following the loss of Lapita ceramics from the archaeological record is something of a dark age in many parts of Oceania, and nowhere more so than in the Solomon Islands. In those areas where ceramics continued to be made, sequences are generally poorly defined and poorly dated, and serve as little more than a marker of human presence. In areas where ceramics stopped or were never produced there is only an ephemeral record at best for the first millennium AD, followed by a gradually increasing density of remains until the historic period. For at least the last 500 years a surface record is to be found everywhere in the Solomons in the form of stone platforms, shrines, wharves, old villages, artificial islands, terracing, irrigation works and fortifications. The religious shrines, often with deposits of human remains and votive offerings, form one of the most visible and enduring components of the cultural landscape of the Solomon Islands. Their nineteenth- and early twentieth-century forms are preserved for us as one of the most common subjects in the photographic record of early missionaries and administrators (e.g. Brown, 1909), and their continuing importance as respected markers of ancestral history means they are preferentially preserved and brought to the attention of archaeologists (Figures 6.1 and 6.2).

Although anthropologists and linguists are struck by the cultural and linguistic diversity of the Solomon Islands, for archaeologists the study of the development and maintenance of such diversity represents a major challenge. Archaeology is hindered by the difficulties of resolving the sort of variability marked by language and ethnicity, although it can resolve some of the temporal and spatial patterns of regional variation in the archaeological record that may underlie the development of that diversity. In the following sections we review the archaeological record of the last two millennia and look at some of the key data types that are both archaeologically accessible and relevant to a study of the development of cultural diversity. We also review the historical and ethnographic data and, where possible, use it to supplement the archaeological record. The sections below deal with the Northern, Central and Eastern Solomon Islands, and the following chapter looks in more detail at the Western Solomon Islands, for which there is a greater body of archaeological data relating to the late prehistoric and early historic sequence.

The Northern Solomon Islands

The island of Bougainville and its small neighbour to the north, Buka, together form the largest landmass in the geographical Solomon Islands at approximately 9300 square kilometres (Figure 6.3). Together with the Shortland Islands this makes up the Northern Solomons region. This is considerably larger and wider than the second largest island of Guadalcanal at 5320 square kilometres. Although Bougainville is more mountainous than Guadalcanal or any of the other Solomon Islands – a considerable portion of the island is over 1600 m in height – what sets it apart is the south Bougainville plain, Buin, which forms a large part of the southern half of the island. This area today supports a very large number of people with a population density among the highest in the Solomon Islands. As Terrell

THE LAST 2000 YEARS

Figure 6.1. Historic photo of a Western Solomon Islands shrine, Simbo Island (from Hocart, 1922: fig. 1, 'Skull houses at Pa Na Gunda').

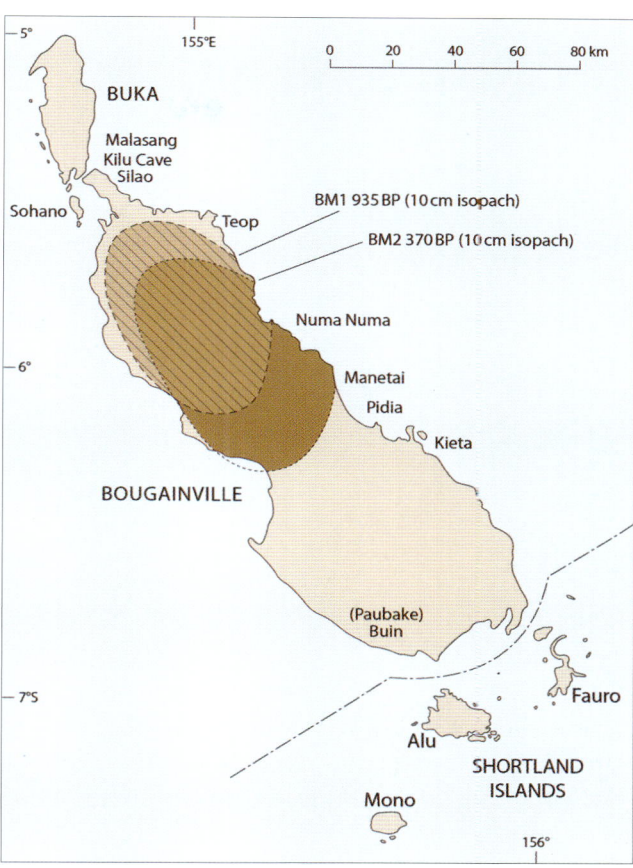

Figure 6.3. Northern Solomons, showing the distribution of volcanic ash deposits.

Figure 6.2. Historic photo of a Western Solomon Islands shrine, Simbo Island (from Hocart, 1922).

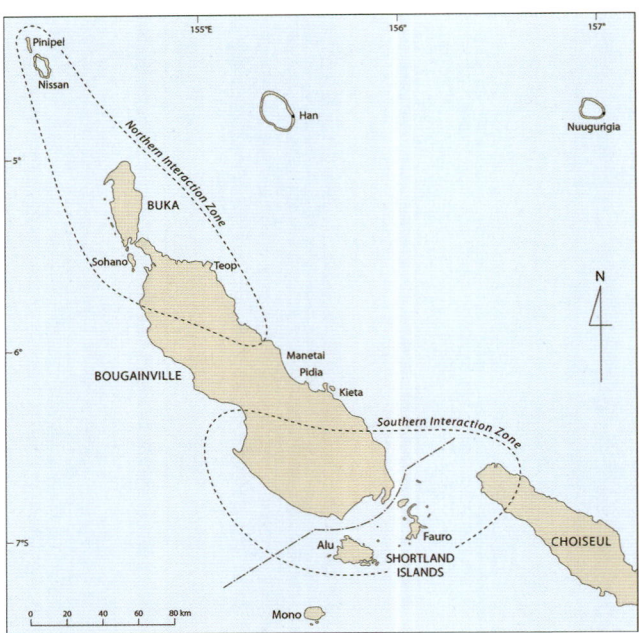

Figure 6.4. The Northern Solomons showing interaction spheres and production zones (after Blackwood, 1935; Guppy, 1887; Oliver, 1955).

volcano has generated considerable pyroclastic deposits throughout southernmost Bougainville during numerous eruptions from 31,000 BP to 3000 cal BP. At least five events occurred in the Holocene. As Spriggs has noted (1992, 1997) it seems probable that these eruptions have strongly shaped the cultural history of the island, creating at times large, uninhabitable zones that would have repeatedly isolated the northern and southern regions. For much of the Holocene, Bougainville would have provided pyrotechnic effects visible throughout the Northern Solomons. Such explosive forms of volcanism are not found south of Bougainville until you reach Tinakula in the Reef Islands.

A complicated linguistic picture matches the geographical distinctiveness of Bougainville. Today there are 11 Austronesian and eight non-Austronesian (NAN) languages spoken on Bougainville and Buka, while the languages of the Shortlands and Choiseul are Austronesian. This concentration of NAN languages is not found elsewhere in the Solomons (Dunn et al., 2005). This linguistic diversity and the implied complicated history makes Bougainville a seemingly ideal location for investigating the relationships between language, culture and biology (Friedlaender, 1987; Spriggs, 1992; Terrell, 1976). Most Austronesian language speakers are found on the coast and most NAN speakers live in the generally mountainous interior: this suggests Austronesian speakers have intruded into a previously NAN area. The movement of Austronesian speakers most probably occurred as a wave of advance from the Bismarck Archipelago to Buka and north Bougainville and then in a series of short hops over existing NAN communities south to Choiseul, with subsequent movement to the Shortlands and the west coast of Bougainville.

(1976) has noted, the geography of land systems correlates closely with population distribution; and the fertile soils of the Buin Plain region, showered with ash from Holocene volcanic eruptions in Central Bougainville (Rogerson et al., 1989, fig. 6.3), support intensive traditional agriculture (Oliver, 1991). The large island of Choiseul and the smaller islands of the Shortland group are only a short distance south of Buin (Alu 5 km, Choiseul 48 km) and the people were and are closely related. Canoe travel over these distances was routine, and interisland interaction within the region is geographically easier than movement either to the north or south.

Bougainville is unique within the Solomons, too, for the considerable number of large volcanoes along the central spine of the island: seven volcanoes are recorded as having been active in the last 10,000 years. Bagana, located in the central region, is currently active, with recorded eruptions since 1842, and Billy Mitchell, its neighbour to the northeast, has been repeatedly active since the late Pleistocene (17,000, 13,800 cal BP). In the last 2000 years there have been two major eruptions, at about 900 years ago and 350 years ago, which produced pyroclastic flows that covered much of the northern half of the island to a depth of more than 40 cm and extended 25 km to the east coast. The 900 cal BP Billy Mitchell eruption appears to have blanketed virtually the entire northern half of the island with ash that is still 10 cm thick some 75 km north of the crater (Rogerson et al., 1989:69, fig. 2.27). At the south end of the island the Loloru

The archaeology and ethnography of the Northern Solomons demonstrate the presence of a number of interaction spheres within which there is considerable cultural similarity; this indicates a lengthy period of shared history (Figure 6.4). At the northern end is the Nissan–Buka–northern Bougainville interaction sphere centred on the Buka Passage region (Blackwood, 1935:439–57), and to the south is the Bougainville Straits interaction sphere, which extends from southern Bougainville across to the Shortland Group (Alu, Mono, Fauro) and south to northern Choiseul (Guppy, 1887; Oliver, 1955). These zones of interaction are documented historically and through oral tradition (e.g. Terrell & Irwin, 1972). But one of the features of the Northern Solomon Islands is that there is a continuous ceramic record which extends from the Lapita period up to, in places, the present day, and this allows this interaction to be tracked into prehistory in a manner not possible elsewhere in the Solomons.

The ceramic record

Pottery production in the Northern Solomons appears to have been focused on a series of production centres scattered from Buka down through Bougainville and across to the Shortlands and northern Choiseul (Blackwood, 1935; Guppy, 1887:202; Irwin, 1972; Ogan, 1970; Specht, 1969, 1972; Terrell, 1976). Pottery was not made in the historic period outside of the Northern Solomons, but within this region the rich ceramic record allows us to look closely at stylistic variation and regional interaction on a much finer scale than is currently possible outside this area – either to the north or south. Although in recent years research has been limited on Bougainville, the broad picture can be seen in the work of Specht, Terrell, Irwin, Spriggs and Wickler. What it shows is a pattern of increasing regionalisation; for although ceramic production is important throughout the Northern Solomons, over time, local interaction spheres or traditions of ceramic manufacture and exchange developed. It currently seems probable that at least three regions or overlapping ceramic production zones can be distinguished: the Buka Passage region, central Bougainville and the Bougainville Straits region.

Jim Specht pioneered much of the archaeology work in the Northern Solomons and the Bismarck Archipelago, and he established the Buka pottery sequence in his 1969 PhD dissertation. Specht's sequence has since been slightly revised by Wickler (2001) (see Chapter 5). On Buka, Specht found 46 sites in a 22-kilometre stretch of coast, with survey concentrated around modern towns (Figure 6.5). He visited another 27 other locations on Buka and surveyed on Bougainville on the south side of Buka Passage. At Hangan, one of three traditional pottery manufacturing sites on the east coast of Buka, Specht excavated two large test trenches which provided material that formed the basis for his sequence.

Specht (1969) identified six ceramic styles which formed a chronological series. He argued that this series could be split into two ceramic traditions, with the early Buka style seemingly unrelated to the apparently later Sohano style. The Buka style was characterised by open bowls with shell and calcareous temper and a decorative component that included dentate stamping, linear incision and appliqué. Specht (1969; see also Chapter 5) described this late Lapita ware as differing from subsequent styles in a number of ways (Specht, 1969:193, 218).

1. It was often heavily tempered with finely ground shell.
2. It included slab building for thick sherds.
3. There was a dominance of Specht's (1969) Type 5 lip modification (crenulated lip).
4. There was a small amount of dentate stamping.

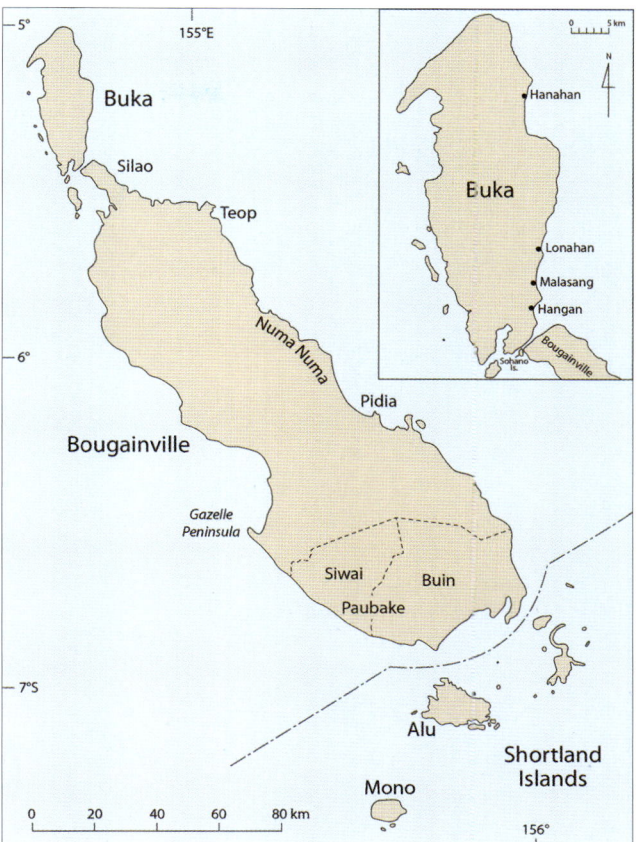

Figure 6.5. The location of archaeological sites and other places on Bougainville referenced in text.

5. Angular contoured (carinated) pot forms were present and possibly also flat-bottomed bowls.

Specht (1969: 218) argued that these features disappeared abruptly in the Sohano and subsequent styles.

Terrell, in his review of the Buka sequence, suggests continuity between the Buka and Sohano styles; he notes that Specht's data reported some shell temper in ceramics of Sohano style (Terrell, 1976:230). Wickler (2001) has also argued for continuity; he points out that Sohano pottery styles were mixed, with Buka styles in at least three (DBE, DKC, DAF) of the four sites containing Buka-style pottery that he investigated. Unfortunately, poor sample sizes and disturbed deposits make it very difficult to resolve the temporal relationship between the two styles (Wickler, 2001:144). It would also seem to be methodologically problematic to assign small, plain sherds to either style without using the circular argument that defines Buka style as shell-tempered. Indeed, Wickler reports some Sohano-style sherds with calcareous temper, and work by Summerhayes (1987) suggests that similar clay fabrics (clay and temper inclusions) were used in the production of both

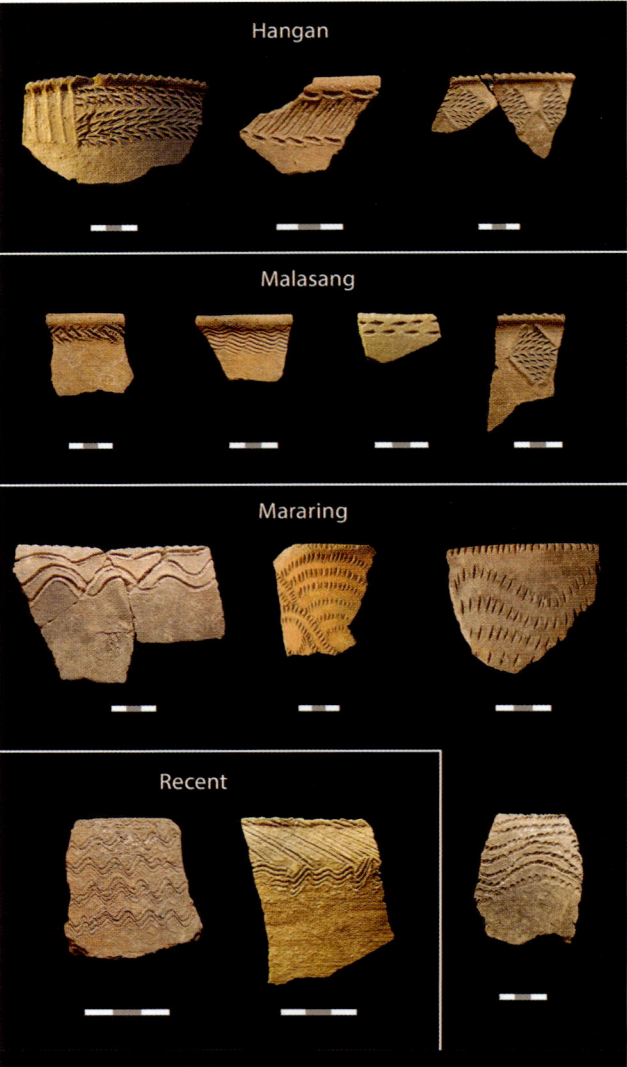

Figures 6.6 (above) and 6.7 (right). Examples of pottery showing changes through the Buka sequence (with permission of Jim Specht).

styles. Wickler concludes by suggesting that Sohano is simply 'a continuation of the process of simplification seen in Buka Style pottery' (Wickler, 2001:243). This sequence of change proposed by Wickler on Buka is also found in the Western Solomons (Felgate, 2003). In both areas, late Lapita ceramics are found in intertidal sites, followed by assemblages where both dentate stamping and complex angular pot forms disappear. In Roviana the most striking change is the loss of shouldered pots, although both Terrell and Wickler limit the importance of this feature in their discussions.

This argument about the relationship between the Buka and Sohano ware has been framed in the cultural continuity versus cultural replacement dichotomy. We favour a general argument for continuity in the ceramic tradition, and see the differences between Buka and Sohano wares as a manifestation of a process that is congruent with the distribution of Lapita ceramics. It is a reflection of a fundamental, pan-Lapita loosening of the design strictures placed on the pottery, wherein the pottery tradition carries the code for its own systematic simplification. This loosening of Lapita strictures may also be seen in the sudden demise in obsidian exchange; obsidian is represented by about six flakes in Sohano deposits (Wickler, 2001:243) and a few in Western Solomon Islands sites. Wickler and Terrell are undoubtedly correct in arguing for cultural continuity, but the Buka to Sohano change reflects a transformation that would appear to be more profound than those that follow.

Whichever way the change from the Buka style is interpreted, there seems to be little debate over proposed regional continuity in the following style series which, Wickler argues, provides no evidence for 'non-local introductions or replacement in the form of pots, or by extension, populations' (2001:168). Wickler describes the Sohano style as having fewer vessel forms than the Buka style, with less decoration, fewer motifs and simpler designs. Punctation becomes the principal form of decoration in early Sohano, although rectilinear incision and appliqué strips are also common. Vessel forms change only gradually and are limited to large bowls with constricted mouths and direct or incurving rim courses. Figures 6.6 and 6.7 illustrate the basic changes in vessel decoration throughout the Buka sequence.

The following Hangan style, which lasted from 1400 to 800 cal BP, represents a gradual development out of Sohano: sherds at the DJQ site show attributes common to both styles. Manufacturing techniques are still based on the coil and strip method but wall thickness is reduced. Vessel forms are vertical-sided to slightly restricted, with rounded bases. Applied relief becomes a more important decorative technique, and decoration of interior lips and rims appears for the first time.

The Malasang style appears, again, as a gradual transition from the Hangan style; Specht (1969) identified three sub-styles that reflect that gradual change. Malasang pottery is technologically similar to that from the preceding Hangan style, although surfaces are increasingly smoothed. Pot forms are predominantly globular with restricted mouths and thicker walls. A key change in decoration is the appearance of comb incising on transitional pottery of Hangan-style vessel forms, perhaps using a shell, which comes to dominate Malasang assemblages over time. This decorative technique is also applied to rim interiors.

Specht (1969:211–13) made 59 surface collections and amassed around 12,000 sherds during his survey of Buka, Sohano and neighbouring islands. In 38 collections both Mararing and Recent styles were present; only the Mararing style was present at eight sites; and only the Recent style at 13 sites. On the basis of this separation Specht argued for a temporal distinction between styles. Wickler describes Specht's Mararing and Recent styles within one phase because the chronological relationship between the styles is, he argued, poorly resolved in the surface collections. Mararing ceramics appear to date after 1500 AD, based on a date associated with Malasang-phase ceramics at the DJO-D site (Wickler, 2001:245). Pottery of Mararing and Recent styles is made from the same smoothed paste as the Malasang style. A majority of the vessels are globular with slightly restricted orifices and rounded to pointed bases. A series of new introductions appear at this time: these include pointed-base vessels, loop handles, and the spouted kepa bowls that were used historically to cook coconut oil in a ceremonial context (Specht, 1969:207). Modern Buka pottery manufacture, use and distribution are well described by Blackwood (1935) and Specht (1972).

The Buka ceramic series is distributed throughout Buka and across Buka Passage to the Silao Peninsula, where the ceramics recorded by Terrell fall within those styles, although he did not record any of the early Buka style (Terrell, 1976:238). To the north, Sohano-style pottery is reported from Nissan, and the abundance of Malasang to Recent Buka pottery on the island indicates extensive interaction after 800 AD. Over time, Buka ceramics appear further south on Bougainville. Terrell (1976) reports Sohano pottery at Teop Island and increasing amounts of Buka ceramics along the north coast after the Hangan period. By the Mararing period Buka ceramics are found as far as Numa Numa, 90 km south of Buka. By the historic period, pottery manufacture on Buka was restricted to three neighbouring villages – Lonahan, Malasang and Hangan – on the southeast coast of the island (Specht, 1972).

In the historic period the next pottery manufacturing centre south of Buka was at Kieta (Ogan, 1970) on the east coast of Bougainville, 160 km south of Buka. As recently as the 1980s pottery was being made at Pidia on the Kieta Peninsula. Archaeological research indicates that this separate pottery tradition has some antiquity: Kieta pottery was distributed north as far as Teop (Black, 1977) over the last 700 years (Spriggs, 1992). At the Sivu rockshelter site near Pidia, Spriggs (1992) has defined three ceramic styles that cover the last 1500 years. The modern ware (Pidia style) dating to the last 300 years is generally plain untempered thick ware with plain or notched lips. Earlier pottery (the Asio style), which overlaps chronologically with the recent style and extends back to 1000 cal BP, is a thin ware (2.5–5 mm) with notched lips and straight-line incised designs. The oldest style, which is dated back to 1500 cal BP, is a calcareous-tempered, thin plain pottery with a plain lip (Sivu style) (Spriggs, 1992:419, 1997:171). At the site of Teobebe on Teop Island, Black recovered 6129 sherds of which 1.7% were identified as coming from the Kieta region, over 100 km to the south. This attribution was based on the presence of a distinctive temper (Dickinson, 1975) and pottery with strongly everted collar rims and sherds bearing geometric incised fine-line decoration. The everted rims appear to have belonged to pots called nanava (Teop language), which were likely equivalent to the Buka kepa forms and were used in a similar ceremonial manner. Terrell describes them as a 'heavy, round-bottomed vessel with a strongly everted collar-rim, that may have been notched' (Terrell, 1976:242). These pots were made historically in the Kieta area, where they were known as otao in the Nasioi language.

Although pottery manufacture in Kieta seems to share little relationship with that on Buka – perhaps partly due to the volcanic impacts on North Bougainville that must have repeatedly severed regular interaction – links into the Buin region, located less than 70 km south, are well attested. In addition, Spriggs states that the modern pottery technique is identical to that found on northern Choiseul, and that surface pottery found there is similar to Asio-style ceramics (Spriggs, 1992:420).

Figures 6.8–6.11. Examples of pottery manufacture in the Paubake of Bougainville in the 1960s. Figure 6.8 (left top). Koriniai processing clay beneath her house (Terrell, 1976: Plate 6.2a) (Anthropology Photo Archive Auckland PID602892). Figure 6.9 (right top). Koriniai building up the walls of a pot (Terrell, 1976: Plate 6.3a) (Anthropology Photo Archive Auckland PID602082). Figure 6.10 (right middle). Firing the pots at Moru (Terrell, 1976: Plate 6.5b) (Anthropology Photo Archive Auckland PID602220). Figure 6.11 (right). Removing fired pots (Anthropology Photo Archive Auckland PID602176).

Historically, pottery was manufactured in various centres in Siwai and Buin. It seems probable that, like the other modern centres to the north, the manufacturing tradition there has deep roots, although the chronology is poorly resolved. Oliver describes the nature of pot use and manufacture in Siwai as follows.

> Every Siuai household uses clay pots for cooking but pot-making is centred in northeast Siuai, partly because the best clay is to be found there and partly because it is customary for men of that region to specialize in pot-making. There are, to be sure, a few potters scattered through the other regions of Siuai but even they purchase clay from the north-east. Not all men even in the north-east can make pots, however; I estimated that only about half of them can turn out a usable product and only about one in eight produce pots for sale. (Oliver, 1955: 297)

Pottery manufacture is notable in Siwai for the fact that it was carried out by men; among their Buin neighbours women make pottery, as is the case in all other manufacturing centres in the Solomons. The historic pottery of both Buin and Siwai is very similar in appearance. Pots are all thick-walled, collared with notched lips and made from untempered clay. There are differences in the bases, which are rounded in Siwai but conical or sub-rounded in Buin. Larger pots were used to cook pigs in the ritual context of 'men's houses' (Terrell, 1976:353).

Archaeological data on the ceramic sequences of the south Bougainville Plain is based primarily on the work of Terrell in the Paubake region. Observation in 1970 of pot manufacture by a woman who had last made pots immediately after WWII provided a modern baseline for study of the ceramics of the region. Gorbey's description of pot manufacture by Koriniai of Morou village is reported in detail by Terrell (1976:365) (Figures 6.8–6.11). These pots were manufactured by coiling and thinning using the paddle and anvil technique. Of particular note is the absence of deliberate tempering of the clay: this historically is recorded only on Buka where, Blackwood reports, a reddish sand from a nearby mountain is added (Blackwood, 1935:396) – although Specht, who has visited the source, notes it is more yellowish than reddish (Specht 1972:127–28) – and on Choiseul, where added temper appears to be a black placer sand (alluvial sand deposit) from a local riverbed (Terrell, 1976:460). Pottery decoration in south Bougainville is distinctive in its historic use of painting with red-orange clay. This clay 'paint', applied in crude bands and dots, turns reddish-brown when fired. Thin painting is characteristic of historic pottery, while 'thick' painting with an appliqué of clay would appear to be an older trait. Unfortunately, well-stratified sites with good ceramic collections were not discovered in the Paubake survey; therefore, the chronology of ceramic change is elusive. Terrell (1976:460) suggests that ceramic manufacture started in the Paubake area sometime in the interval from 900 to 1300 AD, possibly as the result of immigration or of intermarriage with people from the Shortland Islands. Early tempered thin pottery was decorated with band appliqué, punctate appliqué and incising – all techniques that Terrell sees paralleled in the Shortland sequence described by Irwin (1974). Following this, Terrell postulates devolution of the appliqué bands, first to 'thick' painting and finally to 'thin' painting on thick ware, as was made historically.

The postulated links from south Bougainville to the Shortlands are most clearly demonstrated in the Lanlapana site where, although the surface collections had clear relationships to Paubake pottery, the assemblage excavated by Irwin (1972) looked to Terrell to be foreign. Well-made, thin untempered ware decorated with incising, band appliqué, punctate appliqué or plain styles dominated the assemblage. A date on a large fireplace that contained most of these 'Shortland' sherds falls within the late sixteenth to early seventeenth centuries AD (Terrell, 1976:283, 257) which is in the middle of the Shortlands Middle ceramic period.

The Shortland ceramic sequence is based on the study of 30 assemblages from Alu and two from Mono by Irwin (1972). These have been seriated to provide a relative chronology of three periods, supported by limited radiocarbon dating. The Early Period is represented by thin plainware sherds from one site (Purupuru). A date on charcoal from the bottom (Layer C, assemblage Z-5) of a small two-metre-square excavation gives a calibrated age range (95.4% HPD) of 1156–690 cal BP (ANU-796 1040 ± 95) (Irwin 1972:103). The Middle Period, which includes the majority of the assemblages, and comprises sherds decorated by incising and brushing plus small amounts of appliqué and carved-paddle impression, is estimated to date from 1000 to 200 cal BP. In the Late Period, which essentially grades into the historic, appliqué and especially paddle-impressed ware becomes more important (see Guppy (1887) for a description of historic pottery production in the region). Among Solomon ceramics the use of a carved paddle as a decorative technique is unique to the Shortland Islands (Irwin, 1974).

In summary there looks to be a broad similarity in early ceramics, stretching from Kieta in the north, through Buin to the Shortlands. The early sequence at Kieta, with thin, plain, tempered (Sivu-style) pottery changing to thin, tempered, incised (Asio-style) pottery is paralleled in the Early to Middle Period transition in the Shortlands at about 1000 cal BP (Spriggs, 1992). In Buin, Terrell's sequence from Paubake again starts with thin, tempered pottery decorated by incising and appliqué (Terrell, 1976:460). It seems however, based on the Buka and the Western Solomons situation, that although the earliest deposits in this region at present only date back to 1600 cal BP, earlier material may well be found in intertidal sites in lagoon and sheltered bay settings, especially in the Bougainville Strait region. It is probable that throughout this region the sequence of ceramic change starts from a common late Lapita base and that the plain calcareous-tempered ceramics from Kieta, although they are later in time, are linked in a general sense to the plain calcareous-tempered Buka ware and the Early Period thin plainware of the Shortlands. Alternatively, the thin ceramics of the earliest Kieta and Shortland sites may relate more directly to the thin ceramics that appear at the same time in the Hangan style of Buka (see Wickler, 2001:158), despite the lack of decoration in the former. It is possible that the Buka and Sohano periods are represented, south of Buka, in as yet undiscovered intertidal sites like those from the Western Solomons, where terrestrial plainware sites date to c. 1400 AD and probably earlier. At present, our understanding of all these sequences is limited by very small sample sizes of badly preserved ceramics and poorly resolved chronology (see Wickler, 2001:144 for Buka). Although distinctive ceramics and tempers clearly demonstrate interaction throughout the area in later periods, it seems unnecessary at this point to link ceramic production to introductions from Austronesians later than at the time of late Lapita. The oral history of the Torau migration (Terrell & Irwin, 1972), for example, does record historic interaction and movement between the Shortlands and the east coast of Bougainville, possibly into an area previously vacated after volcanic eruptions (Spriggs, 1997:200); however, it is not necessary to call on similar earlier movements of Austronesian speakers, who were subsequently assimilated, to explain ceramic production among non-Austronesian speakers in Bougainville.

Settlement patterns and subsistence systems

Although the archaeological interpretation of prehistoric settlement patterns must rely heavily on site distribution data, which is itself skewed towards ceramic sites, the historic record is rich and provides a good model for late prehistoric land use. Historically, the settlement pattern of Bougainville is characterised by almost continuous coastal settlements in the north, scattered hamlets in the mountainous interior and dispersed interior hamlets on the Buin Plain (Terrell, 1976:95–120). Blackwood reports a string of coastal villages around Buka and the northern coast of Bougainville, each containing around 120 to 150 inhabitants (1931:201, 1935:17). The explorer Louis Antoine de Bougainville commented on the very dense settlement on the eastern and northern coasts of Buka, and in recent times the population has exceeded 240 per km^2 (Terrell, 1976:102). Specht's surveys on Buka reported 46 archaeological sites in a 22-kilometre stretch of coastline, while Terrell reported 52 locations designated as archaeological sites along 15 kilometres of coastline in the Silao Peninsula area of northwest Bougainville, although these actually formed a near continuous distribution. Furthermore, ceramic evidence suggests that these distributions have considerable time depth (Terrell, 1976:237).

In contrast to the northern coasts, a survey of 19 kilometres of coastline in the Teop region produced only 19 sites represented by abundant ceramic and shell midden along a swampier coastline. Nineteenth-century reports comment, too, on the thinly populated southern coast in contrast to the densely populated Buin Plain. However, Oliver (1949:8) suggests there were formerly large settlements of Austronesian speakers along the southern and southwestern coast, but when German New Guinea became Australian Mandated Territory (AMT), the imposition of custom barriers curtailed native interisland trade and led to the abandonment of the coastal Siwai villages (Oliver, 1955:196) and a movement inland. Terrell (1976:103; 1978), citing publications and maps from the 1880s, suggests that Oliver's model of movement inland after WWI is in error. He argues that there were never more than a few coastal villages along this swampy coast and that the number of villages may actually have increased at the beginning of the AMT. However, we might also consider the possibility that attacks on coastal settlements for captives, launched from the neighbouring Shortland Islands (15 km to the south), reduced coastal settlement in the late nineteenth century (Ribbe, 1903). Clearly the straits region has been a dynamic zone where the intersection of a number of factors (Terrell, 1978) – such as an inhospitable environment, headhunting and related exchange, its later decline, colonial administrative developments and possibly disease – have produced considerable fluctuations in population location and density during the late nineteenth and early twentieth centuries. Such dynamism is well expressed in the traditions of the nineteenth-century movement of Austronesian-speaking peoples between Shortland (Alu), Mono (Treasury Group) and southern Bougainville (Terrell & Irwin, 1972).

All observers agree, however, that before WWI the Buin Plain of south Bougainville was densely settled with scattered small hamlets of around 50 people, and men's houses joined by a network of paths. Political organisation in the region was based on the competitive power politics of 'big men' whose influence could provide some cohesion above the hamlet level. Each big man controlled a clubhouse within which was a large ceremonial slit gong. The clubhouses were situated beside major paths between hamlets and served as regional centres for meeting and feasting (Oliver, 1955). Dryland taro (*Cyrtosperma* and *Colocasia*) was the main subsistence crop and it was cultivated in extensive swidden (slash-and-burn) systems (Blackwood, 1935:272; Oliver, 1955:123; Terrell, 1976). There is no evidence of irrigation systems of any kind, nor any evidence of breadfruit storage, and none of the archaeological research in the area has reported any evidence of terracing or signs of agricultural intensification. Oliver (1955) reports that the Siwai people left their swidden systems fallow for as little as six years (versus 10–20 years in Choiseul). This was very likely facilitated by the presence of soils enriched with volcanic ash (Sillitoe & Shiel, 1999). Beyond the root-crop base, the nut-tree harvest was of great importance and was a time of feasting (Oliver, 1955:138). During that time pigs that had been raised for special events were also killed and consumed. Fishing is relatively unproductive on the south coast of Bougainville, which may account in part for the limited coastal population or archaeological sites.

Although the history of volcanic activity on Bougainville has had a major impact on settlement and population distribution since first occupation, the archaeological record

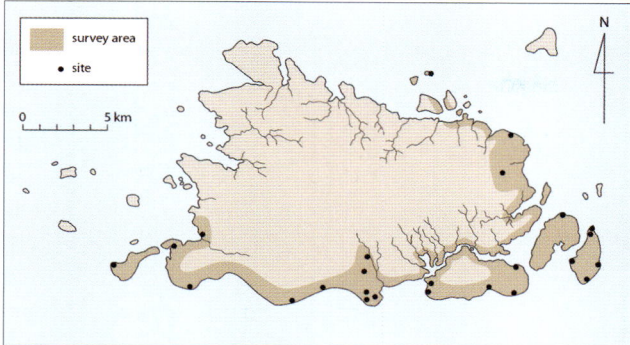

Figure 6.12. The location of archaeological sites on Alu Island, Shortland Island group, recorded by Irwin (after Irwin, 1973: figs 6.6 and 6.7).

of this is as yet very limited. Spriggs' (1992) excavation of a rockshelter at Manetai in the Evio region of central Bougainville, some 20 km southeast of the Billy Mitchell crater, showed volcanic ash halfway through the section which is attributed to the 350 cal BP eruption. Spriggs argues that the devastation of central Bougainville caused by that eruption and the earlier one at 900 cal BP accounts for a gap in population between the north and south. People were apparently moving permanently back into the Manetai region from the mountains only in the twentieth century. Although volcanic ash will ultimately enhance soil fertility, the raw ash would have inhibited occupation for some time. Pyroclastic flows are of course much more destructive, and a large flow running east from the last Billy Mitchell eruption covered 300 km² out to the coast, leaving the area deserted up to the time when European plantations were established.

Shortland Islands

The settlement pattern in the Shortlands, as observed by Irwin in 1970 (Irwin, 1972, 1973), consisted of coastal villages opposite reef passages with some interior hamlets or garden houses occupied for short periods of time. This pattern is consistent with that reported by Guppy (1887) in the late nineteenth century. Irwin's work is notable for his study of settlement-pattern change over time on Alu, where he managed to locate 40 archaeological sites concentrated on the south coast of the island in areas of raised coral and alluvium (Figure 6.12). This remains one of the few studies of its kind in the Solomons. Using ceramics recovered from test excavations or surface collections, Irwin was able to create a stylistic seriation, and this allowed him to place the sites into a four-stage chronological scheme (Early, Middle, Late and Modern) that started c. 500–1000 AD. Irwin's analysis suggested that factors that affected site distribution have remained essentially unchanged. Due to the need to keep a proportion of arable land fallow,

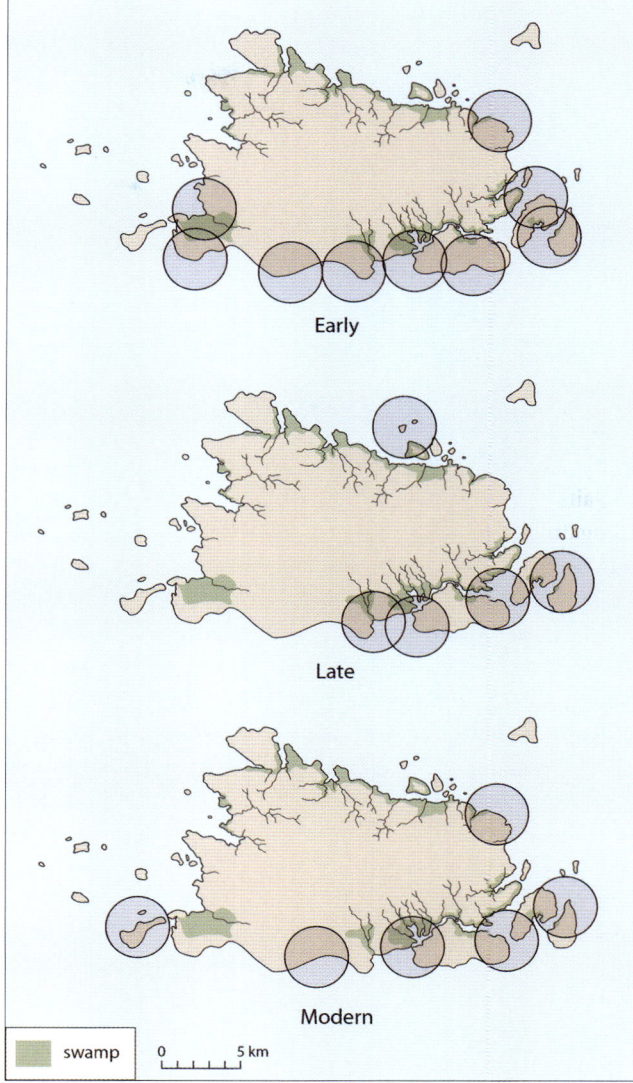

Figure 6.13. Alu Island settlement patterns as modelled by Irwin (1973).

there was a minimum distance at which villages would be expected to lie from one another; on Alu this proved to be approximately two kilometres. Shifts in population meant that there was a tendency for the actual distances between villages to fluctuate slightly around the two-kilometre range, but no major shifts in the forces influencing settlement were noted (Figure 6.13). The data does, however, appear to reflect some change in Alu population over time, with a noticeable decline in the nineteenth century. Irwin (1973:249) is cautious in his interpretation, but a major decline at this time is consistent with historical records, which report the devastating impact of European disease (Guppy, 1887:176; Thurnwald, 1912: vol. 3, 76). Prior to this decline some villages appeared to have had comparatively large populations: the site (A9) of Paramata was reported to have had a population of 300 in 1884 (Ribbe, 1903:31). Of the 40 sites that Irwin recorded, only one appears to have been a defended ridge location. The subsistence base on the Shortlands, as reported by Guppy (1887), consisted of crops of banana, some breadfruit and sweet potato, although the last was a recent introduction (Guppy, 1887:85; Irwin, 1973:229; Scheffler, 1965:10). *Cyrtosperma* and *Colocasia* were grown in dryland plots. Marine resources were most important in local subsistence systems, and pigs were apparently raised mainly for ceremonial occasions. None of the food staples were stored or preserved (Irwin, 1973:230).

Central Solomon Islands

The Central Solomon Islands includes Guadalcanal, Malaita and Makira, which are the largest islands east of Bougainville, as well as the Nggela (Florida) Group between Guadalcanal and Malaita, Savo off the coast near Honiara, Maramasike and Ulawa, which continue the line of islands southeast from Malaita towards Makira, and the smaller islands of Santa Ana and Santa Catalina off the coast of Makira (Figure 6.14). Malaita and Guadalcanal have the highest population densities in the Solomon Islands today: Guadalcanal 18 and Malaita 33 people per km^2. These high population densities reflect the fact that they have a large number of modern inland settlements, unlike most of the rest of the Solomon Islands, where population is today concentrated almost entirely along the coast – although archaeology reveals pre-1900 AD interior populations in most islands (see Chapter 7). This makes the modern densities in the Central Solomons – especially for Malaita – somewhat anomalous. How did Malaita maintain its large interior populations when other islands seemingly only support remnant coastal populations? Perhaps it is a function of size and travel distance to the coast, and the differential impact of European diseases and warfare in the late nineteenth century. Further research is needed on these islands: although Roe has conducted some archaeological research on Guadalcanal, most of the island is yet to be studied, while Malaita is virtually unknown to archaeology.

Guadalcanal is a geologically complex island whose interior mountainous ranges are composed of igneous and metamorphic rocks (Hackman, 1980) that reach a maximum elevation of 2449 m at Mt Popomanaseu. The ranges drop sharply on the southern or weather coast: this creates an orographic rainfall effect, which makes that coast very wet (up to 5000 mm per year) and the seas very rough. The sheltered north coast is considerably drier, with areas of grassland along the slopes behind and west of Honiara. This may reflect a combination of anthropogenic and climatic effects, although rainfall is still very high in this region (Figure 6.15). To the east of Honiara lie the northern alluvial plains which, at 450 km^2 in area, form the largest such area in the Solomon Islands. These plains were used to develop large coconut plantations from the end of the nineteenth century, and this displaced some population from what may potentially have been an area of high population density.

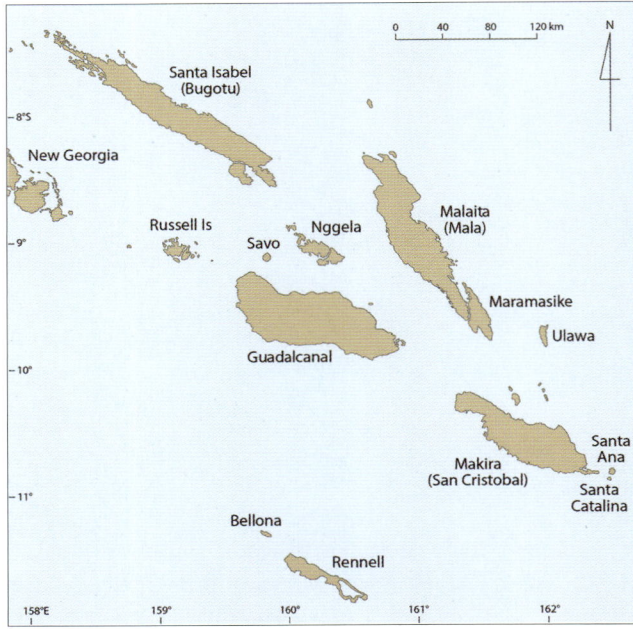

Figure 6.14. The Central Solomons.

Like Guadalcanal, Malaita has a central southeast–northwest spine of very hilly to mountainous land rising from a narrow coastal strip to a maximum elevation of 1430 m. The main island is separated to the south from Maramasike or Small Malaita by the very narrow Maramasike Passage. The small island of Ulawa lies 40 km to the east of Maramasike. Geologically these islands consist of a basaltic core overlain by a thick strata of sedimentary rock, primarily limestone, which was emplaced when the Pacific plate rode up over the Australian plate during the formation of the Solomons chain (Cowley et al., 2004). The limestone, which extends from southeast Isabel through to Ulawa, contains large amounts of very high-quality chert in a wide variety of colours that can be found as cobbles in most riverbeds (Sheppard, 1996). This material was used to make a range of stone tools, including adzes (Ross, 1970), and was distributed historically to neighbouring islands in the Central and Eastern Solomons. Malaita also stands out for the lagoon systems that extend along the western and northeastern portions of the island. The Lau and Langalanga systems contain artificial islands (Ivens, 1930); those in Langalanga, such as Lolasi, are famous for the production of shell money that was distributed historically

Figure 6.15. The Guadalcanal grasslands on the Honiara Plain (photo by authors).

throughout the Solomons and north into Bougainville and beyond (Connell, 1977).

Makira is the smallest of the 'large' islands of the Central Solomons at 3090 km² (compare 5336 km² for Guadalcanal and 4225 km² for Malaita). It also has a much lower population density at around 12 people per square kilometre, although, like Malaita and Guadalcanal, it retains a large inland population base. In many respects Makira is topographically and geologically similar to Guadalcanal: they share a common tectonic history and position. As on Guadalcanal, the south coast of Makira rises sharply to above 1000 m; this forms a narrow, steep watershed in the south, and a long, more gradual watershed in the north that results in a swampier alluvial plain. The geology of Makira (Petterson et al., 2009) and neighbours is much like that of Guadalcanal – essentially basement basaltic volcanics with a small amount of ultramafic rock overlain by calcareous sandstones and basaltic/sandstone breccia. Cherts are commonly associated with a formation known as the 'early Waihaoru sedimentary group', and this formation may have produced chert used to make flaked-stone tools. However, it is unlikely that chert from that source was widely used as it is not as high-quality as that from Ulawa or Malaita (Petterson et al., 2009).

As ceramics are absent, site visibility in the Central and Eastern Solomon Islands is low and the distribution of sites is less clearly understood than in either the Northern or Western Solomons. The SESP teams have carried out surveys and limited excavation programmes in parts of Makira, Ulawa, Uki Island and Santa Ana, and the Polynesian Outliers of Rennell and Bellona have had enough work done to define the broad outlines of a sequence. There have been a number of small-scale surveys by teams from the Solomon Islands Museum, but the most comprehensive coverage is from Guadalcanal, where cave sites in the Poha Valley have preserved reasonable stratigraphic coverage. Drawing on the Poha Valley excavation data plus the results of a survey programme in the Visale region of northwest Guadalcanal, David Roe has proposed a full sequence for the island (Roe, 1993). There are also some historical and ethnographic studies to supplement the archaeological data.

The Guadalcanal sequence

The Guadalcanal sequence was defined by Roe largely on the basis of his work in the Poha Valley (Roe, 1993). The most important site there was Vatuluma Posovi, which Roe interpreted as containing five occupation phases. He argued that Phase 1 (discussed in Chapter 4) represented a very limited and possibly disturbed mid-Holocene occupation between 6000 and 4000 cal BP – although we argued for a more conservative interpretation of 4200 cal BP for the basal cultural horizons, which still leaves it as the only possible candidate for a pre-Lapita horizon east of Buka.

Phase 2 (3000–2900 cal BP)
There is a hiatus of 1100 years in the radiocarbon and stratigraphic record at Vatuluma Posovi between the end of Phase 1 at 4000 cal BP and the start of Phase 2. Phase 2 is a short archaeological event bracketed by two dates (I-2874 and ANU-5845) that calibrate at one sigma to provide the age range for this phase. The artefacts are indistinguishable from the small sample from the later part of Phase 1; they include *Trochus* shell fishhook blanks and armlets, as well as a small chert chip. The major differences from the very fragmented and limited range represented in Phase 1 (Roe, 1993: Table 1) are an increase in shell density and species diversity, and the relative emphasis on marine species. This implies a possible change in economic emphasis from terrestrial to marine environments, although this apparent trend may owe something to sample size biases (Roe, 1993:70). This phase spans the putative period of late Lapita activity in the Solomon Islands, but there is no direct record of a Lapita presence in the Vatuluma Posovi sequence.

Phase 3 (2700 cal BP)
This phase is defined by radiocarbon samples P-1943 and P-1942 and is stratigraphically separated from Phase 2 deposits by a rockfall layer, although this is interpreted as a very minor pause in the occupation sequence (Roe, 1993:70). The artefacts from this layer include two volcanic stone adzes (recovered by Russell and Tedder) that are argued to be from this phase, a nut-cracking anvil and hammer stone, and a small ground shell bead. The high relative use of marine molluscs continues from Phase 2. Oven stones and fire features were also recorded in Phase 3 deposits.

Phase 4 (1300–1200 cal BP)
The age of this phase is not particularly clear because the radiocarbon samples and stratigraphy are difficult to reconcile. It could be argued that this phase dates to about 500–700 cal BP, which would bring it in the range of Phase 5, but this would make little difference to wider site interpretations as the content of this phase is little different from Phase 5 – or from Phase 3, for that matter. The artefacts include *Trochus* arm-ring fragments and fishhook blanks, a perforated shell disc and a perforated *Spondylus* valve. Freshwater and marine shell species are present, but the marine shell component is less varied than that of Phase 3.

Phase 5 (700 cal BP – recent)
Again, the radiocarbon dates are difficult to correlate with stratigraphy but the deposits appear to record a 'sporadic, and fairly recent, settlement of the site, probably within the last 700 years' (Roe, 1993:73). Layers defining this phase are stratigraphically separated from those of Phase 4. The artefacts of Phase 5 are similar to those of the preceding phase and include chert chips and *Trochus* fishhook blanks. The midden shell is also similar, but these layers contain the first record at Vatuluma Posovi of *Phalanger* sp. and dog or pig.

Drawing on Simon Haberle's (1996) palynological work, Roe (1993, 2000) has constructed a three-phase sequence for Guadalcanal. In the following description we have adopted Roe's (1993) chronology.

Hoana (Forest) Phase (6400–2200 cal BP)
The Hoana Phase is discussed in more detail in Chapter 4. It can be summarised as representing a generalised forest edge and riverine hunting and gathering regime. There was some population mobility, as cherts from elsewhere on Guadalcanal and possibly from Malaita were present in the Poha Valley sites.

Hamosa (Grasslands) Phase (2200–1500 cal BP)
During this phase there was increased forest clearance, erosion and the expansion of the extensive grasslands that characterise modern northwestern Guadalcanal. Roe argues that settlement shifted away from the inland caves towards the occupation of open settlements on the ridge crests and slopes. The palaeoenvironmental evidence from this period documents an increase in sedimentation rates as a result of the expansion of shifting dry-field agriculture, and in some areas this may have led to a partial failure of the hill-slope gardens. This is indicated archaeologically by the first appearance of occupation horizons in forest-zone rockshelters, which suggest a reorientation of economic patterns. There was also an increase in the sedimentation rate of the swamps of the north Guadalcanal plains and coast, and in the Visale area irrigated agriculture began to expand (Roe, 1993:176). The faunal assemblages of the Hamosa Phase show a marked reduction in the presence of forest fauna. Based on their appearance in the succeeding phase, Roe argues that the cuscus and the pig probably appeared in the Hamosa Phase (Roe, 1993:183).

Moru (Garden Regrowth Vegetation) Phase (1500–150 cal BP)
During the Moru Phase there was some forest regrowth, and expansion of irrigation systems and further human penetration of the interior forests. What are probably Malaitan cherts become increasingly common relative

to Guadalcanal sources during this phase, but given the proximity of Malaita and the known distribution of Malaitan stone to the remote islands of Temotu Province since Lapita times, it is probable that Malaitan material was widely available in Guadalcanal for most of the sequence. The quantity of *Canarium* nutshells increases in the upper levels of Vatuluma Posovi, and they include a much wider range of sizes and shapes, suggesting that many trees were present in the area. Nut-cracking anvils are also common from this phase.

The Guadalcanal sequence is based on limited excavation data recovered under difficult circumstances, and as such the resolution is quite low. But the broad-scale patterns that Roe describes are important. First we note a general continuity in material culture. This is reflected in the manufacture of shell ornaments as well as in the use of imported stone. *Trochus* arm rings and similar items are found in Lapita assemblages, but the Guadalcanal record would suggest that they were present in the Solomon Islands before Lapita and they continue well into the recent past. The sequence also records a long-term tradition of mobility, reflected in the movement of stone resources. The use of Malaitan or Ulawan and distant Guadalcanal chert sources suggests that the resource networks that are visibly part of the Lapita systems in the Reef–Santa Cruz region and are well attested ethnographically, have been an integral part of Solomon Island economies for possibly up to a millennium before the arrival of Lapita. We have argued that the Hoana Phase might be best considered as a two-phase period split at c. 2600 cal BP, after which both the midden data and palynological record show changes in economic practices that are well established by the beginning of the Hamosa Phase (2200 cal BP). Allowing for the vagaries of the dating, this is approximately the period when late Lapita settlement was occurring in the Western Province and late Lapita-derived plainware traditions were established in the eastern outliers, and it seems to mark a major period of change throughout the Solomon Islands.

Sites and settlement patterns

In 1568 Spanish explorers reported finding dense settlement along the Guadalcanal plains and extending into the foothills (Amherst & Thomson, 1901:15–176). In one coastal location a continuous settlement was said to extend for a distance of three leagues (16.7 km). By the early twentieth century this dense settlement pattern no longer existed on northwest Guadalcanal (Paravicini, 1931:60), supposedly because of the impact of headhunting raids from the west (Roe, 1993:23). Roe was unable to find any archaeological evidence of large coastal settlements in the Guadalcanal plains, something he attributed to twentieth-century disturbance in the form of palm plantations, road building and extensive bulldozing during WWII (Roe, 1993:32). In the northwest tip of Guadalcanal he did, however, find a deep midden deposit at the site of the Visale Roman Catholic Mission. The bottom of the deposit provided a date that suggested initial occupation in the fifteenth century. Survey of the interior of the Poha and Vuru valley systems and the *Themeda* grasslands of the northwest cape produced little in the way of village sites other than occasional terraces, house platforms and chert scatters on the ridgetops, suggesting small hamlets. Survey and excavation of known historic interior settlements failed to find any archaeological evidence (Roe, 1993:179) – an indication of the low archaeological visibility of such sites.

Hendren (1976) and Ward (1976) report a similar pattern from Ulawa. Coastal evidence seems most commonly to consist of U-shaped stone structures that formed the base of canoe houses, and small stone shrine enclosures. At the site of Haradewi (BS-UW-1) located at the back of the coastal strip on a raised beach, Ward (1976:165) excavated evidence for a small village occupation. It was located on a 'long low mound' with surface scatters of midden and worked chert fragments. There were no other obvious village features on the surface other than a small shrine enclosure which is undated. Radiocarbon dates are reported for the Upper and Lower deposits that suggest occupation over some hundreds of years beginning in the eighth or ninth century AD (Ward 1976: Table 11).

There is almost no archaeological evidence reported from Malaita, but the ethnographic record and modern settlement patterns conform to a model that Roe (2000) refers to as the 'bush–saltwater divide'. This is a reference to the distinction in the Solomon Islands between people who live on the coast and get their living from the sea, and those who live in the interior and work forest gardens – 'man blong solwata' and 'man blong bus' respectively in Solomon Islands Pijin. The distinction between bush and saltwater people is currently more apparent in Malaita than anywhere else in the Central Solomons where there are both dense coastal settlements and a heavily occupied interior. In the extensive lagoon systems of Lau and Langalanga, artificial islands have been constructed to support quite densely occupied settlements (Figure 6.16). Coral platforms, walls and jetties have been built well out into the lagoons, and line the edges of the mainland shores. These were described in some of the earliest European accounts of the nineteenth century and probably define a settlement pattern that extends well into prehistory. Langalanga is also a main centre for the production of shell money, which is still used in a variety

Figure 6.16. Langalanga lagoon artificial island settlements (photo by authors).

of traditional transactions (Goto, 1996). When Sheppard surveyed the coast in 1989 between Auki and Buma looking for chert sources he noted large quantities of chert debitage, including drill points and discarded cores, on islands in the Langalanga Lagoon. It is likely that the archaeological evidence for the production of shell valuables will prove widespread if coastal surveys are carried out.

Malaita also supports an inland-based settlement pattern that is best exemplified by the Kwaio communities that Roger Keesing has described (1970, 1982). Although his ethnographic work took place in the mid-twentieth century (after at least a century of European influence), Keesing has reconstructed Kwaio settlement patterns at the time of European arrival on the basis of information from Kwaio informants.

> The Kwaio were at the time of European invasion a bush people, swidden cultivators of taro and yams whose tiny mountain settlements were shifted every few years. Small descent groups, ideally agnatic but often with some non-agnatic affiliates, held primary interest in small estates, conceptually defined in terms of focal shrines … Relations between groups were maintained by bonds of inter-marriage and alliance in mortuary feasting, and sundered periodically by ramifying blood feuds. (Keesing, 1987:432)

Keesing's description of Kwaio society provides an excellent model for archaeology, although it is interesting to note that when Daniel Miller carried out a brief survey in the East Kwaio district of Malaita he found it very difficult to locate any surface evidence of the small hillside hamlets that Keesing had described (Miller, 1979:109). Clearly the Kwaio settlement patterns leave a faint archaeological signal. Miller did note, however, that the small hilltop forts (labu) that Keesing had also described were sometimes visible where stone walling was used to augment natural defences.

The surface evidence of settlement in Makira contrasts quite markedly with that of Guadalcanal and Malaita. There, coastal villages are marked by the presence of clusters of often sizeable mounds of midden debris and dense distributions of stone features in a variety of forms. On Santa Ana (Owa Raha), Swadling (1976: fig. 34) mapped a coastal village at Mwaroqorafu (BB-8-3), a kilometre north of the modern village of Gupuna, which sits at the base of a large, sheltered harbour on the west coast of the island. The site is over 600 m long and 200 m wide and consists of numerous intersecting stone walls, stone-lined pathways, mounds, wells, burial enclosures (ratanapaqora) and a 'sacred' canoe house (Figure 6.17). Swadling interprets the intersecting stone walls as having formed protective field enclosures for valuable crops. The site was dated to around 1500 AD from scattered charcoal in a stone oven, and the upper layer of a midden gave an age of about 1750 AD (Swadling, 1976:128–29). The anthropologist Bernatzik (1936) has described a very similar set of features on the east side of the island in and around the village of Nafinuatogo. Oral tradition states that Nafinuatogo was the oldest place of settlement on the island. Members of the Mendaña expedition landed on Santa Ana and Santa Catalina in July 1568, and their account indicates that both the east and west sides of Santa Ana were settled at that time (Davenport, 1972a).

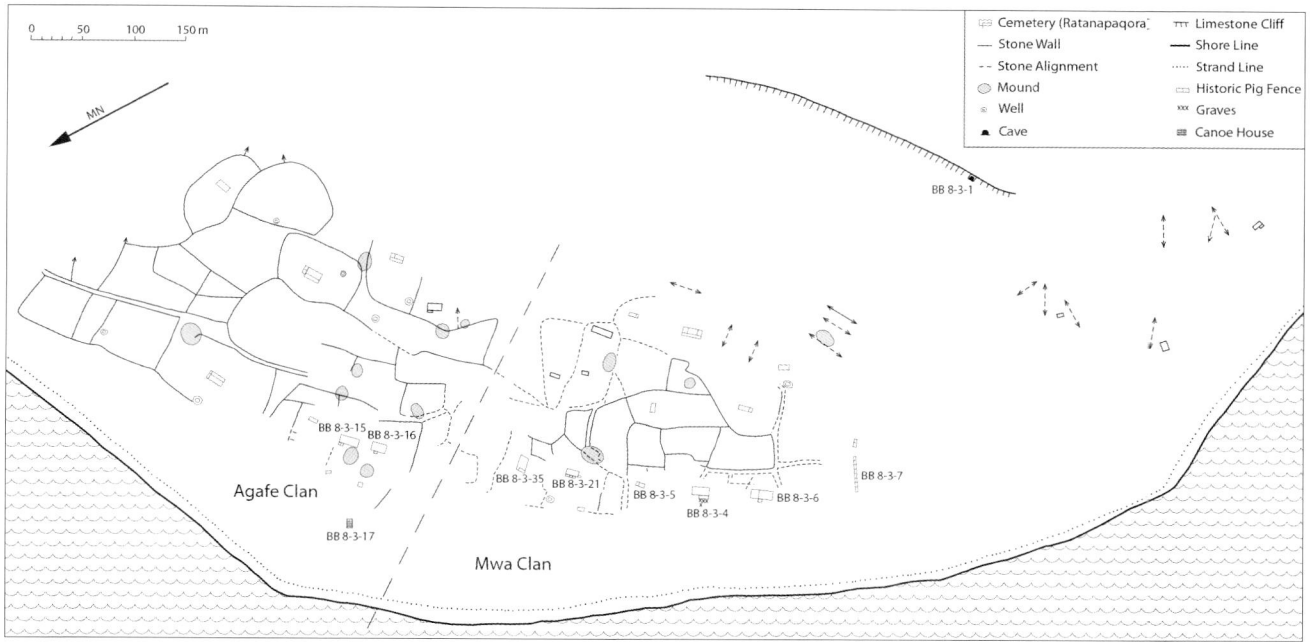

Figure 6.17. Plan of the Mwaroqorafu Site on Santa Ana (Central Solomons) (after Swadling, 1976).

At Star Harbour on Makira, Green found a similar record with numerous sites marked by low mounds ranging from a few metres to 20 metres in diameter (Miller, 1979:90). The largest site (Na Mugha BB-8-4) consisted of seven mounds and three burial enclosures like those of Santa Ana, distributed over an area of about 80 x 120 m (Green, 1976e: fig. 38). Green notes that although this site is comparable to that mapped by Swadling, nowhere in the Star Harbour area are mounds as high as those recorded on Santa Ana or Santa Catalina, where they can be up to 4 m in height and up to 40 m in diameter; these latter mounds are composed mostly of sand (Green, 1976e:137). The Na Mugha site provided a date (I-6180) from an oven beside a burial enclosure that suggested first occupation in the mid-seventeenth century AD, although the majority of the site is suggested to date to the late eighteenth to early nineteenth century AD, based on the historic artefacts recovered (Green, 1976e:143). A similar settlement, marked by the presence of two large mounds, was located on the small island of Uki off the northwest coast of Makira (see below).

Shrines and burial structures of various forms are found throughout the Central Solomons, although there appears to be some regional patterning, with somewhat more elaborate structures recorded in the east. On central and northwest Guadalcanal, Roe (1993:32–34) notes the presence of a number of features associated with burials or sacred beliefs and practices. These include shrines that commonly take the form of small stone cairns (peo), or deposits of shell valuables (moi), which are typically hidden. Burial structures (ngginggilu) also have some of the characteristics and function of shrines; they are usually rectangular or semicircular, curbed, stone-filled platforms containing human remains. Such structures are sometimes associated with prominent men. Deposits of exhumed bones (mbeku) are another class of ritual site; these are generally found in hidden locations such as caves, or in small stone slab-roofed crypts covered with vegetation and soil.

Roe notes that archaeologically it might be very difficult to distinguish between the various classes of stone cairn features on structural criteria (Roe, 1993:34). The evidence provided by human remains or shell valuables cannot be depended on as these remains were often moved when a settlement was abandoned. Peo are typically found on elevated locations and, when associated with village sites, on the up-slope side. Peo, ngginggilu and mbeku may be found in any combination at old village sites. Typically the stone cairns associated with these features are subcircular to subrectangular in plan, less than two metres in maximum dimension and less than half a metre in height (Roe, 1993: app. 2). Although we have limited data it appears that the features of central and northwestern Guadalcanal are more similar to those of trading partners in Malaita than to those of Makira.

Large, rectangular stone platforms (ratanapaqora in Santa Ana) have been recorded in Santa Ana and Star Harbour. They have low walls of stone and contain multiple burials, and in both areas they are found with settlements. Although it is not entirely clear from the published plan,

Figure 6.18. Figure of a Malaohu boy (from Ivens, 1927).

and with the ritual seclusion of young men in a tradition known as the Malaohu or Maraufu, which was a central part of the ritual life of the community (Fox, 1925; Ivens, 1927; Mead, 1973a) (Figures 6.18–6.20). In the Eastern Solomons, Swadling notes that on the weather coast of Santa Ana such structures (aofa) were surrounded by stone walls to protect them from storm surges; however this was not the case on the sheltered coast at Mwaroqorafu, where no identifiable structure was found (Swadling, 1976:126). Today the only extant canoe houses are located at Nataghera just south of Nafinuatogo, where the old houses have been rebuilt after being destroyed in the 1971 cyclone that devastated the island. These richly carved houses contain chiefly burial canoes, skull containers, ceremonial bowls and weapons. In the past they also contained bonito fishing canoes.

Miller (1979) carried out an extensive coastal survey of northwest Makira in which he compared his findings with the site and settlement-pattern descriptions of Fox (1925). As on Malaita, he noted difficulties in matching the archaeological record to the ethnographic texts. Burial enclosures (hera) like those from eastern Makira and Santa Ana were the most common feature found and were described as rectangular enclosures surrounded by coral walls up to 1 metre high and up to 10 metres long (Miller, 1979: fig. 5.4; see also Scott, 2007:168). Another feature that Fox (1925) described is a rectangular stone platform or mound (ariari) which may be associated with a hera. Miller (1979: fig. 5.8) recorded 13 features that he described as ariari, and noted that while they varied widely in form, most seemed to be rectangular in plan. A large example is represented by site SB-2-20: a low, grass-covered mound 14 m long and 3.3 m wide (Miller, 1979:103, fig. 5.5). Miller also recorded a category of small shrine (pirupiru) in northwest Makira. These are small stone enclosures or mounds, usually less than two square metres in size, apparently dedicated to sacred beings or tasks (e.g. shark shrines, grinding stones) (Miller, 1979:105). On Ulawa, Hendren (1976) and Ward (1976) noted both small shrines and U-shaped canoe-house structures at coastal hamlet sites. The small shrine features that Miller (1979:109) noted in East Kwaio on Malaita may be similar in form; however neither was described in detail.

Martin Gibbs and Natalie Blake have worked recently at Pamua on northwestern Malaita, where they have demonstrated considerable continuity between the archaeological record of that region and that of eastern Makira as recorded by Green during the SESP work (Blake & Gibbs, 2013). This is something that Miller has already remarked on (1979). Although Gibbs' (2011) research has focused on investigation of the Spanish settlements of the

there appear to be at least six of these structures at the site of Mwaroqorafu on Santa Ana mapped by Swadling (1976), and 11 at Nafinuatogo. The burial enclosure excavated by Green at Star Harbour contained few associated grave goods, however the surface of other platforms contained small samples of shell arm-ring fragments (*Trochus*, *Tridacna*, porcelain), chert flakes, pearlshell lures, pig bones and teeth (Green, 1976e:146). Dating of such structures is often problematic but an oven beside the structure gave a date that suggested use from around the sixteenth or seventeenth century.

Other common structures of Makira, Santa Ana and Santa Catalina – and also found in Ulawa – are the foundations of canoe houses located beside the beach in front of villages. The canoe houses were associated with the bonito cults,

Figures 6.19 (top) and 6.20 (bottom). Custom houses at Nataghera on Santa Ana (Central Solomons) showing burial canoes and carvings (photos by authors).

Solomon Islands, study of the Spanish remains located at Pamua Bay involved mapping and excavation at the site of Mwanihuki (SB-4-6) that was first studied by Green and Kaschko (Allen, 1976) as part of the SESP programme. The site consists of a series of stone platforms and mounds or middens like those that Miller (1979) described further west. Blake and Gibbs (2013) also note considerable similarities with the archaeological and ethnographic record (Scott, 2007) that stretches from northwestern Makira to Star Harbour in the east. Excavation has revealed burials – both primary internments and comingled secondary burials – associated with large (13 x 8 m) coral-faced rectilinear enclosures and large (12 x 12 m) circular mounds demarcated by coral limestone rubble. Radiocarbon dating of these features indicates deposition in the late prehistoric period (1500–1800 AD). No shell valuables were found in association with any of the burials; however, a metal aiglet (a European clothing fastening) was recovered in direct association with the chest area of an individual excavated from Feature 5, and Blake and Gibbs (2013:77) tentatively suggest that this burial may be associated with the short-term Spanish occupation of the area, indicated by the recovery of considerable Spanish ceramic from Pamua.

Archaeology on Uki Island

Uki (or Ugi) Island is a small, raised-coral reef island lying in the straits between Malaita and Makira about 50 km southwest of Ulawa. Roger Green carried out the first survey on Uki in 1970 as part of the SESP project, and located a number of sites (Figure 6.21), of which Su`ena appeared to provide the best opportunity for more detailed investigation.

The village of Su`ena is located about 600 m inland, and the site itself (BB-2-7) consists of two midden-rich mounds from which local members of the community had previously recovered chert adzes and various other items of material culture. Excavations carried out in 1972 and in 1973 resulted in the collection of large assemblages of material culture and faunal remains from the site, which for many years remained largely undescribed. In the 1990s Richard Walter, in collaboration with Roger Green and students from the University of Otago, began a lengthy period of laboratory analysis of the Su`ena assemblages, which culminated in the publication in 2011 of a comprehensive account of the Su`ena site (Walter & Green, 2011).

The BB-2-7 site is situated in an area of shell midden scatter (120 x 30 m) on a coral bench behind the modern village of Su`ena (Figure 6.22). Excavation revealed a total depth of deposit of 1.8 m in one of the mounds, but the entire site comprises three major layers that represent a continuous deposition over a period of 500 years, commencing in the

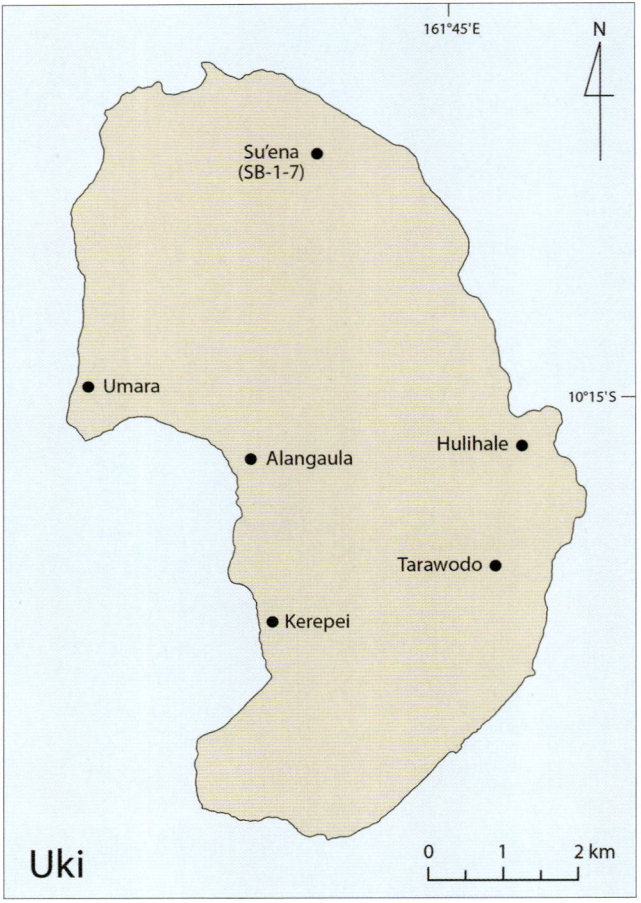

Figure 6.21. The location of archaeological sites on Uki Island (Central Solomons) recorded by the SESI team (from Walter & Green, 2011).

early sixteenth century (Walter & Green, 2011:28). The mound appears to have served as a rubbish dump and one interpretation is that it accumulated as a result of 500 years of household clearance. Green noted that rubbish disposal during his visit consisted mainly of householders sweeping waste into baskets and dumping it onto a communal refuse pile behind the houses.

Uki Island lies in an area known ethnographically to have experienced high levels of social interaction and exchange (Fox, 1925; Ivens, 1927; Mead, 1973b), and characterised as the Eastern Triangle culture area (see below). The area includes Sa`a on the southeastern tip of Malaita, Ulawa, and Makira with its offshore islands – Santa Ana and Santa Catalina in the east, and Uki and the Three Sisters in the north (Walter & Green, 2011:7) (Figure 6.31).

The aims of the Su`ena analysis were to describe the material culture and subsistence systems in a chronological context, and to develop an understanding of the site within the historical framework of the wider culture area.

Subsistence

The Su'ena subsistence economy was rich and varied. Although the community was 600 m inland, fishers took advantage of all fishing zones including the outer pelagic zone where bonito (*Katsuwonus pelamis*) is usually taken on lures – a practice that reached cult status in the Eastern Solomons (Davenport, 1971; Ivens, 1927). The inshore zones were exploited using hooks and nets to catch reef fish, with a particular emphasis on parrotfish; and invertebrates were taken from all available microenvironments on the reef and elsewhere on the littoral zone (Walter & Green, 2011:73). Pig and dog were present from the earliest layers, but chicken has not been positively identified from secure horizons. Forest hunting was important throughout the sequence, as evidenced by the presence at high relative abundance in all levels of cuscus and flying fox. The midden data does not point to any substantial impact on terrestrial fauna over the length of the Su'ena occupation, but there is some slight evidence of impact on molluscan resources in terms of a size decline in *Turbo setosus* and a widening of harvesting zones through time (Walter & Green, 2011:76).

Material culture

The material culture of Su'ena was dominated by chert tools, which were used to manufacture adzes and drill points, and a range of fairly generalised flake-tool classes (Figure 6.23). The chert appears, on hand specimen identification, to have derived from Ulawan or Malaitan sources, and some had arrived at Uki in the form of river cobbles that were broken down onsite (Walter & Green, 2011:76). More than 50 complete chert adzes were recovered, and many examples of broken specimens (Walter & Green, 2011:43–49) (Figure 6.24). The sheer abundance of adze-making debitage at the site suggests that Su'ena was a centre for adze manufacture and redistribution within the Eastern Triangle Furthermore, the lack of any indication of change in the availability of chert through the sequence provides good evidence for the stability and economic importance of the communication and exchange networks that traversed the Eastern Triangle over the last 500 years of prehistory (Walter & Green, 2011:74). In addition to the chert adzes, a small sample (n=18) of volcanic and metamorphic stone adzes in similar size ranges to the chert examples were also

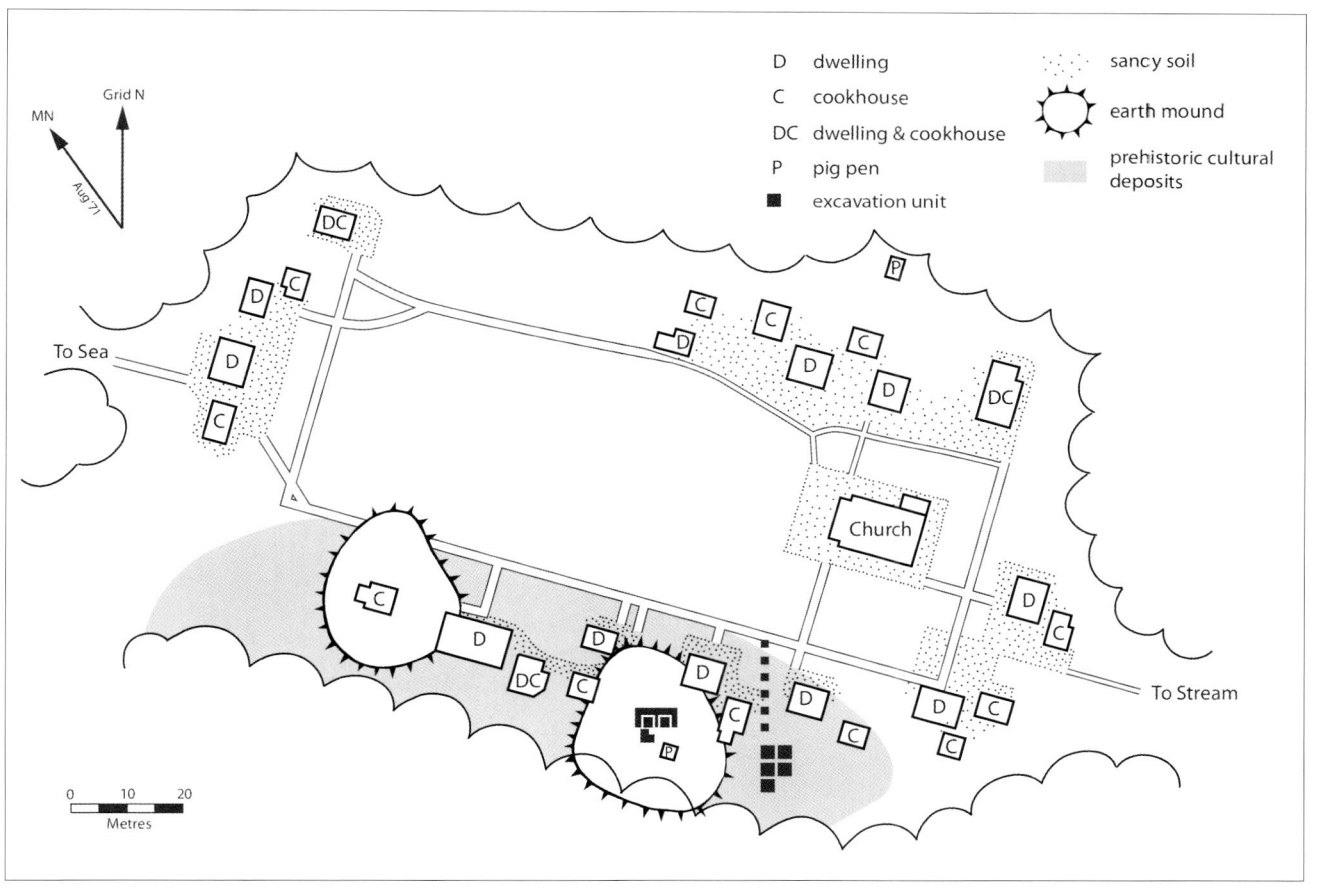

Figure 6.22. Plan of the Su'ena Site (BB-2-7) Uki Island (Central Solomons) (from Walter & Green, 2011).

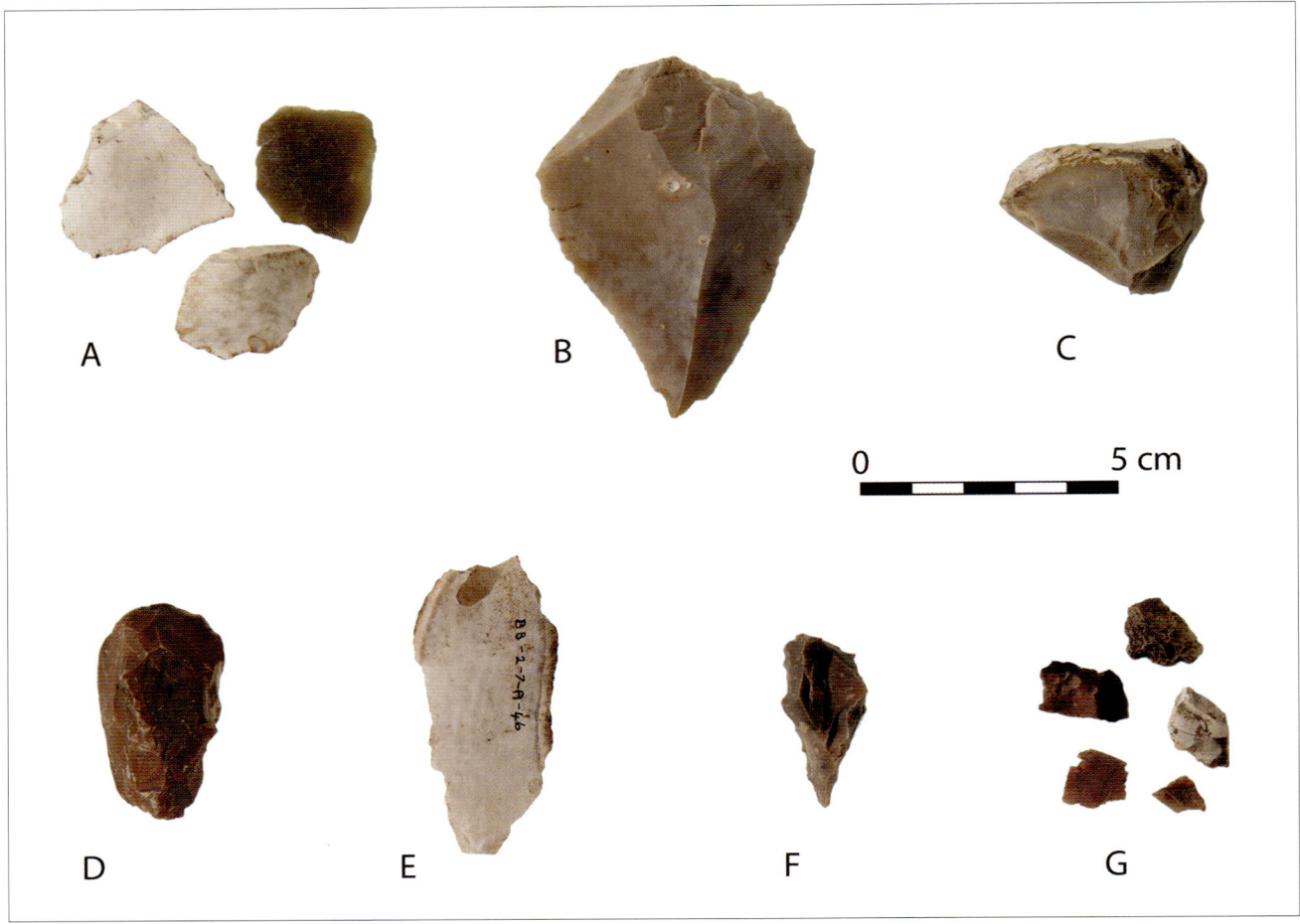

Figure 6.23. A selection of chert tools excavated from the Su`ena Site, Uki Island (Central Solomons) (from Walter & Green, 2011)

recovered (Figure 6.25). It is unclear where they originated from geologically, but they were certainly imported.

Su`ena also produced a diverse range of kastom money units and ornaments. The latter included personal items of adornment such as shell arm rings, necklace units of cowrie shell and animal teeth, and shell inlay pieces that were probably once inset (or intended for inset) into wooden items, perhaps even canoe structures (Figures 6.26–6.28). The Eastern Triangle is renowned for its carving tradition, which specialises in the application of nautilus inlay units. Bonito cult imagery, including the use of the frigatebird motif, dominates the art of wood carving (Mead, 1973b). Many of the ornaments and decorative items from Su`ena have equivalents in the ethnographic record and in museum collections, and this includes items that display the frigatebird motif. The frigatebird motif was found as an armband decoration in the earliest layers at Su`ena but Walter and Green have pointed out that while there is continuity in symbolism, the decorative systems have not remained static (Figures 6.29 and 6.30).

Only two of the motifs that are most strongly associated with the art and symbolism of the bonito cults are present in the early period suggesting that while these symbols have great time depth, there has also been change in their role and significance through time. Other changes were noted over time in the application of design principles and the selection of motifs within the arm ring assemblage. (Walter & Green, 2011:76)

Horticultural systems

The nature of prehistoric horticultural practices in the Central Solomons has proved something of a mystery, as the nineteenth-century documentation and archaeological record appear to be at variance with the picture painted by the Spanish explorers in the sixteenth century (Yen, 1976). The narratives of Mendaña and his companions report a densely occupied landscape in Guadalcanal and Makira with villages of over 200 houses and 'small villages of about 300 Indians' (Amherst & Thomson, 1901:308–20). Gomez Hernandez Catoira's description of gardens in the interior of Guadalcanal, to the west of modern Honiara, is

THE LAST 2000 YEARS

Figure 6.24. A selection of chert adzes excavated from the Su`ena Site, Uki Island (Central Solomons) (from Walter & Green, 2011).

Figure 6.25. A selection of meta-basalt adzes excavated from the Su`ena Site, Uki Island (Central Solomons) (from Walter & Green, 2011).

THE LAST 2000 YEARS

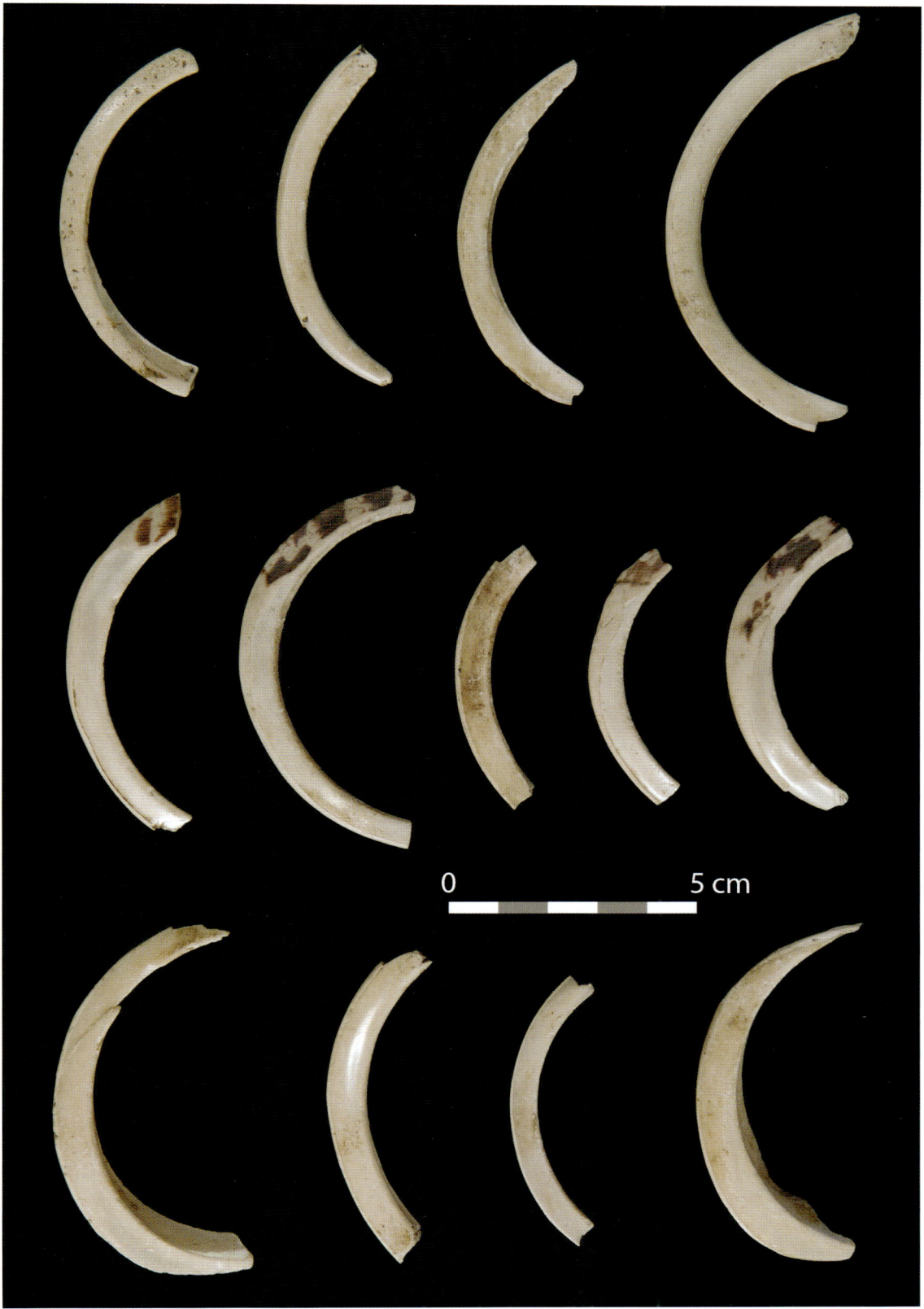

Figure 6.26. A selection of personal ornaments excavated from the Su`ena Site, Uki Island (Central Solomons) (from Walter & Green, 2011).

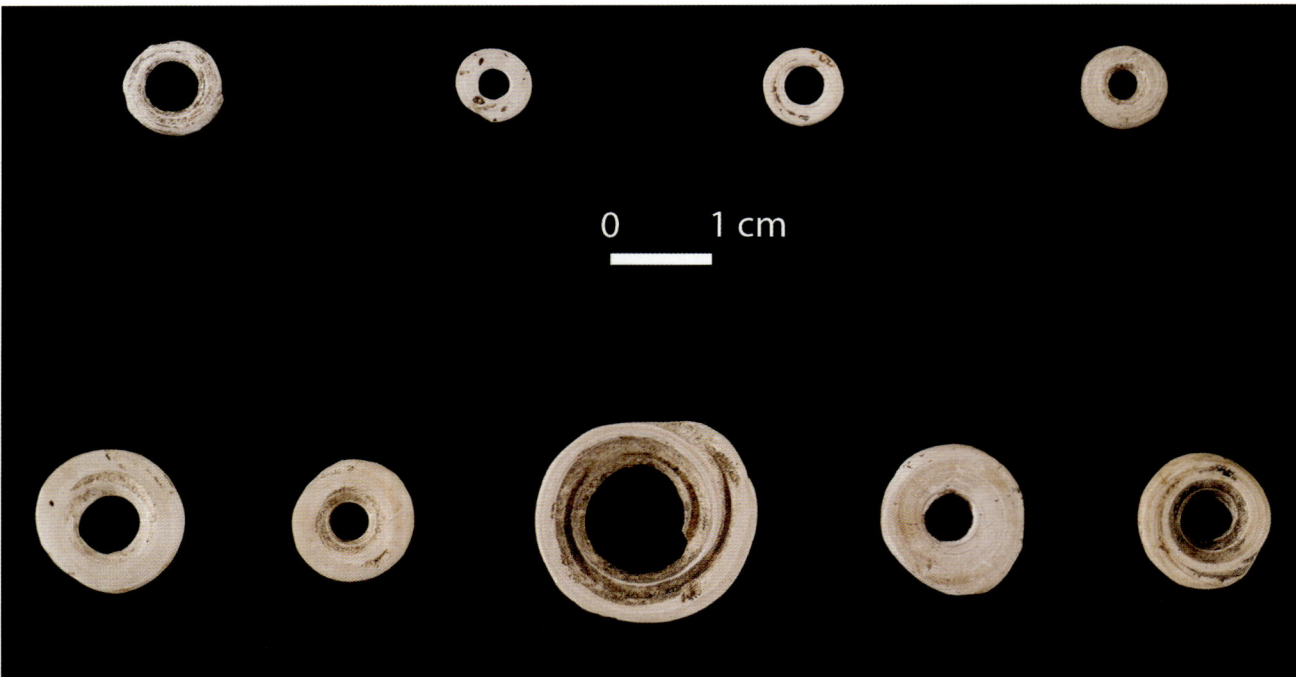

Figure 6.27. A selection of personal ornaments excavated from the Su`ena Site, Uki Island (Central Solomons) (from Walter & Green, 2011).

Figure 6.28. A selection of personal ornaments excavated from the Su`ena Site, Uki Island (Central Solomons) (from Walter & Green, 2011).

Figure 6.29. A selection of shell armbands excavated from the Su`ena Site, Uki Island (Central Solomons) (from Walter & Green, 2011).

Figure 6.30. Motifs found on the decorated shell armbands excavated from the Su`ena Site, Uki Island (Central Solomons) (from Walter & Green, 2011).

of particular note: 'We saw many villages upon the hills and many plantations (chacaras) of food on the slopes, arranged very well so that they could irrigate them, which they did. It was well laid out; and by each cleft there was a stream of water' (Amherst & Thomson, 1901:306). At the time of Yen's (1976) review of agricultural systems there was no reported evidence of irrigation systems in the entire Central Solomons including Guadalcanal, although there was evidence of enclosed field systems, suggesting some degree of intensification. Stone-walled garden complexes and terraces are apparently common on Ulawa, and Hendren (1976:154) reported frequent 'large areas of adjoining stone-walled enclosures on the coastal flats of the island'. One of these consisted of 35 enclosures in an area of over 2 hectares. Ridgetop variants of these systems included combinations of enclosures and stone-faced terraces that extended down valley slopes. Roe failed to find any evidence of irrigation systems in the vicinity of Honiara; however, using aerial photography, he did ultimately find seven irrigated pond fields in the interior valleys of the northwest cape of Guadalcanal (Roe, 1993:159). All of these consisted of a series of contiguous ponded fields, usually defined by stone-walled banks that averaged a metre in height. In the Kolevu III system at Visale the ponds spread over a distance of 600 m with an approximate area of 9 hectares, although it is possible they once extended further into modern coconut plantations. Dating of these systems is difficult, but one date (ANU-6730) from the T1 excavations at Kolevu III produced an age range of 672–266 cal BP (92.8% HPD), which Yen believed probably dated the commencement of the cultivation phase.

The SESP surveys recorded only a few examples of agricultural systems in the Makira region. Yen (1976:64) recorded a substantial enclosure with walls up to a metre high and varying in width from 40 to 150 cm as an example of a walled yam garden on Santa Ana. But Green's survey at Star Harbour on Makira and on the island of Uki did not find any surface evidence of horticultural field systems.

Culture areas and exchange systems
Historically the area of Malaita, Ulawa, Makira, Santa Ana, Uki and the Marua Sound region of southeast Guadalcanal were bound by social networks that involved trade in canoes, captives, food and the movements of shell valuables in both ritual and commodity exchanges. These exchange relationships were almost impossible to separate from other social interactions and institutions (Walter & Green, 2011:7–22). Mead (1973b), for example, describes dance exchange visits as overlapping the trade in indigenous currency and canoes in Makira. The movement of fine chert from Malaita and Ulawa, metamorphic and igneous adzes from Marau Sound and shell beads from Haununu on Makira are examples of exchange relationships that show up in the archaeological record (Fox, 1925; Green, 1976a; Ivens, 1927). An additional network appears to have linked western Guadalcanal, the Florida Group and Malaita in an exchange of chert, shell beads and numerous perishable goods (Roe, 1993:29). The archaeological evidence from this region, although fragmentary, suggests a considerable antiquity to this exchange. Extensive deposits of chert throughout the limestones of Malaita and Ulawa were exploited for the manufacture of a variety of tool forms, including flaked adzes as found in the Su`ena assemblage (Figure 6.23). The Ulawa chert industry has been documented by Ward (1976): it seems that considerable chert moved south from there toward Makira – although it is very difficult to distinguish cherts from Ulawa from those of Malaita. There is limited evidence for trade to Ulawa, but Ward (1976:179) reports adzes of green-grey metamorphic rock, probably from Marau Sound, that are found infrequently on Ulawa, although none were recovered in his excavations. On Guadalcanal the Vatuluma Posovi site demonstrates that chert was moving around from at least 4200 cal BP, and the sequence from there reflects some changes in source areas through time. At the nearby cave site of Vatuluma Tavuro, Roe noted that, beginning in Phase Three (ANU-6990, 1173-681cal BP 95.4% HPD), chert decreases in size and quantity and changes from a predominantly coarse material attributed to the Mbirao volcanics of Eastern Guadalcanal to the brown glassy chalcedony characteristic of Malaita (Roe, 1993:178).

Within the Central Solomons there are areas where there has been sufficient interaction over a lengthy period of time to allow shared cultural traditions to emerge (Mead, 1973b, Walter & Green, 2011). The ethnographic accounts of Ivens (1927), Fox (1925) and others describe an area we refer to as the Eastern Triangle – a place where there are sufficiently high levels of regular interaction underpinned by a basic similarity in technology, art style and cultural practice to justify referring to it as a 'culture area' (Walter & Green, 2011).

Of all the social and ritual practices of the Eastern Triangle, the one that dominated social life and permeated all aspects of art style and traditions was the bonito cult in its various permutations. Throughout the Eastern Triangle males were taken as young boys into a period of seclusion in the canoe houses where they learned the mysteries of bonito fishing: the technology, the rituals and the mythology (Ivens, 1927). At the end of the seclusion period the boys emerged as men, ready to participate in village life. In the Eastern Triangle the imagery of bonito fishing permeates most artwork and

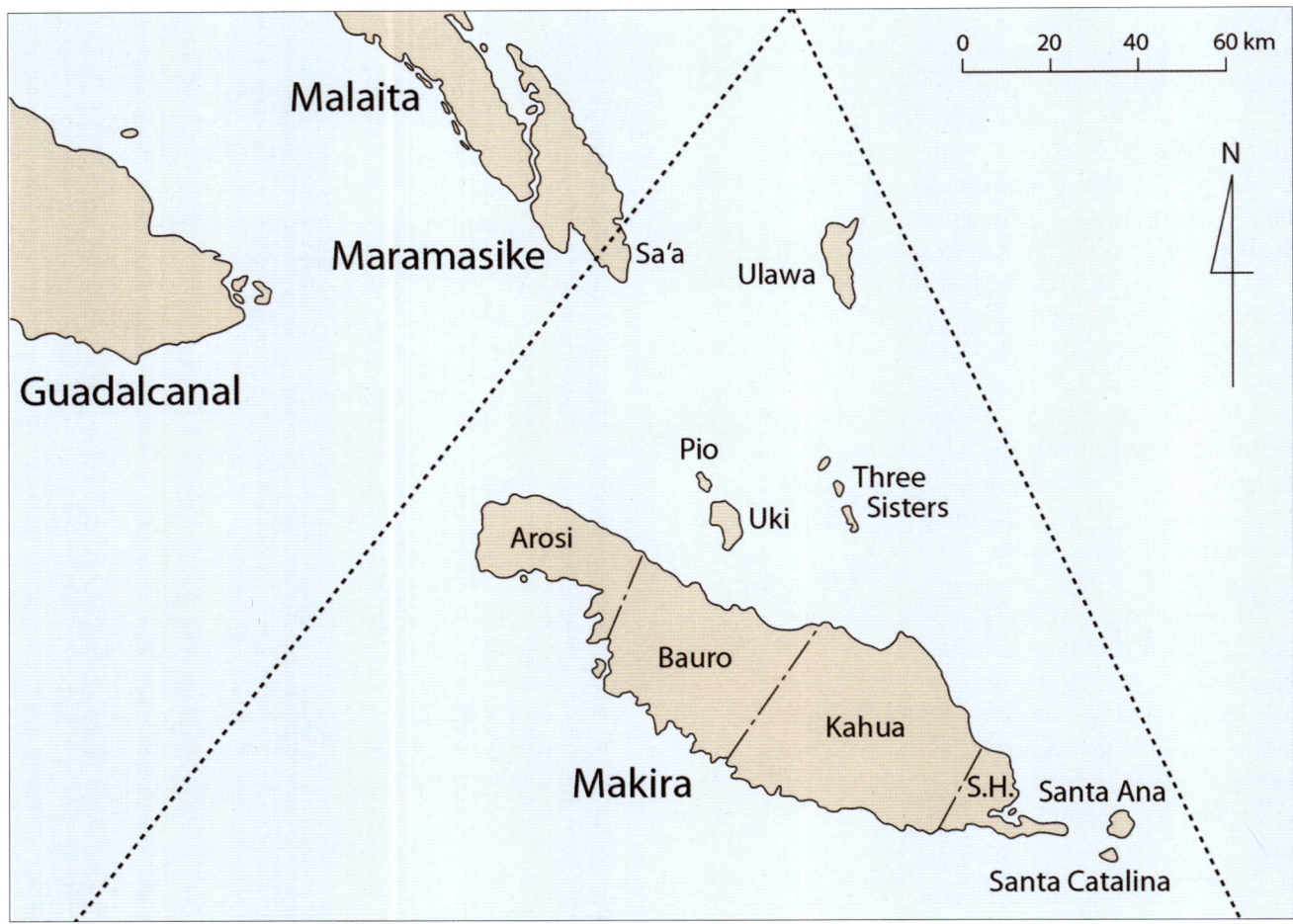

Figure 6.31. The Eastern Triangle culture area (from Walter & Green, 2011).

ritual life. There is not much archaeological evidence for bonito fishing in the midden record anywhere in the region, although canoe houses, possibly associated with bonito cults, were tentatively identified at Santa Ana and elsewhere in the Eastern Triangle (Swadling, 1976). But the Su`ena record contained convincing evidence for the long-term importance of bonito cults, in the form of stylised motifs of bonito and of the swooping frigatebird, which follows the bonito schools. The motifs appear on armbands from the earliest period of occupation and in a variety of other media throughout the Su`ena sequence. They are often located in association with motifs representing sharks and swordfish – all powerful symbols of the bonito hunt (Davenport, 1971). According to the symbolic record, then, rituals and symbolism relating to the fishing of bonito may go back at least 500 years, to the beginning of the Su`ena sequence.

The interaction systems operating within the Eastern Triangle in the nineteenth and early twentieth century articulated with other systems in Maramasike, Malaita, Guadalcanal and elsewhere in the Central and Eastern Solomons. These systems involved the circulation of shell valuables, trade in canoes and other commodities including captives, and regular movements of people involved in dance ceremonies, marriage exchange and various other transactions or ceremonial activities (Walter & Green, 2011: ch. 2). Most of these exchange events are invisible archaeologically, but patterns of prehistoric mobility and exchange are visible in the movement of raw materials. Davenport (1972a:171, 183) recovered chert flakes from sources on Ulawa or Malaita in all of his excavations on Santa Ana – suggesting that the movement of this material commenced at the time of first settlement of the island c. 2700 cal BP (Black & Green, 1975:30). At Na Mugha in Star Harbour, Green found several thousand chert flakes, adzes and drill points as well as a nodule of unworked chert he attributed to sources on Ulawa or Malaita. He also found polished adzes from surface collections of a grey-green metabasalt that was likely brought in from Marau Sound on Guadalcanal (Green, 1976e:140, 144). Chert flakes were also abundant in the sites recorded and excavated in the Arosi district of northwest Makira (Miller, 1979:91), and a similar pattern is seen on Uki, where chert flakes and adzes were ubiquitous throughout the excavated mound. At present, it is proving difficult to identify the source of cherts with great precision but, given the quantity of cherts moving throughout the region and into the Reef–Santa Cruz sites, fine-scale sourcing work would be an excellent means for teasing out long-term changes in networks.

Although Makira lies at the centre of this sphere of interaction, there are distinctive zones of interaction with neighbouring islands at each end of Makira, and from central Makira through Uki and the Three Sisters across the 30-km gap to Ulawa. These comparatively short water gaps facilitated regional interaction, and although the crossing to Guadalcanal or Malaita is 60 km from the west end of Makira, the people of Marau Sound on Guadalcanal share a common linguistic history and pattern of interaction with peoples of the Eastern Triangle. It is at this point that the pattern of interacting with neighbours on near, visible islands, which extends back into island Southeast Asia, comes to a halt. To the east, no islands were visible or within a few days' sail of the Central Solomons. Between Santa Ana and the Reef–Santa Cruz Islands there is a boundary created by a 360-km water gap that does not appear to have been crossed from settlements within the Solomons during the early Lapita colonisation. This separates the Lapita zone of the Eastern Solomons from the Central Solomons, which did not appear to receive Lapita settlers – although there was movement of chert from Ulawa and Malaita to the Reef–Santa Cruz region during the early Lapita settlement. In the historic period, contact with Santa Cruz was made primarily by castaways from the Eastern Solomons who managed to come ashore at Santa Ana.

The Eastern Solomon Islands

The Eastern Solomons comprise the high volcanic island of Santa Cruz (Nendö), the active volcano of Tinakula and the small, generally lower islands of the Reef Islands, the Duff (Taumako) group, Vanikoro, Anuta and Tikopia. Although they are a relatively small group compared to the Solomon Islands chain, the islands of the Eastern Solomons have attracted a relatively high level of archaeological attention. In addition to the SESP work and follow-up studies of Lapita, there is now a good synthesis of the post-Lapita phases in work by Moira Doherty (2007, 2009). The post-Lapita prehistory of the Reef–Santa Cruz Islands is intriguing, as it provides a potential case study in the archaeology of ethnicity or cultural difference. The linguistic picture is complex, with considerable past debate over whether some languages spoken there should be classified as Austronesian or mixed Austronesian/non-Austronesian (AN/NAN) languages. One major focus of Doherty's work was to see how well the hypothesis of multiple linguistic inputs or migrations might be reflected archaeologically. In that work she failed to identify any evidence of a break in cultural tradition that might be consistent with multiple migrations, and recent linguistic research concludes that these languages are in fact AN without any NAN mixture (Ross & Næss, 2007).

Doherty (2007, 2009) has divided the Reef–Santa Cruz sequence into four periods. The date ranges for these periods, given below, are based on our interpretation of the record and of the radiocarbon dates as presented in Doherty's (2007) Table 2.2.

Period 1 – Decorated Lapita 3000–2600 cal BP

The dentate Lapita period has been discussed in Chapter 5, including a detailed review of the data from the three major sites of this period: SZ-8, RF-2 and RF-6. The remaining excavated decorated Lapita-period site is Mdailu (SZ-33) on Santa Cruz, which contains two layers (VII and V) with a few ceramic sherds and ephemeral evidence of occupation (McCoy & Cleghorn, 1988).

Period 2 – Plainware 2600–2500(?) cal BP

Although this is designated a plainware ceramic phase, this is based on the lack of decoration on the body of the vessels; there are, however, occasional decorated elements on the vessel lips. Plainware sites include Mdailu (I–IV), where McCoy and Cleghorn (1988) report evidence for round houses delineated with coral edging and with coral pavements. The material culture includes *Tridacna* adzes, one-piece fishhooks, stone adzes and flake tools in chert and obsidian, and *Spondylus* shell ornaments (Doherty, 2007:54; McCoy & Cleghorn, 1988). At the Növlaö rockshelter, Layers VIII–XXI contained a similar material culture as well as shell arm-ring fragments. This shelter site also contained shallow pit burials and some superimposed house foundations. The Ngatoponu site (RF-19) is a mound site measuring approximately 45 x 30 m, excavated by Green in 1979. The mound itself seemed to be built largely of discarded materials, midden, ovenstones and scatters of pottery, although it did contain a few postholes and oven features (Doherty, 2009:183). The chronology associated with this site provides a challenge for the notion of a simple progression from decorated Lapita through to a later plainware phase. Two dates have been obtained (Wk-7849 2920 ± 60, Wk-7852 2850 ± 55) on *Turbo* marine shell (Doherty, 2009). Calibration of these dates using the delta R value (-81 ± 64), determined previously for RF-2 (Jones et al., 2007), provides ages in the range of 3002 to 2438 cal BP (95.4% HPD), which overlaps completely with the later decorated Lapita sites. The pottery from these mound sites is highly fragmented and seemingly of poor quality, but there is nothing to suggest that it is a biased subset of a decorated Lapita assemblage. The site itself is uncharacteristic of earlier Lapita sites as it appears to be primarily a midden deposit formed through secondary deposition; such midden deposits are characteristic of the later period sites in the Reef Islands. It is possible that the shells dated from this site were old shell incorporated, during cleaning, into younger midden deposits.

Not a great deal is known of the settlement patterns or nature of the settlements themselves, but Doherty makes a strong case for continuity, in the ceramic tradition of Period 2, from the earlier decorated Lapita assemblages: 'There are no new distinctive vessel forms, or parts (e.g., handles or spouts) nor any form of body decoration ... that suggest external influence or would allow the source of any influence to be traced' (Doherty, 2009:196). The tempers in the Mdailu and Növlaö pottery assemblages appear to be of local origin (Doherty, 2009:200).

Period 3 – Early aceramic 2500–? cal BP

This period is only known from undated layers (V–VII) at Növlaö. In fact, there are no defining characteristics to the phase other than the absence of ceramics or other items typical of the earlier ceramic sites (McCoy & Cleghorn, 1988:114).

Period 4 – Late aceramic, protohistoric, historic 600 cal BP–historic

This phase includes all other sites recorded in the Reef–Santa Cruz surveys: Naiavila (SZ-12) and Mateone (SZ-26) on Santa Cruz, Dai (SZ-11) and Növlaö (SZ-47) Layers I–IV on Tömotu Neo, and Sie (RF-3) on the Main Reef Islands. These sites are represented by surface features including mounds, abandoned village complexes and various forms of stone structure. They do not form any coherent archaeological grouping in terms of uniquely shared characteristics, but together with the historical and ethnographic accounts they document the emergence of historical Reef–Santa Cruz societies.

Sites and settlement patterns of the late aceramic to historic period

Some of the earliest historical accounts of traditional Oceanic societies come from the Spanish records of visits to the Reef–Santa Cruz Islands in the late sixteenth century.[1] They visited Graciosa Bay in 1595 and described 10–12 villages, each consisting of about 20 round houses, two longhouses and several wells (Markham, 1904:51). This description, though vague, does suggest a distinction between domestic (the round house) and communal structures (the longhouse, perhaps men's houses) – which is well reflected in the archaeological record and later historical and ethnographic accounts. In 1767 British naval officer and explorer Philip Carteret described quite dense settlement patterns around the north of Santa Cruz, especially at the western end of the island, where he described the settlement patterns on both sides of the passage between Tömotu Neo and the mainland as 'towns' with 'swarming' populations (Hawkesworth, 1775:292). French explorer Antoine Bruni d'Entrecasteaux confirmed the higher population densities of the north coast when he visited the island in 1793; he also noted small settlements with stone walling close to the water's edge along the southern coast (Rossel, 1808:372–74). There were certainly inland populations at the time of the Spanish visits, perhaps even quite densely settled areas, but there are no known direct accounts, and by the early twentieth century the interior villages were mainly abandoned (Doherty, 2007:136). When Davenport carried out his ethnographic work on Santa Cruz in the 1960s there were 33 villages, all sited close to the shore. On the Outer Reef Islands he noted that the settlements were located on the lagoon edge of the lee side of the islands (Davenport, 1972b). Yen mapped and test-excavated at Naiavila (SZ12), a historic village 4 km inland from Graciosa Bay. He estimated that it covered an area of 6000 m^2 (Yen 1976:204).

Throughout the Reef–Santa Cruz Islands, Davenport noted that villages were oriented with male and female sides and that there were generally four main types of structure within the settlement: men's house, family dwelling, cult house and dance circle (Davenport, 1964b, 1969, 1972b). The men's houses were located on the seafront: these were where trading activities took place and specialists practised their craft. Adolescent and unmarried men slept in the men's house, and it was the venue for various social activities. The men's house is likely to have some antiquity: Carteret described what appear to be men's houses on his visit to the island in 1767 (Doherty, 2007:139). At the Naiavila site on Santa Cruz, Yen (1976) identified two clusters of structures outlined by stone foundations and joined by a stone 'pig fence', and a series of other features that appear to have comprised rectangular house foundations. These include large structures that a former inhabitant has identified as men's houses. McCoy and Cleghorn (1988) recorded a very similar site at Dai village (SZ-11) on the tip of Tömotu Neo,

---

1. The review of historical sources in this section draws heavily on the work of Doherty (2007:131–98).

where there was a total of 35 stone structures, including a centrally located dance circle, in a tightly clustered area of 4900 m². Informants pointed out five rectangular structures that they identified as men's houses. Another candidate for a men's house was identified at Mateone; it contained evidence for the working of *Trochus* shell (McCoy & Cleghorn, 1988:110–11). The sizes of these archaeological structures varied between about 15 and 60 m².

Whether men's houses can be accurately identified archaeologically is unclear, but there are clearly two classes of structure implied by the platform sizes of the structures in the late-period sites: small structures of up to around 30 m² may be equated with dwellings, and larger structures of between 30 and 60 m² equated with the men's house.

The cult house or 'ghost house' is another class of structure described by Davenport (1964b). The exact function of these seems to have varied, but they were found throughout the Reef and Santa Cruz Islands in the mid-twentieth century and appear to have some antiquity: there are descriptions in various historical accounts going back as far as the time of Pedro Fernandez de Quiros's visit in 1595 (Doherty, 2007:158–61). Although the cult houses would be larger than most dwellings, it is debatable whether there would be anything to distinguish such structures archaeologically. Local informants pointed out two in the Dai village site to McCoy and Cleghorn (1988).

The dance circles or dancing grounds were places where men's associations sponsored community entertainments (Figures 6.32 and 6.33). The activities involved feasting and dancing over several days, and the events had both ritual and secular functions. The men's groups hosted visiting groups at the entertainments, and at some point in the future this would be reciprocated, in a dance cycle that lasted several years (Davenport, 1975a). The dance circles appear to have been up to 20 m in diameter and were often edged with coral slabs or rough rocks. McCoy and Cleghorn identified a total of eight dance circles in the site survey of Santa Cruz but these structures do not appear, on either historical evidence or archaeological grounds, to have great antiquity. Excavations at Mateone village (McCoy & Cleghorn, 1988:110) show that the floor was refurbished, as Davenport (1975a:40) described. Radiocarbon dates from the site, however, indicate that the dance circle, as a village feature, was probably less than 200 years old (Doherty, 2007:163).

The most noteworthy features missing from the Reef–Santa Cruz Islands, compared to the wider Solomon Islands, are the ancestral skull shrines that are commonly found elsewhere. There have been various references in the historical literature to 'shrines' or sacred places, but where any structural evidence for these is described it is usually

Figure 6.32. Dance circle on Santa Cruz at Graciosa Bay (photo by authors).

Figure 6.33. Dance circle at Nanggu Villae, Santa Cruz (photo by authors).

of above-ground wooden structures, and there is no clear reference to the stone piles, mounds or platforms with human remains and votive offerings that characterise many shrines to the west of the Reef–Santa Cruz Islands (Doherty, 2007:172).

In the Reef–Santa Cruz Islands human remains have been found archaeologically in association with houses – which was in keeping with the custom of retaining the bones of ancestors in or under houses, as reported by various visitors (Doherty, 2007:156–57). At Naiavila a pile of human skulls and bottle fragments was found in a corner of the house that was identified as belonging to the chief (Yen, 1976:210). At Dai village, human burials were present in three of the four excavation areas but absent from the dance circle excavation. Some were articulated burials while others were jumbles of bones from different individuals buried in shallow pits (McCoy & Cleghorn, 1988:111). Two human burials were found in the Növlaö rockshelter in areas dating to before 2000 cal BP and seemingly associated with ovens and house foundations.

Midden mounds

An interesting and unusual type of site in the Reef–Santa Cruz Islands is the rubbish mound. These mounds vary in size up to about 50 x 30 m, and up to 3 m high, but usually less. They have been identified as components of a number of sites in the Reef Islands including RF-5, RF-7, RF-19, RF-27, RF-28, RF-32, RF-33, RF-34 and RF-39 (Doherty, 2007:164–65). The sites are either components of abandoned village sites, or appear alone on the landscape. They consist of midden debris, including ceramics, but some also contain very recent material, which suggests that they span much of the occupation sequence. Only one mound feature was found on Santa Cruz but, in total, 12 of the 16 sites classified as 'old villages' in the SESP survey contained at least one such feature, and most contained two or more. The midden mound appears to be a standard component of the Reef–Santa Cruz village settlement layout and represents a specific type of discard behaviour that is not seen widely in the Solomon Islands. However, as noted above, similar features were recorded at the Su`ena site on Uki Island and in many locations on Makira. This suggests that the midden mound is a common, and probably unique, component of habitation complexes in the Eastern Solomon Islands.

To date there is little archaeological evidence for horticultural practices in the Reef–Santa Cruz archaeological record. Despite having carried out considerable survey in the region, Yen (1976) reported no physical evidence of field systems. This would appear to be a function of the elaboration of arboriculture in the Reef–Santa Cruz Islands, including the use of breadfruit fermentation pits and smoked and dried breadfruit, although traditionally the swidden system of yam and taro cultivation was also important. Yen suggests that the eastern end of the Central Solomons and the Reef–Santa Cruz Islands was a region where forest swidden systems dominated, in contrast to the Western Solomons where water-controlled irrigation appears to have been important (Yen, 1973b:43, 1976:62).

At least one feature at Naiavila was identified as a breadfruit fermentation pit (Yen, 1976:216–17). A possible breadfruit pit was also identified in the Lapita RF-2 site, and similar structures have been putatively identified in other Lapita sites on Niuatoputapu and Tongatapu islands (Kirch, 1988b). There is as yet insufficient evidence, however, to determine whether the use of breadfruit fermentation pits in the Reef–Santa Cruz Islands was a retention from Lapita or a later introduction from Polynesia; the latter seems more likely, given the historical prevalence of breadfruit fermentation in Polynesia.

Exchange

Although the Reef–Santa Cruz Islands are small and relatively isolated, the archaeological record shows that they have always played a part in wider regional networks. The practice of voyaging and exchange was introduced by Lapita and included, for the first century or so, the importation of obsidian from the Bismarck Archipelago 2000 km to the west. A more localised interaction sphere embraced the southern end of the Central Solomons extending south to the Banks Islands, and would have included Tikopia and perhaps Anuta. Cherts from Malaitan and Ulawan sources moved into the region through the ceramic phases, and Banks Island volcanic glass shows up in all periods – attesting to continuous contact with Northern Vanuatu. There seems to have been some contraction during the Lapita period, and that trend apparently continued until the historic-period pattern of interaction was established. Chert which, during the Lapita period, was predominantly sourced from Malaita and Ulawa along with a small quantity sourced to the Duffs, is not reported from the late-period sites excavated by Yen, and it is perhaps significant that McCoy and Cleghorn (1988) do not report any from the Dai village site. Some volcanic glass from the later period sites has been provisionally assigned a Banks Island source – indicating interaction to the south, possibly through Vanikoro – although modern Vanikoro people professed no knowledge of the Banks Islands until the mission period (Davenport, 1964a:135).

Figure 6.34. Red feather money units photographed in use in Santa Cruz in the 1960s by William Davenport. (Copyright 2005 University of Pennsylvania Museum of Archaeology and Anthropology)

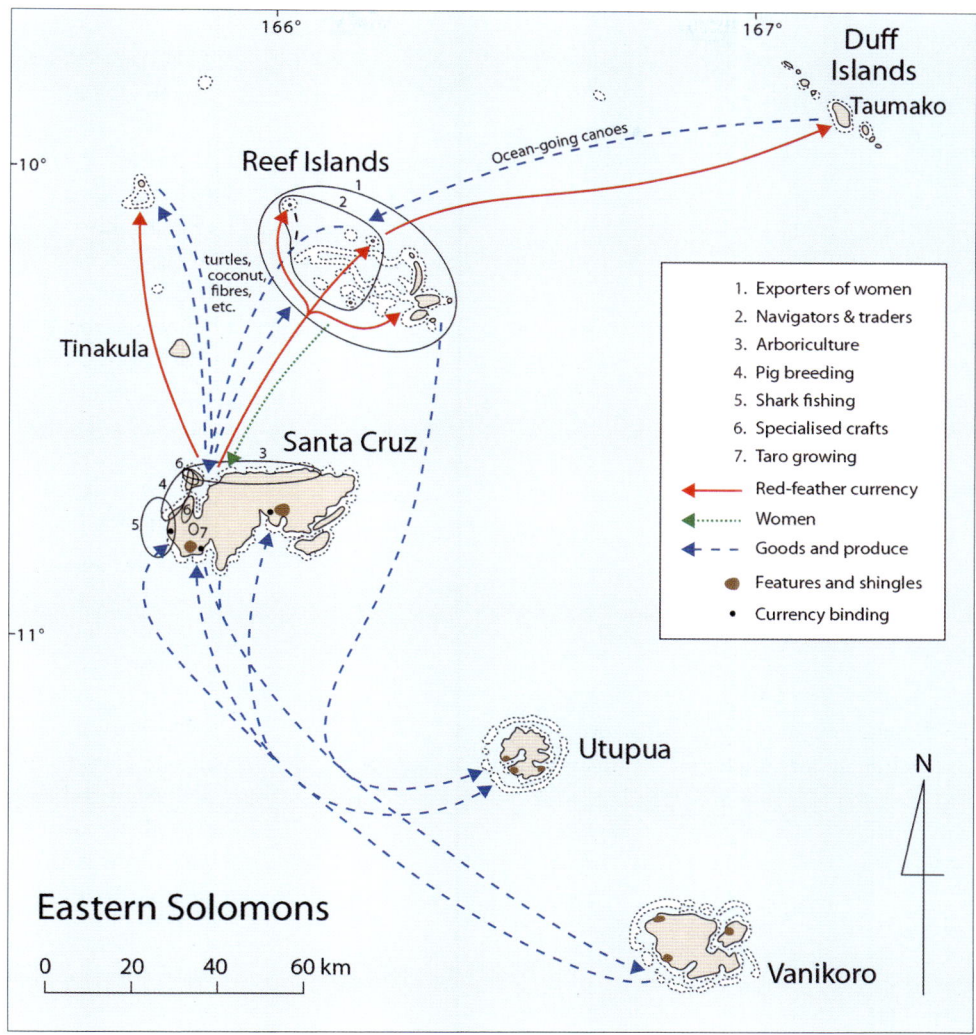

Figure 6.35. A model of the red-feather money cycle (after Davenport, 1962).

In the historic past the Reef–Santa Cruz Islands have been part of the well-known red-feather money exchange system (Beasley & Jones, 1936; Davenport, 1962; Pycroft, 1935). Belts made of red feathers from the scarlet honeyeater, *Myzomela cardinalis* were made up into long coils (Figure 6.34); each coil used the feathers of around 350 birds that probably all died in the process, although there is debate on this point (Houston, 2010:63). These coils were manufactured in Santa Cruz and circulated within an exchange system that stretched from the Duff Islands in the north, through the Reef Islands, Santa Cruz, Utupua and Vanikoro (Figure 6.35). The red-feather money was used in the purchase of items such as pigs; it was also paid as bride price, and it was used in a range of ritual and quotidian services. Given the perishable nature of these exchange valuables it is unlikely that archaeology can inform directly on this system, but it may be able to provide indirect evidence of the trade that accompanied such interactions.

Although the web of interisland exchange that sustained the red-feather system included the Duff Islands (Taumako), the Reef Islands and Santa Cruz, as well as Utupua and Vanikoro to the south, the core of the historic system involved very frequent interaction within the Reefs and Santa Cruz where the red-feather money circulated in direct support of the subsistence and prestige economy. Interactions with the remote end-points of the system appear to have been more specialised and less frequent. They involved sailing voyages on large canoes by men of the Western Reefs who traded red-feather money to the Duffs for te puke sailing canoes (Figure 6.36), and shell beads to Utupua and Vanikoro for unprocessed feathers (the latter islands were outside the red-feather money system). Historically there seem to have been no regular ties to the Central Solomons other than occasional drift or accidental voyages (Davenport, 1964a).

Figure 6.36. Te puke canoes used in the trade cycles of Te Motu Province (Eastern Solomons), photographed by William Davenport in Santa Cruz in the 1960s. (Copyright 2005 University of Pennsylvania Museum of Archaeology and Anthropology)

The chronology of change in the Reef–Santa Cruz sphere of interaction awaits more detailed dating and material analysis of the post-Lapita period sites in the region, in particular that from the Mdailu (SZ-33) and Növlaö (SZ-47) sites. The loss on Vanikoro, in 1788, of two French frigates under the command of Comte de Lapérouse provides a unique opportunity to examine the distribution of the iron and other European goods from the wrecks over the 40-year period before Peter Dillon recorded the wrecks while investigating the fate of Lapérouse. Clark (2003) has argued that the distribution to Vanikoro, Utupua and Tikopia, but not to Santa Cruz, marks the distinction between formal exchange network relationships between Vanikoro and Santa Cruz and informal and more opportunistic networks among the other islands, including the more distant Tikopia.

Polynesian influence in Reef–Santa Cruz

The Reef–Santa Cruz Islands were colonised by Lapita, and many aspects of the Lapita tradition persisted long after the decorated pottery was lost. The plainware tradition was Lapita-derived, and the shell tool and ornament complex that spans the sequence was introduced by Lapita – if not necessarily a Lapita innovation. Polynesian-speaking (Pileni [Vaeakau–Taumako] language) communities migrated into the Reef Islands and introduced new traits, including certain stone adze forms and probably the breadfruit fermentation pit. They also adopted practices that are definitely non-Polynesian in origin and this has resulted in the emergence of an identifiable culture area that cross-cuts all linguistic boundaries. There have clearly been a number of migrations into the Reef–Santa Cruz region but there is no archaeological evidence to support the idea of large-scale migrations or population displacements that the current linguistic and biological diversity implies (Doherty, 2007:473).

Taumako

After a survey by Roger Green in 1970 as part of the SESP, Leach and Davidson carried out major work on Taumako in 1977. They described a four-phase sequence for the island (Leach & Davidson, 2008:296).

Tavatava period (3000–2400 cal BP)
This is the Lapita colonisation phase represented by the excavations at the Tavatava cave site – the only representative site of this period located on Taumako (see Chapter 5). The

material culture bears a strong resemblance to that of the Kiki Phase in Tikopia and, to a lesser extent, to Zone E on Anuta (see below). We also note the close agreement with the dates, and this strongly suggests all three outliers were settled as part of the same expansion of late Lapita voyaging, perhaps out of Vanuatu to the south.

Pig, dog and two species of rat (*R. exulans* and cf. *R. praetor*) were present in the Tavatava period and throughout the sequence, which suggests they were introduced with the first arrivals. Chicken was absent, however. The fish assemblage was quite diverse compared to later periods, and Katsuwonidae and Thunnidae – both pelagic species that are caught offshore on lures – appeared only in these early levels. Turtle and bird were both present in Tavatava-period deposits but at low density. In relation to turtle, this is an interesting contrast with the Reef–Santa Cruz, Tikopia and Anuta settlement phase sites, where turtle was an important food source.

Lakao period (2400–1000 cal BP)
The Lakao phase is represented by what is thought to have been a small village occupation outside the cave site at Tavatava. The site consists of a build-up of coral gravels from a series of house floors, spanning what was possibly a continuous occupation of 1400 years (Leach & Davidson, 2008:296). The material culture of the Lakao period does not appear to be greatly changed from the Tavatava period, although the density of artefacts was very low. The period is, however, marked by the appearance of a new artefact form – a cowrie shell vegetable peeler, which indicates the importance of crop production. The faunal assemblage was marked by a lower relative abundance of the molluscs *Nerita*, *Haliotis* and *Asaphis*, but both dog and pig were still present.

Namu period (1000–200 cal BP)
There are three sites dating to this period: Ana Tavatava (Layer 3A), Kahula and the large burial ground of Namu. The material culture of the Namu period is particularly well represented from the Namu burial site, which contained a rich array of personal ornaments, and from Kahula, where more utilitarian items, including shell and stone adzes, were recovered. The faunal assemblage suggested general continuity with previous periods in terms of fishing and shellfish gathering. Presumably chicken was introduced sometime in the Namu period, as Quiros was provided with fowl when he visited in 1606 (Markham, 1904:230).

The excavators grouped Layer 3A at Ana Tavatava with Layer 3B, but with some uncertainty because the 3B artefacts were similar to those from Layer 4 (Tavatava period) (Leach & Davidson, 2008:297). Layer 3A is included in the Namu period on the basis of the radiocarbon dates, but contained little in the way of material culture or faunal remains to greatly advance an understanding of change from the Tavatava period.

The Kahula site was a low mound that contained several circular stone enclosures and was covered with a variety of occupation debris, including artefacts (Leach & Davidson, 2008:255). The function of the stone-walled enclosures was never resolved, but the nature of the other finds in the site suggest it was a general habitation zone of some sort. Excavations revealed an assemblage that expanded on the Namu material by providing a good sample of the non-ornament classes. A range of shell adzes were located that were comparable to assemblages from the Reef–Santa Cruz and eastern outliers. Three stone adzes were also recovered: these were in characteristic Western Polynesian forms and could all be assigned to one or other of the Samoan adze types defined by Green and Davidson (1969) although, on petrographic grounds, the excavators also thought they could be from Samoan sources (Green & Davidson, 1969:259; Leach & Davidson, 2008:430). Geochemical analysis of these adzes has supported a Samoan origin (Best et al., 1992). Stratigraphically, the adzes at Kahula appear in the earliest levels, which would make their appearance on Taumako slightly earlier than the appearance of Western Polynesian stone tools in Tikopia (see below). Perhaps this signals the commencement of the voyaging phase out of that region. Shell ornaments overlap those from Namu, but are not as varied or abundant. A small assemblage of arrow or spear points was found: similar items are known from northern Vanuatu and Santa Cruz from the early historic record (Leach & Davidson, 2008:269).

The Namu burial ground is a low mound about 7–8 m in diameter and standing about 70 cm above the surrounding surface. It contained the skeletal remains of over 200 individuals, of which 190 individuals were brought to New Zealand for study. (The human remains have subsequently been returned to the Solomon Islands National Museum in Honiara for repatriation to Taumako.) The burials appear to have been placed either on the ground or extremely close to the surface, as there is no evidence of either burial cuts or intercutting of graves (Leach & Davidson, 2008:142). The individuals were buried with a wealth of grave goods that are illustrated and described in Leach and Davidson (2008:149–200). The grave goods are mainly personal ornaments, including tavi shell discs of *Tridacna*, *Conus* and *Nautilus* discs and pendants, *Trochus* arm rings, ivory reel necklace units, various cowrie-shell limb ornaments, strings of drilled flying-fox teeth, and the remains of what may have been red-feather money from Santa Cruz (Leach & Davidson, 2008:200) (Figure 6.37). Many of the items were of forms that were familiar to the Taumako workers on the site, and this assemblage, which spans the last 450 years or so of prehistory, represents the development of the ornament tradition as described in the ethnographic literature of the wider Reef–Santa Cruz region. Tavi, for example, are similar to the *Tridacna* breast pendants that have been described by Beasley (1939) on Santa Cruz and which exist in various forms throughout the wider area as far as Tikopia (Firth, 1951); today similar examples are made with turtleshell fretwork overlay. There is also evidence of change in the use of ornament types, however. The workers at Namu were very clear that tavi were worn only by men, yet they were found in the burial layer associated with men, women and children – although that is not necessarily an indication that they were worn by women and children in life.

The Namu burial site contained an important collection of shell adzes (12 *Tridacna* and two *Cassis*). Only one of these was unequivocally associated with a burial; but the high proportion of complete forms in comparison with other assemblages from the island suggested to the excavators that these were probably burial items (Leach & Davidson, 2008:193). Namu also produced a single small potsherd that contained feldspathic temper sand and was almost certainly imported (Leach & Davidson, 2008:301)

All the Namu burials were laid on their back and aligned with the head inland and the feet facing towards the beach, and there were other subtle variations in orientation and body position that indicated the presence of specific burial norms (see Leach & Davidson, 2008: Table 6.10). One particularly interesting observation was the apparently deliberate mutilation of hands and feet after death. A conservative estimate suggests that this had occurred in 27 of the 190 burials, and it cannot be ruled out in an additional 78. Given the difficulty of removing hand and foot bones from a fleshed corpse it is likely that the removal took place after the body had partially decomposed – which suggests a custom of exposure of the corpse for some time before burial. This is not uncommon in many parts of Melanesia.

Tahua period
The Tahua period is the historic period commencing with the arrival of European influences on Taumako life, around 1800 AD. This was not explored archaeologically.

Tikopia

The Tikopia sequence, described by Kirch and Yen (1982), outlines the effects of Oceanic production systems on island ecosystems: it is a case study of the domestication of an island environment. The four-phase sequence documents the colonisation of the island, the early effects of forest clearance and the expansion of swidden gardening on lowland landscapes (Figure 6.38). As the Tikopian communities settled in, their production systems changed. This was partly to take advantage of the new zones opened up through forest clearance and erosion, and partly in response to the losses of some species as a result of hunting and other indirect effects of humans in the landscape. Cross-cutting the influences of these feedback processes, Tikopia also experienced major population movements that affected core aspects of social life, including economic systems and technology. Kirch and Yen's analysis drew heavily on the work of Firth (e.g. 1936, 1959, 1961, 1967), which formed an ethnographic baseline for the study.

Kiki Phase (2900–2100 cal BP)
This is the Lapita phase discussed in some detail in Chapter 5. It represents the occupation of a pristine island by Lapita settlers who brought with them a ceramic technology that included dentate stamp decoration. The pristine nature of the environment is reflected in the presence of turtle and large molluscs in the middens, and in the bones of forest and sea birds, including megapodes. During the Kiki Phase the island was only about 72% of its total 1970s area; the change was the result of erosion processes that began with the introduction of forest clearance and swidden agriculture (Kirch & Yen, 1982:325). The settlers brought pig, chicken, dog and rat, and the presence of *Cypraea* shell abraders and anthropophilic land snails associated with crop plants is further indirect evidence – along with the sedimentation record – for the presence of horticulture. The Kiki Phase communities were not isolated: imported material included chert, possibly from the Malaita or Ulawa sources (Sheppard, 1996), metavolcanic rock from the Central Solomons, a few pieces of obsidian from the Bismarck Archipelago and volcanic glass from the Banks Islands in Vanuatu.

Sinapupu Phase (2100–c. 800/500 cal BP)
The transition from the Kiki to the Sinapupu Phase was sudden and dramatic. According to Kirch and Yen (1982:329) it represented the arrival of new influences from Vanuatu to the south, as well as changes in the environment, which affected production systems. They listed the most striking differences between the Kiki and Sinapupu phases as follows:

1. Cessation of local manufacture of pottery and the importation of an incised, Mangaasi-style ceramic ware characteristic of Vanuatu.
2. The abandonment of certain ornament types (*Spondylus*

THE LAST 2000 YEARS

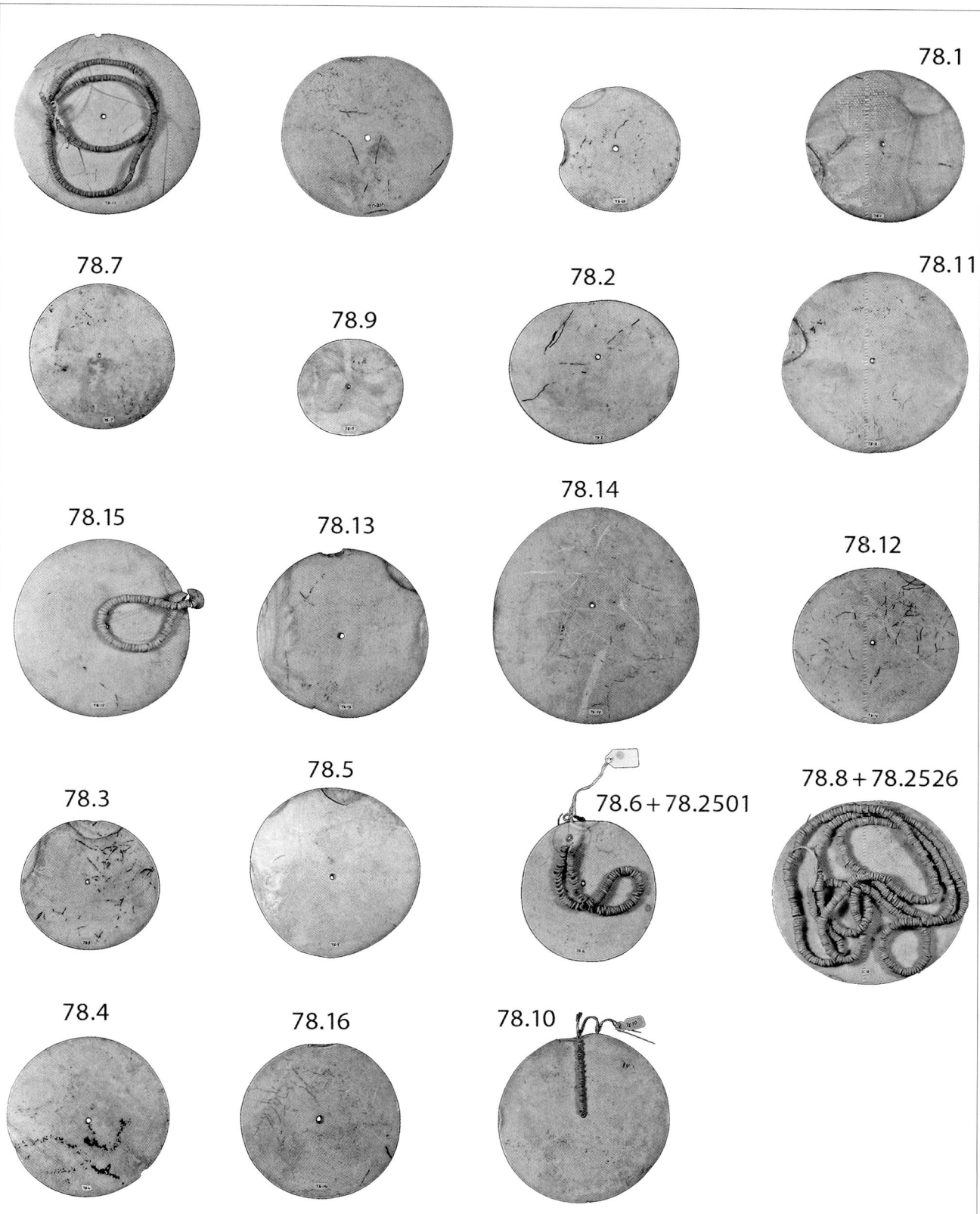

Figure 6.37. A selection of tavi ornaments from Namu; a full reference to the artefact number and provenance can be found in the original (Leach & Davidson, 2008: fig. 6.13) from where this illustration was taken with permission.

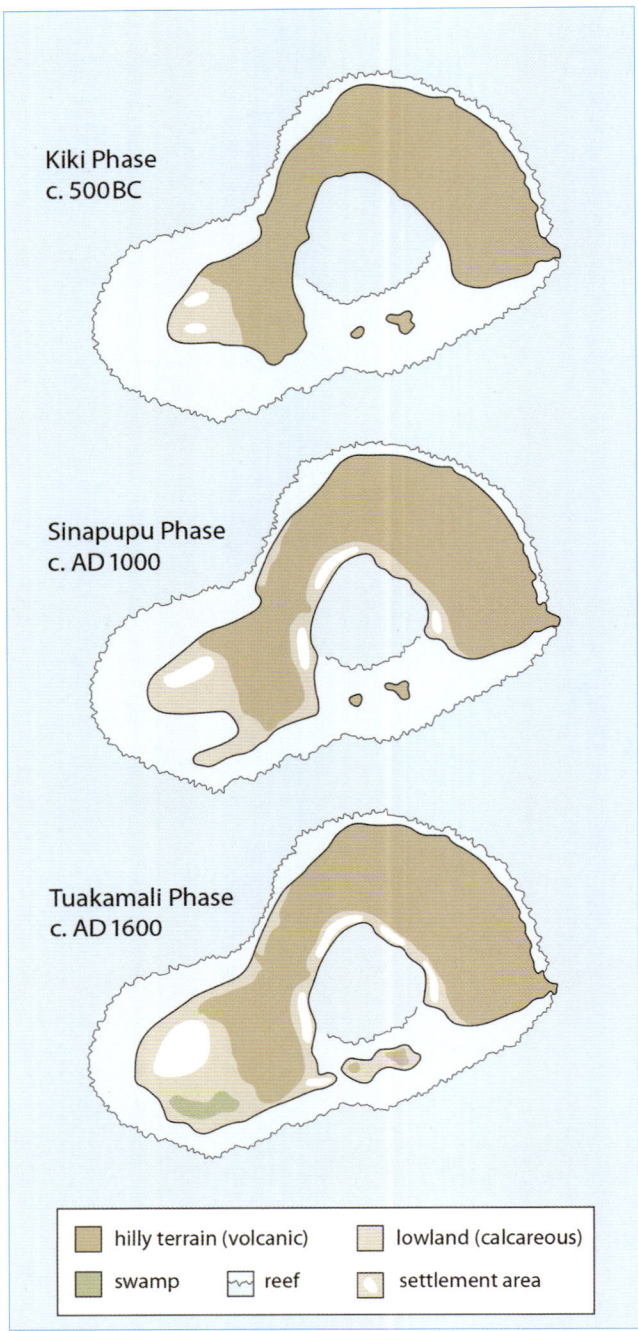

Figure 6.38. The Tikopia sequence (after Kirch & Yen, 1982).

migrants – although there is no suggestion of cultural replacement. The transition from decorated Lapita to incised-ware ceramics occurs more generally in the pottery traditions of Remote Oceania and has parallels in the ceramic sequences of the Bismarck Archipelago and in the Western Solomons (see above). Bedford (2006:181–83) has reviewed the putative connections to Vanuatu and has concluded that there is now no clear basis for this assignment based on either petrographic or stylistic grounds, and that the earlier arguments linking 'Mangaasi-style' to a widespread post-Lapita ceramic tradition are not well supported (see also Bedford & Spriggs, 2008; Clark, 1999). The appearance of an incised ceramic phase, in our opinion, owes more to the loss of dentate stamping and the retention of incision and appliqué, which are common in the Lapita decorative repertoire, than the 'appearance' of a new style. The absence of the incised-ware phase following the loss of Lapita decorated wares in the Reef–Santa Cruz Islands is an interesting phenomenon. It suggests that the forces driving ceramic change were not uniform throughout the region. This regional variability developed despite the fact that contact between the eastern outliers and the Reef–Santa Cruz region continued throughout the post-Kiki phases.

The economy of the Sinapupu Phase seemed to involve expansion of the terrestrial production system and, at first, the increased importance of pig husbandry. Late in the Sinapupu Phase pig was entirely abandoned.

Tuakamali Phase (c. 1200–c. 1800 AD)

The Tuakamali Phase is the Polynesian phase and represents the beginnings of modern Tikopian society. The landscape underwent major transformation during this phase and production systems responded accordingly. Arboriculture was expanded, along with taro production, and the breadfruit fermentation pits that were an important part of historic Tikopian economies appear in the archaeological record.

The Tuakamali Phase is aceramic, but many aspects of material culture continue. The most important new introductions were trolling lures, pig-tooth necklaces and various shell ornaments and bone needles – all signs of the new Polynesian influence. More direct evidence in the material culture is the appearance of adzes made of oceanic basalts from West Polynesia. The Polynesian influence is also seen in the architecture: the use of angular slabs to delineate house foundations; erection of 'god stone' uprights; and construction of marae-like ritual structures. Connections to the Banks Islands are also signalled by the presence of volcanic glass. These connections might appear to be part of a general expansion of trade or exchange systems

shell bracelet units) and the introduction of new forms (biconvex pendants).
3   The loss of turtle as part of the subsistence economy.
4   A dramatic increase in the use of pig.

The new pottery tradition is not only the most archaeologically visible change, it may signal new connections to the south and perhaps the arrival of new

(Reepmeyer, 2009) in Northern Vanuatu, or perhaps a sign of greater overall mobility at the time of Polynesian arrival in the region.

Historic Phase (1800 AD–)

The first European visitor to Tikopia was Quiros in 1606. His visit had little apparent impact but by the early 1800s metal was replacing stone tools and the society was changing. The landmark ethnographic works of Raymond Firth (1936, 1959, 1961, 1967) describe historical and 'traditional' Tikopian society.

Anuta

The Anutan sequence has some parallels with the Tikopian sequence but is not as secure, as it derives mainly from one site excavation (AN-6). It also has some intriguing differences.

The initial sequence from Anuta was published by Kirch and Rosendahl (1973b) based largely on the stratigraphy of the AN-6 site at Rotoapi village, excavated in 1971. The sequence they proposed was based on the assumption of an 'essentially uniform stratigraphic regime with three major layers' (Kirch & Rosendahl, 1973b:98). Layer III was the basal (presumably colonisation) layer, where the material culture was represented by a plainware pottery tradition with a range of *Turbo* hooks, *Tridacna* and *Cassius* adzes and various ornaments and manufacturing tools. The phase continued until about 500 AD, at which time there was a major hiatus in occupation, followed around 1600 AD by the arrival of Polynesians representing the beginnings of the modern Anutan cultural tradition. This sequence was criticised on various grounds by a number of authors (Bayard, 1976; Davidson, 1974, 1975) and, unable to re-excavate for logistical reasons, Kirch reviewed the original field notes and published a revision of the sequence (Kirch, 1982). The revised sequence was based on the realisation that Layer III was not uniform; instead it consisted of three stratigraphic horizons, with the hiatus in occupation occurring somewhere in the upper portion (Kirch, 1982:247). Correlating the various transect and test-pit excavations at Rotoapi, he reorganised the sequence in terms of five zones. The dates for the zones are ours; they are rough estimates based on a reading of Kirch (1982).

Zone E (commencement at c. 2950 cal BP)

This is the colonisation phase, as described in Chapter 5. It includes the introduction of Lapita-derived plainware ceramics with a very minor decoration component (less than 2%). Artefacts included hinge section *Tridacna* adzes, *Turbo* fishhooks, pendants, shell rings, *Trochus* armbands and vegetable peelers (the latter implying horticulture).

Zone D (undated)

Although there is a reasonably well defined stratigraphic change between the Zone E and Zone D horizons, this has not been dated and there is an overall continuity between the zones in terms of content. The use of *Turbo* hooks continues and there is a small amount of plainware pottery.

Zone C and Hiatus (2300–1500 cal BP)

The stratigraphic horizons designated as Zone C represent a relatively short period of dune construction that capped the seaward portions of the Zone E and Zone D layers. It is assumed that this was caused by a major cyclone (Kirch, 1982:248). A period of abandonment followed – thus the hiatus period is now located within Zone C.

The dating of this zone is problematical. Kirch (1982:247) estimates that the deposition of Zones E and D spanned 600 to 1000 years, which would place the commencement of Zone C dune-building no earlier, but perhaps several centuries later, than 2300 cal BP. The actual deposition of the dune sands may have been a relatively short event. The commencement date of the hiatus period is unknown and is only defined at the end point with the deposition of the Zone B materials.

Zone B (c. 1400 cal BP)

This represents the recolonisation of the island and, sometime during the Zone B phase, the commencement of Polynesian influences. Although Kirch (1982) suggests that the Zone B phase commenced around 1400 cal BP, he sees the arrival of Polynesians occurring sometime later – about 400–500 cal BP.

This revision of the Anutan sequence reconciles many of the problems of the first sequence and is more compatible with the oral traditions which suggest that the apukere (the autochthonous inhabitants replaced by the Anutan's Polynesian ancestors) were around much longer than the earlier model allowed. But it is based on a small sample and the proposed hiatus, and the Polynesian arrival event would benefit from further investigation. In our view, it seems more likely that the Polynesian arrival event on Anuta was coincident with that of Tikopia, which is more securely dated to the Tuakamali Phase commencing at c. 800 cal BP. It is interesting to note that the archaeological record of Anuta does not reflect the same levels of external contact as we see in the Tikopian sequence. There is evidence of contact with the Banks Islands, but archaeological evidence of contact with Tikopia is restricted to Zone A, despite the view of the authors that Anuta and Tikopia were probably settled as part of the same expansion of late-Lapita voyaging.

Zone A (1800 AD–)
This is the historic zone and is influenced by the same general historical events and processes as occurred on Tikopia.

Comments on the origins of Solomon Island diversity

It is commonplace to speak of Melanesian diversity, but of course diversity is determined by what is being observed and at what scale observations are being made. Linguists report around 70 extant languages in the Solomon Islands and, given the comparatively small land area, this means the Solomons is linguistically diverse. However, with the exception of 14 non-Austronesian languages, all are Austronesian, and neighbouring languages are generally very similar. The degree of divergence among the Austronesian languages is for the most part not great and an overarching cultural tradition based on a shared linguistic origin can be argued to underlie the cultural pattern (Shore, 1996). Similarly the economies of the historic Solomon Islands are, with a few exceptions – such as the arboriculture of Santa Cruz and the limited irrigation systems of the Western Solomons – almost identical non-intensive slash-and-burn horticultural systems based on dryland taro and yam crops, supplemented by the use of domesticated animals and foraged wild game and nuts. Nowhere do we see the sort of agricultural intensification that is apparent in the archaeological record in many places in East Polynesia. On top of this economy we do, however, see regionalisation expressed in patterns of interaction founded on maritime geographical propinquity, where interaction is promoted by efficient water transport. This creates systems of economic exchange which develop associated shared patterns of culture. Typically these are at adjacent ends of neighbouring islands in the chain and associated smaller islands. Good examples of this are found in the Bougainville Straits, the Eastern Solomons network linking Makira with islands to the east and north, and the network indicated by the red-feather exchange system. Such a pattern can best be predicted as systems of interaction based on nearest-neighbour (Terrell, 1986) and least-effort models. Left undisturbed, such forces should lead to regular predictable patterns of cultural and linguistic variation. However, the growth of other internal regional forces, or the impact of external forces, may distort the predicted pattern. For example, the historical accident of the movement of Polynesians west into the Eastern Solomons created an unexpected diversity unlike anything found in the Main Solomons; while in the Western Solomons the development of a powerful sociopolitical system based on headhunting, and intersecting with the arrival of a European economic structure, rearranged the linguistic map and overprinted previous diversity with a dominant cultural pattern. We describe the details of this latter case as a study of a regional evolution in the next chapter.

7

Regional prehistory in the Western Solomons: Process and history

The setting

The Western Solomons is dominated by the islands of the New Georgia Group. These include New Georgia itself as well as Vangunu, Gatokae, Rendova, Kolombangara, Ghizo, Vella Lavella, Ranongga, Tetepare and Simbo (Figure 7.1) . Along with the Shortland Islands this set of islands makes up the modern Western Province. In this study we have grouped the Shortland Islands with the Northern Solomons and included Choiseul and Santa Isabel within the Western Solomons. The reason for treating Choiseul and Santa Isabel as part of the Western Solomons is that they maintained strong cultural ties with the other islands of that grouping, and were part of a well-defined Western Solomon Island sphere of interaction in late prehistory. Choiseul and Santa Isabel are poorly known archaeologically; the best surveyed regions are the eastern end of Choiseul and the western (Kia) end of Santa Isabel, plus the islands in the strait between those two islands. That region lies less than 60 km from north New Georgia and Vella Lavella, and during late prehistory and into the historic era there were strong cultural ties between these regions.

European visitors in the nineteenth century seem to have arrived in the Western Solomons during a period of great political upheaval, and the distribution of the indigenous populations they encountered was strongly influenced by those events. Key among these events was the rise of the Roviana Chiefdom and the expansion of warfare and headhunting associated with the Roviana politico-religious system. Oral traditions and historical records (McKinnon, 1975; Sheppard et al., 2004) tell of drastic reorganisation of settlement patterns in the Santa Isabel region as a response to headhunting and the abandonment of entire regions (White, 1991). Indeed, some large islands were abandoned at that time and remained unoccupied well into the nineteenth century. For example, early European visitors reported that Kolombangara had a limited population in the mid-nineteenth century, and the modern provincial capital of Ghizo and the island of Tetepare had been recently abandoned. In fact the nineteenth-century expansion of Roviana politics is still felt in the region; at 110 km^2, Tetepare is one of the largest unoccupied islands in the Pacific today (Thomas, 2009).

As discussed in Chapter 4, the New Georgia Group was formed by comparatively recent volcanism and most islands have one or more high volcanic centres. Kolombangara boasts the highest peak at 1770 m, but the interiors of the islands of the Western Solomons are generally hilly rather than mountainous and are cut by small rivers and streams. Most of the islands are narrow, so the centre is never more than half a day to a day's walk from the coast. Tradition tells of a longstanding distinction between coast and bush people in the past, but today only Choiseul and Santa Isabel have any inland settlements, and even on those islands all communities are closely connected with the coast, both physically and socially. The interiors of the large islands of New Georgia, Vella Lavella and Rendova are largely uninhabited today, but they contain a record of a more extensive use of the inland in the past.

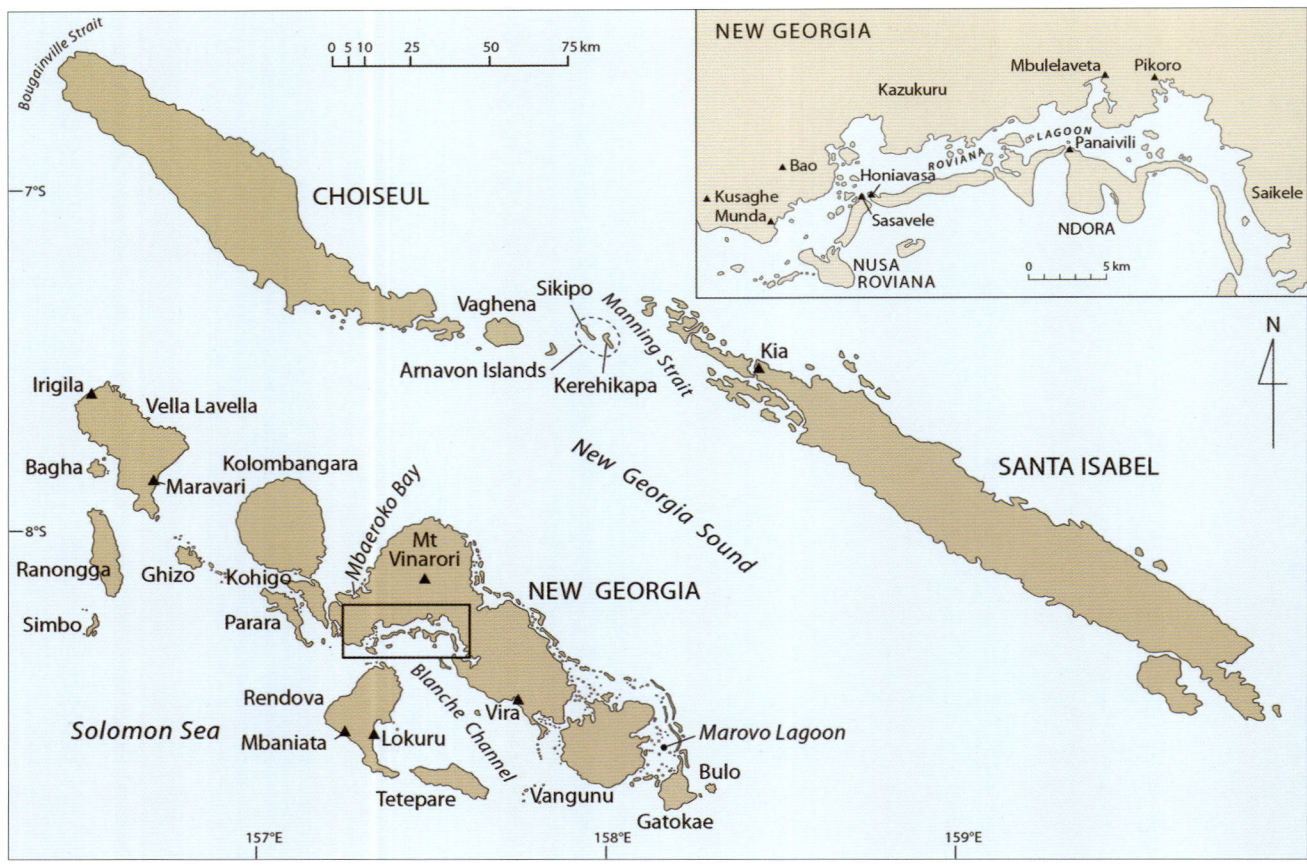

Figure 7.1. The location of archaeological sites in Western Solomons discussed in text.

The interior of the islands is heavily forested in a lowland rainforest similar to that of island Southeast Asia and New Guinea (Malesia), although with a more impoverished range of taxa (Whitmore, 1969:261). Logging companies have had a major impact over the last four decades (Figure 7.2), but there are still extensive tracts of 'pristine' forest. Yet even these apparently undisturbed tracts of forest are actually the product of 'strong disruptive influences operating on a species-poor flora' (Whitmore, 1969:270), the most important of which has been prehistoric swidden agriculture and indigenous 'agroforestry' (Bayliss-Smith et al., 2003; Hviding & Bayliss-Smith, 2000; Whitmore, 1969:264).

The most outstanding feature of the Western Solomons' coastal geography is the sheer number and size of lagoon systems with their attendant barrier islands and mangrove-lined coastlines and waterways (Figure 7.3). New Georgia is ringed with rich inshore marine systems (Aswani, 1997), and Marovo Lagoon of eastern New Georgia is often listed as the largest such system in the world. As with the inland topography, the lagoon systems are in part a product of recent complex tectonic processes (Mann et al., 1998; Sheppard & Walter, 2009), including subsidence created by the weight of the volcanic mass. This led to periods of flooding of the coastal plains, punctuated by episodes of uplift created by subduction of the Australian plate under the Pacific plate.

Not all the coasts, however, are equally hospitable. Where lagoons are present there are also sheltered landings and arable land, along with abundant marine resources. Roviana and Marovo stand out as places with particularly favourable resources for human settlement: sheltered landings, freshwater streams and rivers, rich and varied coastal resource zones and flat to gently sloping horticultural lands. Roviana Lagoon is also located in the geographical centre of the region and its physically hospitable shores and easy access to the rest of the Western Province quickly made it the centre of European trade in the mid-nineteenth century (Bennett, 1987), just as it would appear to have facilitated making Roviana the dominant power in the region during late prehistory.

Much has been made of island Melanesia as a sea of islands and a safe voyaging corridor, and nowhere is this more true than in the Western Solomon Islands. There, most of the population can look out from their villages and see

Figure 7.2. Logging operations in Roviana from the air (photo by authors).

Figure 7.3. Roviana lagoons and islets (photo by authors).

Figure 7.4. Tomoko (mon type) war canoe in Roviana (photographer John Thurston, 1894, Munda, used with permission from the Solomon Island National Museum).

Figure 7.5. Ancestral skull shrine showing wooden skull house, Munda, Roviana, early twentieth century (photographer Rev. George Brown, 1899, Munda, courtesy Methodist Archives Auckland).

Figure 7.6. Roviana canoe house showing slots to accommodate the high stern and prow of the canoe (from Charles Woodford photographs; London Illustrated News 1889).

another island within 50 km, and often much closer. Only populations on the outer margins of the region look out on empty seas, and the historic distribution of settlement suggests that these areas outside of the internal interaction zone were less heavily populated (Sheppard et al., 2010b). Although very few places in the Solomon Islands were ever truly isolated for any great length of time, the Western Solomons does exhibit patterns of cultural homogeneity, showing some levels of independent cultural development. Thus a Western Solomon Island culture area can be defined in terms of shared elements of custom, tradition, material culture and ideology (Waite, 1990; Waite, 1979; Walter & Green, 2011). At the end of the nineteenth century most groups in the Western Solomons were participating in the headhunting cultural complex and the economic, political and religious systems that were an integral part of it. Therefore, throughout much of the region we see the use of the mon-type plank-built war canoe capable of holding 30 or more people (Figure 7.4); large canoe houses designed to hold these canoes and serve as chiefly men's houses (Figure 7.6); a common set of shell valuables used in exchange, including the bakiha (Roviana), a shell chest ornament that is a symbol of chiefly status, authority and mana (Figure 7.7); and specialised ancestral skull shrines under the control of chiefs and priests at which the support of ancestors could be invoked (Figure 7.5). Local variants of these forms were evident at the end of the nineteenth century; however, this pattern cut across all language areas, both AN and NAN, in the Western Solomons. Archaeology helps us document these patterns of similarity and variation and provides insight into the cultural processes that have strongly shaped the history of this region.

The Western Solomons is perhaps the most linguistically diverse region within the Solomon Islands (Figure 7.8). In addition to 24 Austronesian languages of the Northwest Solomonic family of Western Oceanic, there are two

Figure 7.7 Chief Ingava of Roviana with his wife; he is wearing a bakiha. Photograph taken around 1902 by Rev. George Brown (Thomas W. Edge-Partington Album 2, British Museum, used with permission).

extant NAN (East Papuan) languages: Mbilua, which is the single language on Vella Lavella; and Touo (Mbaniata), spoken on the south coast of Rendova, which shares the island with Austronesian speakers. Formerly, Kazukuru, an extinct language in the interior of west New Georgia behind Munda, was considered to be NAN (Capell, 1969); however Dunn and Ross (2007) have recently concluded it was an Oceanic Austronesian language. Roviana is the largest language group in the region and its influence is felt throughout the area, both as an early lingua franca used by the Methodist mission and, as will be discussed below, through the impact of headhunting raids on its neighbours both near and distant. As with population distributions, some of the current language distribution can be explained as a reaction to headhunting. Headhunting raids sometimes pushed populations out of areas, causing the incorporation and extinction of languages (as in the Kazukuru case); and sometimes they simply decimated populations along with their dialects or languages (White, 1991).

In 1996 the authors initiated the New Georgia Archaeological Survey (NGAS), a four-year programme of field survey and excavation in Roviana Lagoon in partnership with the Solomon Islands National Museum. The NGAS research had two aims: the first was to construct an archaeological sequence of human occupation of Roviana and adjacent regions supported by a radiocarbon chronology, and the second was to contribute to the anthropological study of Melanesian diversity and the evolution of 'traditional' Melanesian societies by documenting the development of the Roviana Chiefdom. We discuss the Roviana Chiefdom below before turning to the larger programme of sequence construction in New Georgia.

The Roviana Chiefdom

The Spanish explorers of the sixteenth century and the French explorers of the late eighteenth century visited the Western Solomons but did not leave any accounts of New Georgia or its people. The first regular contact with the West occurred at the end of the eighteenth century when the Bougainville Strait became an important route to the east for ships sailing out of Australian ports. By the 1820s British and American whalers were increasingly active in the Western Solomons as the Atlantic whaling grounds were becoming exhausted and the Pacific grounds were opening up (McKinnon, 1975:292).

In 1844 the trader Andrew Cheyne established a trading base on Simbo (Shineberg, 1971). By this time there was already a thriving indigenous trade network in the Western Solomons, and Hocart (MSS) provides a list of some of the active trading groups. According to Hocart the people of Simbo were trading with the following regions: Vesu Gogoto (Ranongga), Vella Lavella, Ghizo, Nduke (Kolombangara), Lueori, Roviana in the wide sense, Siakile, Lokuru (southeast Rendova), Hareo, Kusaghe (north New Georgia), Mbaniata (west Rendova), Hoava (central New Georgia), Marovo, Vagunu (Vangunu), Pondakana (southeast New Georgia), Viru (central New Georgia) and Panono. They also had 'head-hunting relationships' with the islands of Choiseul and Santa Isabel, which could include friendly relations with certain communities and kin relations through captives. Soon after establishing his trading base, Cheyne travelled with his Simbo guides to New Georgia (Shineberg, 1971). There, in what was probably Roviana Lagoon, he reported attacks on trading parties from Simbo, and violence directed towards himself and his crew. Thus in the earliest written accounts of both indigenous and Western trade in the Western Solomons,

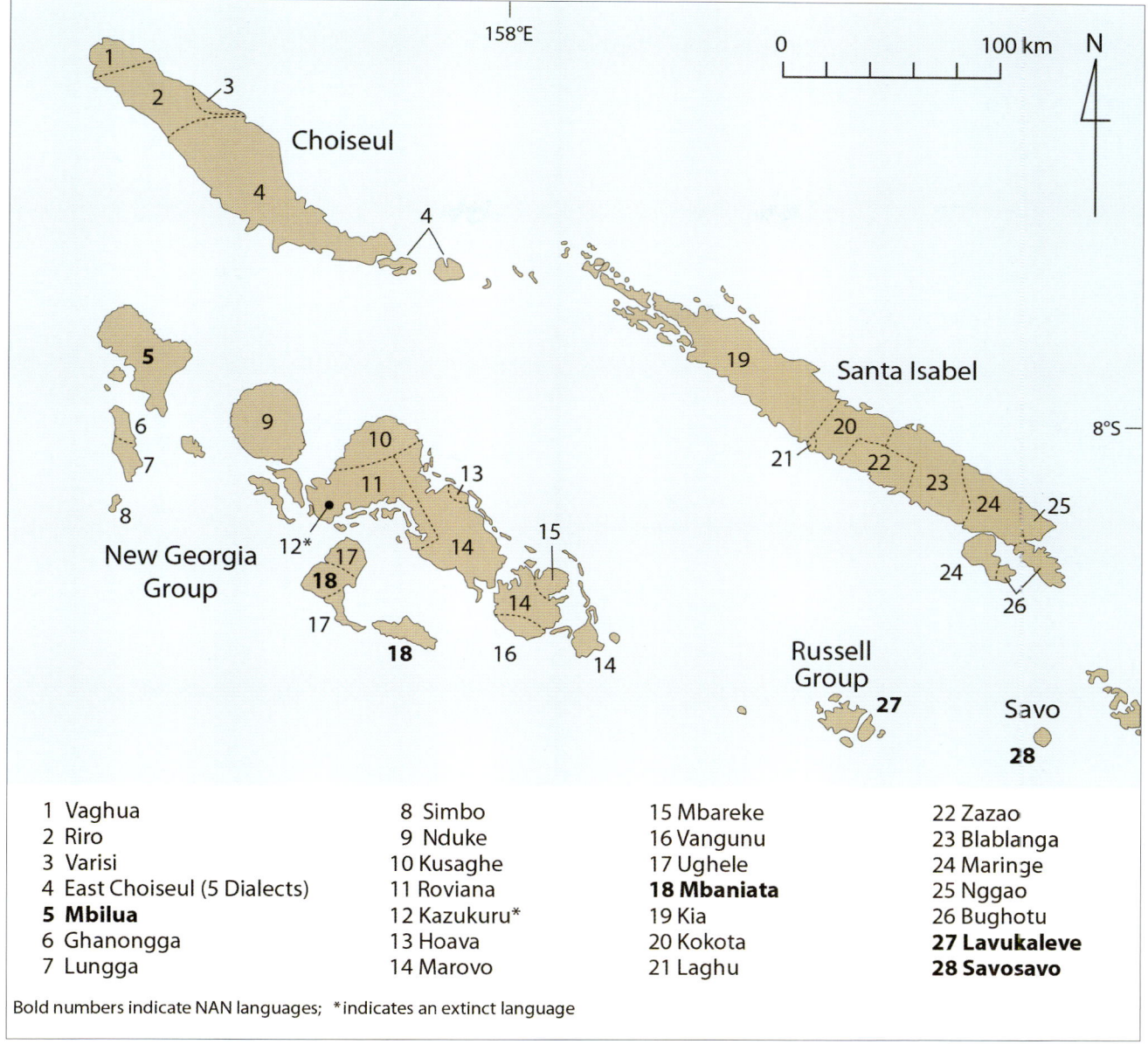

Figure 7.8 The distribution of language groups in the Western Solomons (from Sheppard et al., 2010b).

these activities were directly linked with raiding and violence.

As more European traders visited the New Georgia Group in the early nineteenth century to explore the possibilities of trade, they found the people eager to engage, and Western commerce was soon tied in to the existing exchange networks. This introduced new commodities into the local exchange systems and endowed traditional goods and quotidian products of the New Georgia environment with new values. By far the most important trade item was the shell of hawksbill turtle (McKinnon, 1975; Bennett, 1987), and by the 1850s chiefs from Roviana Lagoon dominated this trade (Zelenietz, 1979). At first the traders targeted foraging hawksbill turtles from their own inshore reefs and lagoons, but the absence of hawksbill rookeries in New Georgia (McKeown, 1977) quickly incentivised headhunter raiding parties into Santa Isabel and Choiseul, where the real target was the nesting sites in Manning Strait, especially the Arnavon Islands (Walter, 2011). These islands currently support the largest rookery for hawksbill turtles in the Oceanic South Pacific (Mortimer, 2002). The Roviana chiefs sought iron in return, and would trade for little else (McKinnon, 1975). The iron was used to fashion axes that were employed in the headhunting raids that dominated the Roviana politico-economic and religious system.

By the late nineteenth century headhunting and the turtleshell trade were entirely enmeshed, with ongoing feuds and retaliatory raiding: 'It appears that taken together trading [for turtle shell] and raiding [for slaves and heads] formed part of an interlocking system that built up its own momentum and led to an ever increasing level of violence' (Sheppard et al., 2000). In the early twentieth century Gumi, a chief of Kekehe in Roviana, related the following to his grandson regarding a raid in Choiseul that resulted from competition over the turtle grounds in the Arnavon Islands.

> One day, only a few years ago, a large party came over from [Nusa] Roviana on a turtle hunting expedition … and found the Lauru [Choiseul] men poaching on our hunting grounds. They thought we were not aware of their presence and hoped by hiding to take us by surprise or to escape in the darkness of the night. We laid our plans, and just before daylight we fell upon them. They were all killed … Hiqava [Ingava], Vonge and Miabule took part and killed many men. We took two hundred heads back to Munda. (Carter, 1981:6)

The impact of such raids throughout the Western Solomons was severe. By the end of the nineteenth century they had resulted in the depopulation of many regions, including Ghizo, Tetepare and much of Kolombangara. Traders and administrators reported that large areas of eastern Choiseul and western Santa Isabel were also emptied (Woodford, 1890:204). Among the Cheke Holo people of central Santa Isabel this time period is remembered as the grikha glehe or 'flight from death' (White, 1991). Many of these raids seem to have wiped out whole communities. White reports one Maringe man whose parents told him of a raid 'that killed so many people, and left so few survivors that they could not observe the proper burial practices for everyone. Instead, bodies were heaped in the shade of a mango tree. Those who remained began their migration to other areas' (White, 1991:89).

The Roviana people entirely dominated the trade by the late nineteenth century, and the small island of Nusa Roviana had become the religious and probably the military centre of the Roviana Chiefdom. By this time the exchange and raiding network spanned the islands of the Western Solomons (White 1979; Zelenietz, 1979), with occasional forays as far away as Guadalcanal, some 200 km to the southeast (Bathgate, 1985). The missionary Rev. George Brown described the Roviana people in the last decades of the nineteenth century as follows.

> They were a very numerous and a very powerful race in those days [1880s], and were known and feared by the adjacent islanders. They were indeed the Vikings of the Western Solomons, and the sight of a Roviana war tomoko (war canoe) caused fear and consternation whenever one of them appeared in the neighbourhood of any village on any of the larger islands of the Western Solomons. (Brown, 1909:343)

The British Navy – concerned at the increasing violence which, by this time (the 1890s), had included the death of two European traders (Bennett 1987:60) – targeted Roviana in an attempt to curtail the violence that accompanied trade activity. In 1891 the HMS *Royalist* under the command of Captain Davis (Davis, 1892) attacked villages on Nusa Roviana and the Munda coast. Nusa Roviana, in particular, was targeted because it was home to some of the largest canoe houses as well as the most sacred shrines in Roviana, including one dedicated to the mythological figure of Tiola, who taught the people how to construct war canoes (Sheppard & Walter, 1998) and was strongly associated with warfare and the defence of the island. The *Sydney Morning Herald* (12 December 1891) relates that most of the skull shrines, houses and canoe houses in the western part of the lagoon were destroyed and approximately 150 war canoes were burned – although those figures are likely exaggerated (Lawrence, 2014:156; Schneider, 1996:114).

From about that time the political centre appears to have shifted from Nusa Roviana to Munda, where the first European traders had set up base. It was at Munda that Ingava, the last of the warrior chiefs, resided and conducted business with European agents. Ingava's base seemed to have been spared in the British naval raids, and from Munda he organised one of the last of the large-scale headhunting raids in 1893. This was directed against the island of Santa Isabel, 170 km by sea to the northwest, and involved 500 men, 20 canoes, two English-built boats and over 300 rifles (Elkington, 1907:99). The final raid of the Roviana headhunters probably occurred in about 1900, two years before the arrival of the Methodist mission at Munda.

Given the pervasive nature of violence and raiding in the late nineteenth century there has been some speculation that these activities might have been sparked by interactions with Western commerce and technology. Certainly headhunting, and the politico-religious systems of which it was a part, thrived and expanded as a result of European trade. For example, the French explorer d'Urville asked to see skulls in the Bugotu region at the eastern end of Santa Isabel in 1838 but was unable to satisfy his curiosity (Jackson, 1975:65); yet by the 1850s headhunting was present in the region, introduced, as Ivens (1930:66) suggests, from New Georgia. However, there is no doubt that headhunting and raids for captives (McDougall, 2000) were part of the political and economic life of the Western Solomons long before the arrival of European traders. Cheyne, who was the first trader

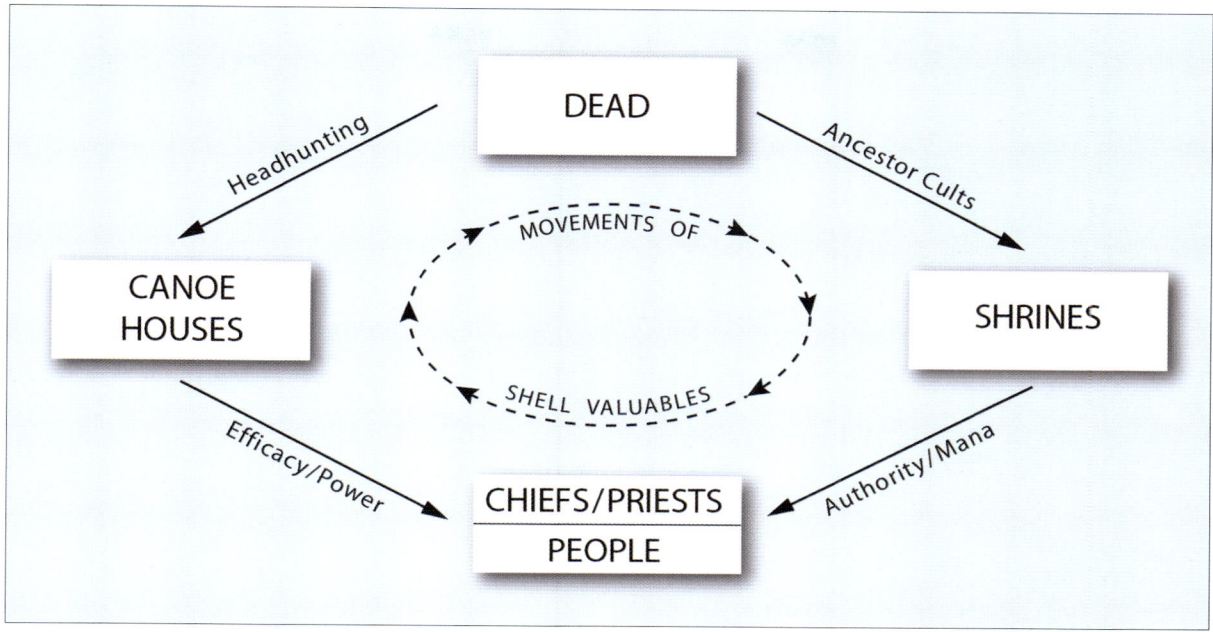

Figure 7.9. Representation of materialised power relationships and relationship to headhunting (after Sheppard et al., 2000).

in the Western Solomons, described a thriving indigenous trade in skulls and captives.

> At the time of my visit [1844], Eddystone [Simbo] natives had just returned from a war expedition, in which they had come off conquerors; and had brought home with them – including men, women, and children – no less than ninety-three human heads! On my landing, I was horrified to observe those very heads hanging along the wall-plates of their war-canoe house. (Cheyne, 1852:66).

It is clear that headhunting was an indigenous phenomenon – a key component of a ritually charged politico-economic and religious system that evolved in a regionally distinctive form in the New Georgia Group during prehistory. Central to this system were ancestor cults, the war canoe and canoe houses as sites of male power, the circulation of shell valuables, and headhunting as a source of material wealth and mana. The oral traditions and archaeological record (see below) both suggest that these elements all existed before the influence of European trade (e.g. Cheyne, 1852:66). A primary focus of the NGAS work was to track their emergence, evolution and fusion over time to form the basis of the political economy and ritual systems of the Roviana Chiefdom. To address this goal we drew on ethnographic accounts and oral histories to construct a model of the ideology of power and ritual life in late prehistoric Roviana. According to this model, in nineteenth-century Roviana society, power and efficacy derived from ancestors were materialised, channelled and circulated through an interconnected set of cultural media (ancestors–skulls–shrines–priests/chiefs–exchange valuables–skulls–ancestors) (Figure 7.9).

In Roviana cosmology the worlds of the living and the dead were intimately entwined (Sheppard et al., 2000; Aswani, 2000). The ability to act as a successful political or social agent depended on the flow of power from the dead to the living. Skilled priests officiating on the ancestral shrines could traverse the interface between these two worlds and negotiate on behalf of their patrons. Thus power could be channelled to the world of the living and expressed as mana – the central concept of power and status in Melanesian societies, and the currency of political efficacy (Codrington, 1891:118; Dureau, 2000). The authority and ability to act in all matters political, economic or ceremonial was signified in part through the acquisition of trophy skulls taken in headhunting raids; these became material tokens of ancestral sanction, and demonstrated the mana of the chiefs who funded and participated in the raids (Walter & Sheppard, 2001:297). The skulls taken on the raids were used to adorn the houses of the tomoko or war canoes – the most potent symbols of Roviana power. The skulls of Roviana chiefs themselves were conserved in the hope (ancestral shrines) and provided a material manifestation of powerful ancestors: 'Thus the canoe houses and shrines, both adorned with human skulls, were places of sacred connection between the worlds of the living and the dead, and were the sites of ritual and ceremonial acts that cemented power relations and demonstrated religious sanction for chiefly authority' (Walter & Sheppard, 2001:297).

An archaeological sequence for Roviana Lagoon

The first aim of the NGAS research was to develop an archaeological sequence for the Roviana region. Our work was guided in large part by local chiefs and our Solomon Island field crew, who took us to visit the kastom sites or tambu ples (sacred or tapu places) of which their tribes were aware, and shared stories about those places. We were also particularly interested in identifying sites associated with Lapita movement into the Solomon Islands chain. To do this we concentrated on rockshelters close to major passages and onshore transect surveys and intertidal sites. We found a strong late-Lapita 'signal' throughout the Western Solomons: wherever we looked in lagoon settings from northern Vella Lavella to Marovo Lagoon we found intertidal ceramic sites, and the limited evidence from eastern Choiseul suggests the presence of such sites in that area too, although active subsidence in the region might blur the record there.

Based on our survey results we define a four-phase archaeological sequence for Roviana Lagoon (Figure 7.10). The first two phases have been documented in earlier chapters. We summarise this material briefly below, then focus on the Munda Tradition, whose two periods trace the emergence of the Roviana Chiefdom.

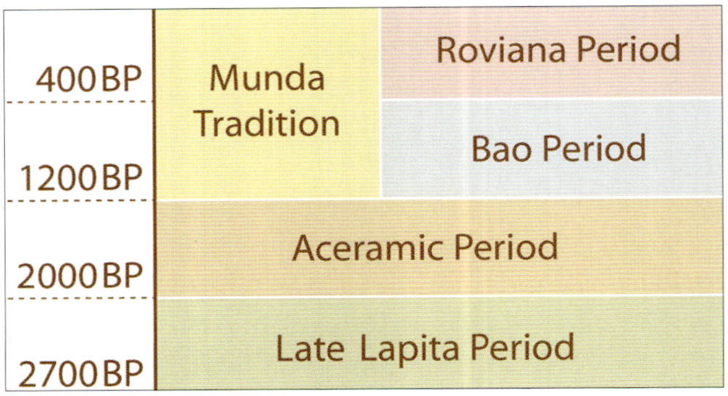

Late Lapita period

The early Roviana record was summarised in Chapter 5, where we showed that a spike in charcoal from pollen cores suggests the commencement of gardening around the lagoon edges c. 2700–2600 cal BP. The ceramic sites associated with this early evidence of gardening are predominantly intertidal. We have found ceramic evidence of land-based sites possibly from this period only in very disturbed deposits in the village of Irigila in north Vella Lavella, and in surface scatters around Nyamae village on eastern Ranongga, and on Sikopo Island in the Arnavon Island group between northwest Santa Isabel and Choiseul. It is probable, however, that food production was adopted by the first wave of Lapita migrants who moved into the interior of the islands by the end of this intertidal period. After integrating the results of radiocarbon and thermoluminescence dating on eight sherds from Roviana intertidal sites, Felgate (2003:465) has suggested that the ceramic sequence in Roviana had a minimum temporal span of about 600 years from 2550 cal BP. He has also proposed (Felgate, 2003:480–81) a set of possible seriations of the ceramics from nine sites in the western end of Roviana Lagoon; and Sheppard and Walter (2009:84) have suggested another. Although there are internal differences, both seriations suggest the Panavili site (see Chapter 5) is located towards the younger end of the sequence. A date on a

Figure 7.10. The Roviana sequence based on the work of the authors.

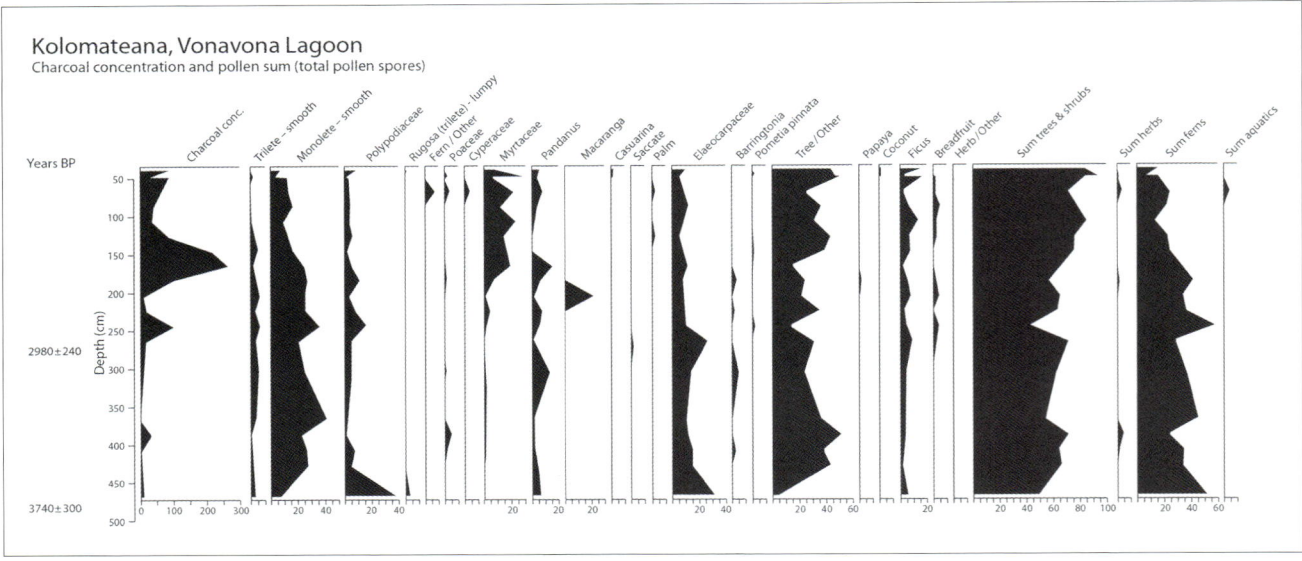

Figure 7.11. A pollen sequence from Kolomateana, Vonavona Lagoon (from Grimes, 2003).

Figure 7.12. Team members taking pollen cores in New Georgia.

charcoal inclusion in a Panaivili sherd (AA-3504, 2130 ± 90) provides a calibrated age range of 2320–1878 cal BP (95.4% HPD). Therefore current data indicates that the intertidal ceramic sequence probably ended around 2000 cal BP. Up until that time, the Western Solomons had been part of a ceramic tradition with linkages to the north into the New Ireland region and, based on temper studies (Felgate & Dickinson, 1998), outside of the Solomons across the Coral Sea to Woodlark Island in the Massim region of New Guinea (Sheppard et al., 2015b; Tochilin et al., 2012). At 2000 cal BP these linkages apparently broke, and development became more regional in nature. A similar pattern can be seen in the Bougainville Sohano ceramic series, where long-distance linkages contracted and a regionally distinctive tradition emerged in the same time period.

Aceramic period

With the virtual disappearance of ceramics around 2000 cal BP the archaeological record becomes extremely hard to identify until around 800 cal BP. We do not believe the region was abandoned; indeed it is highly probable that the prime settlement locations near passages and fresh water (which were the favoured intertidal site locations) continued to be occupied after the ceramic tradition ended. However, the lack of either ceramics or a monumental stone-working tradition rendered it effectively invisible in the wet, mobile environments of New Georgia. Only the pollen record provides some insight into human activity in this time period. Pollen records from Roviana Lagoon and Rendova to the west indicate near-continuous burning from c. 2600 cal BP to the present. At the modern village of Mbulelavata in central Roviana, a pollen sequence shows fern dominance from just after that time to the present; this suggests continuous occupation of this prime riverside location on Roviana Lagoon (Grimes, 2003:143) (Figures 7.11 and 7.12).

Munda Tradition

Based on our survey and dating results we have defined the Munda Tradition, which commenced with the emergence of an archaeological landscape dominated by the construction of stone and coral religious sites, platforms and associated residential complexes and material culture, including shell rings and other valuables. These sites are not all known or named by the people of Roviana, but they are recognised as part of the architectural repertoire of their immediate ancestors and many are known generically as hope or shrines. Most hope and – particularly in the Late Lapita period – the associated living platforms and terraces are concentrated along a narrow coastal zone, especially around the passages and on the barrier islands. Given the familiarity of these classes of site to the Roviana people, we assumed they were of relatively recent construction – possibly spanning the last 300–400 years before European arrival. Roviana oral tradition also insists that there was an earlier phase of inland habitation. There are no inland villages in Roviana today, but there is a good knowledge of bush tracks and forest resources, so we carried out a series of surveys in the forests above Roviana Lagoon and elsewhere in the Western Solomons. There we found other monumental sites that were also recognised by our Roviana colleagues as hope, but which differed in form, spatial relationships

Period	Wall construction	Human bone	Table stones	Shell valuables
Bao (n = 24)	Basalt	None	Common	Absent (n = 24)
Late Bao (n = 8)	Coral slabs	None	Uncommon	Absent (n = 3)
				Present (n = 5)
Roviana (n = 79)	Coral rubble	Present (n = 46)	Absent	Absent (n = 14)
				Present (n = 32)
		None (n = 33)	Absent	Absent (n = 13)
				Present (n = 20)

Table 7.1. A simple seriation of shrine features showing differences between Bao and Roviana Period structures.

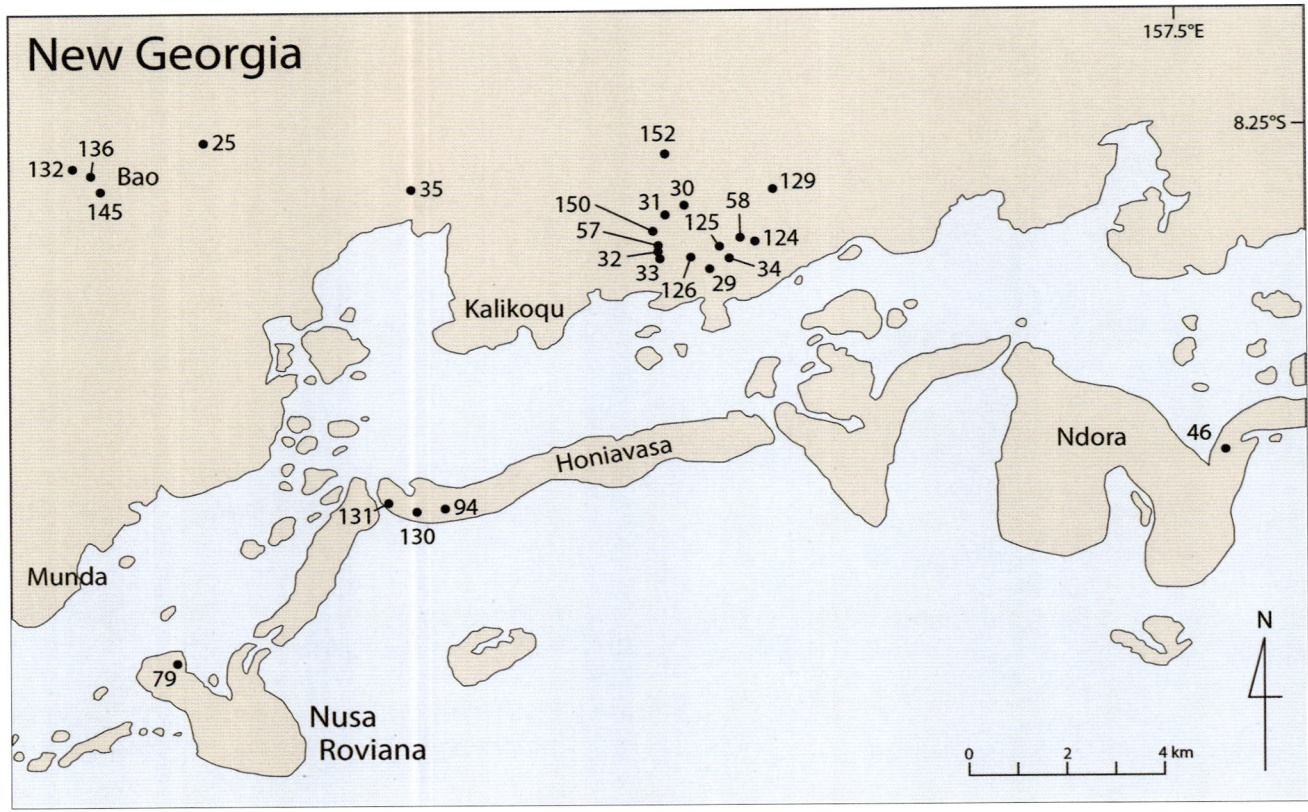

Figure 7.13. The location of Bao period archaeological sites in Kalikoqu district of New Georgia, Western Solomons.

and content. Our survey and later dating programme show that the Munda Tradition spans a period of approximately 700 years and that it traces the development of the political, economic, religious and ceremonial complex we know as the Roviana Chiefdom. We have divided the Munda Tradition into two time periods: the earlier Bao period (1200–1550 AD) and the subsequent Roviana period (1550 AD to historic). The distinction between these two periods is based on differences in the construction and content of religious features, material culture and settlement patterns. This is summarised in a simplified seriation presented in Table 7.1. These names of the two periods reflect a shift in geographic focus from the mainland interior of New Georgia during the Bao period to the coast during the Roviana period.

Bao period (1200 AD–1550 AD)

The Bao period is characterised by a highly dispersed settlement pattern that is heavily biased towards inland occupation (Figure 7.13). The most distinctive sites are earthen platforms faced with basalt slabs, and the majority of sites and site complexes are in isolated positions at some distance from presumed habitation or gardening zones. The material culture of the Bao period is not well known, especially in contrast with the Roviana period. This is because the rich material culture of the latter period is mainly represented by the votive offerings placed on the shrine sites; this appears not to have been part of Bao-period religious practice.

Conducting fieldwork in the dense inland forests of the Western Solomons is difficult, and finding archaeological deposits is especially so. Although logging in the Solomons brings its own set of problems, it facilitated our survey of the interior of New Georgia at the western end of Roviana Lagoon by allowing us access via the logging roads. In a region known as Kalikoqu (Lio Zuzulongo-Tagosaghe) (Figure 7.13) we were able, in collaboration with the local landowners, to map a series of monumental sites and to record exposures of cultural deposits, including shell midden and other settlement remains. The most common site type of the Kalikoqu interior was earthen platforms faced with basalt slabs and columns, which were scattered along the ridgetops behind the coastal flats (Figure 7.14). These hope sites are important to the Roviana people, as knowledge of their whereabouts is used to support land claims. But they are seen as surviving from a distant past and are not part of the same shrine tradition as is represented by the coastal hope.

Excavation on the Bao-period shrine sites revealed

Figure 7.14. A shrine in the Kalikoqu district of New Georgia mainland, Western Solomons.

Figure 7.15. Bao-period shrine site (Site 145), Roviana.

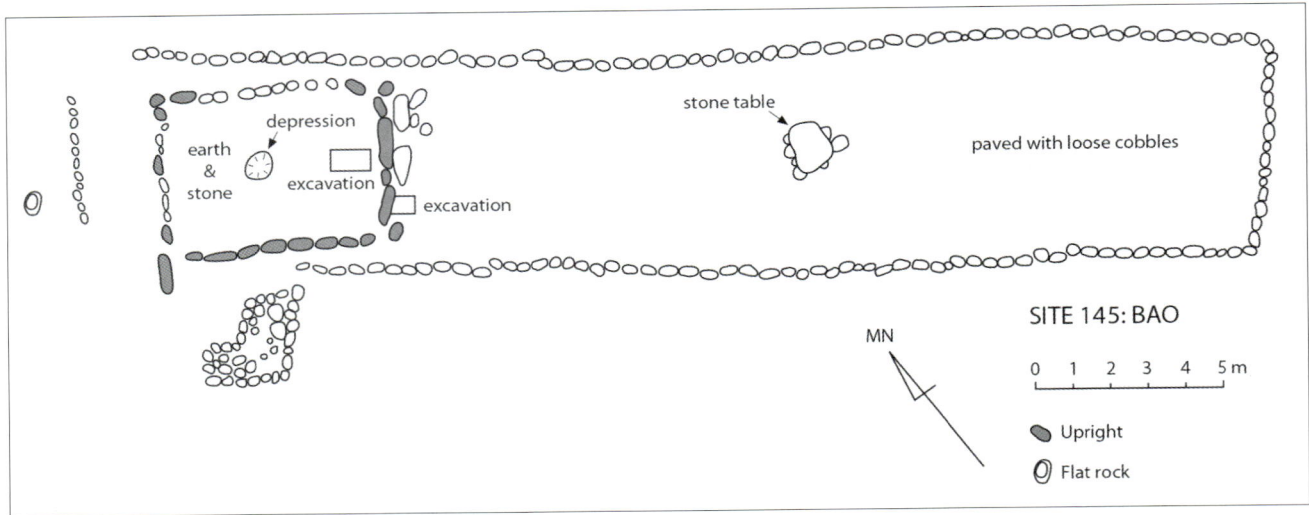

Figure 7.16. Plan of excavations of site 145 on the Bao ridge, Roviana.

them to be almost devoid of any artefacts, human bone, food waste or evidence of ovens (Table 7.1). They were, however, frequently associated with adjacent basalt 'table' stones – a basalt slab balanced on a low supporting structure formed from basalt rocks or rubble. These shrines were not obviously associated with any settlement zones or house sites; instead they sit as isolated structures or small clusters of structures along the ridgelines.

Additional survey in the Kazukuru region behind the modern town of Munda revealed similar platforms to those seen in Kalikoqu. The most important concentration was at Bao itself, where we visited a series of shrines along a high ridge that looks out towards north New Georgia and the Mbaeroko river drainage (Hall, 1964). At the eastern end of the Bao ridge is a very large, high, faced platform (Site 145) that the Roviana people consider to have particular significance in the history of their tribes. As at Kalikoqu, excavation on the Bao sites (including small-scale excavations at Site 145) failed to reveal any faunal remains, human bone or artefacts associated with the platforms or immediate surrounds (Figures 7.15 and 7.16). Dating these faced platforms is difficult but we obtained a series of dates from the platform fills (Figure 7.17). Of these the oldest is 804–637 cal BP (91.4% HPD) (NZA-10855 830 ± 60 charcoal; NZA-10856 789 ± 70 charcoal) from the large platform (Site 145) in the Bao region. All dated faced platforms are older than 1500–1550 AD.

Although most sites assigned to the Bao period are in the mainland interior, we identified at least three locations on the barrier islands where there were sites that we assigned to this period, based on architectural form, the use of slab construction and the incorporation of basalt elements; and radiocarbon dating later confirmed that these sites did

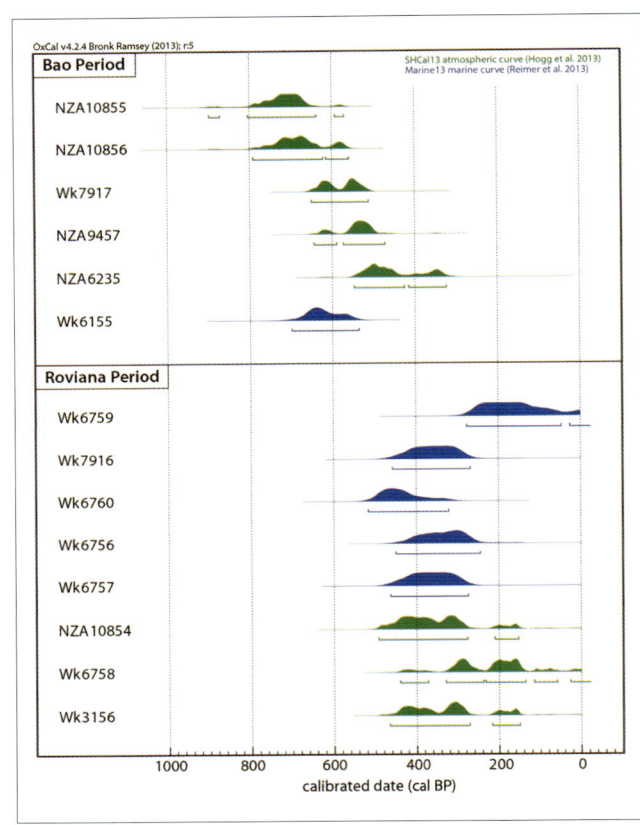

Figure 7.17. Plot of radiocarbon dates on faced Roviana shrines (Bao period) (OxCal v.4.15).

indeed all belong to the late Bao period. The barrier island sites comprised clusters of stone platforms, many of which had coral-cobble walls faced with sheet coral (in contrast to the basalt facing used on the inland shrines of the Bao period). Several of the barrier island sites also contained large uprights or structural elements of columnar basalt, some of which measured more than a metre in length and would have exceeded 200 kg in weight. There are no exposures of basalt along the mainland coastline so these stones would have been transported from the interior of New Georgia at considerable effort.

At Nusa Roviana, Site 79 is a shrine complex incorporating multiple basalt columns. On Honiavasa Island we recorded large coral-faced platforms close to what may have been a settlement zone, and on Ndora island in the eastern end of the lagoon we found a similar set of features at the Kekehe site. The Kekehe site included platforms constructed of basalt boulders that would have had to have been transported from the mainland. The basalt on these barrier island sites links them to the mainland. These sites also share the other characteristics of the mainland sites: the lack of cultural remains, ovens and skulls; and the presence of stone tables.

The Bao-period shrines of the New Georgia interior are not found close to any identifiable habitation zone. This suggests a settlement pattern involving low-density habitation around the garden land, and the placement of religious sites on prominent ridges at some distance from the domestic zones. Actual evidence of the habitation zones is slight. Above the Hura River, which is one of the larger rivers in the lagoon and provides canoe access some 5 km into the interior, large middens of lagoon shellfish (*Anadara* sp.) were exposed by road building, and a nearby road cut exposed a plainware pottery-bearing midden (Site 25) dated at 547–323 cal BP (95.4% HPD) (R-21360 468 ± 62, *Canarium* charcoal). Despite considerable walking of road cuts, test pitting out from shrine sites and surveying up rivers, we found no other evidence of inland settlement in the Kalikoqu region.

The barrier island sites of the Bao period seem to reflect a change in settlement patterns with the move to the coast. In all three of the regions where shrine sites of this period were located, they were found in fairly close association with other platforms and features: this suggested they might have been part of a generalised occupation space that incorporated both secular and sacred areas.

We have no direct evidence of the economic basis of the Bao-period settlements; however, subsistence would certainly have been founded on talo (taro) cultivation and exploitation of groves of *Canarium*. *Canarium* trees are common in the vicinity of shrines and old settlements in the New Georgia Group. Roviana people make use of two varieties of *Canarium*: okete (*Canarium indicum*), a large nut-bearing form; and tovinia (*Canarium salomonense*), a smaller form. They also distinguish between a cultivated okete and a wild form, okokete (Waterhouse, 1949:175). Taro cultivation was important until the introduction of sweet potato and the impact of the taro blight after World War II, when sweet potato came to dominate the diet (Allen, 2005). Waterhouse (1949:183) records 18 varieties of taro and notes that this list is probably incomplete. Among these is talo ruta, which is described as grown in fresh water. Small taro irrigation systems are known as ruta in Roviana, although the term does not appear on its own in Waterhouse (1949). Other than the occasional smallholding of swamp taro near modern villages, we have recorded only one small irrigation system along a stream inland from Mbulelavata (Sheppard & Walter, 2013). Local elders suggest that there may be a small number of similar systems elsewhere in Roviana, but nowhere are there large systems like those described elsewhere in the New Georgia Group (i.e. Kolombangara, Marovo, northwestern New Georgia). Roviana people note that such things are found along the larger rivers in north New Georgia in the Kusaghe region. Tedder and Barrus (1976) have reported on the large irrigation systems on the Mase River, which drains the extensive crater of Mt Vinarori that forms the central mass of north New Georgia. In total they estimated 200 hectares of irrigated taro may have existed in the Mase basin. It seems probable that similar systems existed in the other large rivers of northwest New Georgia, including the Mbaeroko river basin which drains north for 5 km from the interfluve between Kalikoqu (Lio Zuzulongo area) in Roviana and north New Georgia to the coast at Mbaeroko Bay. Most Roviana taro appear to have been grown as dryland swidden, and the extent of this may be seen in the widespread distribution of secondary forest in the interior of New Georgia (Bayliss-Smith et al., 2003). However, trade in many items was common with the Kusaghe region (Tedder & Barrus, 1976) and this may well have included taro.

Roviana period (1550 AD – historic)

The Roviana period is characterised by the appearance of new architectural forms, settlement patterns and material culture. The most distinctive site type is the coral-rubble hope (skull shrine), which was a common feature of the historic Roviana landscape and was frequently noted and photographed by early traders and missionaries (Figure 7.18). These are small, rectangular cobble constructions which supported a skull house (oru) in a variety of forms. Some skull houses represented in photos took the form of wooden boxes mounted on posts; others were constructed from sheet coral. Sometimes skulls were simply placed in crevices or fissures in upraised coral outcrops adjacent to the small platform of coral cobbles. In almost all cases a cooking hearth or oven, often rectangular and edged with cobbles shrines with different functions (Nagaoka, 1999). Many of the shrines are small and may contain only one or two skulls; however others, generally described as chiefly skull shrines, have multiple levels and shelter more than 10 skulls.

These unfaced coral-cobble shrines are commonly found along the barrier islands, often within the precincts of modern or old villages. On Nusa Roviana they are found in large numbers within former settlement areas, and many important shrines are located within a large fortified complex on the ridge that forms the central axis of Nusa Roviana. Other large shrine complexes are found on very small islands in the lagoon, opposite modern settlements. These are generally described by Roviana people as being important chiefly skull shrines. One such example is the skull shrine of Ingava, the last major headhunting chief of Roviana (Edge-Partington, 1907), whose shrine was moved from his area in Munda west into Vonavona Lagoon, where tourists today are taken to see it on Kundu or 'Skull Island'.

Fortification and settlement at Nusa Roviana

In addition to shrines, the island of Nusa Roviana is densely covered with other coral-cobble features. There is a wide variety of these within the settlement areas, including wharves on the coast, foundations for canoe houses, shell-ring production areas, walled shrine complexes and house platforms with associated ovens (Walter & Sheppard, 2001). In total we have assigned 1012 unique identification numbers to features in a 1.05 km² area that corresponds with most of the non-swamp, inhabitable portion of northwestern Nusa Roviana (Figure 7.19). Of these features

Figure 7.18. Ancestral shrine from Simbo photographed by Arthur Hocart in the early twentieth century. Labelled 'Kundahelo's garden shrine Mbulolo'. Cambridge Museum of Archaeology and Anthropology. Used with permission under creative commons licence (http://maa.cam.ac.uk/category/collections-2/catalogue/).

and filled with oven stones, was placed adjacent to the platform: oral traditions say that these were used to prepare offerings for the shrine, and faunal remains (pig, fish, etc.) were frequently found adjacent to the fire features. The hope were just one of a large number of types of coral platform found in the Roviana-period settlements. All of the hope and many of the other coral-rubble platforms contained artefacts, often in large numbers, deposited on the surface or under sheet-coral slabs and frequently in association with human skulls (Thomas, 2003). The most common artefact types are shell rings in a variety of forms (Aswani & Sheppard, 2003) including the arm rings (hokata) that warriors are seen wearing in historic photos, and bakiha, the symbol of chiefly authority, made from fossil *Tridacna* shells most probably recovered from the raised coral of the barrier islands. Other durable items found on the surface of shrines are conch shells, pieces of fossil *Tridacna* and chert cobbles imported from Santa Isabel and, on historic shrines, glass bottles, iron, broken weapons and other durable trade goods. Much of this material was deposited when broken or, in some cases, deliberately broken before deposition. Almost all of the wooden boxes and posts have rotted away and today most skulls are sheltered in small box-like containers of sheet coral on the surface of the coral-cobble platforms. Historically there was a considerable variety of

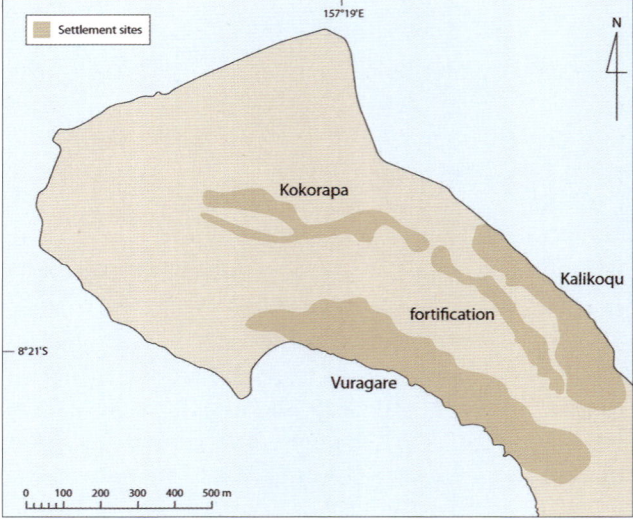

Figure 7.19. The distribution of archaeological features on Nusa Roviana Island, Roviana.

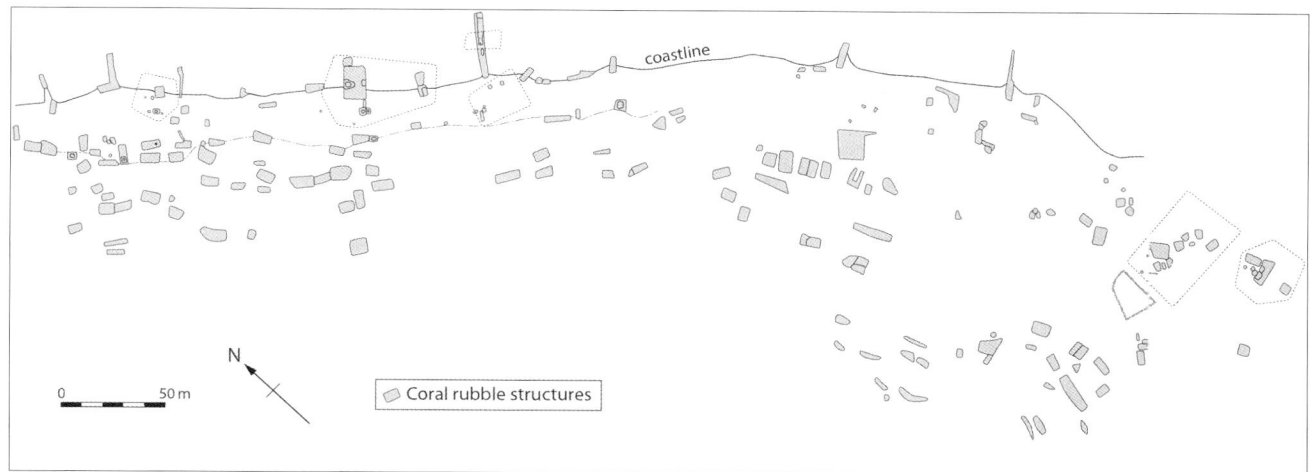

Figure 7.20. The distribution of archaeological features in the Kalikoqu section of Nusa Roviana Island, Roviana.

all but 43 are made of loose coral cobbles derived from the surface or the lagoon, or are cut into bedrock (e.g. some terraces and ditches). Many of these features comprise contiguous structures which share the same number, so the actual density is higher than the unique numbers might suggest. Although we have not generally mapped artefacts as individual items, a count of finished items of material culture (European and Roviana manufacture) in shrine features gives a figure of 1001 artefacts, of which most are finished shell rings of various forms (Thomas, 2003). The labour investment represented by the stone features is very considerable. The 783 features that have been mapped as closed polygons represent an area of 17,916.5 m². Even with a very conservative allowance of 25 cm height per feature this is a large volume of rock that has been transported and piled.

When the ethnographer Maurice Hocart visited in 1908 much of this area was uninhabited, yet it seemed to have been only recently abandoned. The burning of the villages on Nusa Roviana as part of a police action by Captain Davis of HMS *Royalist* in 1891 and the impact of European disease probably resulted in the abandonment of much of this area in the late nineteenth century.

Today archaeological features are concentrated on the coastal flat in three clusters which correlate with named sociopolitical groupings. On the east the interior lagoon side is known as Kalikoqu[1] (bay side); on the west side which looks out to the open sea is Vuragare (where the wave breaks); and on the northern end of the island where the modern village lies is Kokorapa (middle). Most features on the Kokorapa flat have been destroyed by activity during

Figure 7.21. Shrine (Site 33) on the mainland of New Georgia (Roviana) (from Walter & Sheppard, 2001: fig. 7).

World War II and by recent village growth; however a series of skull shrines remain within the modern village. We assume Kokorapa was once similar to the Kalikoqu and Vuragare settlement complexes, which contain a dense array of domestic dwelling features, shrines, wharves, manufacturing zones and specialist structures within a near-continuous low-density zone of midden and artefacts (Nagaoka, 2011).

The Kalikoqu settlement provides a model for Roviana-period coastal settlements on the Nusa Roviana coast. Kalikoqu stretches over an area of approximately 5.4 hectares. Within that space we identified 18 sites as shrines (Figures 7.20 and 7.21). Traditional accounts note four major shrine types: ancestral (skull) shrines, garden shrines, fishing shrines and shrines used in certain acts

---

1. Not to be confused with Kalikoqu district on the mainland of New Georgia, where Bao-period settlements were recorded.

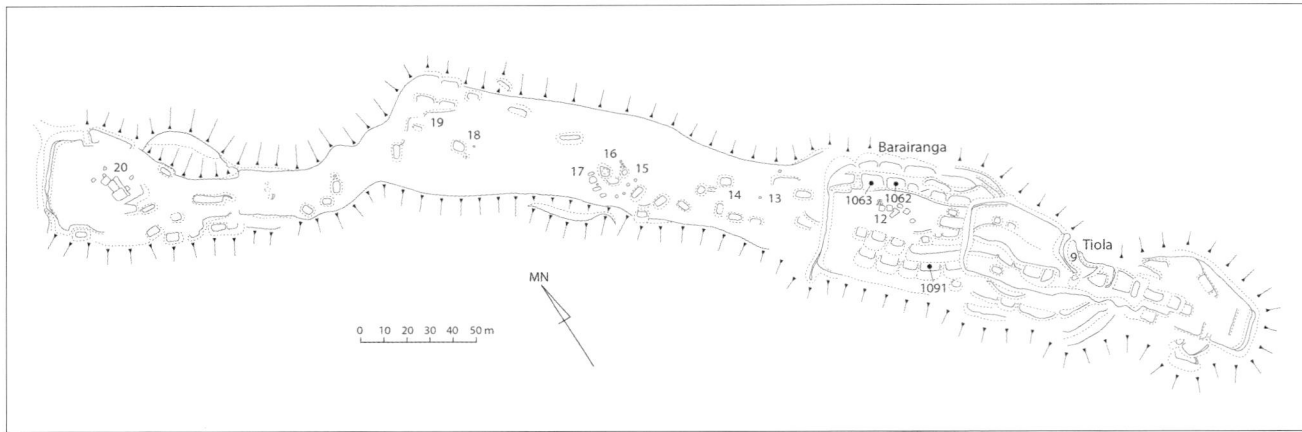

Figure 7.22. Plan of the central fortification on Nusa Roviana Island.

of purification (Walter & Sheppard, 2001:301). All the Kalikoqu shrines consisted of rectangular, square and irregularly shaped coral-rubble platforms. The ancestral shrines, of which we recorded four, contained skulls, and the other platforms were identified as shrines by the presence of shell valuables or other items in positions that suggested these were votive offerings. It is likely that other platforms recorded in Kalikoqu were also once used as shrines but no longer have visible remains of skulls, skull houses or shell valuables. One of the shrines, identified locally as a garden shrine, contained 43 broken shell rings. Many of the shrines were associated with other features – coral uprights, platforms and walls.

In addition to shrines, stone wharves extended out into the tidal zone and were often associated with onshore structures that were almost certainly canoe houses. Small artificial islets or isolated wharf features were often found nearby. Wharves and canoe houses were male precincts and played both a functional and a ritual role in Roviana society. Several of the Kalikoqu wharves reflected ritual activity through the presence of shell valuables, while others contained debris associated with the production of these items. The distribution of wharf sites along the Kalikoqu and Vuragare coasts certainly suggests their association with tomoko, but the early resident commissioner Charles Woodford also reported the use of wharves in Roviana as pens for keeping fish and turtles (Lawrence, 2014:91).

The majority of coral platforms and faced terraces in Kalikoqu were probably foundations for house structures (Nagaoka, 2011) and they contain no skulls or votive offerings. These structures are scattered over the coastal strip, often in distinct clusters, and stretch up the lower slopes of the hill. The whole area is densely covered with midden shell, and shell artefacts (adzes and ornaments) are commonly found lying on the surface.

A fourth major zone of feature concentration is on the low ridge behind the Kokorapa settlement where a fortified area extends over 700 m to the southern end of the ridge (Figure 7.22). This fortified zone (Sheppard et al., 2000) consists of a series of sectors isolated by four large stone walls that cut laterally across the ridge. The northernmost wall is a ditch and bank feature; the bank is faced and topped with coral cobbles. The second wall, 300 m south of this, is a very high cobble wall that isolates the Barairanga ('wall for shouting') area. This sector is isolated to the south by a high wall and, just beyond it, a large ditch cut into the rock at the highest point of the ridge. Between the wall and the ditch is a small area where we found the last of a series of shrines (Site 9), scattered along the ridge. Finally, at the southern end is another low stone wall, halfway down the steep slope that descends from the ridge. Other prominent features within the fortified area include shrines and probable house terraces. There is a series of terraces arranged in ranks down the slope on either side of the ridge, and the slopes are covered in many places with scattered shell.

The series of 10 shrines or hope spread along the top of the ridge within the fortification served a variety of functions. Some are traditional chiefly skull shrines but others are reported to be places of ritual associated with warfare or headhunting, or shrines associated with powerful ancestors or mateana spirits from whom the chiefly lines of Roviana descend (Sheppard et al., 2000; Thomas et al., 2001). All are named locations, and some of these names are replicated on the mainland (e.g. Liozuzulongo), suggesting affinity to regions on the mainland. The last and highest shrine, Site 9, is especially important to Roviana as it contains the remains of a dog sculpture that is reported to be Tiola, the watchman of Roviana (Figure 7.23).

Without a detailed dating programme of a much larger sample of features it is difficult to provide a chronology for

Figure 7.23. The Tiola Shrine in the fortification on Nusa Roviana Island.

the development of the Nusa Roviana settlement (Figure 7.17). However, the set of dates that we do have indicates that considerable construction was taking place throughout the island before 1700 AD. Only one of our dates has provided a 'modern' age (post-1800 AD). Taken at face value our data suggests that occupation was most intense well before the nineteenth century. The age of the hillfort is of particular interest. The main wall of Barairanga dates (Wk-6757) to c. 1600 AD or slightly earlier, and this date compares quite well with the date (Wk-6156) of the shrine oven just inside the wall and the age of the fill (NZA-10854; Wk-7916) of one of the lower terraces on the slope just below the dated shrine. Statistically none of these dates can be distinguished from one another, and together they make a strong argument for the creation of the most labour-intensive and strongest part of the hillfort at a time near 1600 AD or slightly earlier. Other segments of the hillfort may date earlier or later. Roviana elders state that an earlier tribe known as Koloi made some of the hillfort, but most was constructed after the time of the chief Ididubanara. Probably the first low wall and some of the shrines along the central portion of the site date before the Barairanga portion.

The fortification was certainly fully functional and in use right into the early nineteenth century. Roviana oral tradition indicates that warfare with Vella Lavella was common at some early point; in particular, numerous sources relate a story involving the attack by 1000 Vella Lavella warriors on the hillfort at Nusa Roviana. Rev. George Carter translated the following version from a Roviana text provided by an unknown Roviana informant: the Roviana individuals identified in this story would indicate it dates to around the time of the Roviana chief Qutu at about 1800 (Schneider, 1996: fig. 7).

During the time when Tungahanika was *mbangara* [chief] in Roviana Kokorapa there occurred a great fight at [Nusa] Roviana Island. Over 1000 men from Mbilua [southern Vella Lavella] came up and attacked Roviana Island. The Roviana leader was Nggiro. Those who came from Mbilua followed Nggevi. This man called Nggevi was part Mbilua (and part Roviana). When the Mbilua raiding party arrived, the Roviana people were on the top of the hill. There was a stone wall there. When the raiding party arrived at the shore they hid their war canoes. Nggevi went up the hill and told the people, 'A thousand Mbilua warriors are at the beach and they will follow me and attack at dawn,' he said. The people at Roviana prepared. When dawn came the army went up the hill and the fighting began. Nggevi was among the Rovianas, Nggiro went and speared the leading fighter from Mbilua and he died. The Mbiluans then ran away. The wall was broken down and the Rovianans both men and women fell on the enemy and killed them. Nggevi also fought the Mbilua people. A bold *mbangara* at Roviana, Pepeho, called out defiantly to Munda, calling Munda people to intercept the enemy. Only 20 people returned to Mbilua. (Anonymous, 1963)

Other sites on the Roviana barrier islands

Nearly everywhere we surveyed, especially in and around modern villages, we found examples of sites similar to those of the Nusa Roviana coast. Many were in small clusters; some appeared in isolated positions but were probably associated with unrecorded living zones. Nowhere along the barrier islands was there a density of domestic and ritual sites as great as on Nusa Roviana. The best example of a well-defined site complex outside of Nusa Roviana was located at the far eastern end of the lagoon, 25 km from Nusa Roviana. This was a small fortification known as Patu te Malukete on the eastern end of Ndora Island in the Saikile region (Figure 7.24). There a flat area (145 m long and 25 m wide) of upraised coral, backed by a steep 15 m cliff, is walled off by two high coral-cobble walls that run from the sea back to the cliff. The platform itself is well hidden from the sea and supports a complex arrangement of occupation and manufacturing sites.

The eastern end of the complex is defined by a coral-rubble wall 1.8–2 m in height that cuts across the coral shelf between the sea and the raised makatea cliff. It contains a narrow doorway close to the cliff and a narrow 'window' that is reminiscent of a gun-firing position. The wall is clearly defensive, and as we found a musket barrel in some rubble fill on the western end of the complex it is possible that the wall was designed for musket defence. A concentrated area of shrines, skull houses and coral platforms lies just inside the wall. Skull houses occur either as isolated

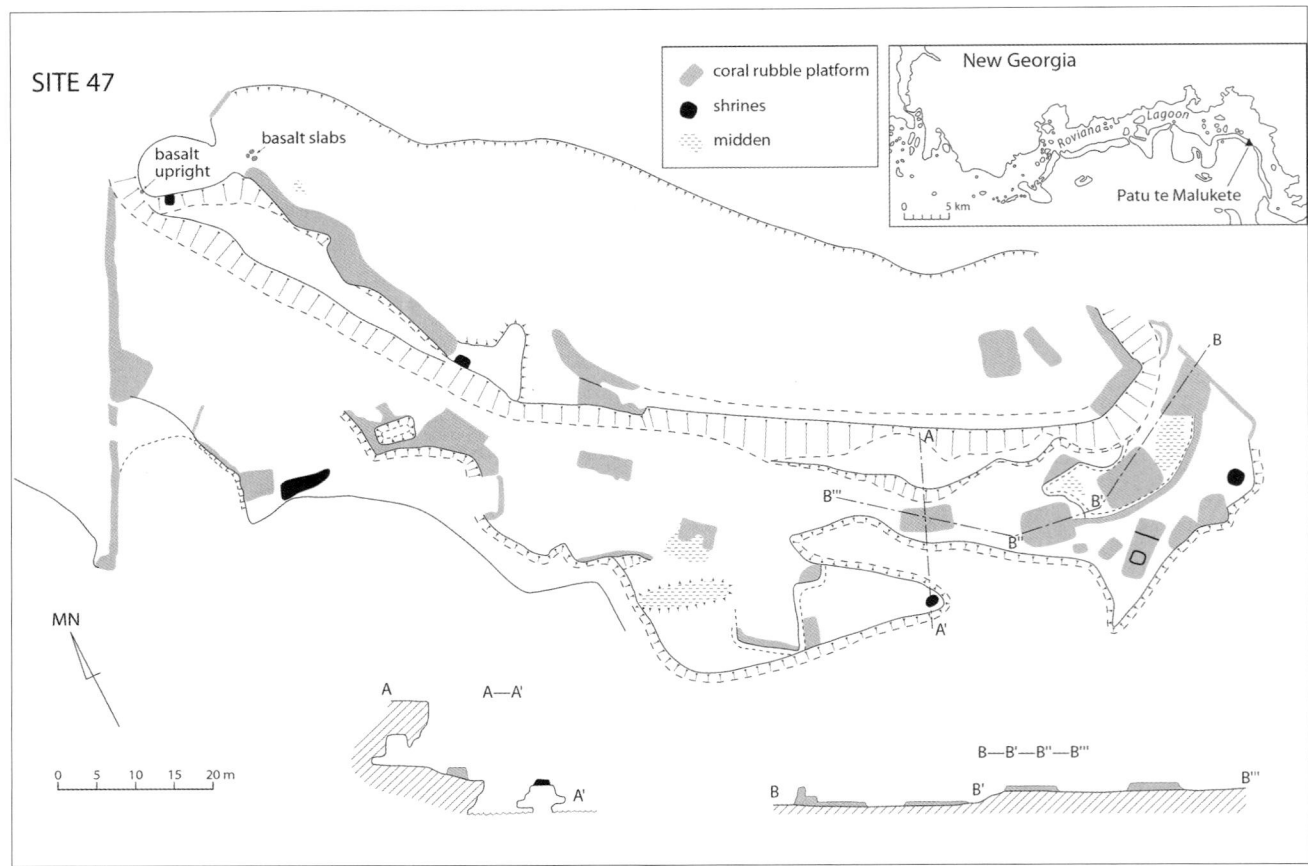

Figure 7.24. Plan of the Patu te Malukete Site in Roviana with inset map showing location of site in the Saikele District.

features consisting of coral slab enclosures a metre or so in length, placed on a foundation of coral rubble, or as similar constructions built as adjunct components on the top of larger platforms. All the skull houses contain skulls and most contain shell valuables. This portion of the site has a large and diverse range of artefacts. Whole and broken portions of fresh *Tridacna* shell occur in small clusters on the shrines and on the surrounding surface. Fossil *Tridacna*, including worked portions, is found in similar locations. Other artefacts found on the shrines include shell adzes, bakiha and various types of *Trochus*, *Tridacna*, *Terebra* and *Conus* shell ornaments that are traditionally used to decorate the tomoko. Basalt and coral uprights are located on several of the platforms, and were also found in isolated positions on the surrounding ground surface. Basalt was not as widely used here as at Kekehe, but the fact that it was imported from the Saikile mainland and used to adorn ceremonial structures suggests a continuity in its ritual significance. Several of the shrines have basalt paved sections.

Further west along the coral shelf of Patu te Malukete there are more platforms and at least one more shrine with a skull house, but the concentration of structures is less dense than to the east. About 120 m from the western wall the shelf drops down from a series of platforms, slumped walling and paved areas to a narrow bay. Here, a section of flat land between a sandy beach and the back cliff contains several platforms and a complex skull shrine built onto a remnant portion of reef. A coral-rubble wall 80 cm wide and 1.6 m high runs out from the back cliff, across the western margin of the bay for a distance of 50 m, terminating on the intertidal flats. This structure and the eastern wall serve to enclose the entire site. The wall contains a low step on the inner, eastern edge that may have served as a firing platform, and like the eastern wall it contains a narrow doorway. The bay adjacent to this wall is the only area within the fortified section of the site where canoes could be beached, and it is likely that this is where the tomoko were housed. A large platform adjacent to the shrine complex and another built into the wall may have supported canoe houses. There are also a few platforms on the top of the cliff.

According to oral accounts, in about the 1780s there was a division in the Nusa Roviana Chiefdom, at that time under chief Taebangara. His cousin the chief Odikana moved into the eastern lagoon and established Patu te Malukete (Parker, 1994). Although we have no radiocarbon dates from this site the nature of the defensive works suggests much of it dates to the nineteenth century.

The development of the Roviana Chiefdom

The oral traditions of New Georgia record the Roviana Chiefdom, with its ancestor cults and predatory headhunting, emerging out of an environment of changing demographics and shifting tribal relationships over a period of time that is measured genealogically (Aswani, 2000; Sheppard et al., 2000:10). These traditions ascribe the development of late-period Roviana society to a series of acts by individual chiefs and other players, and provide detailed accounts of key historical events in that trajectory. Archaeology cannot work at that level of resolution or scale, but its methodology and data sets enable it to expose long-term processes of cultural change in ways that are not accessible to any other historical discipline. In the case of Roviana, the archaeological record of change in settlement patterns, material culture and in the form, content and spatial relations of shrine and other monumental features traces out the essential developments that led to the emergence of the Roviana Chiefdom.

Our record of the Roviana Chiefdom begins in the forests of the New Georgia mainland some 700 years ago, during the Bao period. Here the settlement patterns were highly dispersed. Although no house platforms have yet been identified it is likely that the domestic zones comprised small clusters of houses that were scattered at a low density over the planting soils and along the ridges. The shrines occurred in small clusters (as at Bao itself) or as isolated structures, and they were always isolated from the settlement zones, suggesting a deliberate separation of sacred and secular space. The early shrines comprised basaltic stone uprights and large table stones – flat rocks mounted on stone foundations. The shrine tradition seemed to have involved quite different rituals and practices to that of the later Roviana period. If these shrines were associated with ancestor cults, the heads of the ancestors were certainly not placed in any permanent position on the shrines. Nor is there any indication that the shrine tradition was associated, as it later was, with the circulation of shell valuables or the presentation of votive offerings of any kind, as there are no remains of material culture or fauna. Indeed, there is little in the archaeological record to suggest how the shrines were used.

Along the barrier islands of Roviana Lagoon there are seven sites that we assign to the Bao period. The Bao-period shrines of the barrier islands all contain slab-built walls, like those of the mainland, and oral tradition supports the interpretation that these appear relatively early in the Roviana sequence. This is supported by the lack of information about who built and used the sites. Unlike the majority of sites in Roviana, only one has any tradition attached: a small slab-built shrine complex on Nusa Roviana that is linked in oral tradition to the chief Ididubanara, who is also associated with the early Bao settlement.

Although the barrier island sites are structurally similar to the mainland Bao sites, they also show interesting differences. The barrier island shrines continue the slab construction tradition, but they are generally built of coral slabs rather than basalt slabs. The most outstanding exceptions are three basalt shrines within the Kekehe site, Site 79 on Nusa Roviana, and several other small sites on the ridge above Kokorapa village on Nusa Roviana that also contain basalt components. The basalt for these structures must have been transported from the mainland, which suggests that the Kekehe sites represent an early transferral of the Bao shrine tradition from the mainland, and that the use of basalt might have a symbolic dimension – perhaps a reference to a tribal homeland. Four of the barrier island shrines are also the only such sites of the Bao period that contain any shell valuables. These were dominated by bareke, which are considered to be the oldest of the Roviana shell valuables (Aswani & Sheppard, 2003). As on the mainland, the Bao-period shrines of the barrier islands were not used for depositing human remains or votive offerings. However, the small number of crude shell rings found on the barrier island shrines of this period probably mark the start of the Roviana shell valuables tradition and its association with the shrine tradition.

The Bao sites of the barrier islands also display a different use of space to those of the mainland. At Kekehe and Honiavasa, which are the sites with the best-preserved features, the shrines and domestic house platforms are scattered along the peripheries of flat plantation land. They are not particularly clustered and certainly do not comprise a nucleated settlement, but the shrines and house platforms are much closer together than on the mainland and appear to form a single, integrated settlement zone. There is, however, still a distinct separation of sacred and secular space, and shrines are rarely found close to – and never directly attached to – house platforms.

Radiocarbon dating has not provided sufficient precision to define the relative age of all the Bao-period sites but we consider it likely on typological grounds, and with the strong support of the oral traditions, that the Bao sites of the barrier islands represent the late part of the Bao sequence.

The sites of the Roviana period represent a continuation

of the trajectory of change in site form, artefact association and settlement patterns that we see in the transition from mainland to barrier island sites during the Bao period. The shrines of this period have coral-rubble walls and a high incidence of human bone, shell valuables or both. The shrines come in a variety of forms and sizes, and often contain ancillary features such as skull houses of sheet coral. Skulls are often contained within the skull houses, and other human remains may be found lying on the surface of the shrines or inserted into the fabric of the coral walling. Artefacts are also frequently found scattered over the shrines, including shell-ring manufacturing debitage, different forms of shell valuables and a variety of ceramic and metal historic artefacts. Ovens or oputu are often located within several metres of a shrine, along with associated faunal remains. Traditional accounts of shrine use tell us that ovens were used to prepare sacrificial offerings to the ancestors. Many shrines are part of larger clusters made up of other shrines and various types of platform and walls.

The settlement pattern at Nusa Roviana at the end of the Roviana period is highly nucleated. The shrines and house platforms are all located within a single living space, where the area between features is rich with midden and broken artefacts (Nagaoka, 2011) – of both utilitarian and ceremonial items. There is a very high ratio of shrines to house platforms (Sheppard et al., 2000:36) and the shrines are scattered among the house platforms; indeed, many are attached to house platforms. The shrines and house platforms start about 50 m or so inland of the intertidal mangrove zone where the wharves, canoe houses and shell-valuable manufacturing floors are located. Thus the settlement space of the Roviana period was permeated with religious symbolism and residues of religious acts. By the mid- to late nineteenth century when the Roviana Chiefdom was at its height we see a near fusion of sacred and secular space and a merging of the worlds of the living and the dead.

Munda tradition beyond Roviana: Rendova and Tetepare

The trajectory of change in site form, material culture and settlement pattern described above traces the emergence of the Roviana Chiefdom with its attendant ancestor cults, headhunting practices and exchange systems, and identifies the shorelines and offshore islands of Roviana Lagoon as the centre of these developments. It is apparent, however, that many of the archaeological changes documented in Roviana also occurred elsewhere in the Western Solomons.

The large, high volcanic island of Rendova is located 3 km across the Blanche Strait from Roviana. Roviana people have close ties with Rendova, especially with the speakers of the closely related Ughele language who live directly across from Nusa Roviana on the north coast of Rendova. Much of the southern part of Rendova is occupied by speakers of the non-Austronesian language Touo (Mbaniata). The NGAS team carried out preliminary work in the Lokuru region of southeastern Rendova in 1999, and Tim Thomas (2009) subsequently conducted more extensive research there and on the large unoccupied island of Tetepare, 3 km east of the southeastern tip of Rendova.

Neither NGAS nor Thomas found intertidal ceramic-period sites, although a few pieces of ceramic were recovered from near a spring at Log Point in Busana Bay. The exposed beaches of southeastern Rendova do not provide suitable locations for such sites, although the lagoons and barrier islands of north Rendova would appear to have considerable potential. Thomas has recovered a late prehistoric sequence from the Lokuru region that is very similar to that from Roviana, but sites and shrines there are concentrated in defensive positions on the interior ridges and not on the coast in the vicinity of modern villages. Remains of gardens and some house platforms are found below ridges near river bluffs; above these, at the head of the ridge, is a first set of shrine complexes oriented out to sea; behind them, further up the ridge, are defensive works and house platforms; and behind them, at the highest point on the ridge, are often additional shrines (Figure 7.25). The shrines are identical in most respects to those of the Roviana period, with numerous skulls, shell valuables, food remains and earth ovens (Thomas, 2009:133). The most significant difference is that they are constructed of locally available basalt river cobbles rather than coral cobbles; however Thomas notes that some coral cobbles and branch coral are often incorporated, in the same way as basalt is often incorporated into Roviana coral-cobble shrines as uprights. Defensive works consist of ditches cut across the ridge at narrow points, and steep terracing. The largest defensive feature was at Hasiri (RDV 15) where, on a steep slope from the river, a 40-metre-long ditch and bank was backed by a 1-metre-high coral-cobble wall. Four radiocarbon dates on these sites date them as no earlier than 1650–1700 AD.

The Bao period is represented by a set of three faced platform sites located to the north of Lokuru in the Haforai area. Each elongated earthen mound is faced with basalt slabs, and supports one or more stone platforms on top. Each mound has a large basalt upright at the downslope end. Thomas (2009:136) notes their striking similarity to the Bao-period shrines of Roviana: this is seen in their elongated shape, basalt facing, absence of artefacts and

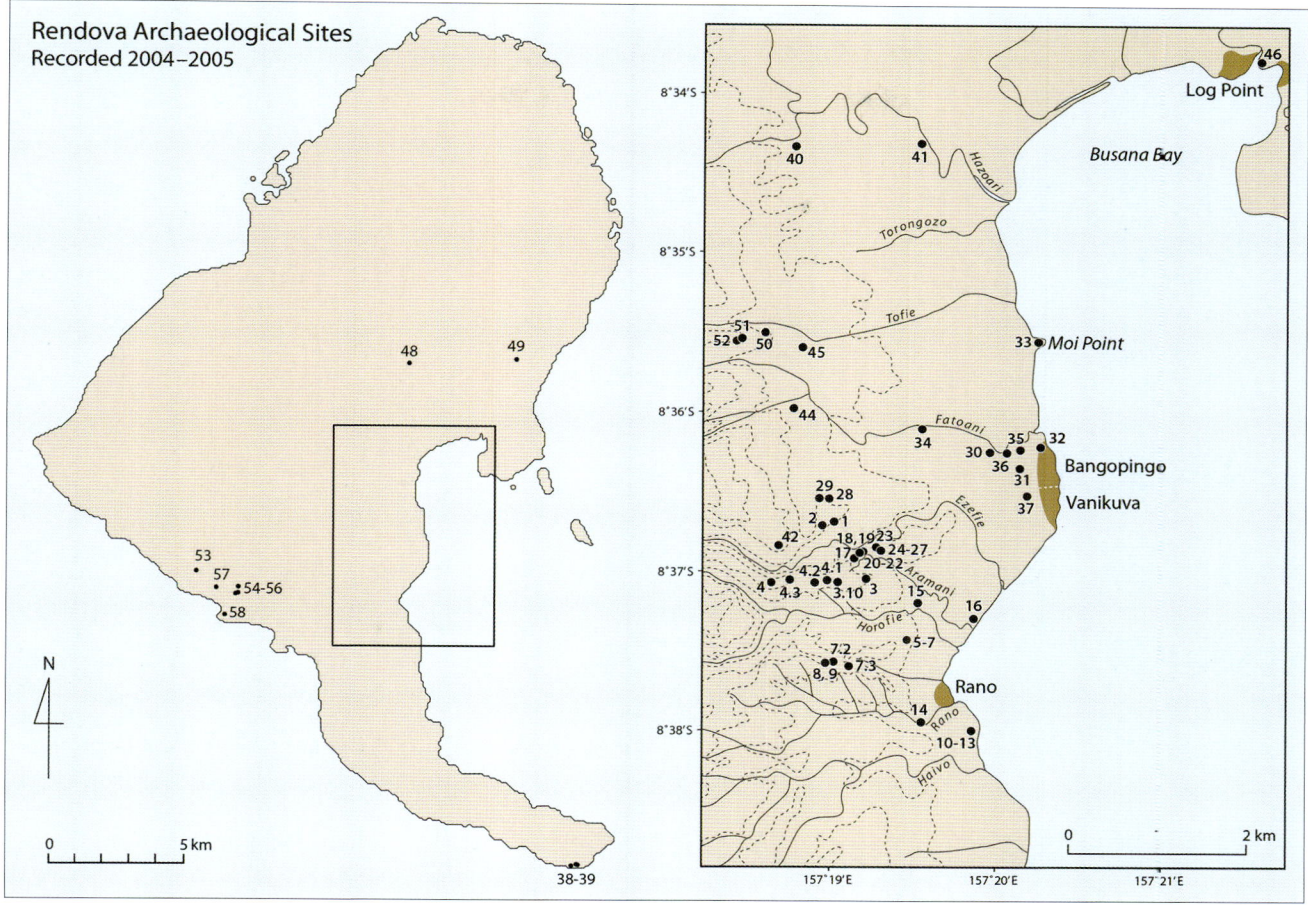

Figure 7.25. The location of archaeological sites in the Lokuru area on Rendova Island (from Thomas, 2009, with permission).

human remains, and their isolated locations. One of these mounds (RDV 49) was dated to c. 1450 AD (WK-22393 431 ± 30 charcoal), which places it towards the end of the Bao period.

Tetepare is today unoccupied; however, a landowners' association based on New Georgia claims land rights on the island, mostly through women who were taken as captives or otherwise married into Roviana and other areas within the New Georgia Group during the late 1700s or early 1800s. Oral tradition indicates the island was abandoned sometime after the death of chief Odikana from Saikile (Patu te Malukete) in Roviana, who was wounded in an attack on Tetepare. This would suggest abandonment in the 1800s.

As in Rendova, settlement sites are located on ridgetops between rivers, or on raised makatea coastal bluffs (Figure 7.26). However, many sites are close to the coast and in less defensive locations than on Rendova – although a number are surrounded by low walls. Oral tradition suggests older settlement was at the western end of the island, and people gradually moved to the east to avoid attacks from Roviana

(Thomas, 2009). Only one site (TET 40) appears on typological grounds to date to the Bao period (Figure 7.27). It is a rectangular platform with three faced steps and with basalt and coral facing stone (Thomas, 2014:53). The presence of only a few skull houses made of sheet coral makes it hard to distinguish house and shrine platforms in the absence of other artefacts. Sites identified as shrines vary from those seen in Roviana and Rendova: most are elongated basalt and coral-cobble mounds that have indented cists or depressions on their surface. A common form is a platform 'with dual elongate mounds placed in parallel on top' (Thomas, 2009: 139), within which crania and other human bones are found – unlike Roviana, where only skulls are kept. Despite these differences the complement of other artefactual material found at these shrines is like that from Rendova and Roviana. Dates on six sites on Tetepare fall between 1500 and 1800 AD, and most sites postdate 1600 AD. The earliest dates are associated with an apparent settlement formed by a cluster of platforms containing earth ovens in their centres (TET 44), and with an apparent ritual enclosure. No items of European origin were recovered from the sites.

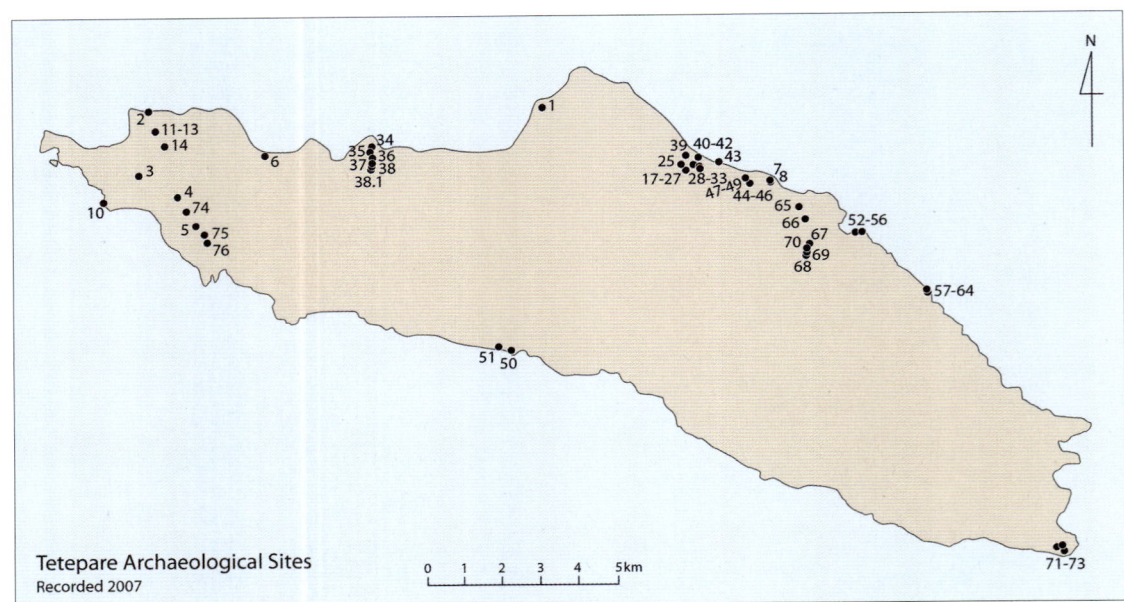

Figure 7.26. The location of archaeological sites on Tetepare Island (from Thomas, 2009, with permission).

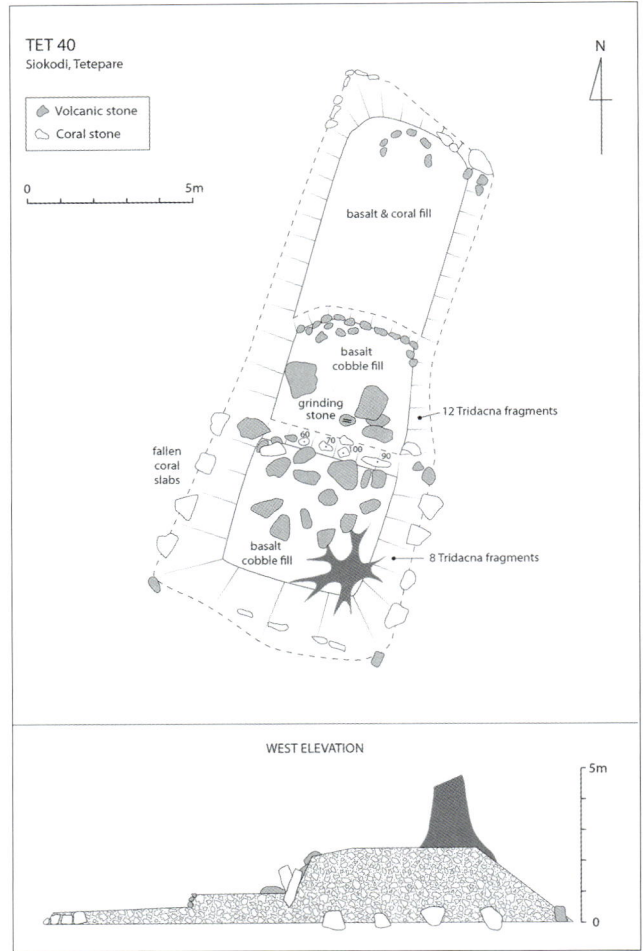

Figure 7.27. Plan of the TET 40 site on Tetepare (from Thomas, 2009, with permission).

Vella Lavella

The Roviana Chiefdom developed among Austronesian-speaking people and drew on some basic Austronesian principles, ideologies and symbols – yet there are good accounts of Roviana-style canoes carrying warriors from Vella Lavella embarking on headhunting trips with all the paraphernalia associated with the chiefs of Roviana Lagoon (McKinnon, 1972). It is clear that Vella Lavella adopted and participated in much of the headhunting and shrine complex, despite being made up of non-Austronesian societies. Indeed it is clear they adopted these practices successfully, given that warriors from Vella Lavella were able to launch a major attack on the stronghold of the Nusa Roviana fortification sometime around 1800 (see above). We were interested in documenting similar aspects of the archaeological record of Vella Lavella that we focused on in New Georgia, in order to see if the trajectories were the same or whether there were any key differences.

The island of Vella Lavella is 70 km northwest of Munda in Roviana, and can be reached by sheltered sailing or paddling through Vonavona Lagoon, past the high volcano of Kolombangara, through the lagoons of Ghizo Island and across a narrow channel to Vella Lavella (Figure 7.1). Like Rendova and New Georgia, Vella Lavella is formed through the coalition of a series of volcanic centres. A narrow coastal flat of a few hundred metres quickly gives way to steep slopes and interior ridges cut by small rivers and streams. The major exception to this is the large Oula river basin on the southwestern side of the island (Figure 7.28). The interior is rugged, but most ridges within 5 km of the coast

REGIONAL PREHISTORY IN THE WESTERN SOLOMONS: PROCESS AND HISTORY

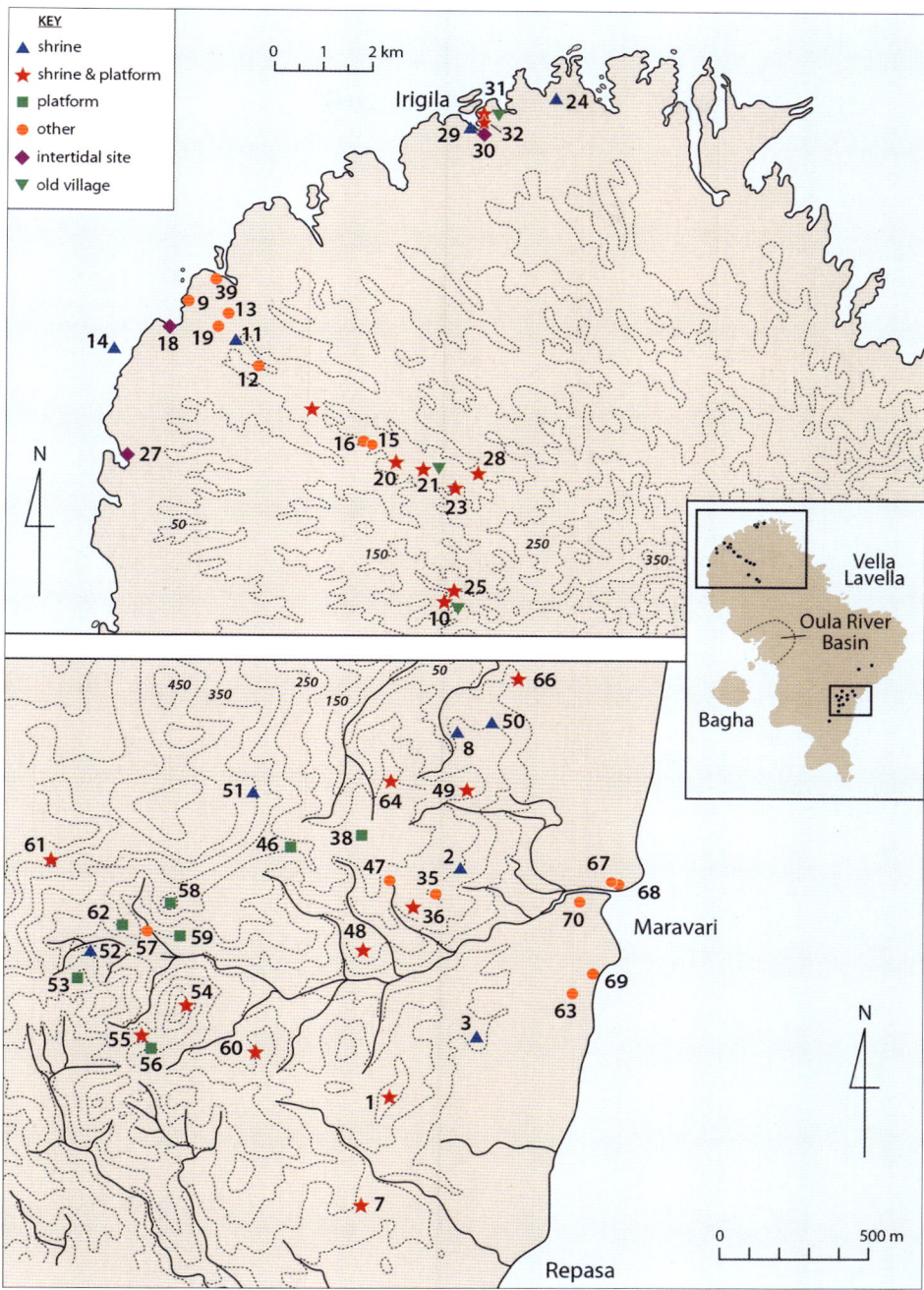

Figure 7.28. The location of archaeological sites on Vella Lavella.

do not exceed 400 m in altitude. As is the case in the rest of the New Georgia Group, modern villages are located on the coastal flat; however, they have been established there only since the early twentieth century when mission stations were set up and headhunting ended. All of the people are Mbilua speakers, which makes Vella Lavella the largest concentration of non-Austronesian speakers in the Solomon Islands, outside of Bougainville. Most people also speak or understand a neighbouring Austronesian language, however, and many of the matrilineages trace their descent back to a woman who either was captured or married in from an Austronesian group (Sheppard & Walter, 2014; Sheppard et al., 2010b).

We initiated the Bilua Bifoa project in 2004 as a combined programme of archaeological, palaeoenvironmental and anthropological research focused on two field sites: Maravari in southeastern Vella Lavella and Irigila in the northwest. Results of this work are for the most part as yet unpublished

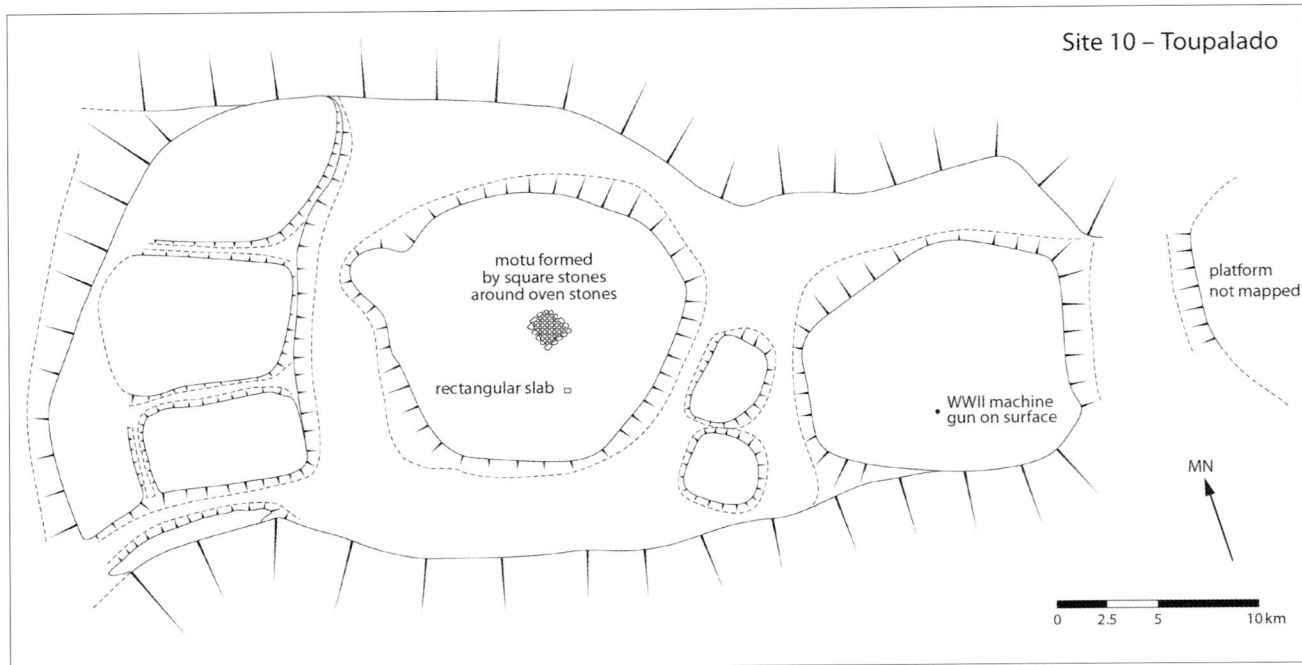

Figure 7.29. Plan of Toupalado (Site 10) on Vella Lavella.

(McKenzie, 2007; Sheppard & Walter, 2008; Sheppard et al., 2010b). The primary goal of our research was to build on the basic research conducted on Vella Lavella by Chikamori (1965) in the early 1960s, and to use this to compare developments there with those in Roviana. We were particularly interested in whether the distinctive patterns and models of Austronesian New Georgia would be reflected in the prehistory of non-Austronesian Vella Lavella.

Chikamori (1965) did not find any ceramics in his research in the interior of the west of the island, north of the Oula basin. Nor did our team find any ceramics in the Maravari region but, as discussed in Chapter 4, we found a number of intertidal ceramic sites in the lagoons around Irigila in north Vella Lavella as well as ceramic scatters in Irigila village and surrounds, as originally reported by Reeve (1989). Unfortunately the deposits at Irigila village are heavily disturbed by crab activity, which has churned them to a depth of more than a metre. Although the ceramics from the intertidal sites are as yet undated they are stylistically identical to those recovered in Roviana and elsewhere in the Western Solomons, which would suggest they are younger than 2700 BP. Results of pollen core analysis are not yet available, but it seems probable that they will provide a similar pattern to that reported for Roviana, which indicates that gardening started at the time of the appearance of the intertidal ceramics. Taro cultivation would have been the foundation of subsistence for the hamlets that covered the interior of Vella Lavella; however, at least in late prehistory, it appears to have been based primarily on dryland swidden. Chikamori (1965) did not find any irrigation systems during his research, which involved travel up the Oula River, although he did map and report systems on the Lupa River in north New Georgia. During his stay at Paramata village on the west coast of Vella Lavella, people reported to him that they formerly grew two varieties of wetland and eight of dryland taro but that, by 1965, wetland taro was no longer grown. One of the goals of our work was to investigate the possible use of such systems; however, as in Roviana, we found only a few stands of taro in swamps adjacent to modern villages. Chiefs and elders who had knowledge of ruta in north New Georgia and Kolombangara stated that such cultivation systems were not used in Vella Lavella, and that they specialised in growing bananas.

Chikamori (1965) located a series (48 at Veala) of settlement sites situated along ridgetops in the interior in the vicinity of Mts Veala and Tu`umbou, about 5 km from the coast on the southern side of the volcanic centre that forms north Vella Lavella. Oral tradition describes that area as an ancestral location for the people of Vella Lavella from which they dispersed throughout the island (Chikamori, 1965). These sites appear to be hamlets of up to 11 rectilinear to oval platforms that were probably house foundations, dispersed around a large, circular foundation 7–12 m in diameter within which is located a round oven or fireplace.

The settlement pattern that Chikamori saw is repeated at sites we recorded in the Irigila and Maravari regions. At

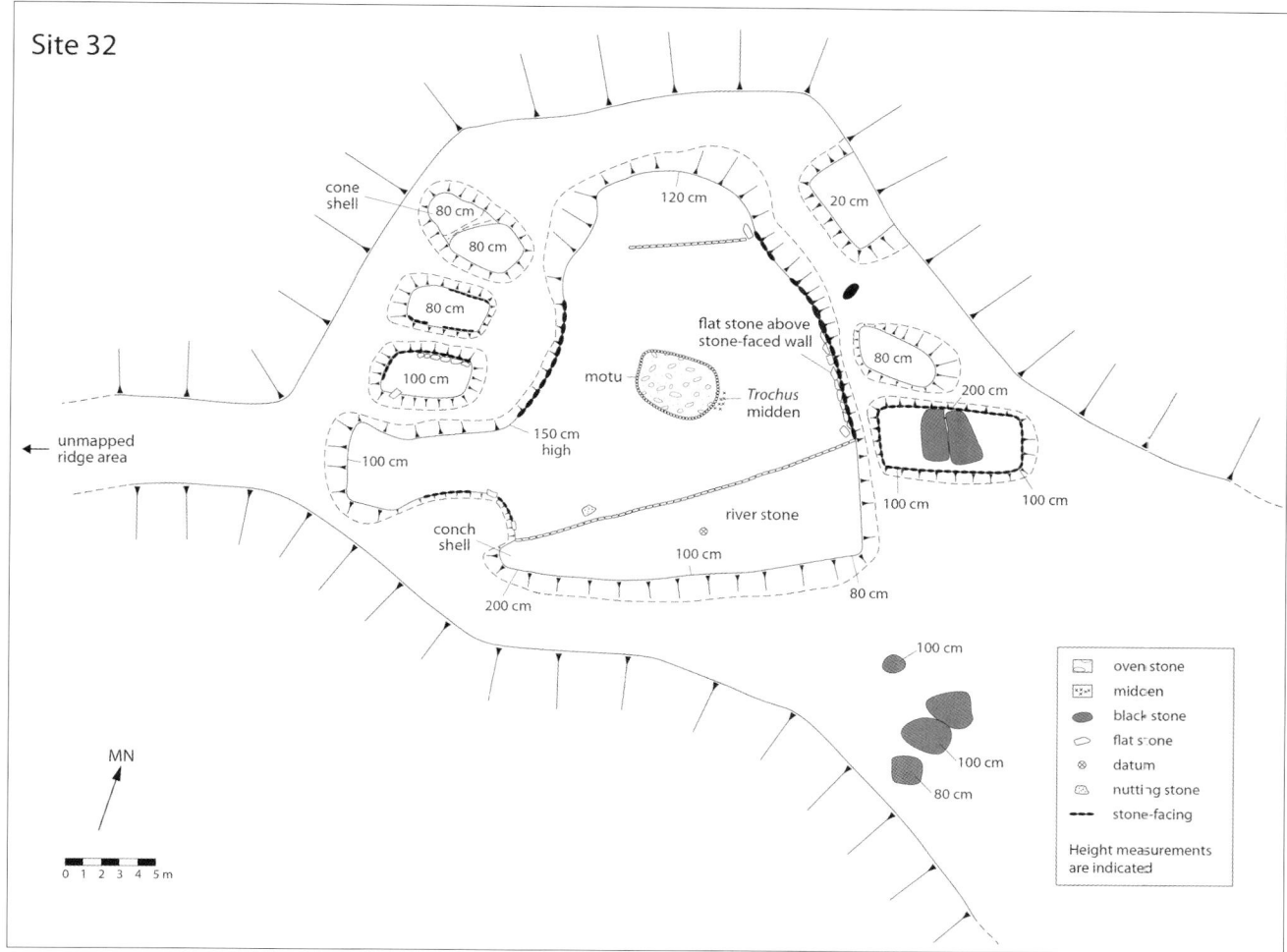

Figure 7.30. Plan of Site 32 on Mundimundi ridge, Vella Lavella.

Toupalado (Site 10) on a narrow ridge on the north side of Mt Tu'umbou, a series of rectangular and oval platforms are adjacent to a large, circular platform that contains a large stone oven (Figure 7.29). Two transverse ditches serve as defensive features. Oral tradition associates this location with a settlement area occupied prior to movement to the coast in 1902. Sites 26 and 32 on the Mundimundi ridge southwest of Irigila present very similar patterns (Figure 7.30). Dating of both of these sites returned Modern ages suggesting use in the nineteenth century. In the Maravari region we did not find such a distinctive pattern, although large circular foundations with central ovens are associated with platform complexes in what are probably residential areas below at least two skull shrines (Figure 7.31).

Skull shrines are common on Vella Lavella. They appear in historic photographs (Nicholson, 1925), and Lawrence Foana'ota (1974) produced an early report on them while he was working for the National Museum of the Solomon Islands. We have recorded a small number of shrines during our research on the coast and in the vicinity of modern villages, but these are generally small and often contain only a single skull; one was located beside a Christian grave. It is our impression that most of these shrines are historic and date to the point at which people moved down to the coast in the early twentieth century. Although canoe houses were located on the coast, until the end of headhunting, people lived in hamlets dispersed across the interior ridges.

Our research in the Maravari region has closely surveyed the drainage area of the Maravari River up to 3 km inland, and recorded 24 sites in an area of about 2 km² (Figure 7.28). Of these, 10 sites contain platforms with skulls and often other human remains, and are generally located high on ridges overlooking the drainage area.

The skull shrines of Maravari share the basic characteristics of skull shrines from elsewhere in the Western Solomons. Skulls are placed or cached on platforms along with shell valuables of a wide variety of forms, but mirroring in most respects shell valuables from Roviana.

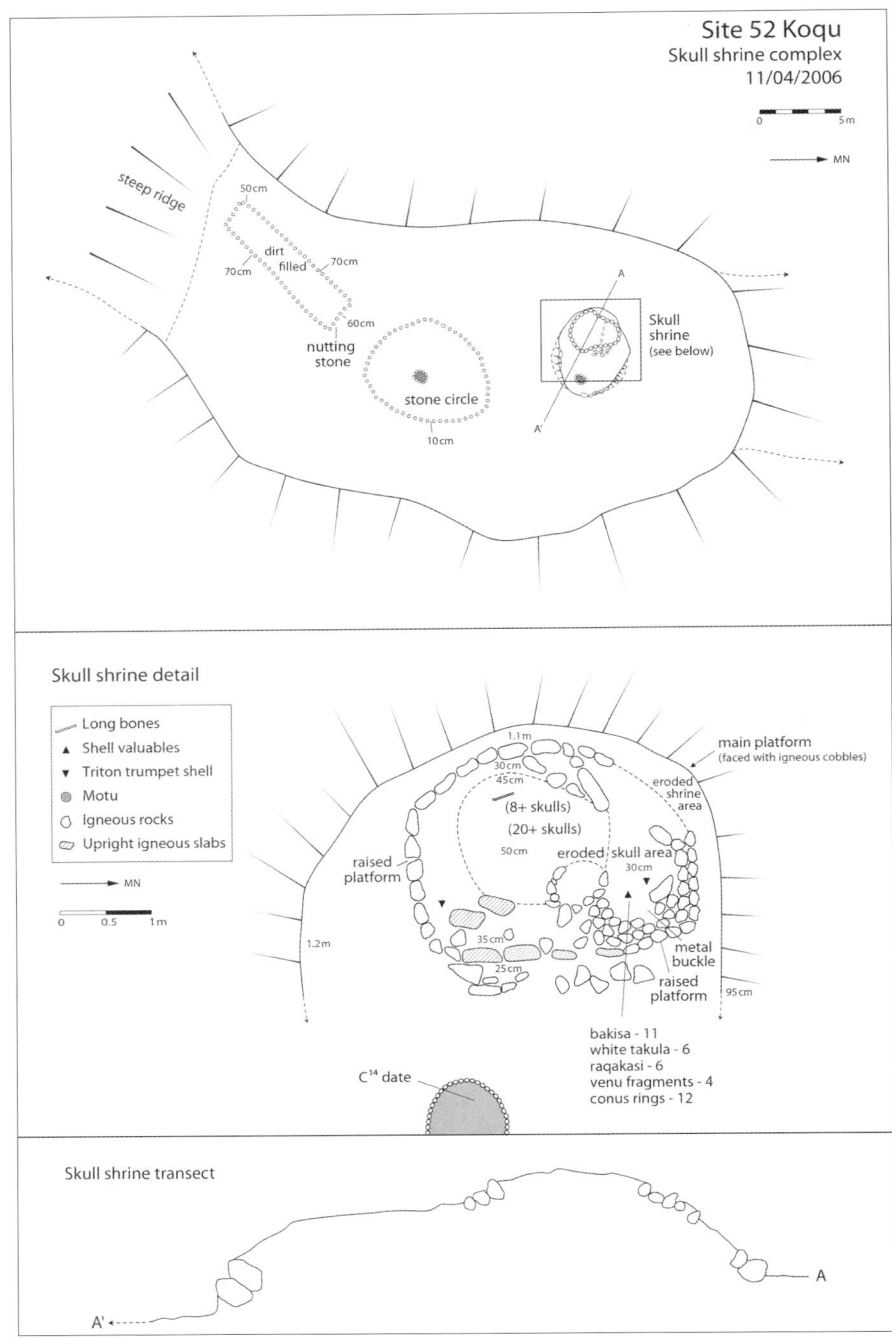

Figure 7.31. Plan of Site 52 on Vella Lavella.

Other items of material culture include chunks of fossil *Tridacna*, chert nodules and a wide variety of European trade goods, including gun parts. Adjacent to the platform or platforms is an oven and often igneous uprights, which may also be incorporated in the platform fabric. The shrines are constructed from coral or basalt cobbles (sometimes both), and as in Roviana there is considerable diversity in platform size and details of construction (McKenzie, 2007); many are adapted to the natural landform. Where these shrines often differ markedly from those seen in Roviana is in the presence of dual identical platforms (four sites) containing large numbers of skulls and often human bones other than skulls. A good example of such a shrine is Niatukubo (Site 1), located high on the first ridge southwest of Maravari village (Figure 7.32). In this site more than 23 skulls are visible on the surface of platform F, and more appear to be

REGIONAL PREHISTORY IN THE WESTERN SOLOMONS: PROCESS AND HISTORY

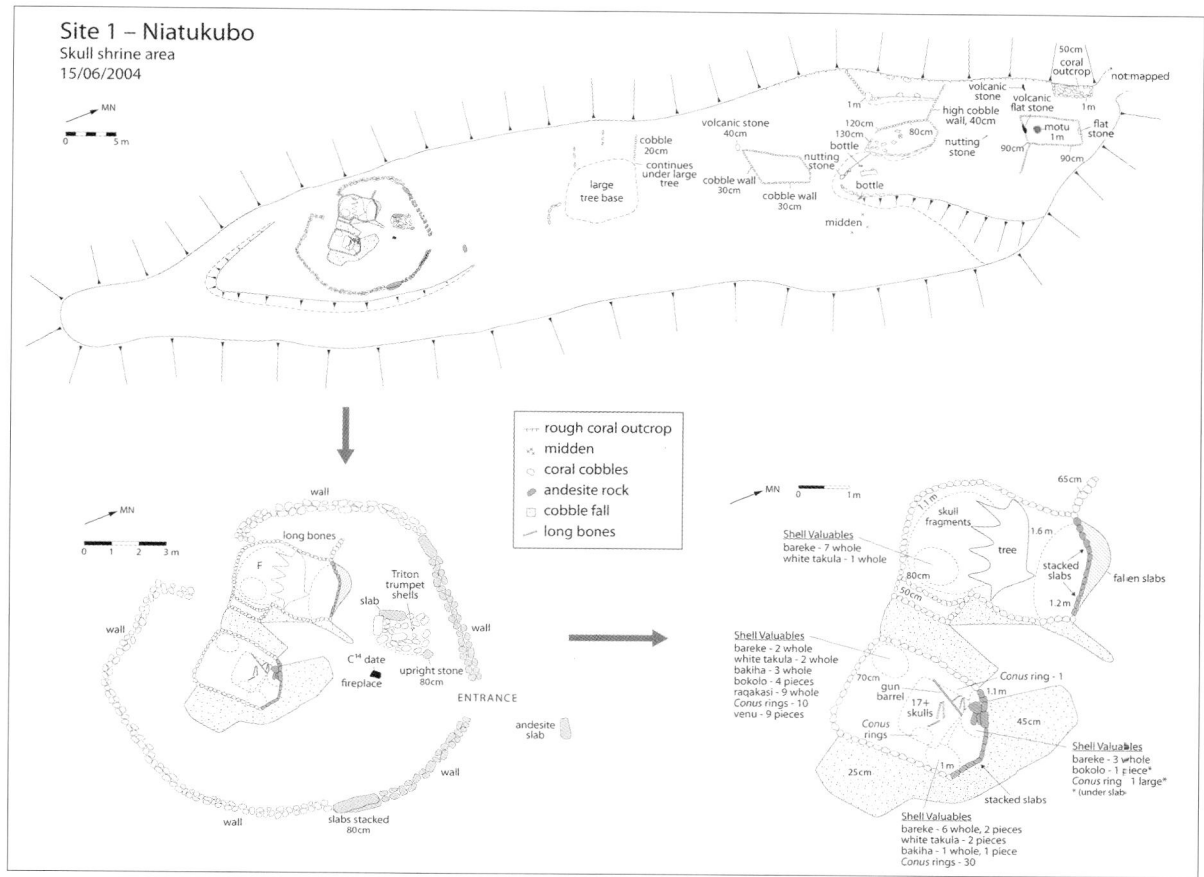

Figure 7.32. Plan of Niatukubo (Site 1) on Vella Lavella.

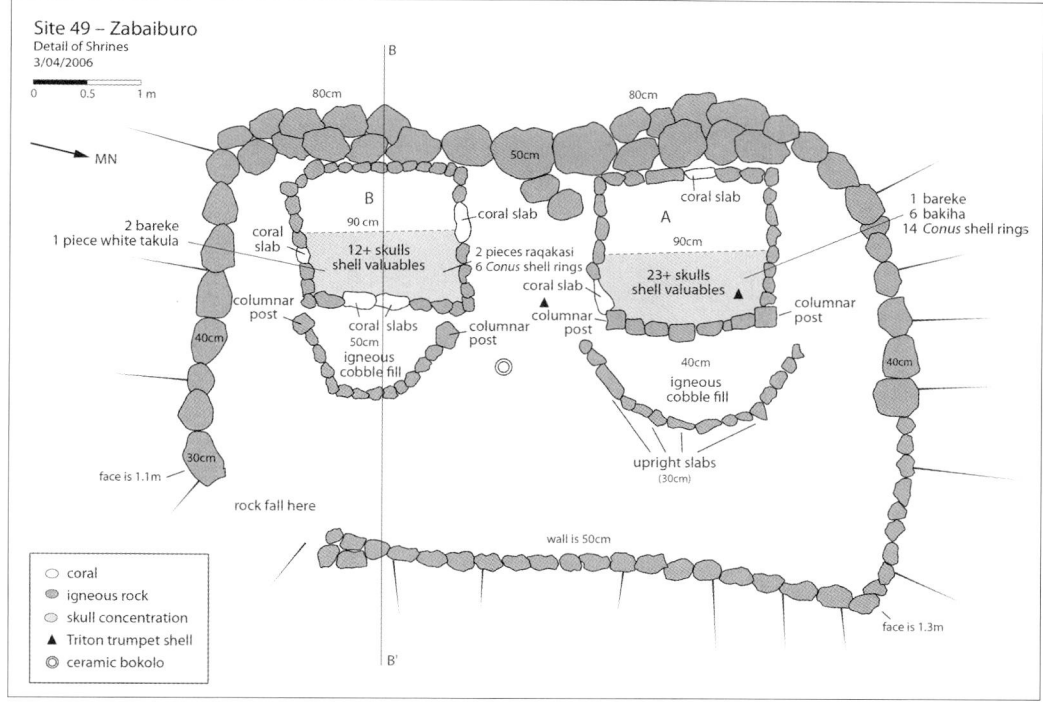

Figure 7.33. Plan of Zabaiburo (Site 49) on Vella Lavella.

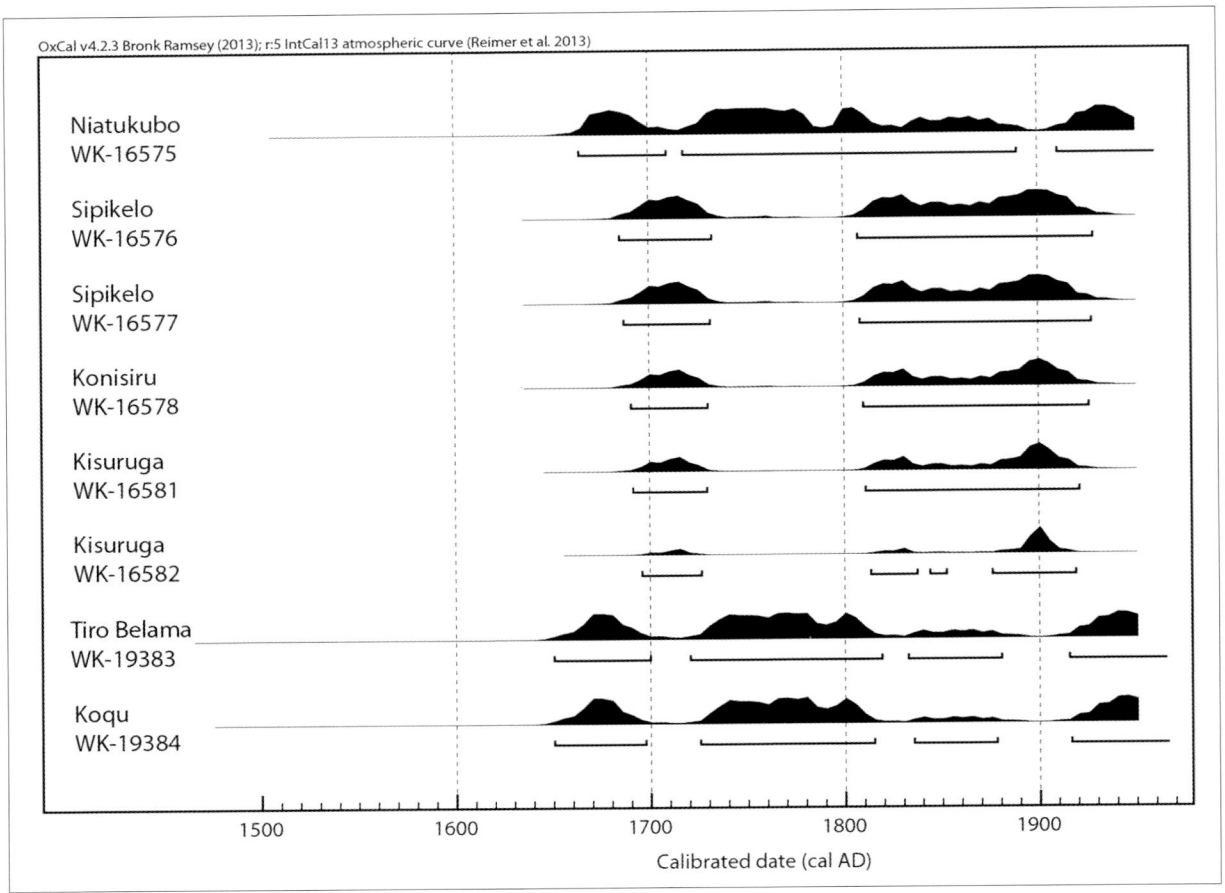

Figure 7.34. Plot of radiocarbon dates on Vella Lavella shrines (OxCal v.4.15).

present inside both platforms, which also contain a variety of other subcranial human remains (ribs, long bones), shell valuables, a rifle barrel and conch shells. In the adjacent area surrounding the coral-cobble platforms are dense midden, nut-cracking stones and glass bottles. Beside the small earth oven (C) is a large igneous slab sitting on coral cobbles. This structure is similar to the table stone features from the Bao period of Roviana. An additional example of this type of shrine layout can be seen at Site 49 (Zabaiburo) located in a similar position on the first high ridge to the northwest of Maravari (Figure 7.33). Maravari elders associated with the Niatukubo shrine state that each platform is associated with a different matrilineage: one is the elder autochthonous land-owning lineage and the other is a foreign matrilineage whose land rights are conferred by the elder lineage.

Some shrines in Maravari are isolated from any other platforms, but most have a small number of adjacent platforms, terraces and walls, generally running down a narrow ridge from the zone containing the shrine platform. This is well illustrated in Figure 7.32, which shows the features immediately down-slope from the Niatukubo shrine. This is a relatively simple complex; other shrines have more extensive features. All would appear to be adjacent to residential areas, and Maravari elders suggest the features immediately below the shrine represent the residence of the priest. It is possible, especially where features are more extensive, that these are remains of normal hamlets, however other house platform complexes such as those in the headwaters of the Maravari Stream have no associated shrines.

Dating of these surface features is difficult; most dates have been obtained on charcoal from the bottom of the shrine oven, creating the possibility that the date is on the last use of the oven. Of the eight dates obtained on six shrines, five are modern – suggesting nineteenth-century use. The other three (Niatukubo Site 1, Tiro Belama Site 51, Koqu Site 52) date with greatest probability to the late seventeenth century (1670–1750) AD (Figure 7.34). If we accept these dates as representing the time of establishment of skull shrines on Vella Lavella, it is 100 to 150 years later than the start of the Roviana period of the Munda Tradition and the appearance of comparable shrines in Roviana. Two of the earliest dates

(Niatukubo and Tiro Belama) are on dual platform shrines, and it is possible that this is an early form of shrine. The Vella Lavella dual platform shrines are almost identical, including the incorporation of subcranial elements, to those reported by Thomas (2009) from Tetepare, which appear to be contemporaneous with or to date slightly earlier than those on Vella Lavella.

Archaeology, history and regional development

As Miller (1980b) has noted, Solomon Island oral tradition often reports cultural origins as being in the high interior of islands, with subsequent movement to the coast – a pattern we have observed in both the histories and the archaeology of Roviana and Vella Lavella. Although, as Miller suggests, this pattern may be a basic symbolic structure and not necessarily related to history in a simple linear fashion, it is also possible that it reflects the fundamental bush–coast dichotomy, which is underlain by unequal access to resources (Roe, 2000). It may be a fundamental structuring principle of Solomons history, reflecting constant tension between the bush and the coast and a long history of movement from bush to coast. This movement has played out repeatedly throughout the Solomons; the last movement was at the start of the twentieth century in Roviana and many other areas, when the bush people of most islands came down to the coast. For recent populations of the Solomons, history literally has been a movement from the interior to the coast.

In the Western Solomons the archaeological record, and the cultural record that it reflects, have been profoundly shaped within the last 500 years by the rise of the headhunting complex. Whether we accept all the details of the developmental sequence for Roviana – and there does appear to be some confirmation of the sequence from Rendova (Thomas, 2009) – there is no doubt that the geographical distribution of sites and populations, and the nature of the construction and types of cultural items included in sites such as shrines, are constrained by headhunting. Outside of Roviana, people have sought refuge in small hamlets in the hills – although this did not stop them from maintaining canoe houses on the coast, as in Vella Lavella. In some areas, populations were completely displaced and islands abandoned. In the New Georgia Group everyone participated in the headhunting complex – there was little option, and it was perhaps the only mechanism around which group defence or political organisation could be mobilised above the hamlet level.

Participation in the headhunting complex involved adopting the fundamental properties of the overall system: this includes the shell-valuables economy that underwrote the system, with particular emphasis on the use of bakiha as a mark of chiefly authority; the ancestral shrines that enabled chiefs to obtain power (mana); and the large canoe houses and war canoes and related material culture. All of these elements are found in various forms and elaborated to different degrees within the Western Solomons. For example, shell rings and valuables are found everywhere within the Solomons, and even within the New Georgia Group there are some local varieties or forms. Everywhere in the New Georgia Group, however, the bakiha is the most important form and is associated with the headhunting complex. Similarly, shrine forms vary; and in the case of Vella Lavella and Tetepare, the dual platform form may be associated with the adoption of the large chiefly ancestral skull shrine by matrilineal groups who needed to adapt forms used by people like the Roviana, who have cognatic kinship systems where descent is traced on both maternal and paternal sides. Of course, the cognatic system may itself have been something that has developed along with the headhunting complex.

In the Western Solomons, and particularly in the New Georgia Group, it is the amalgamation of all the key elements of the headhunting complex and the ultimate amplification of the system that mark this region off from the rest of the Solomons. This raises an interesting question: Did the headhunting complex and the sociopolitical developments that went with it develop first in Roviana? Unfortunately, dating skull-shrine construction is rather difficult, and radiocarbon dating in the last 400 years is made problematic by our inability to date within the last 200 years and by the variability within the calibration curve after 1600 AD. It seems clear that the construction of large fortifications on Nusa Roviana occurred early and is unmatched anywhere else in the New Georgia Group or the Western Solomons. Comparison of the ages of shrines in Roviana and Vella Lavella would suggest that those on Nusa Roviana are earlier. Certainly headhunting in the nineteenth century was driven from Roviana, and large-scale interisland raids occurred within the New Georgia Group in the early nineteenth or late eighteenth centuries, with Roviana a focus of such activity. This raises a second question: Why did a headhunting and ancestral shrine tradition lubricated by shell currency develop in Roviana and not somewhere else?

As noted above, Roviana has some geographical advantages. It is located at the centre of the New Georgia Group. This facilitated movement and trade and exchange within the area – something that was appreciated by early Western traders, although protection by the most powerful polity in the region was also a concern. Roviana has rich marine resources but there is no evidence of intensification of food production based on taro irrigation such as can be seen in Marovo Lagoon at the eastern end of New Georgia (Hviding & Bayliss-Smith, 2000; Sheppard & Walter, 2013). It may, however, have been the absence of such local opportunity for intensification of food production that led to an intensification of the economy of mana through headhunting as a means of developing political power and integrating local populations in Roviana. Although manufacture of shell valuables was important in Roviana and the resources needed to produce shell valuables were common, Roviana had no monopoly on such production. Roviana chiefs may simply have been well situated at the geographical centre of the regional shell-valuables economy, which facilitated their procurement of food and other resources both through exchange and through social ties that extended across the region. In turn they could convert these into mana and power through the headhunting system. Such power allowed them to amass shell valuables in the name of the butubutu (lineage) through a variety of daily social transactions and special mechanisms (Aswani & Sheppard, 2003).

Thomas (2009) has described the peoples of the New Georgia Group as participating in a 'community of practice' that developed over time in a dynamic fashion, and he has argued that 'complex aggregate practices do not have pin-point origins'. Similarly Renfrew's (1986) peer-polity model of island development in the Eastern Mediterranean suggests how such communities of practice may arise within regions in an interactive fashion without diffusion from a centre. As we have seen there is variation in the archaeological record within the region and people have actively modified or created aspects of the headhunting complex. We do not know if all components originated in Roviana, and it is highly unlikely: the mon-type canoe form clearly has an independent history, and the origin of shell valuables such as the bakiha is unknown and may well be outside Roviana. However, Roviana clearly energised this system, at least in the nineteenth century, and although not all groups in the region acted in a simple reactive fashion, for many in the later stages of the system, especially those in the greater Western Solomons, there was little option.

The goals of this chapter were to describe in some detail the archaeology of the Western Solomons, based on our research. Another goal, however, was to examine how regional 'communities of culture', represented by distinctive archaeological records, might develop. Our work suggests that a number of generalisations or factors need to be considered when examining regional prehistory in the Solomons. These include:

1. the impact of external cultural forces
2. the long-term dynamic tension between bush and coastal populations
3. the geographical configuration of islands and distribution of resources, facilitating the creation of a regional economy and sphere of social interaction.

Specific responses to these factors result in regions moving along dissimilar paths and creating different histories. Alternative configurations of culture are created out of the cultural material provided by their common heritage. Rates of change or the impact of change may also vary. In some areas, such as the Eastern Solomons, ongoing external input into the region from populations to the north and east may have created sudden changes in culture and language. Elsewhere in the Solomons, change may have been gradual and may have occurred in relative isolation, resulting in patterns of regional diversity. In still other areas, regional interaction may have produced communities of culture that share some aspects of cultural practice but not others, depending on the intensity and the mechanism of interaction. For example, sharing the bonito cult in the Central Solomons has created a community of practice in that area, but it does not have anywhere near the impact on societies and their economic practices that the headhunting complex of the Western Solomons has. The linguistic picture in the Western Solomons suggests that such high-impact systems have not existed there in the distant past. Headhunting was a very powerful system that imprinted most aspects of regional culture after it began; however, it does not appear to have destroyed regional cultural diversity. Nevertheless, by the nineteenth century intensified Roviana headhunting was rapidly wiping out linguistic diversity in the Western Solomons, creating regions of linguistic homogeneity and expanding Roviana until it became the largest language group in the region. Such processes of regional expansion of powerful systems should leave signs in the Solomons linguistic picture, but this is not evident – which suggests that such events were rare. It was only with the impact of the Western world system that we see the creation of a common Solomons cultural system and language in Pijin. Yet even then, very considerable linguistic, cultural and religious diversity has been maintained.

8
Conclusion

The geographical position of the Solomon Islands as a long, linear archipelago stretching east to the edge of Remote Oceania gives it a unique role in the prehistory of Oceania. Although the Solomons can be considered a westward extension of the Bismarck Archipelago, the sea gap from New Ireland to Buka may have been a major (130–170 km) barrier or filter before the emergence of the Pleistocene-age raised atolls of the Green Islands (Nissan and Pinipir), midway between the two. Nowhere to the east of Buka does an atoll serve as a key stepping-stone in the Solomons chain. At the eastern end of the Main Solomon Islands chain, a water gap of 360 km between Santa Ana and Santa Cruz became the first major challenge to sailing and navigation in the chains of islands that extend back through island Southeast Asia to mainland Asia. The Solomon Islands thus provide the secure base from which the initial exploration and settlement of Remote Oceania was launched.

The other important geographical characteristics of the Solomons archipelago are perhaps not so unique, from the perspective of the cultural historian. The Main Solomons chain is about 1000 km long and consists of a line of long, narrow, intervisible islands. With the exception of Bougainville these are of moderate size, averaging about 160 km in length. The geography of this archipelago makes for great ease of communication and interaction, and nowhere in the interior of these islands – with the exception of Bougainville – is much more than half a day's walk from the coast. Furthermore, each island is a comparatively easy paddle from its nearest neighbour, as the historical records attest. Although not all coasts provide equally easy landing, and currents can make some passages more difficult than others, the use of paddling as opposed to sailing canoes makes for efficient water access throughout the archipelago. The people of the Main Solomons routinely travelled along the coast and between neighbouring islands in a variety of craft, from single-person dugouts to 30-man plank-built trading and raiding canoes. However, once into Remote Oceania, in the Eastern Solomons, specialised navigation and sailing craft were required to provide communication as interisland distances increased. This requirement – and a tradition of specialised long-distance maritime communication – are shared with the archipelagos of Fiji and island groups to the east.

In the late Pleistocene the water gap between the Northern Solomons and the Bismarck Archipelago appears to have been minimal. People made the crossing to Buka – as evidenced by remains at Kilu Cave – and presumably also to Greater Bukida, which at that time extended southeast to near modern Guadalcanal. Whether people moved along this large landmass is unknown, and to date no late Pleistocene archaeological deposits or convincing artefacts dating to that period have been discovered east of Buka. Nor have early Holocene deposits been found, although cladistic analysis of the scattered, highly variable non-Austronesian (Papuan) languages of the Solomons suggests to some linguists (Dunn et al., 2007) that there was a break-up in the very early Holocene. Progress in our understanding of that time period in the Solomons will have to await future research in regions with numerous caves and rockshelters that lie close to what was the late Pleistocene coastline. The volcanic islands of the Western Solomons where we have focused our research have not provided such settings;

perhaps the limestones of Malaita and Ulawa might prove more fruitful.

With the establishment of mid-Holocene sea levels the modern island geography was essentially formed, although sea levels of +1–2 m might have created coastlines a short distance inland of where they are today. It is at this time that we see the earliest dates from the cave of Vatuluma Posovi on Guadalcanal. Although the link between the dates from the lowest levels and the cultural remains is unclear, it is not unreasonable to expect human occupation at this time when the cave would have been a short distance from the coast. If people were present in the Central Solomons, then it is perhaps from this point that a very low-density hunting and collecting settlement pattern characteristic of the late Pleistocene may have begun to focus on the newly established lagoons with their rich marine resources. The result might have been localised higher population densities than what could previously have been supported. Whether this scenario has any validity remains to be seen. The fact that to date there are no definitive finds in the Solomons of distinctive mid-Holocene artefact forms such as those reported by Torrence and Swadling (2008) in the Bismarck Archipelago might suggest that the Solomons had a history of settlement unlike that of the Bismarcks.

The Lapita archaeological culture appeared in the Bismarck Archipelago in the late Holocene, after 3500 BP. Whatever the origins or developmental history of Lapita, it is clear that people in the Bismarck Archipelago at that time developed or obtained enhanced sailing capability. This is dramatically evidenced by the first movement out beyond the Main Solomons to the Eastern Solomons, which indicates the ability to cover long distances out of sight of land, find small targets and safely return. Settlement on Santa Cruz by 3000 BP also indicates Lapita expansion occurred possibly within a few generations of the appearance of Lapita in the Bismarcks. Such speed of expansion argues against simple models of settlement driven by demographic pressures. The early Lapita settlers of the Eastern Solomons were of course familiar with the Main Solomon Islands. Their sailing capability would have made exploration of the Solomons chain comparatively easy, and the Solomons would have served as an important voyaging corridor for canoes setting out into Remote Oceania. Direct evidence of contact with the Ulawa–Malaita region at the eastern end of the Main Solomons is provided by quantities of chert flakes and cores in the early Lapita sites in the Eastern Solomons. These rocks are sourced, using microfossils, to the marine limestones of either Ulawa or Malaita, where high-quality brown chert is very common in coastal streams. Evidence of contact, however, is not necessarily evidence of settlement. To date there is no record of early Lapita settlement anywhere in the Main Solomons.

The Lapita sites of the Main Solomons are all intertidal deposits from the later end of the Lapita ceramic sequence. Dating these deposits is difficult. Perhaps the oldest is the intertidal site (DJQ) on Buka, which contains a comparatively high proportion of dentate stamped ceramics that Wickler (2001) dates to c. 2700 BP, based on comparison with similar dated assemblages in the Bismarcks. This estimate is very close to the earliest dates (c. 2600 BP) on inclusions in pottery from the Western Solomons. All of these intertidal assemblages from the Western Solomons and Buka appear to share a style and a common post-Lapita developmental tradition related to that from the New Ireland region. The dating of the end of this regional sequence is poorly known but rough estimates place it around 2000 BP. There is still the question, however, of whether we are simply missing the earlier Lapita ceramic record in the Main Solomons. If our model of the Lapita period in the Main Solomons was based merely on the absence of early Lapita deposits then one might conclude that more research will eventually fill in the gap. However, we argue that a model of an early rapid 'leapfrog' movement out into Remote Oceania, which bypassed the Main Solomons, followed by a late Lapita movement from the New Ireland region eastward into the Western Solomons, actually fits better with the known cultural variation as well as being the best interpretation of the current archaeological record in both the Solomons and Remote Oceania.

The major cultural division in the Solomons Islands is that between the peoples on either side of the Tryon-Hackman Line, which bisects the Solomons at the eastern end of Santa Isabel. Although this marks a major linguistic division, with all Austronesian languages to the east out through Remote Oceania sharing a common ancestor, it also marks a clear biological distinction. For the people of the Solomons this division is salient and appears to be of long standing, and irrespective of our understanding of the Lapita period, requires explanation – although the most obvious explanation would simply be that the boundary formed at that time. Additional evidence is supplied by the more recent archaeological record. In Bougainville and Choiseul there is a ceramic record which lasted into the historic period. Although there is no corresponding historic ceramic record in the Western Solomons, even the earliest archaeological survey in the region recovered a low-frequency but ubiquitous record of late prehistoric plainware ceramics, which was presumably trade ware from further west. In the area east of the Tryon-Hackman Line no ceramics from any period have ever been recovered, with the exception of a handful of very poor-quality plain sherds from extensive excavations on Santa Ana, which date to c. 2500 BP. It might be argued that the record is the result of limited research, but in fact the SESP conducted much more intensive research in the Eastern Solomons than the rapid National Museum surveys conducted in the Western Solomons, which turned up pottery in many locations. And within the Central Solomons the large-scale excavations on Guadalcanal at Vatuluma Posovi, which included Lapita-period deposits, failed to recover ceramics from any period. The ceramic and other evidence shows clearly that the areas east and west of the Tryon-Hackman Line have had distinctive culture histories and that these differences have had an important and long-lasting impact on the region.

That the Eastern Solomons was first settled in the early Lapita period is undisputed. Recent redating (Sheppard et al., 2015a) of what has been considered to be the oldest site in the Eastern Solomons, at Nanggu (SE-SZ-8) on the south coast of Santa Cruz, has shown that it, like virtually all of the earliest sites in Remote Oceania, dates to c. 3000 cal BP. This very large site is well positioned adjacent to a sheltered bay and nearby lagoon, and Utupua, the next island to the south, can be seen from it. This site may well have served as a short-term staging post for exploration and settlement into the south and east; however, it seems probable that other early sites existed in the sheltered areas of Graciosa Bay and northeastern Santa Cruz where numerous Lapita sites have been and continue to be found. After what might have been a short period as a way-station for the settlement of the western Pacific, the islands of the Eastern Solomons settled into a period of regional development that lasted for as long as 1000 years, until some of the descendants of the early Lapita explorers returned from the east.

Once populations in the islands to the east of the Eastern Solomons (Tuvalu, Tokelau, Samoa) were sufficiently large it was perhaps only a matter of time before the prevailing westerly winds drove sailors back towards the Solomons, providing the last piece in the Solomons cultural puzzle. During this period the Polynesian Outliers were settled by people who spoke Samoic languages: they found refuge on the small remote islands that fringed the Solomons and which, because of their sailing capabilities, were viable places for permanent settlement. As in Vanuatu, some of these people were also able to establish themselves on islands within archipelagos that were already occupied by earlier inhabitants and, as with the people who live on the atolls of the Outer Reef Islands in the Reef-Santa Cruz group, use their tradition of deep-ocean sailing to provide specialised services to their neighbours. It is also possible that the Polynesian Outliers in the Solomon Islands were the islands from which East Polynesia was settled. This radical revision of the commonly accepted model of East Polynesian settlement out of West Polynesian is based on a recent revision of Polynesian linguistic subgrouping (Wilson, 2012) which posits a subgrouping of Northern Solomon Island outliers with unique shared innovations with the languages of East Polynesia.

There is also evidence for interaction with Micronesia, as seen in the material culture of the northern Polynesian Outliers and the Reef-Santa Cruz region, where distinctive forms such as the backstrap loom indicate prolonged contact. As in the case of the Polynesian Outliers, this may be in part a function of population growth in eastern Micronesia, possibly at the time of the expansion into East Polynesia.

With the settlement of the Polynesian Outliers the Solomons resumed slow regional differentiation which, until the arrival of Europeans, was exposed to only occasional influences from the east and north.

The Solomons position downwind of Western Polynesia has ultimately had an effect on culture history. However, we should not forget that the southeast coast of Papua New Guinea and its fringing archipelagos and, ultimately, the coast of northern Queensland, are downwind of the Solomons. It may be that for most of prehistory the paddle canoes lost at sea from the Solomons failed to survive or had little impact, but during the Lapita period sailing canoes were in use and may have facilitated more successful interaction across the Coral Sea. Some tantalising evidence for this is provided by late Lapita ceramics from the Western Solomons. Felgate and Dickinson (1998) have discovered small quantities of exotic hybrid granitic ceramic temper in late Lapita sherds from intertidal sites in the Western Solomons. Dating of zircons in this temper (Tochilin et al., 2012) has indicated that the most likely source is Woodlark Island, west of the Western Solomons, 475 km across the Coral Sea in the Massim region of Papua New Guinea. This temper suite has subsequently been identified in other intertidal sites in the Western Solomons, which suggests ongoing interaction with the source region and indicates routine interaction across the Coral Sea during the late Lapita period (Sheppard et al., 2015b).

In the last 1000 years the pattern of external influences and forces operating within a regionally variable framework of geographic interaction, which together shaped Solomon Island culture history, was essentially set until the arrival of large numbers of Europeans in the nineteenth century. Although local processes and agencies will always have played a role, it is perhaps only in the last 1000 years of Solomons prehistory that we can see the highly localised histories developing. Our research in the Western Solomons has showed the outlines of one such regional history, which is perhaps an exemplar of similar, regionally distinctive histories played out across the Solomons. Among the most obvious processes influencing the direction of prehistory in the Western Solomons has been the tension between a tendency for regional divergence versus historical forces encouraging homogeneity. The pattern of linguistic diversity across short distances suggests that for much of prehistory, although people would have interacted with their neighbours and many were probably multilingual, there were no forces operating that were powerful enough to counteract a tendency towards regional diversification.

There are 14 languages found within 100 km of Nusa Roviana, in Roviana Lagoon on the south coast of New Georgia, and it seems probable that there were more in the past. Today most languages are Austronesian; however two – Mbilua, which covers all of Vella Lavella, and Touo, which is found on the eastern end of Rendova – are NAN. Although it is harder to measure the degree of other elements of cultural diversity in the region, there is also considerable variation in systems of kinship descent and in items of material culture. This diversity suggests that for most of prehistory, slow regional diversification was the dominant process in the area.

In the last 400 years countervailing historical forces have dominated, leading to decreased linguistic diversity, major changes in language and cultural geography, and an overlay of shared cultural forms. These forces stem from the growth and expansion of the headhunting complex with its associated religious, economic and political features. An obvious linguistic effect of this process was the establishment of Roviana as the most widespread and dominant language group in the region. We have documented and explained the processes of change that led to the emergence of the Roviana Chiefdom, but the ultimate cause of this development is unclear. Underlying the Roviana development may have been the bush–sea tension that is common in the Solomons. Certainly Roviana oral history sees proximate causality in the desire of chiefs of the interior of New Georgia to come down and exploit the resources of the coast. The rich marine resources of the Roviana and Vonavona lagoons and the centrality of Roviana in the New Georgia Group made the coastlines strongly attractive. This is recounted in the oral traditions of Roviana, which tell of fighting among the peoples of the lagoon and the interior over control of this prime location. There is direct evidence of this in the archaeological record in the form of the large hillfort constructed on Nusa Roviana circa 1600 AD, and the dense settlements that came to surround it.

Oral history also speaks of aggregation of different groups by leaders whose bases of power were centred on Nusa Roviana. However, consolidating groups and maintaining large settlements and defensive works would have required innovation in sociopolitical organisation and the cultural structures that underpinned it. The archaeological record shows a major change in the form of stone shrines at this time, with the incorporation of ancestral skulls and shell valuables. We have argued that this marks the development of new forms of chieftainship that were legitimised through success in attracting mana or efficacy from ancestors which, in turn, was materialised through accomplishment in conducting and financing headhunting. It was this latter development that transformed what might have been a local struggle for resources into a region-wide phenomenon. The search for heads and for economically useful captives drove Roviana to raid its neighbours, and they in turn were pushed to adopt the headhunting complex as a means of transforming their own sociopolitical systems, as a defensive measure.

With the arrival of European traders in the Western Solomons in the mid-nineteenth century, a new set of economic and cultural forces came into play. The headhunting complex and Roviana expansion had clearly begun before there was any relevant European presence; but the new Western demand for turtleshell and a local demand for Western goods, including guns and axes, intensified the process. Headhunting and turtle hunting became entwined as chiefs turned their attention to Choiseul and Santa Isabel and the turtle nesting sites of Manning Strait. Large-scale raids depopulated eastern Choiseul and western Santa Isabel, pushing populations to the opposite ends of those islands. It is also possible that, at this time, islands closer to Roviana such as Tetepare, Ghizo and Kolombangara became depopulated. This expansion of Roviana and the headhunting complex was ultimately halted at the end of the nineteenth century under the combined effects of Western disease and the imposition of British colonial control: one of the main tasks of the latter was to end violence in the Western Solomons and its negative impact on commercial activity.

Were the headhunting complex and the cultural features with which it was intimately entwined solely a Roviana innovation that spread to neighbouring groups? It seems unlikely. Keeping ancestral skulls in shrines of various forms is a practice recorded throughout the Solomons in the nineteenth century, although it was arguably most elaborate in the Western Solomons. Similarly, the use of shell valuables is common throughout island Melanesia although, again, the very elaborate set of shell valuables and especially the use of fossil shell is a feature of the Western Solomons, while the bakiha form is probably a Roviana innovation. Other important items of material culture such as the mon-type plank-built canoe used in headhunting have a wide distribution in the Western and Northern Solomons. It seems most probable that Roviana adopted cultural forms and ideas from elsewhere and that the headhunting complex itself, although driven from Roviana, developed over time as an interactive process of neighbours reacting to and in turn influencing regional development. The final form of the headhunting complex, seen in the late nineteenth century, appears – based on our Vella Lavella work – to have varied across the islands of the Western Solomons: in Vella Lavella, for example, it seems to have been adopted after developments in Roviana. More detailed understanding of this process and its timing will require much more work in the region.

The prehistory of the Solomon Islands is barely known; yet what we do know reveals that it is marvellously rich, and one of the most complicated stories in the southwestern Pacific. Explaining the cultural and linguistic pattern of the Solomons requires an understanding of large-scale historical processes such as the impact of major cultural traditions and distinctive economies which include early Papuan settlers, Austronesian horticultural society and finally European colonialism and the world system it represented. The distinctive geography of the Solomons has also shaped history. At the island level the tension between coast and interior seems to be important in understanding local history; and while the ease of communication within this archipelago facilitated economic and cultural interaction, it also exacerbated the effects of violence. At the larger, geographical scale the position of the Solomons as a long zone of landfall downwind of the islands of Western Polynesia facilitated the initial settlement of Remote Oceania. It also made the Solomons the long-term recipient of influence from the east as the world system of the Pacific grew after 3000 BP. Onto these major forces were projected local historical contingencies and agencies. Variations in geography made some areas of the Solomons more or less resource rich and more or less central, and this ultimately led to them becoming the focus of cultural change within regions, as in the case of Roviana. Changes in population structure from the low-density hamlet settlement pattern characteristic of most of the Solomons led to changes in sociopolitical organisation. Such changes in turn built on regional cultural variation, which provided the cultural structure and content underlying new forms of organisation. It seems probable that such local processes, including those driven by factors other than variation in population density, have waxed and waned across the Solomons throughout its long prehistory. Unfortunately it is only in the more recent past that we are able to resolve them archaeologically and, most importantly, with the aid of oral history.

Today the Solomon Islands, like many nations in the developing world, struggles to create a modern nation state that will provide for all of its people. Working to form unified nations in areas of great linguistic and cultural diversity is a challenge. How do you respect diversity yet build a future based on shared values and goals? Education ultimately plays an important role. In the Solomons the spread of Pijin helps bridge linguistic barriers that may exist between regions. It is our hope that the work of archaeologists and the National Museum of the Solomon Islands may also provide information that helps bridge cultural barriers and which highlights the long history of diversity but also the shared history that has played such an important role in the Southwest Pacific.

References

Alejandra, C. & Gregory, H.A., 2005. Biogeography of mammals on tropical Pacific islands. *Journal of Biogeography* 32, 1561–69.

Allen, J., 1976. New light on the Spanish settlement of the Southeast Solomons: An archaeological approach. In Green, R.C. & Cresswell, M.M. (eds) *Southeast Solomon Islands Culture History: A preliminary survey*. Wellington: Royal Society of New Zealand, pp. 19–29.

Allen, J., 1993. Notions of the Pleistocene in Greater Australia. In Smith, M.A., Spriggs, M. & Fankhauser, B. (eds) *Sahul in Review: Pleistocene archaeology in Australia, New Guinea and Island Melanesia*. Occasional Papers in Prehistory. Canberra: Department of Anthropology, Australian National University, pp. 139–51.

Allen, J., Gosden, C. & White, J.P., 1989. Human Pleistocene adaptations in the tropical island Pacific: Recent evidence from New Ireland, a Greater Australian outlier. *Antiquity* 63, 548–61.

Allen, J. & Green, R.C., 1972. Mendaña 1595 and the fate of the lost *Almiranta*: An archaeological investigation. *Journal of Pacific History* 7, 73–91.

Allen, J. & O'Connell, J., 2007. Getting from Sunda to Sahul. In Clark, G., Leach, F. & O'Connor, S. (eds) *Island of Inquiry: Colonisation, seafaring and the archaeology of maritime landscapes*. Terra Australis 29. Canberra: ANU E Press, pp. 31–46.

Allen, J. & O'Connell, J.F., 1995. *Transitions: Pleistocene to Holocene in Australia and Papua New Guinea*. Oxford: Antiquity Publications.

Allen, M.G., 2005. The evidence for sweet potato in Island Melanesia. In Ballard, C., Brown, P., Bourke, R.M. & Harwood, F. (eds) *The Sweet Potato in Oceania: A reappraisal*. Oceania Monographs. Sydney: Oceania Publications, pp. 99–108.

Ambrose, W., 1996. Obsidian hydration dating of the Reef/Santa Cruz Lapita sites. In Davidson, J., Irwin, G., Leach, F., Pawley, A. & Brown, D. (eds) *Oceanic Culture History: Essays in honour of Roger Green*. Dunedin: New Zealand Journal of Archaeology Special Publication, pp. 387–410.

Ambrose, W., 2007. The implements of Lapita ceramic stamped ornamentation. In Bedford, S., Sand, C. & Connaughton. S.P. (eds), *Oceanic Explorations: Lapita and western Pacific settlement*. Terra Australis 26, Canberra: ANU E Press, pp. 213–21.

Amherst, L. & Thomson, B., 1901. *The Discovery of the Solomon Islands by Alvaro de Mendana in 1568*, vols I & 2. London: Hakluyt Society.

Anderson, A., 2005. Crossing the Luzon Strait: Archaeological chronology in the Batanes Islands, Philippines and the regional sequence of neolithic dispersal. *Journal of Austronesian Studies* 1, 25–45.

Anderson, A., 2009. The rat and the octopus: Initial human colonization and the prehistoric introduction of domestic animals to Remote Oceania. *Biological Invasions* 11, 1503–19.

Anonymous, 1963. Tunahanika. George Carter Papers. University of Auckland Library, Special Collections.

Aswani, S., 1997. Customary sea tenure and artisanal fishing in the Roviana and Vonavona lagoons, Solomon Islands: The evolutionary ecology of marine resource utilization. PhD thesis, University of Hawai`i.

Aswani, S., 2000. Changing identities: The ethnohistory of Roviana predatory headhunting. *Journal of the Polynesian Society* 109, 39–70.

Aswani, S. & Sheppard, P.J., 2003. The archaeology and ethnohistory of exchange in precolonial and colonial Roviana: Gifts, commodities and inalienable possessions. *Current Anthropology* 44 (supplement), S51–S78.

Bailey, R.C. & Headland, T.N., 1991. The tropical rain forest: Is it a productive environment for human foragers? *Human Ecology* 19, 261–85.

Barker, G., Barton, H., Beavitt, P., Bird, M., Daly, P., Doherty, C., Gilbertson, D., Hunt, C., Krigbaum, J., Lewis, H., Manser, J., McLaren, S., Paz, V., Piper, P., Pyatt, B., Rabett, R., Reynolds, T., Stephens, M., Rose, J., Rushworth, G. & Stephens, M., 2002. Prehistoric foragers and farmers in Southeast Asia: Renewed investigations at Niah Cave. *Proceedings of the Prehistoric Society* 68, 147–64.

Barraud, C., 1972. De la chasse aux têtes à la pêche à la bonite. *L'Homme* 12, 67–104.

Bathgate, M.A., 1985. Movement processes from precontact to contemporary times: The Ndi-Nggai, West Guadalcanal, Solomon Islands. In Chapman, M. & Prothero, R. (eds) *Circulation in Population Movement: Substance and concepts from the Melanesia case.* London: Routledge & Kegan Paul, pp. 83–118.

Bayard, D.T., 1976. *The cultural relationships of the Polynesian outliers.* University of Otago Series in Prehistoric Anthropology 8. Dunedin: University of Otago.

Bayliss-Smith, T., Hviding, E. & Whitmore, T., 2003. Rainforest composition and histories of human disturbance in Solomon Islands. *Ambio* 32, 346–52.

Beasley, H.G., 1939. The Tamar of Santa Cruz. *Ethnologia Cranmorensis* 4, 27–30.

Beasley, H.G. & Jones, F.L., 1936. Notes on red feather money from Santa Cruz Group New Hebrides. *Journal of the Anthropological Institute of Great Britain and Ireland* 66, 379–91.

Beavan Athfield, N., Green, R.C., Craig, J., McFadgen, B. & Bickler, S., 2008. Influence of marine sources on 14C ages: Isotopic data from Watom Island, Papua New Guinea inhumations and pig teeth in light of new dietary standards. *Journal of the Royal Society of New Zealand* 38, 1–23.

Bedford, S., 2000. Pieces of the Vanuatu puzzle: Archaeology of the North, South and Centre. PhD thesis, Australian National University.

Bedford, S., 2003. The timing and nature of Lapita colonisation in Vanuatu: The haze begins to clear. In Sand, C. (ed.) *Pacific Archaeology: Assessments and prospects.* Nouméa: Département Archéologie, Service des Musées et du Patrimoine de Nouvelle-Calédonie, pp. 147–58.

Bedford, S., 2006. *Pieces of the Vanuatu Puzzle: Archaeology of the North, South and Centre. Terra Australis* 23. Canberra: Pandanus Books, Research School of Pacific and Asian Studies, Australian National University.

Bedford, S. & Spriggs, M., 2008. Northern Vanuatu as a Pacific crossroads: The archaeology of discovery, interaction, and the emergence of the 'ethnographic present'. *Asian Perspectives* 47, 95–120.

Bedford, S., Spriggs, M. & Regenvanu, R., 2006. The Teouma Lapita site and the early human settlement of the Pacific Islands. *Antiquity* 80, 812–28.

Bellwood, P., 2006. Asian farming diasporas? Agriculture, languages, and genes in China and Southeast Asia. In Stark, M. (ed.) *Archaeology of Asia.* Oxford: Blackwell, pp. 96–118.

Bennett, J., 1987. *Wealth of the Solomons: A history of a Pacific archipelago, 1800–1978.* Honolulu: University of Hawai`i Press, Pacific Islands Studies Program, Center for Asian and Pacific Studies, University of Hawai`i.

Bernatzik, H.A., 1936. *Owa Raha.* Vienna: Berina Verlag.

Best, S.B., 2002. *Lapita: A view from the east.* New Zealand Archaeological Association, Monograph 24. Auckland: New Zealand Archaeological Association.

Best, S.B., Sheppard, P.J., Green, R.C. & Parker, P., 1992. Necromancing the stone: Archaeologists and adzes in Samoa. *Journal of the Polynesian Society* 101, 45–85.

Birdsell, J.B., 1977. The recalibration of a paradigm for the first peopling of Greater Australia. In Allen, J., Golson, J. & Jones, R. (eds) *Sunda and Sahul: Prehistoric studies in Southeast Asia, Melanesia and Australia.* London: Academic Press, pp. 113–67.

Black, S., 1977. *The Excavations at Teobebe.* Reports of the Bougainville Archaeological Survey 10. Chicago: Field Museum of Natural History.

Black, S. & Green, R.C., 1975. *Radiocarbon dates from the British Solomon Islands to December 1973,* Working papers. Auckland: Department of Anthropology, University of Auckland.

Blackwood, B.M., 1931. Report on field work in Buka and Bougainville. *Oceania* 2, 199–219.

Blackwood, B.M., 1935. *Both Sides of Buka Passage: An ethnographical study of social, sexual and economic questions in the north-eastern Solomon Islands.* Oxford: Clarendon.

Blake, N. & Gibbs, M., 2013. Late prehistoric burial structures and evidence of Spanish contact at Makira, southeast Solomon Islands. *Journal of Pacific Archaeology* 4, 69–78.

Blake, N., Gibbs, M. & Roe, D., 2015. Revised radiocarbon dates for Mwanihuki, Makira: A c. 3000 BP aceramic site in the southeast Solomon Islands. *Journal of Pacific Archaeology* 6, 56–64.

Bronk Ramsey, C. 2009. Bayesian analysis of radiocarbon dates. *Radiocarbon* 5, 337–60.

Brown, G., 1909. *George Brown, DD: Pioneer–missionary and explorer.* London: Hodder & Stoughton.

Buhring, K.L., Azemard, C.S. & Sheppard, P.J., 2015. Geochemical characterization of Lapita ceramics from the Western Solomon Islands by means of portable X-ray fluorescence and scanning electron microscopy. *Journal of Island & Coastal Archaeology* 10, 111–32.

Burley, D.V. & Dickinson, W.R., 2010. Among Polynesia's first pots. *Journal of Archaeological Science* 37, 1020–26.

Butler, V.L., 1988. Lapita fishing strategies: The faunal evidence. In Kirch, P.V. & Hunt, T.L. (eds) *Archaeology of the Lapita Complex: A critical review.* Thomas Burke Memorial Washington State Museum Research Report no. 5. Seattle: Burke Museum, pp. 99–115.

Campbell, H.J., 2008. Geological report on nine adzes from the Solomon Islands. In Leach, F. & Davidson, J. (eds) *Archaeology on Taumako: A Polynesian Outlier in the Eastern Solomon Islands.* Dunedin: New Zealand Archaeological Association Special Publication, pp. 427–31.

Capell, A., 1969. Non-Austronesian languages of the British Solomon Islands. In Capell, A., Chowning, A. & Wurm, S.A. (eds) *Papers in Lingusitics of Melanesia 2: Pacific Linguistics*. Canberra: Australian National University, pp. 1–16.

Carter, G., 1981. *Ti-è Varanè: Stories about people of courage from Solomon Islands*. Rabaul: Unichurch.

Carter, M., Roe, D. & Keopo, J., 2012. Recent recoveries of archaeological ceramics on Santa Isabel. *Journal of Pacific Archaeology* 3, 62–68.

Chappell, J. & Shackleton, N.J., 1986. Oxygen isotopes and sea levels. *Nature* 324, 137–40.

Chappell, J., Omura, A., Esat, T., Mcculloch, M., Pandolfi, J., Ota, Y. & Pillans, B., 1996. Reconciliation of late Quaternary sea levels derived from coral terraces at Huon Peninsula with deep sea oxygen isotope records. *Earth and Planetary Science Letters* 141, 227–36. 10.1016/0012-821x(96)00062-3.

Cheyne, A., 1852. *A Description of Islands in the Western Pacific Ocean, North and South of the Equator: With sailing directions, together with their productions; manners and customs of the natives, and, vocabularies of their various languages*. London: J.D. Potter.

Chikamori, M., 1965. Preliminary report on the archaeological researches in the Western Solomon Islands [in translation]. In Itoh, S. & Chikamori, M. (eds) *A Brief Report on Research into the Prehistory and Anthropology of Various Islands in the British Solomon Islands [in Japanese]*, pp. 1–26.

Chikamori, M. (ed.) 1975. *The Early Polynesian Settlement on Rennell Island Bristish Solomon Islands Protectorate: Preliminary report 1975*. Tokyo: Keio University.

Chikamori, M. & Takasugi, H., 1985. *Archaeology on Rennell Island*. Tokyo: Department of Archaeology and Ethnology, Keio University.

Chiu, S., 2007. Detailed analysis of Lapita face motifs: Case studies from Reef/Santa Cruz Lapita Sites and New Caledonia Lapita Site 13A. In Bedford, S., Sand, C. & Connaughton, S.P. (eds) *Oceanic Explorations: Lapita and Western Pacific settlement. Terra Australis 26*. Canberra: ANU E Press, pp. 241–64.

Churchill, W., 1911. *The Polynesian Wanderings*. Washington: Carnegie Institution of Washington.

Clark, G.R. Indigenous transfer of La Pérouse artefacts in the southeast Solomon Islands. *Australian Archaeology* 57, 103–11.

Clark, G.R., 1999. Post-Lapita Fiji: Cultural transformations in the mid-sequence. PhD thesis, Australian National University.

Codrington, R.H., 1891. *The Melanesians: Studies in their anthropology and folk-lore*. Oxford: Clarendon Press.

Connell, J., 1977. The Bougainville Connection: Changes in the economic context of shell money production in Malaita. *Oceania* 48, 81–101.

Cowley, S., Mann, P., Coffin, M.F. & Shipley, T.H., 2004. Oligocene to recent tectonic history of the Central Solomon intra-arc basin as determined from marine seismic reflection data and compilation of onland geology. *Tectonophysics* 389, 267–307.

Cummings, H., 1973. The distribution of compound fishhook types as a gauge of population interaction in the Solomon Islands. *Solomon Island Studies in Human Biogeography* 1. Department of Anthropology, Field Museum of Natural History.

Davenport, W., 1962. Red-feather money. *Scientific American* 206, 94–103.

Davenport, W., 1964a. Notes on Santa Cruz voyaging. *Journal of the Polynesian Society* 73, 134–42.

Davenport, W., 1964b. Social structure of Santa Cruz Island. In Goodenough, W. (ed.) *Explorations in Culural Anthropology: Essays in honour of George Peter Murdock*. New York: McGraw-Hill, pp. 5–93.

Davenport, W., 1968. Anthropology in the British Solomon Islands. *Expedition* 11, 31–34.

Davenport, W., 1969. Social organisation notes on the northern Santa Cruz Islands: The Main Reef Islands. Baessler-Archiv, Neue Folge, Band XX. Berlin: Baessler Archiv.

Davenport, W., 1971. Sculpture of the eastern Solomons. In Jopling, C.F. (ed.) *Art and Aesthetics in Primitive Societies*. New York: E.P. Dutton, pp. 382–423.

Davenport, W., 1972a. Preliminary excavations on Santa Ana Island, eastern Solomon Islands. *Archaeology and Physical Anthropology in Oceania* 7, 165–183.

Davenport, W., 1972b. Social organisation notes on the northern Santa Cruz Islands: The Outer Reef Islands. Baessler-Archiv, Neue Folge, Band XX. Berlin: Baessler Archiv.

Davenport, W., 1975a. Lyric verse and ritual in the Santa Cruz Islands. *Expedition* 8, 39–47.

Davenport, W., 1975b. The population of the Outer Reef Islands, British Solomon Islands Protectorate. In Carroll, V. (ed.) *Pacific Atoll Populations*. Honolulu: University of Hawai`i Press, pp. 64–116.

Davenport, W., 1981. Male initiation in Aoriki. *Expedition* 23, 4–19.

Davenport, W., 1990. The figurative sculpture of Santa Cruz. In Hanson, F.A. & Hanson, L. (eds) *Art and Identity in Oceania*. Honolulu: University of Hawai`i Press, pp. 98–110.

Davenport, W., n.d. Unpublished excavation records, Vatuluma Posovi. Solomon Islands National Museum.

Davenport, W., Russell, R. & Tedder, J.L., n.d. *Excavations at Fotoruma, Poha River, Guadalcanal, British Solomon Islands Protectorate, December 1966 – August 1968: Diary of excavations*. Honiara, Government Printer.

Davidson, J., 1974. Cultural replacements on small islands: New evidence from Polynesian outliers. *Mankind* 9, 273–77.

Davidson, J., 1975. Review of Yen and Gordon, Anuta: A Polynesian outlier in the Solomon Islands. *Journal of the Polynesian Society* 84, 252–53.

Davis, C.E., 1892. *Australian Station, Solomon Islands, 1891: Correspondence respecting Outrages by Natives on British Subjects and other matters, which have been under inquiry during the Year 1891, being continuation of reports of cases dealt with in former years, together with other cases which have since arisen.* Sydney: Government Printer.

Delfin, F., Myles, S., Choi, Y., Hughes, D., Illek, R., van Oven, M., Pakendorf, B., Kayser, M. & Stoneking, M., 2012. Bridging near and remote Oceania: mtDNA and NRY variation in the Solomon Islands. *Molecular Biology and Evolution* 29, 545–64.

Denham, T. & Haberle, S., 2008. Agricultural emergence and transformation in the Upper Wahgi valley, Papua New Guinea, during the Holocene: Theory, method and practice. *The Holocene* 18, 481–96.

Dickerson, R.E., Merrill, E.D., McGregor, R.C., Schultze, W., Taylor, E.H. & Herre, A.W., 1928. *Distribution of Life in the Philippines*. Manila: Bureau of Printing.

Dickinson, W.R., 1973. Temper sands in potsherds from Anuta. In Yen, D.E. & Gordon, J. (eds) *Anuta: A Polynesian outlier in the Solomon Islands*. Honolulu: Dept of Anthropology, Bernice P. Bishop Museum, pp. 109–11.

Dickinson, W.R., 1975. *Petrographic Report on Sand Tempers in Sherds of Buka and Kieta Traditions from Teop Island off Bougainville*. Reports of the Bougainville Archaeological Survey 7. Chicago: Department of Anthropology, Field Museum of Natural History.

Dickinson, W.R., 2006. *Temper Sands in Prehistoric Oceanian Pottery: Geotectonics, sedimentology, petrography, provenance*. Special paper 46. Boulder: Geological Society of America.

Dickinson, W.R. & Green, R.C., 1973. Temper sands in 1595 AD: Spanish ware from the Solomon Islands. *Journal of the Polynesian Society* 82, 293–300.

Dickinson, W.R. & Shutler, R., Jr, 2000. Implications of petrographic temper analysis for Oceanian prehistory. *Journal of World Prehistory* 14, 203–66.

Doherty, M., 2007. Post-Lapita developments in the Reef–Santa Cruz Islands, southeast Solomon Islands. PhD thesis, University of Auckland.

Doherty, M., 2009. Post-Lapita developments in the Reef–Santa Cruz Islands, southeast Solomon Islands. In Sheppard, P., Thomas, T. & Summerhayes, G. (eds) *Lapita: Ancestors and descendants*. Auckland: New Zealand Archaeological Association, pp. 181–213.

Donohue, M. & Denham, T., 2010. Farming and language in island Southeast Asia: Reframing Austronesian history. *Current Anthropology* 51, 223–56.

Donovan, L.J., 1973. A study of the decorative system of the Lapita potters in the Reef and Santa Cruz Islands. MA research essay, University of Auckland.

Dunn, M., Foley, R., Levinson, S., Reesink, G. & Terrill, A., 2007. Statistical reasoning in the evaluation of typological diversity in Island Melanesia. *Oceanic Linguistics* 46, 388–403.

Dunn, M. & Ross, M., 2007. Is Kazukuru really non-Austronesian? *Oceanic Linguistics* 1, 210–31.

Dunn, M., Terrill, A., Reesink, G., Foley, R. & Levinson, S., 2005. Structural phylogenetics and the reconstruction of ancient language history. *Science* 309, 2072–75.

Dureau, C., 2000. Skulls, *mana* and causality. *Journal of the Polynesian Society* 109, 71–97.

Edge-Partington, T.W., 1907. Ingava, Chief of Rubiana, Solomon Islands: Died 1906. *Man* 7, 22–23.

Felgate, M.W., 2001. A Roviana ceramic sequence and the prehistory of Near Oceania: Work in progress. In Clark, G.R., Anderson, A.J. & Vunidilo, T. (eds) *The Archaeology of Lapita Dispersal in Oceania*. Terra Australis 17. Canberra: Pandanus Press, pp. 39–60.

Felgate, M.W., 2003. Reading Lapita in Near Oceania: Intertidal shallow-water pottery scatters, Roviana Lagoon, New Georgia, Solomon Islands. PhD thesis, University of Auckland.

Felgate, M.W., 2007. Leap-frogging or limping? Recent evidence from the Lapita littoral fringe, New Georgia, Solomon Islands. In Bedford, S., Sand, C. & Connaughton, S.P. (eds) *Oceanic Explorations: Lapita and Western Pacific settlement*. Terra Australis 26. Canberra: ANU E Press, pp. 123–40.

Felgate, M.W., Bickler, S. & Murrell, P.R., 2013. Estimating parent population of pottery vessels from a sample of fragments: A case study from inter-tidal surface collections, Roviana Lagoon, Solomon Islands. *Journal of Archaeological Science* 40, 1319–28.

Felgate, M.W. & Dickinson, W.R., 1998. Late-Lapita and post-Lapita pottery transfers: Evidence from intertidal-zone sites of Roviana Lagoon, Western Province, Solomon Islands. In Jones, M. & Sheppard, P. (eds) *Australasian Connections and New Directions: Proceedings of the 7th Australasian Archaeometry Conference. Research in Anthropology and Linguistics* 5. Auckland: Department of Anthropology, University of Auckland, pp. 103–22.

Findlater, A., Summerhayes, G.R., Dickinson, W.R. & Scales, I., 2009. Assessing the anomalous role of ceramics in late Lapita interaction: A view from Kolombangara, Western Solomon islands. In Sheppard, P., Thomas, T. & Summerhayes, G. (eds) *Lapita, Ancestors and Descendants*. New Zealand Archaeological Association Monograph 28. Auckland: New Zealand Archaeological Association, pp. 101–17.

Firth, R., 1936. *We the Tikopia*. London: George Allen & Unwin.

Firth, R., 1951. *Elements of Social Organization*. Boston: Beacon Press.

Firth, R., 1959. *Social Change in Tikopia: Restudy of a*

Polynesian community after a generation. London: Allen & Unwin.

Firth, R., 1961. *History and Traditions of Tikopia*. Wellington: Polynesian Society.

Firth, R., 1967. *The Work of the Gods in Tikopia*. New York: Humanities Press.

Flannery, T., 1995. *Mammals of the South-west Pacific and Moluccan Islands*. Chatswood: Reed Books.

Flannery, T. & White, J.P., 1991. Animal translocations: Zoogeography of New Ireland mammals. *National Geographic Research and Exploration* 7, 96–113.

Foana`ota, L., 1974. Burial sites on Vella Lavella Island. *Journal of the Solomon Islands Museum Association* 2, 22–33.

Foana`ota, L., 1979. *The Solomon Islands National Site Recording System*. New Zealand Historic Places Trust, pp. 29–33.

Foana`ota, L., 1996. The development of archaeologcial work in the Solomon Islands. In Davidson, J., Irwin, G., Leach, F., Pawley, A. & Brown, D. (eds) *Oceanic Culture History: Essays in honour of Roger Green*. Dunedin: New Zealand Journal of Archaeology, pp. 241–43.

Fox, C.E., 1925. *The Threshold of the Pacific: An account of the social organisation, magic and religion of the people of San Cristoval in the Solomon Islands*. New York: A.A. Knopf.

Friedlaender, J.S. (ed.) 1987. *The Solomon Islands Project: A longer term study of health, human biology, and culture change*. Oxford: Clarendon.

Gaffney, D., Ford, A. & Summerhayes, G. 2015. Crossing the Pleistocene-Holocene transition in the New Guinea Highlands: Evidence from the lithic assemblage of Kiowa rockshelter. *Journal of Anthropological Archaeology* 39, 223–46. 10.1016/j.jaa.2015.04.006.

Galipaud, J.-C. & Biran, A.D., 2006. *Naufragés à Vanikoro: Les rescapés de l'expédition Lapérouse à Païou*. Nouméa: IRD.

Galipaud, J.-C. & Swete-Kelly, M.C., 2007. Makué (Aore Island, Santo, Vanuatu): A new Lapita site in the ambit of New Britain obsidian distribution. In Bedford, S., Sand, C. & Connaughton, S.P. (eds) *Oceanic Explorations: Lapita and Western Pacific settlements. Terra Australis* 26. Canberra: ANU E Press, pp. 151–62.

Garling, S., 2003. Tanga takes to the stage: Another model 'transitional' site? New evidence and a contribution to the 'incised and applied relief tradition' in New Ireland. In Sand, C. (ed.) *Pacific Archaeology: Assessments and prospects*. Nouméa: Service des Musées et du Patrimoine, pp. 213–33.

Gentz, F.W., 2005. Mitochondrial haplogroups in island Melanesia. PhD thesis, Temple University.

Gibbs, M., 2011. Brave New World: The failed Spanish colonies of the Solomon Islands. In Joseph, J.W., Leone, M. & Schablitsky, J. (eds) *Historical Archaeology and the Importance of Material Things II*. Special Publication. Rockville: Society for Historical Archaeology, pp. 143–66.

Golson, J., 1968. Archaeological prospects in Melanesia. In Yawata, I. & Sinoto, Y.H. (eds) *Prehistoric Culture in Oceania*. Honolulu: Bishop Museum Press, pp. 3–14.

Golson, J., 1971. Lapita ware and its transformations. In Green, R.C. & Kelly, M. (eds) *Studies in Oceanic Culture History*. Pacific Anthropological Records no. 12. Honolulu: Department of Anthropology, Bernice P. Bishop Museum, pp. 67–76.

Golson, J., 1991. Two sites at Lasigi, New Ireland. In Allen, J. & Gosden, C. (eds) *Report of the Lapita Homeland Project*. Occasional Papers in Prehistory, no. 20. Canberra: Department of Prehistory, Research School of Pacific Studies, Australian National University, pp. 244–59.

Gosden, C., 1995. Arboriculture and agriculture in coastal Papua New Guinea. *Antiquity* 69, 807–17.

Goto, A., 1996. Shell money production in Langalanga, Malaita Province, Solomon Islands. *Traditional Marine Resource Management and Knowledge Information Bulletin* 7, 6–11.

Gray, R.D., Drummond, A.J. & Greenhill, S.J., 2009. Language phylogenies reveal expansion pulses and pauses in Pacific settlement. *Science* 323, 479–83.

Green, R.C., 1972. A site designation code for the British Solomon Islands. *Journal of the Solomon Islands Museum Association* 1, 65–71.

Green, R.C., 1973a. The conquest of the conquistadors. *World Archaeology* 5, 14–31.

Green, R.C., 1973b. Southeast Solomon Islands Culture History Programme. *Royal Ontario Museum Ethnography Monograph* 1, 1–6.

Green, R.C., 1976a. Introduction. In Green, R.C. & Cresswell, M.M. (eds) *Southeast Solomons Cultural History: A preliminary survey*. Wellington: Royal Society of New Zealand, pp. 9–17.

Green, R.C., 1976b. Languages of the Southeast Solomons and their historical relationships. In Green, R.C. & Cresswell, M.M. (eds) *Southeast Solomons Cultural History: A preliminary survey*. Wellington: Royal Society of New Zealand, pp. 9–17.

Green, R.C., 1976c. Lapita sites in the Santa Cruz Group. In Green, R.C. & Cresswell, M.M. (eds) *Southeast Solomon Islands Culture History: A preliminary survey*. Wellington: Royal Society of New Zealand, pp. 245–65.

Green, R.C., 1976d. A late prehistoric sequence from Su`ena village, Uki. Bulletin of the Royal Society of New Zealand, 181–91.

Green, R.C., 1976e. A late prehistoric settlement in Star Harbour. In Green, R.C. & Cresswell, M.M. (eds) *Southeast Solomon Islands Culture History: A preliminary survey*. Wellington: Royal Society of New Zealand, pp. 133–47.

Green, R.C., 1977. *A First Culture History of the Solomon Islands*. Auckland, Auckland University Bindery.

Green, R.C., 1978. *New sites with Lapita pottery and their implications for an understanding of the settlement of the Western Pacific*. Auckland: Dept of Anthropology, University of Auckland.

Green, R.C., 1979. Lapita. In Jennings, J. (ed.) *Prehistory of Polynesia*. Cambridge, Mass.: Harvard University Press, pp. 27–60.

Green, R.C., 1986. Lapita fishing: The evidence of Site SE-RF-2 from the Main Reef Islands, Santa Cruz Group, Solomons. In Anderson, A. (ed.) *Traditional Fishing in the Pacific*. Pacific Anthropological Records, no. 37. Honolulu: Bernice P. Bishop Museum, pp. 119–35.

Green, R.C., 1987. Obsidian results from the Lapita sites of the Reef/Santa Cruz Islands. In Ambrose, W. & Mummery, J. (eds) *Archaeometry: Further Australasian studies*. Canberra: Australian National University, pp. 239–49.

Green, R.C., 1991a. Near and Remote Oceania: Disestablishing 'Melanesia' in culture history. In Pawley, A. (ed.) *Man and a Half: Essays in Pacific anthropology and ethnobiology in honour of Ralph Bulmer*. Auckland: Polynesian Society, pp. 491–502.

Green, R.C., 1991b. A reappraisal of the dating from some Lapita sites in the Reef/Santa Cruz Group of the Southeast Solomon Islands. *Journal of the Polynesian Society* 100, 197–207.

Green, R.C., 1996. Prehistoric transfers of portable items during the Lapita horizon in remote Oceania: A review. *Indo-Pacific Prehistory Association Bulletin* 15, 119–29.

Green, R.C., 2009. An evaluation of sample adequacy for the Lapita-style ceramic assemblages from three sites located in the Reef/Santa Cruz group, outer eastern islands of the Solomons. *Research in Anthropology and Linguistics*. Auckland: Department of Anthropology, University of Auckland.

Green, R.C. & Bird, J., 1989. Fergusson Island obsidian from the D'Entrecasteaux Group in a Lapita site of the Reef Santa Cruz Group. *New Zealand Journal of Archaeology* 11, 87–99.

Green, R.C. & Cresswell, M. (eds), 1976. *Southeast Solomon Islands Cultural History: A preliminary report*. Wellington: Bulletin of the Royal Society of New Zealand.

Green, R.C. & Davidson, J.M., 1969. Description and classification of Samoan adzes. In Green, R.C. & Davidson, J.M. (eds) *Archaeology of Western Samoa*, vol. I. Auckland Institute & Museum, Bulletin 6, pp. 21–32.

Green, R.C. & Jones, M., 2008. The absolute age of SE-RF-6 (Ngamanie) and its relation to to SE-RF-2 (Nenumbo): Two decorated Lapita sites in the southeast Solomon Islands. *New Zealand Journal of Archaeology* 29, 5–18.

Green, R.C., Jones, M. & Sheppard, P.J., 2008. The reconstructed environment and absolute dating of SE-SZ-8 Lapita site on Nendo, Santa Cruz, Solomon Islands. *Archaeology in Oceania* 43, 49–61.

Green, R.C. & Kirch, P.V., 1997. Lapita exchange systems and their Polynesian transformations: Seeking explanatory models. In Weisler, M.I. (ed.) *Prehistoric Long-distance Interaction in Oceania: An interdisciplinary approach*. Auckland: New Zealand Archaeological Association, pp. 19–37.

Green, R.C. & Pawley, A., 1999. Early Oceanic architectural forms and settlement patterns: Linguistic, archaeological and ethnological perspectives. In Blench, R. & Spriggs, M. (eds) *Archaeology and Language III: Artefacts, languages and texts*. London: Routledge, pp. 31–89.

Green, R.C. & Yen, D.E., 2009. The Southeast Solomon Islands Culture History Project. In Sheppard, P., Thomas, T. & Summerhayes, G. (eds) *Lapita Archaeology 2007: Proceedings of the 7th Lapita Conference* 28. Auckland: New Zealand Archaeological Association, pp. 147–72.

Grimes, S., 2003. A history of environmental change and human impact since 3750 BP in the New Georgia Group, Western Solomon Islands. PhD thesis, University of Western Australia.

Guppy, H.B., 1887. *The Solomon Islands and their Natives*. London: Swan Sonnenschein.

Haberle, S., 1996. Explanations for paleoecological changes on the northern plains of Guadalcanal, Solomon Islands: The last 3200 years. *The Holocene* 6, 333–38.

Hackman, B.D., 1980. *The Geology of Guadalcanal*. London: HMSO.

Haddon, A.C. & Hornell, J., 1936. *Canoes of Oceania*, Bernice P. Bishop Museum Special Publication. Honolulu, Hawai`i: Bishop Museum.

Hall, A.H., 1964. Customs and culture from Kazukuru: Folklore obtained after the discovery of the shrine at Bao. *Oceania* 35, 127–35.

Hawkesworth, J., 1775. *An account of the voyages undertaken by the order of His present Majesty, for making discoveries in the southern hemisphere, and successively performed by Commodore Byron, Captain Wallis, Captain Carteret, and Captain Cook, in the* Dolphin, *the* Swallow, *and the* Endeavour: *Drawn up from the journals which were kept by the several commanders and from the papers of Joseph Banks, esq.*, vol. 1. Dublin: James Williams.

Hendren, G.H., 1976. Recent settlement pattern changes on Ulawa, southeast Solomon Islands. In Green, R.C. & Cresswell, M.M. (eds) *Southeast Solomon Islands Cultural History: A preliminary survey*. Wellington: Royal Society of New Zealand, pp. 149–59.

Hocart, M., MSS. Trade and Money. Hocart Manuscripts. Wellington: Turnbull Library.

Hocart, A.M. 1922. The cult of the dead in Eddystone of the Solomons. *Royal Anthropological Institute of Great Britain and Ireland* LII: 71–112, 259–305, pl. V–IX, XVII–XIX.

Houston, D.C., 2010. The impact of red feather currency on the population of the scarlet honeyeater on Santa Cruz. In Tidemann, S. & Gosler, A. (eds) *Ethno-ornithology: Birds, indigenous peoples, culture and society*. London: Earthscan, pp. 55–66.

Hviding, E. & Bayliss-Smith, T., 2000. *Islands of Rainforest:*

Agroforestry, logging and eco-tourism in Solomon Islands. Aldershot: Ashgate.

Intoh, M., 1999. Cultural contacts between Micronesia and Melanesia. In Galipaud, J.-C. & Lilley, I. (eds) *The Pacific from 5000 to 2000 BP: Colonisation and transformations.* Paris: Editions de IRD, pp. 407–22.

Irwin, G.J., 1972. An archaeological survey in the Shortland Islands, BSIP. MA thesis, University of Auckland.

Irwin, G.J., 1973. Man–land relationships in Melanesia. *Archaeology and Physical Anthropology* 8, 226–52.

Irwin, G.J., 1974. Carved paddle decoration of pottery and its capacity for inference in archaeology: An example from the Solomon islands. *Journal of the Polynesian Society* 83, 368–71.

Irwin, G.J., 1992. *The Prehistoric Exploration and Colonisation of the Pacific.* Cambridge: Cambridge University Press.

Irwin, G.J. & Holdaway, S., 1996. Colonisation, trade and exchange: From Papua to Lapita. In Davidson, J., Irwin, G., Leach, B., Pawley, A. & Brown, D. (eds) *Oceanic Culture History: Essays in honour of Roger Green.* Dunedin: New Zealand Journal of Archaeology Special Publication, pp. 225–35.

Ivens, W.G., 1927. *Melanesians of the South-east Solomons.* London: Kegan Paul.

Ivens, W.G., 1930. *The Island Builders of the Pacific.* London: Seeley, Service & Co.

Ivens, W.G., 1931. Flints in the south-east Solomon Islands. *Journal of the Royal Anthropological Institute* 61, 421–24.

Jackson, K.B., 1975. Head-hunting in the Christianization of Bugotu 1861–1900. *Journal of Pacific History* 10, 65–78.

Jones, M.D., Petchey, F.J., Green, R.C., Sheppard, P.J. & Phelan, M., 2007. The Marine ΔR for Nenumbo (Solomon Islands): A case study in calculating reservoir offsets from paired sample data. *Radiocarbon* 49, 95–102.

Keesing, R.M., 1970. Shrines, ancestors and cognatic descent: The Kwaio and Tallensi. *American Anthropologist* 72, 755–75.

Keesing, R.M., 1982. *Kwaio Religion: The living and the dead in a Solomon Island society.* New York: Columbia University Press.

Keesing, R.M., 1987. African models in the Malaita Highlands. *Man* 22, 431–52.

Kelloway, S.J., Gibbs, M. & Craven, S., 2013. The sherds of conquistadors: A petrological study of ceramics from Graciosa Bay and Pamua, Solomon Islands. *Archaeology in Oceania* 48, 53–59.

Keopo, J. & Kawamura, Y., 1999. *Report on National Site Survey: Rereona, Kia District, Isabel Province.* Honiara, Solomon Islands National Museum.

Kirch, P.V., 1982. A revision of the Anuta sequence. *Journal of the Polynesian Society* 91, 245–54.

Kirch, P.V., 1983a. An archaeological exploration of Vanikoro, Santa Cruz Islands, eastern Melanesia. *New Zealand Journal of Archaeology* 5, 69–113.

Kirch, P.V., 1983b. Mangaasi-style ceramics from Tikopia and Vanikoro and their implications for east Melanesian prehistory. *Bulletin of the Indo-Pacific Prehistory Association*, 67–75.

Kirch, P.V., 1984. The Polynesian outliers: Continuity, change, and replacement. *Journal of Pacific History* 19, 224–38.

Kirch, P.V., 1988a. Long-distance exchange and island colonization: The Lapita case. *Norwegian Archaeological Review* 21, 103–17.

Kirch, P.V., 1988b. *Niuatoputapu: The prehistory of a Polynesian chiefdom.* Thomas Burke Memorial Washington State Museum monograph. Seattle: Burke Museum.

Kirch, P.V., 1997. *The Lapita Peoples: Ancestors of the oceanic world.* The Peoples of South-East Asia and the Pacific. Cambridge, Mass.: Blackwell Publishers.

Kirch, P.V., 2000. *On the Road of the Winds: An archaeological history of the Pacific islands before European contact.* Berkeley: University of California Press.

Kirch, P.V. (ed.) 2001. *Lapita and its Transformations in Near Oceania: Archaeological investigations in the Mussau Islands, Papua New Guinea, 1985–1988.* Berkeley: University of California.

Kirch, P.V., Hunt, T.L., Weisler, M., Butler, V. & Allen, M.S., 1991. Mussau Islands prehistory: Results of the 1985–86 excavations. In Allen, J. & Gosden, J. (eds) *Report of the Lapita Homeland Project.* Occasional Papers in Prehistory, no. 20. Canberra: Department of Prehistory, Research School of Pacific Studies, Australian National University, pp. 144–63.

Kirch, P.V. & Rosendahl, P.H., 1973a. Archaeological investigation of Anuta. In Yen, D. & Gordon, J. (eds) *Anuta: A Polynesian outlier in the Solomon Islands.* Pacific Anthropological Records. B.P. Bishop Museum, pp. 25–108.

Kirch, P.V. & Rosendahl, P.H., 1973b. A note on carbon dates for pottery-bearing layers on Anuta island. *Journal of the Polynesian Society* 82, 206–8.

Kirch, P.V. & Yen, D.E., 1982. *Tikopia: The prehistory and ecology of a Polynesian outlier*, Bernice P. Bishop Museum Bulletin. Honolulu, Hawai`i: Bishop Museum Press.

Kraus, B.S., 1945. Preliminary report on the discovery of surface sherds on Mono Island, Treasury Group, Solomon Islands. *American Antiquity* 11, 102–04.

Krose, S. 2016. Same people, different people: Recognition, knowledge and the (re)construction of relationships in Bilua, Vella Lavella. PhD thesis, University of Auckland.

Lampert, R., 1966. Archaeological reconnaissance in Papua and New Guinea: 1966. Canberra: Australian National University.

Lawrence, D., 2014. *The Naturalist and his 'beautiful islands': Charles Morris Woodford in the Western Pacific.* Canberra: Australian National University Press.

Leach, B.F. & Davidson, J.M., 2008. *Archaeology on Taumako: A Polynesian outlier in the Eastern Solomon Islands.* New Zealand Archaeological Association Special Publication. Dunedin: NZAA.

Leavesley, M., 2006. Late Pleistocene complexities in the Bismarck Archipelago. In Lilley, I. (ed.) *Archaeology of Oceania: Australia and the Pacific Islands.* Oxford: Blackwell, pp. 189–204.

Leavesley, M., 2007. A shark-tooth ornament from Pleistocene Sahul. *Antiquity* 81, 308–15.

Leavesley, M., Bird, M., Fifield, K., Hausladen, P.A., Santos, G.M. & DiTada, M.L., 2002. Buang Merabak: Early evidence for human occupation in the Bismarck Archipelago, Papua New Guinea. *Australian Archaeology* 54, 55–56.

Leavesley, M. & Chappell, J., 2004. Buang Merabak: Additional early radiocarbon evidence of the colonisation of the Bismarck Archipelago, Papua New Guinea. *Antiquity* 78, http://antiquity.ac.uk.ezproxy.auckland.ac.nz/ProjGall/leavesley/

Leavesley, M. & H. Mandui, n.d., *Report of the Pioneers of Island Melanesia Project Fieldwork in Bougainville Province, Papua New Guinea.* Leverhulme Centre for Human Evolutionary Studies, Cambridge University.

Loy, T.H., Spriggs, M. & Wickler, S., 1992. Direct evidence for human use of plants 28,000 years ago: Starch residues on stone artefacts from the northern Solomon islands. *Antiquity* 66, 898–912.

MacLachlan, R.R.C., 1938. Native pottery from Central and Southern Melanesia and Western Polynesia. *Journal of the Polynesian Society* 47, 64–89.

Mann, P., Taylor, F.W., Lagoe, M.B., Quarles, A. & Burr, G., 1998. Accelerating late Quaternary uplift of the New Georgia Island Group (Solomon island arc) in response to subduction of the recently active Woodlark spreading center and Coleman seamount. *Tectonophysics* 295, 259–306.

Markham, C.R., 1904. *The voyages of Pedro Fernandez de Quiros, 1595 to 1606.* Works issued by the Hakluyt Society. London: Printed for the Hakluyt Society.

Matisoo-Smith, E., 2007. Animal translocations, genetic variation and the human settlement of the Pacific. In Friedlaender, J. (ed.) *Genes, Language and Culture History in the Southwest Pacific.* Oxford: Oxford University Press, pp. 157–70.

McCoy, P.C. & Cleghorn, P.L., 1988. Archaeological excavations on Santa Cruz (Nendö), Southeast Solomon Islands: Summary report. *Archaeology in Oceania* 23, 104–15.

McDougall, D., 2000. Paths of 'pinauzu': Captivity and social reproduction in Ranongga. *Journal of the Polynesian Society* 109, 99–114.

McKenzie, A., 2007. Ancestral skull shrines: Material dialogues of social interaction in the Western Solomon Islands. MA thesis, University of Auckland.

McKeown, A. 1977. *Marine Turtles of the Solomon Islands.* Honiara: Ministry of Natural Resources.

McKinnon, J., 1972. Bilua changes: Culture contact and its consequences – a study of the Bilua of Vella Lavella in the British Solomon Islands. PhD thesis, Victoria University.

McKinnon, J., 1975. Tomahawks, turtles and traders: A reconstruction in the circular causation of warfare in the New Georgia Group. *Oceania* XLV, 290–307.

Mead, S.M., 1973a. The last initiation ceremony at Gupuna Santa Ana, Eastern Solomon Islands. *Auckland Institute and Museum Records* 10, 69–95.

Mead, S.M., 1973b. *Material Culture and Art in the Star Harbour Region, Eastern Solomon Islands.* Toronto: Royal Ontario Museum.

Mead, S.M., Birks, L., Birks, H. & Shaw, E., 1973. The Lapita pottery style of Fiji and its associations (Memoirs of the Polynesian Society 38:1/2). *Journal of the Polynesian Society* 3, [1–43].

Miller, D., 1978. The archaeology of the Solomons. *Journal of the Cultural Association of the Solomon Islands* 6, 36–53.

Miller, D., 1979. *National Sites Survey Summary Report.* Honiara: Solomon Islands National Museum.

Miller, D., 1980a. Archaeology and development. *Current Anthropology* 21, 709–26.

Miller, D., 1980b. Settlement and diversity in the Solomon Islands. *Man* 15, 451–66.

Miller, D. & Roe, D., 1982. The Solomon Islands National Sites Survey: The first phase. *IPPA Bulletin*, 47–51.

Mortimer, J.A. 2002. *Sea Turtle Biology and Conservation in the Arnavon Marine Conservation Area (AMCA) of the Solomon Islands.* Honiara: The Nature Conservancy.

Moyle, R., 2007. *Songs from the Second Float: A musical ethnography of Takaū Atoll, Papua New Guinea.* Honolulu: University of Hawai`i Press, p. 21.

Næss, Å. & Boerger, B., 2008. Reefs–Santa Cruz as Oceanic: Evidence from the verb complex. *Oceanic Linguistics* 47, 185–212.

Nagaoka, T., 1999. Hope pukerane: A study of religious sites in Roviana, New Georgia, Solomon Islands. MA thesis, University of Auckland.

Nagaoka, T., 2011. Late prehistoric–early historic houses and settlement space on Nusa Roviana, New Georgia Group, Solomon Islands. PhD thesis, University of Auckland.

Nakada, M. & Lambeck, K., 1989. Late Pleistocene and Holocene sea-level change in the Australian region and mantle rheology. *Geophysical Journal – Oxford* 96, 497–517. 10.1111/j.1365-246X.1989.tb06010.x.

Nicholson, R.C., 1925. *The Son of a Savage: The story of Daniel Bula.* London: Epworth Press.

Noury, A., 2007. Lapita period modelled ceramic face from New Caledonia. *Archaeology in Oceania* 42, 28–30.

Nunn, P.D., 1998. *Pacific Island Landscapes.* Suva: Institute of Pacific Studies, University of the South Pacific.

Nunn, P.D. & Heorake, T., 2009. Understanding the place properly: Palaeogeography of selected Lapita sites in the western tropical Pacific Islands and its implications. In Sheppard, P., Thomas, T. & Summerhayes, G.R. (eds)

Nunn, P.D., Matararaba, S., Kumar, R., Pene, C. & Yuen, L., 2006. Lapita on an island in the mangroves? The earliest human occupation at Qoqo Island, southwest Viti Levu, Fiji. *Archaeology in New Zealand* 3, 205–12.

O'Connell, J.F. & Allen, J., 2004. Dating the colonisation of Sahul (Pleistocene Australia and New Guinea): A review of recent research. *Journal of Archaeological Science* 31, 835–53.

O'Connell, J.F. & Allen, J., 2013. The restaurant at the end of the Universe: Modelling the colonisation of Sahul. *Australian Archaeology* 74, 5–31.

O'Reilly, P., 1940. Description sommaire d'une collection d'objets ethnographiques de l'île de Bougainville (groupe des îles Salomon). Vatican City: Pontificio museo missionario etnologico del Laterano. *Annali Lateranensi*, 163–98.

O'Reilly, P., 1948. Un outil néolithique des îles Salomon. *Société des océanistes, Paris: Journal*, 156–57.

Ogan, E., 1970. Nasioi pottery-making. *Journal of the Polynesian Society* 79, 86–90.

Oliver, D., 1949. The Peabody Museum expedition to Bougainville, Solomon Islands, 1938–39. *Studies in the Anthropology of Bougainville, Solomon Islands*. Papers of the Peabody Museum of American Archaeology and Ethnology, Harvard University, 29.

Oliver, D., 1955. *A Solomon Island Society*. Cambridge: Harvard University Press.

Oliver, D., 1991. *Black Islanders: A personal perspective of Bougainville 1937–1991*. Melbourne: Hyland House.

Paravicini, E., 1931. *Reisen in den Britischen Salomonen*. Frauenfeld: Huber.

Parker, R., 1994. *Maekera: The life story of hereditary chief Nathan Kera and the Saikile community of Solomon Islands / as told to Russell Parker*. Brisbane: Solomonesia Productions.

Parker, V.N.M., 1981. Vessel Forms of the Reef Island SE-RF-2 Site and their relationships to vessel forms in other Western Lapita sites of the Reef/Santa Cruz and Island Melanesian area. MA thesis, University of Auckland.

Pawley, A., 1967. The relationships of the Polynesian Outlier languages. *Journal of the Polynesian Society* 73, 289–96.

Pawley, A., 2009. The role of the Solomon Islands in the first settlement of Remote Oceania: Bringing linguistic evidence to an archaeological debate. In Adelaar, A. & Pawley, A. (eds) *Austronesian Historical Linguistics and Culture History: A Festschrift for Robert Blust*. Canberra: Australian National University, pp. 515–40.

Petterson, M., Magu, R., Mason, A., Mahoa, H., Tolia, D., Neal, C. & Mahoney, J., 2009. A first geological map of Makira, Solomon Islands: Stratigraphy, structure and tectonic implications. In Petterson, M. (ed.) *Pacific Minerals in the New Millennium: Science, exploration, mining, and community (The Jackson Lum volume)*. SOPAC Technical Bulletin 11. Suva: Pacific Islands Applied Geoscience Commission (SOPAC), pp. 151–67.

Poulsen, J.I. & Polach, H.A., 1972. Outlier archaeology: Bellona. a preliminary report on field work and radiocarbon dates. *Archaeology and Physical Anthropology in Oceania* 7, 184–214.

Pycroft, A.T., 1935. Santa Cruz red-feather money: Its manufacture and use. *Journal of the Polynesian Society* 44, 173–83.

Reepmeyer, C., 2009. The obsidian sources and distribution systems emanating from Gaua and Vanua Lava in the Banks Islands of Vanuatu. PhD thesis, Australian National University.

Reeve, R., 1989. Recent work on the prehistory of the Western Solomons, Melanesia. *Bulletin of the Indo-Pacific Prehistory Association* 9, 46–67.

Reimer, P.J., Baillie, M.G.L., Bard, E., Bayliss, A., Beck, J.W., Bertrand, C.J.H., Blackwell, P.G., Buck, C.E., Burr, G.S., Cutler, K.B., Damon, P.E., Edwards, R.L., Fairbanks, R.G., Friedrich, M., Guilderson, T.P., Hogg, A.G., Hughen, K.A., Kromer, B., McCormac, G., Manning, S., Ramsey, C.B., Reimer, R.W., Remmele, S., Southon, J.R., Stuiver, M., Talamo, S., Taylor, F.W., van der Plicht, J. & Weyhenmeyer, C.E., 2004. IntCal04 terrestrial radiocarbon age calibration, 0–26 cal kyr BP. *Radiocarbon* 46, 1029–58.

Renfrew, C., 1986. Introduction: Peer polity interaction and socio-political change. In Renfrew, C. & Cherry, J. (eds) *Peer Polity Interaction and Socio-political Change*. Cambridge: Cambridge University Press, pp. 1–18.

Ribbe, C., 1903. *Zwei Jahre unter den Kannibalen der Salomon-Inseln*. Dresden: Beyer.

Richards, R., 2011. A probable Lapita site in the Western Solomon Islands? *Archaeology in Oceania* 46, 139–40.

Riesenberg, S.H. & Gayton, A.H., 1952. Caroline Island belt weaving. *Southwestern Journal of Anthropology* 8, 342–75.

Rieth, T.M. & Hunt, T.L., 2008. A radiocarbon chronology for Samoan prehistory. *Journal of Archaeological Science* 35, 1901–27.

Roberts, R.G., Jones, R. & Smith, M.A., 1990. Thermoluminescence dating of a 50,000-year-old human occupation site in northern Australia. *Nature* 66, 153–56.

Roberts, R.G., Jones, R., Spooner, M.J., Head, M.J., Murray, A.S. & Smith, M.A., 1994. The human colonization of Australia: Optical dates of 53,000 and 60,000 bracket human arrival at Deaf Adder Gorge, Northern Territory. *Quaternary Science Reviews* 13, 575–83.

Roe, D., 1989. The Kolevu Valley terraced taro system, west Guadalcanal. In International Board for Soil Research and Management (ed.) *Soil Management and Smallholder Development in the Pacific Islands: Pacific land*. Bangkok: IBSRAM, pp. 205–11.

Roe, D., 1992. Rock art of north-west Guadalcanal, Solomon Islands. In McDonald, J. & I.P. Haskovec (eds) *State of the*

Art: Regional rock art studies in Australia and Melanesia. Melbourne: Australian Rock Art Research Association.

Roe, D., 1993. Prehistory without pots: Prehistoric settlement and economy of north-west Guadalcanal, Solomon Islands. PhD thesis, Australian National University.

Roe, D., 2000. Maritime, coastal and inland societies in Island Melanesia: The bush–saltwater divide in Solomon Islands and Vanuatu. In O'Connor, S. & Veth, P. (eds) *East of Wallace's Line: Studies of past and present maritime cultures of the Indo-Pacific region*. Rotterdam: A.A. Balkema, pp. 197–222.

Rogerson, R.J., Hilyard, D.B., Finlayson, E.J., Johnson, R.W. & McKee, C.O., 1989. *The Geology and Mineral Resources of Bougainville and Buka Islands, Papua New Guinea*. Memoir 16. Port Moresby: Geological Survey of Papua New Guinea.

Ross, H.M., 1970. Stone adzes from Malaita, Solomon Islands: An ethnographic contribution to Melanesian archaeology. *Journal of the Polynesian Society* 79, 411–20.

Ross, M., 1988. *Proto Oceanic and the Austronesian Languages of Western Melanesia*. Pacific Linguistics C–98. Canberra: Australian National University.

Ross, M., 1989. Early Oceanic linguistic prehistory: A reassessment. *Journal of Pacific History* 24, 135–49.

Ross, M., 2001. Is there an East Papuan phylum? Evidence from pronouns. In Pawley, A., Ross, M. & Tryon, D. (eds) *The Boy from Bundaberg: Studies in Melanesian linguistics in honour of Tom Dutton*. Canberra: Pacific Linguistics, pp. 301–21.

Ross, M. & Næss, Å., 2007. An Oceanic origin for Äiwoo, the language of the Reef Islands? *Oceanic Linguistics* 2, 456–98.

Rossel, E.P.E., 1808. *Voyage de Dentrecasteaux, envoye à la recherche de La Pérouse*. Pub. par ordre de Sa Majesté l'empereur et roi, sous le ministère de S.E. le vice-admiral Decrès, Comte de l'empire. Rédigé par M. de Rossel. Paris: Imprimerie impériale.

Rukia, A., 1989a. Digging. In Laracy, H. (ed.) *Ples Blong Iumi: Solomon Islands the past four thousand years*. Suva: Institute of Pacific Studies of the University of the South Pacific, pp. 1–15.

Rukia, A., 1989b. Early usages of rockshelters and caves in Solomon Islands: Nggela Pile, Central Islands Province. *`O`O: A journal of Solomon Island studies* 2, 26–47.

Russell, T., 2003. *I Have the Honour To Be*. Spennymoor: The Memoir Club.

Sand, C., 1996. Recent developments in the study of New Caledonia's prehistory. *Archaeology in Oceania* 31, 45–71.

Sand, C., 2007a. The eastern frontier: Lapita ceramics in the Fiji–West Polynesia region. In Chiu, S. & Sand, C. (eds) *From Southeast Asia to the Pacific: Archaeological perspectives on the Austronesian expansion and the Lapita cultural complex*. Taipei: Academia Sinica, pp. 214–34.

Sand, C., 2007b. Looking at the big motifs: A typology of the central band decorations of the Lapita ceramic tradition of New Caledonia (Southern Melanesia) and preliminary regional comparisons. In Bedford, S., Sand, C. & Connaughton, S. (eds) *Oceanic Explorations: Lapita and Western Pacific settlement*. Canberra: ANU E Press, pp. 265–87.

Sand, C. & Sheppard, P.J., 2000. Long distance prehistoric obsidian imports in New Caledonia: Characteristics and meaning. *Earth and Planetary Sciences* 331, 235–43.

Scheffler, H.W., 1965. *Choiseul Island Social Structure*. Berkeley: University of California Press.

Schneider, G., 1996. Land dispute and tradition in Munda, Roviana Lagoon, New Georgia, Solomon Islands from headhunting to the quest for the control of land. PhD thesis, University of Cambridge.

Scott, M.W., 2007. *The Severed Snake: Matrilineages, making place, and a Melanesian Christianity in southeast Solomon Islands*. Durham: Carolina Academic Press.

Shapiro, H.L., 1933. Are the Ontong Javanese Polynesian? *Oceania* 3, 367–76.

Sheppard, P.J., 1993. Lapita lithics: Trade/exchange and technology – a view from the Reefs/Santa Cruz. *Archaeology in Oceania* 28, 121–37.

Sheppard, P.J., 1996. Hard rock: Archaeological implications of chert sourcing in Near and Remote Oceania. In Davidson, J., Irwin, G., Leach, B., Pawley, A. & Brown, D. (eds) *Oceanic Culture History: Essays in honour of Roger Green*. Dunedin: New Zealand Journal of Archaeology Special Publication, pp. 99–115.

Sheppard, P.J., 2009. Understanding the who, what and why of Lapita. In Sheppard, P., Thomas, T. & Summerhayes, G. (eds) *Lapita: Ancestors and descendants*. Auckland: New Zealand Archaeological Association, pp. 1–10.

Sheppard, P.J., 2010. Lapita lithic technology. In Sand, C., Bedford, S. & Chambonniere, C. (eds) *Lapita: Ancêtres océaniens/Oceanic ancestors*. Paris: Somogy, pp. 240–50.

Sheppard, P.J., 2011. Lapita colonization across the Near/Remote Oceania boundary. *Current Anthropology* 52, 799–840.

Sheppard, P.J., 2013. Re-dating Feru rock shelter on Santa Ana, Eastern Solomon Islands. Manuscript on file, Department of Anthropology, University of Auckland.

Sheppard, P.J., Chiu, S. & Walter, R., 2015a. Re-dating Lapita movement in Remote Oceania. *Journal of Pacific Archaeology* 6, 26–36.

Sheppard, P.J., Felgate, M.W., Roga, K., Keopo, J. & Walter, R., 1999. A ceramic sequence from Roviana Lagoon (New Georgia, Solomon Islands). In Lilly, I. & Galipaud, J.C. (eds) *The Pacific from 5000–2000 BP: Colonisation and transformations*. Paris: Editions de IRD, pp. 313–22.

Sheppard, P.J. & Green, R.C., 1991. Spatial analysis of the Nenumbo (SE-RF–2) Lapita site, Solomon Islands. *Archaeology in Oceania* 26, 89–101.

Sheppard, P.J. & Green, R.C., 2007. Sample size and the Reef/Santa Cruz Lapita sequence. In Bedford, S., Sand, C. & Connaughton, S. (eds) *Oceanic Explorations: Lapita and* western *Pacific settlement*. Canberra: ANU E Press, pp. 141–50.

Sheppard, P.J. & Pavlish, L.A., 1992. Weathering of archaeological cherts: A case study from the Solomon Islands. *Geoarchaeology* 7, 41–53.

Sheppard, P.J., Trichereau, B. & Milicich, C., 2010a. Pacific obsidian sourcing by portable XRF. *Archaeology in Oceania* 45, 21–30.

Sheppard, P.J. & Walter, R., 2006. A revised model of Solomon Islands culture history. *Journal of the Polynesian Society* 115, 47–76.

Sheppard, P.J. & Walter, R., 2008. The sea is not land: Comments on the archaeology of islands in the Western Solomons. In Connolly, J. & Campbell, M. (eds) *Comparative Island Archaeologies*, no. 1829. Oxford: BAR International Series, pp. 167–78.

Sheppard, P.J. & Walter, R., 2009. Inter-tidal late Lapita sites and geotectonics in the Western Solomon Islands. In Sheppard, P., Thomas, T. & Summerhayes, G. (eds) *Lapita: Ancestors and descendants*. New Zealand Archaeological Association Monograph no. 28. Auckland: New Zealand Archaeological Association, pp. 73–100.

Sheppard, P.J. & Walter, R., 2013. Diversity and networked interdependence in the Western Solomons. In Summerhayes, G. & Buckley, H. (eds) *Pacific Archaeology: Documenting the past 50,000 years. Papers from the 2011 Lapita Pacific Archaeology Conference*. University of Otago Studies in Archaeology, no. 25. Dunedin: University of Otago, pp. 138–47.

Sheppard, P.J. & Walter, R., 2014. Shell valuables and history in Roviana and Vella Lavella. In Burt, B. & Bolton, L. (eds) *The Things We Value: Culture and history in Solomon Islands*. Canon Pyon: Sean Kingston Publishing, pp. 33–45.

Sheppard, P.J., Walter, R. & Aswani, S., 2004. Oral tradition and the creation of late prehistory in Roviana Lagoon, Solomon Islands. *Records of the Australian Museum*, Supplement 29, 123–32.

Sheppard, P.J., Walter, R., Dickinson, W.R., Felgate, M.W., Ross-Sheppard, C. & Azémard, C., 2015b. A Solomon Sea interaction sphere? In Chiu, S., Sand, C. & Hogg, N. (eds) *The Lapita Cultural Complex in Time and Space: Expansion routes, chronologies and typologies*. Archeologia Pasifika 4. Taipei: Center for Archaeological Studies, RCHSS, Academia Sinica, pp. 64–80.

Sheppard, P.J., Walter, R. & Nagaoka, T., 2000. The archaeology of head-hunting in Roviana Lagoon. *Journal of the Polynesian Society* 109, 9–37.

Sheppard, P.J., Walter, R. & Roga, K., 2010b. Friends, relatives, and enemies: The archaeology and history of interaction among Austronesian and NAN speakers in the Western Solomons. In Bowden, J. & Himmelmann, N. (eds) *A Journey through Austronesian and Papuan Cultural Space: A Festschrift for Andrew Pawley*. Canberra: Pacific Linguistics, Australian National University, pp. 95–112.

Shineberg, D. (ed.) 1971. *The Trading Voyages of Andrew Cheyne, 1841–1844*. Canberra: Australian National University.

Shore, B., 1996. *Culture in Mind: Cognition, culture and the problem of meaning*. Oxford: Oxford University Press.

Shutler, R. & Shutler, M., 1964. Potsherds from Bougainville Island. *Asian Perspectives* 8, 181–83.

Sillitoe, P. & Shiel, R.S., 1999. Soil fertility under shifting and semi-continuous cultivation in the Southern Highlands of Papua New Guinea. *Soil Use and Management* 15, 49–57.

Soares, P., Rito, T., Trejaut, J., Mormina, M., Hill, C., Tinkler-Hundal, E., Braid, M., Clarke, D.J., Loo, J.-H., Thomson, N., Denham, T., Donohue, M., Macaulay, V., Lin, M., Oppenheimer, S. & Richards, M.B., 2011. Ancient voyaging and Polynesian origins. *American Journal of Human Genetics* 88, 239–47.

Specht, J., 1969. Prehistoric and modern pottery industries of Buka Island, TPNG [Territory of Papua New Guinea]. PhD thesis, Australian National University.

Specht, J., 1972. The pottery industry of Buka Island, TPNG. *Archaeology and Physical Anthropology in Oceania* 7, 125–44.

Specht, J., 2002. Obsidian, colonizing and exchange. In Bedford, S., Sand, C. & Burley, D. (eds) *Fifty Years in the Field: Essays in honour and celebration of Richard Shutler Jr's archaeological career*. New Zealand Archaeological Association Monograph no. 25. Auckland: New Zealand Archaeological Association, pp. 37–49.

Specht, J., 2005. Revisiting the Bismarcks: Some alternative views. In Pawley, A., Attenborough, R., Golson, J. & Hide, R. (eds) *Papuan Pasts: Cultural linguistic and biological histories of Papuan-speaking peoples*. Canberra: Pacific Linguistics, pp. 235–88.

Specht, J., 2007. Small islands in the big picture: The formative period of Lapita in the Bismarck Archipelago. In Bedford, S., Sand, C. & Connaughton, S.P. (eds) *Oceanic Explorations: Lapita and western Pacific settlement*. Terra Australis 26. Canberra: ANU E Press, pp. 51–70.

Specht, J., 2009. The aceramic to ceramic boundary in the Bismarck Archipelago. In Sheppard, P., Thomas, T. & Summerhayes, G. (eds) *Lapita: Ancestors and descendants*. Auckland: New Zealand Archaeological Association, pp. 11–34.

Spriggs, M., 1990. The changing face of Lapita: Transformation of a design. In Spriggs, M. (ed.) *Lapita Design, Form and Composition: Proceedings of the Lapita Design Workshop, Canberra, Australia, December 1988*. Occasional Papers in Prehistory, no. 19. Canberra: Department of Prehistory, Research School of Pacific Studies, Australian National University, pp. 83–122.

Spriggs, M., 1991a. Lapita origins, distribution, contemporaries and successors revisited. *Bulletin of the Indo-Pacific Prehistory Association* 11, 306–12.

Spriggs, M., 1991b. Nissan: The island in the middle.

Summary report on excavations at the north end of the Solomons and the south end of the Bismarcks. In Allen, J. & Gosden, C. (eds) *Report of the Lapita Homeland Project.* Occasional Papers in Prehistory, no. 20. Canberra: Dept of Prehistory, Research School of Pacific Studies, Australian National University, pp. 222–43.

Spriggs, M., 1992. Archaeological and linguistic prehistory in the North Solomons. In Dutton, T., Ross, M. & Tryon, D. (eds) *The Language Game: Papers in memory of Donald C. Laycock.* Pacific Linguistics, Series C. Canberra: Department of Linguistics, Research School of Pacific Studies, Australian National University, pp. 417–26.

Spriggs, M., 1993a. How much of the Lapita design system represents the human face? In Dark, P.J.C. & Rose, R.G. (eds) *Artistic Heritage in a Changing Pacific.* Bathurst: Crawford House Publishing, pp. 7–14.

Spriggs, M., 1993b. Island Melanesia: The last 10,000 years. In Spriggs, M., Yen, D., Ambrose, W., Jones, R., Thorne, A. & Andrews, A. (eds) *A Community of Culture: The people and prehistory of the Pacific.* Occasional Papers in Prehistory. Canberra: Australian National University, pp. 187–205.

Spriggs, M., 1997. *The Island Melanesians: Peoples of South-East Asia and the Pacific.* Oxford: Blackwell Publishers.

Spriggs, M., 2000a. Can hunter-gatherers live in tropical rainforests? The Pleistocene Island Melanesian evidence. In Schweitzer, P.P., Biesele, M. & Hitchcock, R.K. (eds) *Hunters and Gatherers in the Modern World: Conflict, resistance and self-determination.* Berghahn Books, pp. 287–304.

Spriggs, M., 2000b. The Solomon Islands as bridge and barrier in the settlement of the Pacific. In Anderson, A.J. & Murray, T. (eds) *Australian Archaeologist: Collected papers in honour of Jim Allen.* Canberra: Coombs Academic Publishing, Australian National University, pp. 454–67.

Spriggs, M., 2010. Geomorphic and archaeological consequences of human arrival and agricultural expansion on Pacific islands: A reconsideration after 30 years of debate. In Haberle, S., Stevenson, J. & Prebble, M. (eds) *Altered Ecologies: Fire, climate and human influence on terrestrial landscapes.* Terra Australis 32. Canberra: Australian National University, pp. 239–52.

Spriggs, M., Bird, R. & Ambrose, W., 2010. A reanalysis of the Tikopia obsidians. *Archaeology in Oceania* 45, 31–38.

Steadman, D.W., 1995. Prehistoric extinctions of Pacific Island birds: Biodiversity meets zooarchaeology. *Science* 267, 1123–30.

Steadman, D.W., 1999. The Lapita extinction of Pacific island birds: Catastrophic versus attritional. In Galipaud, J.-C. & Lilley, I. (eds) *South Pacific, 5000 to 2000 BP: Colonisations and transformations.* Nouméa: Orstrom, pp. 375–86.

Steadman, D.W., 2006. *Extinction and Biogeography of Tropical Pacific Birds.* Chicago: University of Chicago Press.

Stoddart, D.R., 1969. Geomorphology of the Marovo elevated barrier reef, New Georgia. *Philosophical Transactions of the Royal Society of London*, Series B, 255, 383–402.

Summerhayes, G.R., 1987. Aspects of Melanesian ceramics. MA thesis, University of Sydney.

Summerhayes, G.R. 2009. Obsidian network patterns in Melanesia: Sources, characterisation and distribution. *Bulletin of the Indo-Pacific Prehistory Association* 29, 109–23.

Summerhayes, G.R. & Ford, A. 2014. Late Pleistocene colonisation and adaptation in New Guinea. Implications for modelling modern human behaviour. In Dennell, R. & Porr, M. (eds) *Southern Asia, Australia and the Search for Human Origins.* Cambridge: Cambridge University Press, pp. 213–27.

Summerhayes, G.R., Leavesley, M. & Fairbairn, A., 2009. Impact of human colonization on the landscape: A view from the Western Pacific. *Pacific Science* 63, 725–45.

Summerhayes, G.R., Leavesley, M., Fairbairn, A., Mandui, H., Field, J., Ford, A. & Fullagar, R., 2010. Human adaptation and plant use in Highland New Guinea 49,000 to 44,000 years ago. *Science* 330.

Summerhayes, G.R. & Scales, I., 2005. New Lapita pottery finds from Kolombangara, western Solomon Islands. *Archaeology in Oceania* 40, 14–20.

Swadling, P., 1976. The occupation sequence and settlement pattern on Santa Ana. In Green, R.C. & Cresswell, M.M. (eds) *Southeast Solomon Islands Cultural History: A preliminary survey.* Wellington: Royal Society of New Zealand, pp. 123–32.

Swadling, P., 2000. Changing marine interests and their implications for the settlement history of Santa Ana, an island in the southeast Solomon Islands. In Anderson, A. & Murray, T. (eds) *Australian Archaeologist: Collected papers in honour of Jim Allen.* Canberra: Coombs Academic, pp. 365–71.

Szabo, K. & Summerhayes, G.R., 2002. Worked shell artefacts: New data from early Lapita. In Bedford, S., Sand, C. & Burley, D.V. (eds) *Fifty Years in the Field: Essays in honour and celebration of Richard Shutler's archaeological career.* Auckland: New Zealand Archaeological Association, pp. 91–100.

Taylor, F.W., Mann, P., Bevis, M.G., Edwards, R.L., Cheng, H., Cutler, K.B., Gray, S.C., Burr, G.S., Beck, J.W., Phillips, D.A., Cabioch, G. & Recy, J., 2005. Rapid forearc uplift and subsidence caused by impinging bathymetric features: Examples from the New Hebrides and Solomon arcs. *Tectonics* 24, TC6005.

Tedder, M.M. & Barrus, S., 1976. Old Kusaghe. *Journal of the Solomon Islands Cultural Association* 4, 41–95.

Terrell, J., 1970. *An Archaeological Survey of Bougainville Island, TPNG.* Chicago: Field Museum of Natural History.

Terrell, J., 1976. Perspectives on the prehistory of Bougainville Island, Papua New Guinea: A study in the human biogeography of the southwestern Pacific. PhD thesis, Harvard University.

Terrell, J., 1977a. Geographic systems and human diversity in the Northern Solomons. *World Archaeology* 9, 62–81.

Terrell, J., 1977b. Human biogeography in the Solomon Islands. *Fieldiana Anthropology* 68, 1–47.

Terrell, J., 1986. *Prehistory in the Pacific Islands: A study of variation in languages, customs, and human biology*. Cambridge & New York: Cambridge University Press.

Terrell, J., 2002. Tropical agroforestry, coastal lagoons, and Holocene prehistory in Greater Near Oceania. In Yoshida, S. & Matthews, P.J. (eds) *Vegeculture in Eastern Asia and Oceania*. JCAS Symposium Series 16. Osaka: Japan Centre for Area Studies, National Museum of Ethnology, pp. 195–216.

Terrell, J. & Irwin, G.J., 1972. History and tradition in the Northern Solomons: An analytical study of the Torau migration to southern Bougainville in the 1860s. *Journal of the Polynesian Society* 81, 317–49.

Terrell, J.E. & Schechter, E.M., 2007. Deciphering the Lapita code: The Aitape ceramic sequence and late survival of the 'Lapita face' (Papua New Guinea). *Cambridge Archaeological Journal* 17, 59–85.

Terrell, J.E. & Schechter, E.M., 2009. The meaning and importance of the Lapita face motif. *Archaeology in Oceania* 44, 45–55.

Terrill, A., 2011. Languages in contact: An exploration of stability and change in the Solomon Islands. *Oceanic Linguistics* 50, 312–37.

Terrill, A. & Keith, B., 2006. Central Solomon languages. *Encyclopedia of Language & Linguistics*. Oxford: Elsevier, pp. 279–81.

Thomas, T., 2003. Things of Roviana: Material culture, personhood and agency in nineteenth century Solomon Islands. PhD thesis, University of Otago.

Thomas, T., 2009. Communities of practice in the archaeological record of New Georgia, Rendova and Tetepare. In Sheppard, P., Thomas, T. & Summerhayes, G. (eds) *Lapita: Ancestors and descendants*. Auckland: New Zealand Archaeological Association, pp. 119–45.

Thomas, T., 2014. Shrines in the landscape of new Georgia. In Martinsson-Wallin, H. & Thomas, T. (eds) *Monuments and People in the Pacific*. Studies in Global Archaeology, no. 20. Uppsala: Uppsala Universitet, pp. 47–76.

Thomas, T., Sheppard, P.J. & Walter, R., 2001. Landscape, violence and social bodies: Ritualized architecture in a Solomon Islands society. *Journal of Royal Anthropological Institute* 75, 545–72.

Thurnwald, R., 1912. *Forschungen auf dem Salomo-insulen und dem Bismarck-Archipel*. Berlin: Dietrich Reimer.

Thurnwald, R.C., 1934. Stone monuments in Buin (Bougainville, Solomon Islands). *Oceania* 5, 214–17.

Tochilin, C., Dickinson, W.R., Felgate, M.W., Pecha, M., Sheppard, P.J., Damon, F.H., Bickler, S. & Gehrels, G.E., 2012. Sourcing temper sands in ancient ceramics with U–Pb ages of detrital zircons: A southwest Pacific test case. *Journal of Archaeological Science* 39, 2583–91.

Torrence, R., 2002. Cultural landscapes on Garua Island, Papua New Guinea. *Antiquity* 76, 766–76.

Torrence, R., Neall, V.E., Doelman, T., Rhodes, E., McKee, C.O., Davies, H., Bonetti, R., Guglielmetti, A., Manzoni, A., Oddone, M., Parr, J.F. & Wallace, R., 2004. Pleistocene colonisation of the Bismarck Archipelago: New evidence from West New Britain. *Archaeology in Oceania* 39, 101–30.

Torrence, R. & Swadling, P., 2008. Social networks and the spread of Lapita. *Antiquity* 82, 600–16.

Tryon, D. & Hackman, B., 1983. *Solomon Islands Languages: An internal classification*. Pacific Linguistics, no. 72. Canberra: Australian National University.

Voris, H.K., 2000. Special Paper 2: Maps of Pleistocene sea levels in Southeast Asia: Shorelines, river systems and time durations. *Journal of Biogeography*, 27, 1153–67.

Waite, D., 1990. Mon canoes of the Western Solomon Islands. In Hanson, A. & Hanson, L. (eds) *Art and Identity in Oceania*. Honolulu: University of Hawai`i Press, pp. 44–66.

Waite, D.B., 1969. Solomon Islands sculpture. PhD thesis. University Microfilms, Columbia University.

Waite, D.B., 1979. Aspects of style and symbolism in the art of the Solomon Islands. *Exploring the Visual Art of Oceania*, 238–64.

Walter, R., 1989. Lapita fishing strategies: A review of the archaeological and linguistic evidence. *Pacific Studies* 13, 127–49.

Walter, R., 1998. *Anai`o: The archaeology of a fourteenth century Polynesian community in the Cook Islands*, New Zealand Archaeological Association Monograph. Dunedin: New Zealand Archaeological Association.

Walter, R. & Green, R.C., 2011. *Su`ena: Five hundred years of interaction in the Eastern Triangle, Solomon Islands*, University of Otago Studies in Prehistoric Anthropology, no. 23. Dunedin: Anthropology Department, University of Otago.

Walter, R., Jacomb, C. & Bowron-Muth, S., 2010. Colonisation, mobility and exchange in New Zealand prehistory. *Antiquity* 84, 497–513.

Walter, R. & Sheppard, P.J., 2001. Nusa Roviana: The archaeology of a Melanesian chiefdom. *Journal of Field Archaeology* 27, 295–318.

Walter, R. & Sheppard, P.J., 2006. Archaeology in Melanesia: A case study from the Western Province of the Solomon Islands. In Lilley, I. (ed.) *Archaeology of Oceania, Austalia and the Pacific Islands*. London: Blackwell, pp. 137–59.

Walter, R. & Sheppard, P.J., 2009. A review of Solomon Island archaeology. In Sheppard, P., Thomas, T. & Summerhayes, G. (eds) *Lapita: Ancestors and Descendants*. New Zealand Archaeological Association Monograph, no. 28. Auckland: New Zealand Archaeological Association, pp. 35–72.

Walter, R., Thomas, T. & Sheppard, P.J., 2004. Cult assemblages and ritual practice in Roviana Lagoon, Solomon Islands. *World Archaeology* 36, 142–57.

Ward, G.K., 1976. The archaeology of settlements associated with the chert industry at Ulawa. In Green, R.C. & Cresswell, M.M. (eds) *Southeast Solomon Islands Cultural History: A preliminary survey.* Wellington: Royal Society of New Zealand, pp. 161–80.

Ward, R.G., Webb, J. & Levison, M., 1973. The settlement of the Polynesian Outliers: A computer simulation. *Journal of the Polynesian Society* 82, 330–42.

Waterhouse, J.H.L., 1949. *A Roviana and English Dictionary, with English–Roviana index and list of natural history objects and appendix of old customs.* Revised and enlarged by L.M. Jones. Sydney: Epworth Printing & Publishing House.

White, G.M., 1991. *Identity Through History: Living stories in a Solomon Islands society.* Cambridge: Cambridge University Press.

White, J.P., Clark, G. & Bedford, S., 2000. Distribution, present and past, of *Rattus praetor* in the Pacific and its implications. *Pacific Science* 54, 105–17.

White, J.P. & Harris, M., 1997. Changing sources: Early Lapita period obsidian in the Bismarck Archipelago. *Archaeology in Oceania* 32, 97–101.

White, J.P. & Murray-Wallace, C.V., 1996. Site ENX (Fissoa) and the incised and applied pottery tradition in New Ireland, Papua New Guinea. *Man and Culture in Oceania* 12, 31–46.

White, M., 2002. The Spanish sherds from San Cristobal. *Journal of the Polynesian Society* 111, 249–54.

Whitmore, T.C., 1969. The vegetation of the Solomon Islands. *Philosophical Transactions of the Royal Society of London: B Biological Sciences*, 259–70.

Wickler, S., 2001. *The Prehistory of Buka: A stepping stone island in the Northern Solomons. Terra Australis* 16. Canberra: Department of Archaeology and Natural History and Centre for Archaeological Research, Australian National University.

Wickler, S. & Spriggs, M., 1988. Pleistocene human occupation of the Solomon Islands, Melanesia. *Antiquity* 62, 703–06.

Wilson, W.H., 2012. Whence the East Polynesians? Further linguistic evidence for a northern outlier source. *Oceanic Linguistics* 51, 289–59.

Woodford, C.M., 1890. *A Naturalist among the Head-hunters.* London: George Phillip & Son.

Woodford, C.M., 1909. The canoes of the British Solomon Islands. *Journal of the Royal Anthropological Institute of Great Britain and Ireland* 39, 506–16.

Yen, D.E., 1973a. Acknowledgements. In Yen, D.E. & Gordon, J. (eds) *Anuta: A Polynesian outlier in the Solomon Islands. Pacific Anthropological Records* 21. Honolulu: Bernice P. Bishop Museum, pp. iv–v.

Yen, D.E., 1973b. Ethnobotany from the voyages of Mendana and Quiros in the Pacific. *World Archaeology* 5, 32–43.

Yen, D.E., 1976. Agricultural systems and prehistory in the Solomon Islands. In Green, R.C. & Cresswell, M.M. (eds) *Southeast Solomon Islands Cultural History: A preliminary survey.* Wellington: Royal Society of New Zealand, pp. 61–74.

Yen, D.E., 1982. The Southeast Solomon Islands Cultural History Programme. *Bulletin of the Indo-Pacific Prehistory Association*, 52–66.

Yen, D.E., 1996. Melanesian arboriculture: Historical perspectives with emphasis on the genus *Canarium*. In Stevens, M.L., Bourke, R.M. & Evans, B.R. (eds) *South Pacific Indigenous Nuts.* Canberra: Australian Centre for International Agricultural Research, pp. 36–44.

Yen, D.E. & Gordon, J. (eds), 1973. *Anuta: a Polynesian outlier in the Solomon Islands,* Honolulu: Department of Anthropology, Bernice P. Bishop Museum.

Zelenietz, M., 1979. The end of head hunting in New Georgia. In Rodman, M. & Cooper, M. (eds) *The Pacification of Melanesia.* Ann Arbor: University of Michigan Press, pp. 91–108.

Index

Page numbers in **bold** refer to maps and illustrations.

aboriculture 122, 128, 130; *see also* forests; tree crops
accelerator mass spectrometry (AMS) 44
Admiralties Group 55, 76, 83
adzes: obsidian adzes 58; shell adzes 25, 58, 79, 83, 85, 119, 125, 126, 129, 148, 150; stone adzes 50, 55, 62, 64, 83, 100, 102, 108, 109–10, **111, 112,** 117, 119, 125
Africa 37
agamids 39
agriculture 64, 92, 102, 117, 130; *see also* animal husbandry; horticulture
Äiwoo language 23, 24
Alocasia spp. 41–42
Alu, Shortland Islands 97, **99,** 99–100
Ambitle 13, 38
amphibolite 83
Ana Tavatava site, Taumako 125
Anadara 50, 145
ancestor cults 34, 35, 139, 151, 152
ancestral skull shrines *see* skull shrines
animal husbandry 64, 78, 130
animals: early to mid-Holocene 50; invertebrates 109; Pleistocene 38, 39; species loss as a result of hunting 126; *see also* biodiversity, terrestrial; bird bones; fishbone assemblages; shellfish; vertebrates; and names of individual species, e.g. rats
Anuta 14, 16, 32, 76, 84–85, 88, 122, 129; location of archaeological sites **84**; Zone A (1800 AD–) 130; Zone B (c. 1400 cal BP) 129; Zone C and Hiatus (2300–1500 cal BP) 129; Zone E (commencement at c. 2950 cal BP) 84, 125, 129
Anutan language 25, 78
Arawe Islands 59
arboriculture 122, 132; *see also* tree crops
archaeology: archaeological knowledge 14–15; early history 29–32; Holocene record 14, 35, 41, 42, 43–51, 164; Lapita peoples 14–15, 32, 35, 64–78, 86; location of fieldwork activities **30**; National Site Survey Project 34, 55–56, 57, 61; Pleistocene record 14, 36–43, **37,** 163; and regional development 161–62; Solomon Islands National Museum 34, 48, 61, 62, 101; Southeast Solomon Island Cultural History Project (SESP) 32–33, **33,** 34, 53, 60, 62, 65, 78, 82 84, 101, 106, 108, 117, 119, 122, 165; underrepresentation of immediate pre-Lapita period 51–52; *see also under* individual regions, island groups and islands
Arnavon Islands 57, **57,** 137, 138, 140
Arosi district, Makira 61, 118–19
arrow or spear points 125
art styles 20, 22
Artocarpus altilis (breadfruit) 46, 78, 98, 100
Asaphis 125
Asio ceramic style 95, 97
atu lou 27
Aua dialect 25
Australia 36, 37; *see also* Wallace Line
Australian plate 45, 100, 132
Austronesian languages 17–18, **18,** 22, 23, 24, 34, 50, 53, 64, 78, 88, 89, 98, 119, 130, 135, 136, 155, 164, 166
Austronesian-speaking peoples 22, 53, 89, 92, 154; *see also* Lapita peoples

backstrap loom 25, **26,** 165
bakiha 135, **136,** 146, 150, 161, 162, 167
Balistidae (trigger fish) 39, 41
bananas 78, 100, 156
bandicoot (*Echymipera kalubu*) 11
Banks Island 25, 76, 77, 80, 83, 88, 122, 126, 128, 129
Bao period, New Georgia 141, 142, **142, 143, 144,** 144–45, 151, 152–53
bareka 151
basalt 56, 68, 100, 101, 128, 141, 142, 144–45, 150, 151, 152, 153, 158
bats 38, 39, 44, 50
Bellona 16, 88; archaeology **31,** 31–32, 101; pottery 32
Bellona language 25, 27
Best, S.B. 66–67, 70, 72
Biak Island 44
Bilua Bifoa project, Vella Lavella 34–35, 155–57

biodiversity, terrestrial: Bismarck Archipelago 11; New Guinea 11, 38; Northern Solomons 11, 38; Remote Oceania 11
bird bones 39, 78, 83, 85, 125, 126
Bismarck Archipelago 13, 28, 163; archaeology 37, 42, 164; canoes and sailing capability 17, 164; DNA studies 22, 24; Holocene social networks 44; languages 20, 24; Lapita homeland 14, 53, 60, 76, 164; Lapita migration to Reef–Santa Cruz Group 86–88, 164; movements of Austronesian speakers before Lapita cultural complex 89; movements of Austronesian speakers to Northern Solomons 92; obsidian 66, 86–87, 122, 126; Pleistocene settlement 37, 38; pottery 58, 59, 62, 77, 128, 164; stilt-house tradition 60; terrestrial biodiversity 11, 38; tools 44, 76; water gap between Northern Solomons 163
Blake, Natalie 106, 108
bones: deposits of human exhumed bones 105, 121; *see also* bird bones; dog bones; megapode bones; and under pigs
bonito *(Katsuwonis pelamis)*: cult and ceremonial rites 20, 23, 106, 109, 110, 117–18, 162; fishing 17, 20, 23, 109, 117, 118
Bougainville 12, 13, 90, 92; archaeology 29, 30, **31,** 44, **93**; carvings 20; compound fishhooks 20; interaction spheres 92, **92,** 97, 98; languages 17–18, 20, 92; plank-built canoes 21; pottery 29–30, 35, 55, 93, 95–97, **96,** 98, 164; sculpture 20; settlement pattern 98–99; tools 44; volcanic activity 92, 95, 98–99; *see also* Greater Bukida (Greater Bougainville)
Bougainville, Louis Antoine de 98
Bougainville Straits 20, 29, 92, 93, 130
Bourewa site, Fiji 65
breadfruit *(Artocarpus altilis)* 46, 78, 98, 100, 122; fermentation pits 122, 124, 128
British Navy 138
Brown, George 138
Buang Merabak, New Ireland 37
Bugotu region, Santa Isabel 18, 20, 22, 138
Buin Plain, Bougainville 30, 35, 90, 92, 95, 96, 97, 98
Buka 12, 13, 38, 90, 163; archaeology 15, 29–30, **31, 37,** 43–45, 98; carvings 20; ceramic and cultural sequences proposed by Specht and Wickler 54–55; compound fishhooks 20; early to mid-Holocene 43–45; interaction spheres 92, **92,** 163; intertidal reef sites 54, 55; languages 17–18, 20, 92; plank-built canoes 21; Pleistocene colonisation 38; pottery 29–30, 35, 54–55, 58, 59, 86, 93–95, **94,** 97, 164; rockshelter habitations 14; sculpture 20; settlement 98; stilt-house tradition 60; *see also* Kilu Cave; Palandraku Cave
Buka Passage **37,** 38
burial customs, structures and shrines 104, 105, 106, 108, 121; ancestral skull shrines 121, **134,** 135, 138, 139; Namu burial site, Taumako 125–26
burning 46, 60, 64, 141; *see also* swidden (slash-and-burn) systems
'bush' (inland) people *see* inland 'bush' people and settlements

cairns, stone 105
Canarium (Pacific almond) species 17, 42, 43, 50, 62, 103, 145; *C. indicum* (okete) 44, 145; *C. salomonense* (tovinia) 44, 145; *C. solomonense* (tovinia) 44, 145
canoe (custom) houses 22–23, 103, 104, 106, **107,** 117, 118, 135, **135,** 138, 139, 146, 150, 157, 161
canoe sculpture 20
canoe travel and transport 12, 16, 17, 24, 25, 28, 51, 130, 154; atu lou 27; deep-ocean sailing 165; drift voyages 25, 28, 62; Lapita technologies 53, 77, 164, 165; Main Solomons 163; Northern Solomons 92; Pleistocene 36, 38; Polynesian Outliers 165; settlement of Buka (longest ocean voyage of the time) 38
canoes: bark (Pleistocene) 36; bonito fishing canoes 23; outrigger canoes 17, 25; te puke voyaging canoes 24, 25, 123, **124;** war canoes (tomoko) 22, **132,** 135, 138, 139, 150, 161; *see also* plank-built canoes
Cape Dunganon 54
Caroline Islands 25, 27
Carter, George 149
Carter, Melissa 35
Carteret, Philip 120
carvings: Eastern Triangle area 110; Santa Cruz and Santa Ana 24; Western Solomons 20
Cassis shell 58, 85, 126
Catoira, Gomez Hernandez 110, 117
Central Solomons 12, 13, 28, 164; archaeology 35; art styles 22; bonito fishing and cult 23, 162; carvings 20; colonisation by Austronesian-speaking peoples 89; contact with Reef–Santa Cruz region 62, 64, 89, 123; differences from Western Solomons 22–23; headhunting and related exchange 103, 138; Lapita period 53–54, 60–64, 86; maps **13, 100;** plank-built canoes 21–22; pottery 60; sculpture 20; *see also* names of individual island groups and islands
Central Solomons, review of last 2000 years 100–19; archaeology 101–10; cultural areas and exchange systems 117–19; horticultural systems 110, 117; sites and settlement patterns 100, 101, 103–10
ceramics *see* pottery
chalcedony 66, 76, 82, 83
charcoal deposition: coconut and *Conarium* 42, 43, 44, 50, 85, 145; dating 53, 61, 62, 65, 78, 79, 82, 85, 104; evidence of burning 46, 64; Nanggu 68
Cheke Holo people, Santa Isabel 138
chert and chert artefacts: Buka and Sohano Island 41, 44, 55; Central Solomons 100, 101, 102–03, 106, 108, 109–10, **110, 111,** 117, 118–19; Guadalcanal 47, 48, 50, 62, 64; Malaita 62, 64, 66, 76, 82, 100, 102–03, 109, 117, 118, 122, 126, 164; Nenumbo site 74; New Georgia 146, 158; Polynesian Outliers 79, 82, 83; proportion of obsidian to chert in Reef–Santa Cruz Lapita sites 66, 67; source of chert, Reef–Santa Cruz Lapita sites 66, 75, 75, **77,** 119, 126; Su'ena site, Uki 109–10, **110, 111,** 119; Ulawa 64, 66, 76,

82, 83, 103, 109, 117, 118, 122, 126, 164; weathering 68
Cheyne, Andrew 136, 138–39
chicken 125, 126; bone, dating 67, 78; *Gallus gallus* 78; Tikopia 83
Chikamori, Masashi 29, 32, 55, 156
Chiu, Scarlett 32, 68, 72, 73
Choiseul 12, 13; archaeology 29, 30, 34, 131; cultural ties to Western Solomons 131; headhunting 136, 137, 138, 166; horticulture 98; interaction spheres 92, **92**, 131, 136; languages 20, 92; pottery 35, 55, 56, 57, 95, 97, 140, 164; sculpture 20; subsidence 56, 86, 140; turtleshell trade 138
coastal environments: early to mid-Holocene 44–46, 50–51, 164; forest clearance and conversion to garden land 46, 50, 60, 64; intertidal zones 54, 55, 56, 57, 58, 59, 60, 64, 65, 86, 88, 94, 97, 140–41, 152; mangrove replacement by muddy-sandy shore environments 50; *see also* lagoon systems
coastal 'saltwater' people and settlements 14, 17, 42, 44–45, 46, 50–51; Bismarck Archipelago 37; Bougainville 50, 92, 98; Buka 50, 98; Central Solomon Islands 100, 103, 104, **104,** 106; New Georgia 58, 131, 132, 141, 142, 145, 147–48, 155; Reef–Santa Cruz Islands 120; shift from coastal to interior settlements 98, 161; shift from interior to coastal settlements 131, 142, 145, 157, 161, 166; Shortland Islands 99; tension between coast and interior 103. 131, 161, 162, 166; Western Solomons 86; *see also* inland 'bush' people and settlements
coconut (*Cocos nucifera*) 44, 85, 100, 117
Colocasia esculenta (taro) *see* taro (*Colocasia esculenta* and *Cyrtosperma*)
colonialism 167
communities of practice 35, 162
conch shells 146
Conus shell 29, 58, 79, 83, 125, 150
Coral Sea 165
coral-rubble/cobble structures 108, 141, 145–47, **146,** 148, 149, 150, 152, 153, 158, 160
Coryphaenidae (dolphinfish) 39
cowrie shell 110, 125
Craven, Anna 34
Crowther, Alison 78
culture: Buka cultural sequence proposed by Wickler 54–55; Central Solomons cultural areas and exchange systems 117–19; communities of culture 162; cultural geography 16–28, 164, 166; differences east and west of Tryon-Hackman Line 18, **18,** 20, 22, 164, 165; Eastern Triangle culture area 108, 109, 110, 117–19, **118**; Melanesian cultural diversity 14; model of connectivity, nearest-neighbour analysis 16, **17,** 20, 130; Northern Solomons interaction spheres 92, **92,** 93, 131; Solomon Islands cultural diversity 14, 16, 90, 130, 162, 165, 166, 167; Solomons cultural and economic interaction 13, 16; Western Solomons cultural and economic interaction 14, 130, 131, 135; Western Solomons cultural homogeneity 135

cuscus or possum (*Phalanger orientalis*) 11, 38, 43, 44, 102, 109
custom (canoe) houses 106, **107**
Cypraea shell 126
Cyrtosperma (taro) *see* taro (*Colocasia esculenta* and *Cyrtosperma*)

Dai village, Tömotu Neo 120–21, 122
dance circles 120, 121, **121**
dance exchange visits 117, 118, 121
Davenport, William 30–31, 47, 48, 61–62, 118, 120, 121, 122, 123
Davidson, Janet 78–82, 124–26
Davis, Captain 138, 147
D'Entrecasteaux Islands 76
Dillon, Peter 124
diseases, European 99, 100, 147, 166
DNA studies: DNA variation, supporting population breakup and dispersal 18; Lapita peoples 88; Micronesian mitochondrial sequences from Ontong Java 27; and pattern of language relationships 18, 20, 22, 24, 27; Polynesian Outliers 27, 88; support of Reef–Santa Cruz direct settlement from Bismarck Archipelago 88
Dodson, John 45–46
dog bones 80, 83, 102, 109, 125, 126
dog sculpture, Nusa Roviana 148
Doherty, Moira 35, 119, 120
domestication: animals 64, 78, 130; plants 42, 43, 78, 126, 130
Donovan, L.J. 66–67, 68–70
Duff (Taumako) Group 14, 76, 78, 122, 123; *see also* Taumako
Dumont d'Urville, Jules Sébastien César 138

East 'Are'are region, Malaita 33, 35, 61, 62
East Polynesia 27, 53
Eastern Solomons 13, 14; archaeology 32–33, **33,** 35; Austronesian settlement 22; carvings 20; cultural geography 23–24, 162; languages 18, 162, 165; Lapita peoples 14, 15, 23, 53, 64–85, **77,** 86, 119, 129, 164, 165; location of sources of exotic stones, Lapita sites **77**; map **13**; Polynesian movement into 53, 130, 162, 165; sculpture 20; water gap between Main Solomons 14, 23, 119, 163; *see also* names of individual island groups and islands, particularly Reef–Santa Cruz Group
Eastern Solomons, review of last 2000 years 119–30; exchange 122–24; sites and settlement patterns of late aceramic to historic period 120–22
Eastern Triangle culture area 108, 109, 110, 117–19, **118,** 130
Echymipera kalubu (bandicoot) 11
economic interactions: before arrival of Lapita peoples 103; Central Solomons 62, 64, 88, 102, 103, 109, 117–19; and climate change, end of Pleistocene 50–51; colonisation-mode exchange 87–88; commodities, including food 24, 117, 118; Eastern Triangle culture area 108,

109, 117–19, **118**, 130; European traders 132, 136, 137, 138–39, 166; exchange of women 24, 118, 153, 155; hunting–horticulture regime 43; kastom money units and ornaments 110; Lapita peoples 53, 64, 66, 75–77, 86–88, 103; long-distance movement of stone 50, 64, 66, 75–77, **77,** 86–87, 88, 103, 117, 118–19, 145, 146, 147, 164; model of connectivity, nearest-neighbour analysis 16, **17,** 20, 130; Northern Solomons 92, **92,** 93, 98, 131; red-feather money exchange system 24, 25, **122,** 123, **123,** 125, 130; Reef–Santa Cruz Group 24, 25, 76, 122–24, 128–29; regional economy 162; Roviana Lagoon 132; shell money 100–01, 103–04; Solomon Islands (generally) 13, 16, 18, 20, 130; turtleshell trade 22, 28, 57, 126, 138, 166; Western Solomons 88, 132, 135, 136–38, 166; woven cloth 24; *see also* headhunting complex and socio-political developments; shell valuables tradition
Elasmobranchii (sharks and rays) 39, 41
Emirau 59
Emo Dune site, Teanu, Vanikoro 65
Entrecasteaux, Antoine Bruni d' 120
environmental change: climate change, end of Pleistocene 50–51; Guadalcanal 62, 64; *see also* coastal environments; sea levels
Erromango 77
Espiritu Santo 65
European disease impacts 99, 100, 147, 166
European visitors and traders 22, 29, 104, 124, 129, 130, 132, 136, 137, 138–39, 166; Spanish visitors and settlements 21, 33, 61, 103, 106, 108, 110, 118, 120, 136

fauna *see* animals
Felgate, Matthew 34, 58, 59, 66, 67, 68, 69
Fergusson Island 76, 83
fern 141
Feru I cave, Santa Ana 30–31
Feru II cave, Santa Ana 30–31, 32, 61–62
Fiji 24, 27, 53, 65, 84, 86, 163
Firth, Raymond 129
fish, wharfs as pens 148
fishbone assemblages: Kilu Cave 39, 40–41; Lapita peoples 78, 80, 85; New Ireland 41; Taumako 125; Vatuluma Posovi (Poha) Cave 50
fishhooks: blanks 48, 52, 62, 102; compound 20, 22; Polynesian Outliers, Eastern Solomons 80, **81,** 83, 84, 85; shell 52, 62, 64, 80, 84, 85, 102, 129
fishing 17, 20, 23, 50, 60, 78, 83, 98, 109, 125; methods 41, 128
fishing shrines 147
Fissoa 58
flint knapping, long flakes 33
flora *see* plants
Florida Group 42, 62, 117
flying fox 109
Foana'ota, Lawrence 34, 157

forests: clearance and conversion to garden land 46, 60, 64, 88, 102, 126; logging **133,** 142; secondary 145; stocking 11; swidden systems 122, 132
Fox, Charles Elliott 33, 117
France 33
frigatebird motif 110, 118

Gafarium 50
Galipaud, Jean-Christophe 65
garden shrines 147, 148
gardening *see* horticulture
Gatokae 13
Gaua 76
genetic studies *see* DNA studies
Ghizo 13, 58, 131, 136, 166
Gibbs, Martin 32, 61, 106, 108
Gorbey, Ken 97
Graciosa Bay, Santa Cruz 33, 120, 121, **121,** 165
grasslands 50, 64, 100, **101,** 102, 103
Greater Bukida (Greater Bougainville) 12, 42, 43, 163
Green Islands 38, 163
Green, Roger 31, 32–33, 34, 47, 60, 61, 65–66, 67, 69, 72, 73–75, 76, 78, 83, 84, 87, 106, 108–09, 110, 117, 118
Grimes, Sarah 34, 45–46
Guadalcanal 12, 13; archaeology 31, 34, 35, 44, 46, 47–50, **48,** 62–64, 100, 103; coconut plantations 100, 117; early to mid-Holocene 14, 44, 46, 47–50, 102; geology and climate 100; grasslands 100, **101;** Guadalcanal sequence 101–03; Hamosa (Grasslands) Phase (2200–1500 cal BP), Guadalcanal 102, 103; headhunting 28, 138; Hoana (Forest) Phase (6400–2200 cal BP) 50, 62, 64, 102, 103; horticulture 64, 110, 117; increasing population mobility 64, 103; lagoons 46; languages 18, 20; Moru (Garden Regrowth Vegetation) Phase (1500–150 cal BP), Guadalcanal 102–03; plank-built canoes 22; Pleistocene period 42; population density 100, 110; schist 76; settlement patterns 102, 103, 105, 110
Gumi, Roviana Chief 138

Haberle, Simon 47, 102
Haliotis 125
Hamosa (Grasslands) Phase (2200–1500 cal BP), Guadalcanal 102, 103
Hangan ceramic style, Buka 55, **94,** 95, 97
Hangan village, Buka 95
Haradewi, Ulawa 103
Hareo 136
Hasiri, Rendova 152
hawks 39
hawksbill turtle 137
headhunting complex and socio-political developments: associated shrines 148; Central Solomons 103, 138; Choiseul 136, 137, 138, 166; development 166–67; Guadalcanal 28, 138; and language distribution 136, 162,

166; materialised power relationships and relationship to headhunting 139, **139**; New Georgia (Roviana) 22, 34, 57, 131, 138–39, 148, 151, 152, 161, 162, 166–67; Northern Solomons 98; population movements and displacement 136, 138, 161, 166; and ritual and shell valuables economy 22, 28, 161, 162; Santa Isabel 22, 136, 137, 138, 166; sculptural symbolism inspired by 20; source of material wealth and mana 139; and turtleshell trade 28, 57, 137–38, 166; Vella Lavella 35, 154, 157, 167; Western Solomons 22, 23, 28, 130, 131, 135, 136, 137, 138–39, 161, 162, 167

Hendren, Gil 31, 103, 106, 117
Heorake, Tony 34
Hoana (Forest) Phase (6400–2200 cal BP), Guadalcanal 50, 62, 64, 102
Hocart, Maurice 147
Hoghoi, New Georgia 64
Holdaway, S. 88
Holocene 38; archaeological record 35, 41, 42, 43–51, 164; development of domesticates in New Guinea highlands 43; expansion and adaptation, Solomon Islands 14, 31, 44, 45, 50–52; production systems 43; rising sea levels 42, 43, 44, 45, 46, 164; *see also* Lapita peoples
honeyeater (*Myzomela cardinalis*) 24, 123
Honiavasa Island 145, 151
hope *see* religious shrines; skull shrines
horticulture 167; Central Solomons 64, 104, 110, 117; Melanesia 43; New Georgia Group 46, 60, 64, 140, 145, 152; Northern Solomons 98, 100, 102; Reef–Santa Cruz Group 65, 78, 122, 125, 126, 128, 129; stoned-walled gardens 104, 117; swidden (slash-and-burn) systems 98, 104, 122, 126, 130, 132, 145, 156; Tamako 80; Western Solomons 132, 156
house mounds 31, 32
house platforms and terraces 29, 103, 141, 142, 145, 146, 148, 149, 151, 152, 160
houses: canoe (custom) houses 22–23, 103, 104, 106, **107**, 117, 118, 135, **135**, 138, 139, 146, 150, 157, 161; cult ('ghost') houses 121; family dwellings 120, 121; human remains in association with houses 121; men's houses 23, 96, 98, 117, 120–21, 135; Polynesian influences 128; Reef Island Lapita site 74; round houses 119, 120; stilt-houses 55, 56, 59–60, 88
hunter–gatherer populations 11, 14, 37–38, 39–40, 42, 164; *see also* Lapita peoples; subsistence practices
hunting–horticulture regime 43, 83, 126, 130
Huon Peninsula, Papua New Guinea 36–37, 42
Hura River, Roviana Lagoon 145

Ididubanara, Roviana chief 149, 151
Indonesia 23
Ingava, Roviana Chief **136**, 138, 146
inland 'bush' people and settlements 17, 100; Bismarck Archipelago 37; Bougainville 50, 92, 98; Buka 50; Central Solomon Islands 100, 101, 102, 103, 104; New Georgia 131, 141, 142, 145, 157, 161; Reef–Santa Cruz Islands 120; shift from coastal to interior settlements 98, 161; shift from interior to coastal settlements 131, 142, 145, 157, 161, 166; Shortland Islands 99; tension between coast and interior 103, 131, 161, 162, 166; *see also* coastal 'saltwater' people and settlements
intertidal ceramics sites 34, 54, 55, 56, 57, 58–59, 60, 64, 65, 86, 88, 94, 97, 140–41, 156, 164, 165
intertidal zones 54, 55, 56, 57, 58, 59, 60, 64, 65, 86, 88, 94, 97, 140–41, 152
Irigila village and region, Vella Lavella 58, 140, 155, 156–57
iron trade 137
irrigation 29, 90, 98, 102, 117, 122, 130, 145, 156, 162
Irwin, Geoff 30, 56, 88, 93, 97, 99
Isa, Henry 34

Kahula site, Taumako 125
Kalikoqu, New Georgia 142, **143**, 145, 147–48; distribution of archaeological features **147**
Kapingamarangi 27
Kaschko, Michael W. 108
kastom money units and ornaments 110
Katsuwonidae 125
Katsuwonis pelamis (bonito) *see* bonito (*Katsuwonis pelamis*)
Kawaio communities 104
Kawaio district, Malaita 62
Kazukuru language 136
Kazukuru region, New Georgia 144
Keesing, Roger 104
Kehehe site, Ndora 145, 151
Keio University archaeological surveys and excavations 29, 32
Keopo, John 34
Kia region 22, 35
Kieta region 30, 35; pottery 95, 97
Kiki Phase, Tikopia 125, 126, **128**
Kiki ware, Tikopia 82–83, 84, 85, 126
Kiko, Lawrence 34
Kilu Cave 38, **39**, 163; abandonment 42, 43; early to mid-Holocene record 38, 41, 42, 43–44; plan of excavation units **40**; Pleistocene record 30, **37**, 38–42; radiocarbon dates 41; stratigraphy of excavations **41**
Kirch, Patrick 65, 82–84, 126, 128–29
Kokorapa, New Georgia 147
Koloi tribe 149
Kolomateana site, Vonavona Lagoon 46, **140**
Kolombangara 13, 55, 56, 57, 58, 86, **87**, 131, 136, 145, 156, 166
Koqu Orovoro site, New Georgia 58
Koqu skull shrine complex, Vella Lavella **158**, 160
Kreslo 59
Krose, Sarah 35
Kundu ('Skull Island'), New Georgia 146
Kusaghe region, New Georgia 136, 145

Kusira, Santa Isabel 57
Kwaio communities, Malaita 104, 106

La Pérouse, Jean-François de Galaup, comte 33
Labridae (wrasses) 39, 41
lagoon systems 164, 165; Langalanga Lagoon, Malaita 62, 100–01, 103–04, **104**; New Georgia (Roviana) **45,** 45–46, **46,** 51, 57, 60, 64, 132, **133,** 166; Western Solomons **45,** 50–51, 132, 140; *see also* Roviana Lagoon and region, New Georgia
Lakao Island 78–82
Lakao period, Taumako 125
Lampert, Ron 29, 30
Langalanga Lagoon, Malaita 62, 100–01, 103–04, **104**
languages: Austronesian languages (AN) 17–18, **18,** 22, 23, 24, 34, 50, 53, 64, 78, 88, 89, 92, 98, 119, 130, 135, 136, 155, 164, 166; breakup of linguistic communities 18; DNA studies supporting pattern of relationships 18, 20; headhunting complex and language distribution 136, 162; linguistic diversity 14, 16, 90, 130, 162, 166, 167; mixed Austronesian/non-Austronesian languages (AN/NAN) 119; non-Austronesian languages (NAN) 17–18, 22, 24, 34–35, 130, 136, 155, 163, 166; Oceanic Austronesian languages 24, 88, 136; Pijin 162, 167; structure provided by linguistics 20; Tryon-Hackman Line 18, **18,** 20, 22; *see also* Northwest Solomonic languages; Polynesian language family; Southeast Solomonic languages; and under individual regions, island groups and islands
Lanlapana site, Bougainville 97
Lapérouse, Jean-François de Galaup, comte de Lapérouse 124
Lapita ceramics 29, 34, 68–73; Buka 29–30, 54–55, 58, 59, 86, 93–95, 141, 164; disappearance from the archaeological record 72, 90, 141; intertidal ceramics sites 34, 54, 55, 56, 57, 58–59, 60, 64, 65, 86, 88, 94, 97, 140–41, 156, 164, 165; Kiki Phase, Tikopia 82–83, 84, 85, 126; Polynesian Outliers, Eastern Solomons 79, 82–83, 84–85; Reef–Santa Cruz Group 54, **68,** 68–70, **69, 70, 71,** 72, 73–75, **74, 75,** 86, 119; Reef–Santa Cruz Group, end of ceramic tradition 72, 73, 76, 77, 120, 128; Roviana Lagoon region 140–41; Western Solomons 55–60, 94, 140, 141, 164, 165
Lapita ceramics, construction, style and form: paddle and anvil construction 54, 82, 84; plainware 64, 72–73, 74, 75, 76, 77, 82, 85, 88, 119–20, 124, 129, 145, 164; pot forms 54, 69, **74,** 74–75, **75,** 82, 85, 93, 120; pre-Buka style ('Lapita') 54, 55; simplified regional style 66, 77, 94–95, 141; slab-building 54, 82, 84; Sohano ceramic style, Buka 30, 55, 93–95, **94,** 97, 141
Lapita ceramics, decoration and tempers **59,** 119, 120; anthropomorphic and zoomorphic designs **68,** 69, **69,** 70; appliqué 55, 56, 57, 58, 59, 60, 77, 82, 93, 128; dentate stamping 53, 54, 55, 58–59, 60, 64, 69, 70, 72, 74, 75, 77, 79, 80–81, 82, 86, 93, 128, 164; face design 70, **70, 71,** 72; incised ceramics 54, 55, 56, 57, 58, 59, 60, 69, 70, 74, 75, 77, 93, 128; lack of decorated ceramics in Central Solomons 60, 64; motifs 66–67, 69–70, **70,** 110, 118; pinched decoration 58, 82; punctation 55, 56, 57, 58, 77, 97; relief 54, 55, 58; rim decoration 54, 56, 57, 58, 82, 93, 119; tempers 54, 55, 60, 68, 82, 93, 120, 165
Lapita peoples: archaeological record 14–15, 32, 35, 64–78, 86; ceramics evidence for changes in settlement patterns 55, 60; date of arrival in Solomon Islands 11, 14, 53; dispersal of early communities 14, 53; economic interactions 53, 64, 66, 75–77, 86–88, 103; horticulture 64, 65; interaction with non-Lapita groups 14, 55; 'Lapita without pots' (Halika Phase) 51–52; 'leapfrog' model for Solomons colonisation 54, 86–89, 164; and Melanesian cultural diversity 14; pan-Oceanic phenomenon 32, 53; regionalisation of stone tools 66, 67; sailing technologies 53, 77, 164, 165; spread of culture 20; stilt-house occupation 55, 57, 59–60, 88; submerged sites 65; *see also under* individual regions, islands and island groups
Lasigi 58
Lau Lagoon, Malaita 100–01, 103
Laukutu Swamp, Guadalcanal 64
Leach, Foss 78–82, 124–26
Lebang Takoroi site, Nissan Island 44
Lokiha, Santa Isabel 57
Lokuru region, Rendova 152
Lonahan village, Buka 95
Lou Island, Admiralty Islands 55, 76
Louisade Archipelago 76
Loy, Tom 41
Luangiua (Ontong Java) language 25, 27
Lueori 136

Main Reef Islands 24
Main Solomons 13, 14, 16; cultural geography 16–23, 28; early to mid-Holocene 44; geography 16–17, 163; languages 24; limits of Pleistocene settlement of Oceanic world 11; map **13;** plank-built canoes 21; water gap between Eastern Solomons 14, 23, 119, 163; *see also* names of individual regions, island groups and islands
Makira (San Cristobal) 12, **13,** 24, 101; archaeology 32, 33, **33,** 34, 60–61, 62, 101; compound fishhooks 20; Eastern Triangle culture area 108, 117, 118–19, 130; geology 101; languages 18; settlement 104, 105, 106, 110, 117
Malaita 12, **13,** 24, 28, 64, 164; archaeology 33, 34, 35, 50, 62, 100, 106, 108; chert 64, 66, 76, 82, 100, 102–03, 109, 117, 118, 122, 126, 164; Eastern Triangle culture area 108, 117, 118, **118;** geology 100; lagoons 46, 100–01, 103–04, **104;** languages 18, 20; population density 100, 110; settlement 100, 103–04, 105, 106
Malaohu or Maraufu tradition 106, **106**
Malasang, Buka 29, 38, 95
Malasang ceramic style, Buka 55, **94,** 95
Malasang Phase 30

mammals 11, 38, 39, 50
mana 139, 162, 166
Manetai rockshelter, Bougainville 99
Mangaasi ceramics tradition, Vanuatu 65, 76, 77, 85, 126, 128
mangrove species 50
Manning Strait 137, 166
Manus, introduced species 11
Maramasike 118
Mararing ceramic style, Buka 55, **94,** 95
Marau Sound, Guadalcanal 46, 117, 118, 119
Maravari village and region, Vella Lavella 35, 155, 156–60
marine resources 11, 78, 80, 100; *see also* fishbone assemblages; fishing; shellfish
Marovo Lagoon, New Georgia 57, 58, 132, 136, 140, 145, 162
marriage exchange 118
marsupials 11
Mase River, New Georgia 145
Matema 16
Matema dialect 25
Matenkupkum, New Ireland 40
Mateone village, Santa Cruz 120, 121
material culture 13, 29, 32, 64; Central Solomons 64, 103, 108, 109–10; Eastern Solomons 83–84, 119, 125, 128, 165; Nissan Island 51–52; Polynesian Outliers 25, 165; Western Solomons 14, 34, 35, 64, 135, 141, 142, 145, 147, 151, 152, 158, 161, 166, 167; *see also* shell ornaments; individual types and items, e.g. fishhook assemblages
Mbaeroko river basin, New Georgia 145
Mbilua langage 136, 155, 166
Mbulelavata, New Georgia 141
McKenzie, Anne 35
Mdailu, Santa Cruz 119, 120, 124
megapode bones 50, 78, 83, 126
Mela Swamp, Guadalcanal 62, 64
Melanesia: archaeology 32–33; cultural diversity 14; cultural history, relationship to Polynesia 32; early phase of colonisation 38, 42; Holocene harvesting of nuts and tree fruits 44; Lapita peoples and Austronesians 53; mana, central concept of power and status 139; Meso-Melanesian linkage 20; plant domestication 42, 126; Pleistocene fluctuations in sea levels affecting western Melanesia 36; regional traditions 77; shell valuables tradition 166; terminal Pleistocene changes 42, 43
Mendaña, Alvaro de 21, 33, 61, 110
men's houses 23, 96, 98, 117, 120–21, 135
Micronesia 25, 27, 28, 165
midden mounds 104, 108, 119, 120, 122
Miller, Daniel 34, 55–56, 58, 62, 104, 106
Mitra shell 25
molluscs 39, 50, 83, 102, 109, 125, 126
mon canoe style 21, **21,** 22, **132,** 135, 162, 167
Mono, Shortland Islands 97
Mopir, New Britain 43
Moru, Bougainville **96**

Moru (Garden Regrowth Vegetation) Phase (1500–150 cal BP), Guadalcanal 102–03
Moser, Johannes 33, 35, 61, 62
Munda, New Georgia **134,** 138, 144, 146, 149
Munda Tradition 141–46; Rendova and Tetepare 152–53, **153, 154**
Mundimundi ridge, Vella Lavella 157, **157**
Mussau 24, 25, 59, 76, 88
Mwanihuki 32
Mwaroqorafu site, Santa Ana 104, **105,** 106
Myzomela cardinalis (honeyeater) 24, 123

Na Mugha site, Makira 105, 118
Nafinuatogo, Santa Ana 106
Nagaoka, Takuya 34, 35
Naiavila site, Santa Cruz 120, 121, 122
Namu burial site, Taumako 125–26, **127**
Namu period, Taumako 125–26
Nanggu dialect 23
Nanggu site, Santa Cruz 32, 53, 65, 165; radiocarbon dates 67, 165
Nataghera, Santa Ana, canoe (custom) houses 106, **107**
National Museum and Cultural Centre, Honiara 34
National Site Survey Project 34, 55–56, 57, 61
Natügu dialect 23
Nautilus shell 125
Ndora 58, 145, 149
Near Oceania 28; archaeology 32–33, 44; dividing line from Remote Oceania 14; early to mid-Holocene 44; hunter–gatherers 14; Lapita settlement 53, 88; linguistic and cultural diversity 14; location of Solomon Islands in relation to 11, **12**; maps **12, 13**; natural resources 11; settlement 11; *see also* names of individual island groups and islands
needles, bone 128
Nendö *see* Santa Cruz (Nendö)
Nenumbo site, Reef Islands 65, **73,** 73–75, **74, 75**
Nerita spp. 39
New Britain 43, 44, 55, 76, 83
New Caledonia 27, 33, 53, 76, 83, 86, 88
New Georgia (Roviana) 12, 42; ancestor cults 34, 35, 139; archaeology 29, 34, **140,** 140–46, **144,** 151; canoe house **135**; ceramic-bearing archaeological sites **56,** 57; cosmology 139; cultural similarity to Santa Isabel 22, 131; dominant power in late prehistory 132; headhunting 22, 34, 57, 131, 138–39, 148, 151, 152, 161, 162, 166–67; Holocene period 14; lagoon systems **45,** 45–46, **46,** 51, 57, 60, 64, 132, **133,** 166; languages 136, 162, 166; logging **133,** 142; pottery **56,** 57, 58, 94; radiocarbon-based chronology for ceramic sequence 58; Roviana Chiefdom system 34, 131, 136–39, 142, 151–52; settlements 131, 132, 141, 145, 151–52, 161, 166; shell valuables economy 22, 139, 162; subsidence 45; trade 136, 138–39, 158; warfare 131, **134,** 138, 139, 148,

149, 154; *see also* Roviana Lagoon and region, New Georgia
New Georgia Archaeological Survey (NGAS) 34, 35, 57, 58, 136, 139, 140, 152
New Georgia Group 13, 88; archaeology 34, **57**; community of practice 162; compound fishhooks 20; European traders 137; formation 45, 131; languages 20, 136, 162; model of late Quaternary reef limestone **46**; plank-built canoes 22; pottery 34, 35, **56,** 57, 58, 164; sculpture 20; stilt-house tradition 60, 88; *see also* names of individual islands
New Guinea: archaeology 42; Australian Mandated Territory (AMT) 98; coastal population interactions 43; development of domesticates in highlands 43; early to mid-Holocene 43; exploration and colonisation of highlands 11, 14; Pleistocene 36, 38, 42; rainforest 132; terrestrial biodiversity 11, 38, 43; *see also* Papua New Guinea
New Hebrides, plank-built canoes 21
New Ireland 38, 163; archaeology 37, 39, 40, 43; canoes 17, 21; introduced species 11, 43; languages 20; Lapita peoples 60, 141, 164; pottery 58, 164
New Zealand 53, 88
Ngamanie site, Reef Islands 65
Ngatoponu site, Reef–Santa Cruz Islands 119–20
Nggela 18, 20, 22, 28, 34, 42, 62
Nginia language 50
Niatukubu shrine, Vella Lavella 158, **159,** 160
Nifiloli 16
Nifiloli dialect 25
Nissan 13, 38, 163; archaeology 44; Halika Phase 51–52; languages 18; Lapita sites 54–55, 58; plank-built canoes 21; pottery 95
Northern Solomons 12, 13; archaeology 29, 43–45; distribution of volcanic ash deposits **91**; early to mid-Holocene 43–45; headhunting 98; Holocene social networks 44; languages 17–18; Lapita sites 53–55, 86; map **13**; plank-built canoes 21; water gap between Bismarck Archipelago 163; *see also* names of individual island groups and islands
Northern Solomons, review of last 2000 years 90–100; ceramic record 93–98, **94, 96**; interaction spheres and production zones 92, **92,** 93; settlement patterns and subsistence systems 98–100
Northwest Solomonic languages 18, **18, 19,** 22, 135; Choiseul 20; and distribution of plank-built canoes 22; Nissan–Buka–North Bougainville 20; Santa Isabel–New Georgia Group 20; South Bougainville–Shortlands 20; West Bougainville (Piva–Banoni) 20
Növlaö rockshelter, Santa Cruz 73, 76, 119, 120, 121, 124
Nuatambu, Choiseul 34, 56
Nuguria 25
Nuiatoputapu Island 122
Nukapu 16
Nukapu dialect 25

Nukumanu 16, 25
Nukuoro 27
Numa Numa 95
Nupani 16
Nupani dialect 25
Nusa Roviana 138, 145; central fortification 148, **148,** 149, 154, 161, 166; distribution of archaeological features **146**; settlement 146–49, 152
nut-cracking anvils 44, 62, 102, 103
Nyamae village, Ranongga 140

obsidians and tools 43, 44, 52, 64; gravers 76; Lapita sites 55, 58, 60, 66, 79–80, 83, 119, 122, 126; New Zealand 88; Polynesian Outliers, Eastern Solomons 79–80, 83; proportion of obsidian to chert in Reef–Santa Cruz Lapita sites 66, 67; source of obsidian, Reef–Santa Cruz Lapita sites 66, 75–77, 86–87, 88; stemmed obsidian tools 44
Oceania *see* Pacific
Odikana (Nusa Roviana chief) 150–51, 153
Oliver, D. 96, 98
Ontong Java 16, 25, **26,** 27, 34, 88
oral history 12, 25–26, 27, 31, 62, 92, 98, 104, 129, 131, 139, 141, 149, 150, 151, 153, 161, 166, 167
ornaments: Reef–Santa Cruz Group 125, 126; selection from Su'ena site, Uki **113–16**; teeth 32, 110, 125, 128; *see also* shell ornaments
Outer Reef Islands 23–24, 28, 120, 165
ovens, earth and stone 44, 74, 78, 104, 105, 106, 119, 121, 144, 145–46, 149, 152, 153, 156, 157, 158, 160

Pacific: first one-way colonisation event 38; Lapita and Austronesians 53–54; Pleistocene colonisation 14, 36–38
Pacific almond *(Canarium)* species 17, 42, 43
Pacific plate 45, 100, 132
Palandraku Cave 44
Pamua, Makira 32, 33, **33,** 61, 106, 108
Panaivili location, Patmos, Ndora 58, 140–41
Panono 136
Papua New Guinea 12, 16, 36–37, 44, 60, 76, 165
Papuan language 24
Papuan settlers, Solomon Islands 167
Paramata, Alu Island 99–100
Patu te Malukete fortification, Ndora 149–51, **150,** 153
Paubake, Bougainville **96,** 97
Phalanger sp. 102; *orientalis* (cuscus or possum) 11, 38, 43, 44, 102, 109
phytoliths 78
Pidia, Kieta Peninsula 95
pigeons 39
pigs: bones 78, 80, 83, 102, 106, 109, 125, 126; ceremonial use 98, 100, 146; cooking 96; husbandry 128; purchase with red-feather money 123; teeth 78, 106, 128
Pijin 162, 167
Pileni Island 16

Pileni language *see* Vaeakau–Taumaki language (Pileni)

Pinipir 38, 163

plank-built canoes 17, 21, 22, 163; binabina style **21, 22**; distribution of styles **21,** 21–22; lisi style 21, **21,** 22; mon style 21, **21,** 22, **132,** 135, 162, 167; ora style 21, **21,** 22

plants: domestication 42, 43, 78, 126, 130; *see also* aboriculture; horticulture; and names of individual species, e.g. taro *(Colocasia esculenta* and *Cyrtosperma)*

platforms 35, 90; coral and coral-rubble 44, 103, 146, 148, 149, 150, 158; earthen 142; faced **143,** 144, **144,** 148, 153, **158**; living platforms and terraces 29, 44, 103, 141, 142, 145, 146, 148, 149, 151, 152, 160; Patu te Malukete 149, 150; Vella Lavella shrines 157, 158, **158, 159,** 160, 161

Pleistocene 13; archaeological record, Solomon Islands 13, 36–43, **37,** 163; fluctuations in sea levels affecting western Melanesia 36; Greater Bukida or Greater Bougainville 12, 42, 43, 163; Kilu Cave record 30, **37,** 38–42, **40, 41,** 43–44, 163; location of archaeological sites in Papua New Guinea–Solomon Islands region **37**; occupation of Solomon Islands 11, 38, 42; settlement of Oceania 11, 14, 36–38; terminal changes 42–43; *see also* Sahul; Sunda

Pliocene 45

Plio-Pleistocene volcanism 45

Podtanean paddle-impressed decoration 76

Poha Valley, Guadalcanal 35, 44, 101, 103; *see also* Vatuluma Posovi (Poha) Cave

political organisation 98

pollen record 46, **47,** 51, 60, 62, 64, 102, 103, 140, **140,** 141, **141**

Polynesian language family 23–24; Nuclear Polynesian subgroup 24, **25,** 27; phylogenetic relationships **25**; Proto-Northern-Outlier–East Polynesia subgroup 27; relationships showing standard model compared with Wilson model **27**; Samoic–Outliers languages 17, 25, **25,** 27, 165

Polynesian Outliers 15, 16, 23, 24, 165; archaeology 31–32, **33**; connections with Western Polynesia 25; cultural geography 24–27, 28; expansion into East Polynesia 27, 165; interactions with Main Solomons 25, 27; interactions with Micronesia 25, 27, 165; languages 24–25, **25,** 27, 165; Lapita sites, Eastern Solomons 78–85; location in the Solomon Islands **26**; settlement of eastern outliers 88; 'stay behind' model 24

population density 14, 42, 50, 64–65, 90, 98, 100, 101, 103, 110, 116, 120, 164, 167

population movements: Austronesian expansion 53–54, 89, 92; Central Solomons 103; chert evidence 50, 103; and climate changes, end of Pleistocene 50–51; and coconut plantations 100; and creation of coastal environment 45, 50; DNA study of population breakup and dispersal 18; and headhunting 136, 138, 161, 166; model of connectivity, nearest-neighbour analysis 16, **17,** 20, 130; Northern Solomons interaction 92, **92,** 97, 98, 163; Polynesian movement into Eastern Solomons 53, 130;

Remote Oceania, Holocene 45, 53, 60, 88; *see also* culture; economic interactions; social networks; stone, long-distance movement

Pororan 20

possum or cuscus *(Phalanger orientalis)* 11, 38, 43, 44, 102, 109

pottery 29, 35; European sherds, Pamua 33; historic record 164; Mangaasi ceramics tradition 65, 76, 77, 85, 126, 128; New Caledonia Puen tradition 76; new styles of decoration and form after 1500 AD 95; paddle-impressed decoration 76, 97; post-Lapita plainware 32, 34, 57, 58, 61, 76, 97, 103; similar post-Lapita transformation in widely dispersed areas 77; southern pottery sequence 30; *see also* Lapita ceramics; and under individual regions, island groups and islands

Poulsen, Jens 31–32

Proto-Oceanic breakup 20

Queensland 165

Quiros, Pedro Ferandez de 121, 125, 129

Qutu, Roviana chief 149

radiocarbon dates: chronology for New Georgia ceramic sequence 58; conventions for reporting ages 11; Feru II cave, Santa Ana 61–62; Guadalcanal 64; Lapita sites 53–55, 58, 65–68, 72–73, 80–82, 85, 119–20; Nanggu 67, 68; Polynesian Outliers, Eastern Solomons 80–82; Reef–Santa Cruz Group 65–68, 80–81, 82, 119–20; Santa Ana archaeological sites **61,** 61–62; Vatuluma Posovi (Poha) Cave 48, 50, 51, **51,** 62, 102; Vatuluma Tavuro Cave 51

rails 39

Ranongga 13, 57, 86, **87,** 136, 140

Rate site, Santa Ana 61–62

rats 38, 50, 78, 126; *Melomys spechti* 39; *Phalanger* 44; Polynesian rat *(Rattus exulans)* 39, 78, 83, 125; *Rattus praetor* 43, 78, 125; *Solomys spriggsarum* 39

red-feather money exchange system 24, 25, **122,** 123, **123,** 125, 130

Reef Islands 14, 23, 78, 120; archaeology 15, **72, 73,** 73–75, **74, 75,** 83, 120; canoes 17; exchange of women with Santa Cruz 24; languages 17, 28; Lapita peoples 14, 64, 124; map **23**; midden mounds 122; red-feather money exchange 24, 123

reef-edge gathering 11

Reef–Santa Cruz Group 14, 23; aboriculture 122, 128, 130; archaeology 32, **33,** 35, **65, 66, 72, 73,** 73–75, **74, 75,** 120; contact with Central Solomons 62, 64, 89, 123; distinctive history and culture of peoples 24, 28, 124; DNA study 24; economic and social interactions 24, 25, 76, 122–24, 128–29; exchange 122–24; first Lapita colonisation of Solomons, from Bismarck Archipelago 86–88; four-period sequence 119–20; historical periods and descriptions 120, 121, 126, 129; horticulture 65, 78, 122, 125, 126, 128, 129; languages 23–24, 28; Lapita settlement and sites 53,

55, 60, 62, 64–78, 119–20, 122, 124–25, 129, 164, 165; long-distance movement of stone 66, 67, 75–77, 86–87, 88, 119, 122, 126; map **23**; midden mounds 122; plot of radiocarbon dates from archaeological sites **66**; Polynesian influence 124–30, 165; possible colonisation of Taumako, Tikopia (Kiki Phase) and Anuta 82, 84, 88; post-Lapita developments 35, 119, 124; pottery 60, 62, 64, **68,** 68–70, **69, 70, 71,** 72, 73–75, **74, 75,** 76–77, 86, 119–20, 124, 126, 128; proportion of obsidian to chert in Lapita sites 66, 67; sites and settlement patterns, late aceramic to historic period 120–21; *see also* names of individual islands

Reeve, R. 57, 58

regionalisation 66, 67, 77, 130, 165; culture 14, 16, 90, 130, 162, 165, 166, 167; economic and social interaction 162; influence of headhunting 167; languages 14, 16, 90, 130, 162, 166, 167; localised histories 166–66; pottery 66, 77, 93, 94–95, 141

religious shrines 90, 121; adjacent basalt 'table' stones 144, 145, 151, 160; associated human bone 141, 152, 153; association with living platforms and terraces 141, 142, 145; Central Solomons 105, 106; New Georgia 141–42, **143, 144,** 144–45, 151, 152, 153; platforms 142, **143, 144, 144;** Simbo Island **91**

Remote Oceania: cultural diversity 14; dividing line from Near Oceania 14; eastern decline in biodiversity and abundance 11; genetic data 27; Holocene population movements 45, 53, 88; intertidal sites 65; languages 14, 20, 24, 164; Lapita settlement 14, 53–54, 60, 64, 164; location of earliest known archaeological sites **54**; location of Solomon Islands in relation to 11, **12;** maps **12, 13;** natural resources 11; pottery 32, 128; relationship of Outliers to patterns of interaction 27, 88; sailing craft and navigation 163; settlement 11, 27, 163, 167; *see also* names of individual island groups and islands

Rendova 13, 35, 42, 46, 131, 136, 141, 152–53, **153,** 161, 166

Rennell 16, 27, 88; archaeology 32, **32,** 101

Rennell language 25

reptiles 38, 39, 44, 50

rock art 62, **63**

rockshelters 14, 29, 42, 64, 95, 99, 102, 140, 163; Feru I and II caves, Santa Ana 30–31, 32, 44, 61–62; Növlaö rockshelter, Santa Cruz 73, 76, 119, 120, 121, 124; *see also* Vatuluma Posovi (Poha) Cave; Vatuluma Tavuro Cave

Roe, David 31, 34, 47, 48–50, 52, 62, **63,** 64, 100, 101–03, 105, 117

Rofe Hill, Santa Isabel 57

Roviana *see* New Georgia (Roviana)

Roviana Chiefdom system 34, 131, 136–39, 142, 154; development 151–52, 166

Roviana Lagoon and region, New Georgia 34, **45,** 45–46, 57, **57,** 132, 161–62, 166; archaeological sequence **140,** 140–46, **144,** 161; barrier islands 46, 58, 141, 144–45, 146, 149–51; decorated ceramic sequence 58–60, **59**; European trade centre 132, 136, 161; Lapita peoples 140–41; uplift and subsidence 86, 132; vegetation and sedimentary changes 60

Roviana language 136, 166

Roviana period, New Georgia 141–42, **144,** 145–46, 151–52

HMS *Royalist* 138, 147

Rukia, Alex 62

Russell Group 18

Russell, Tom 31, 47, 62

Sa'a, Malaita 108

Sahul 36; colonisation by humans 11, 36–37; map **12**

Saikile district, New Georgia 149, 150, **150,** 153

'saltwater' (coastal) people *see* coastal 'saltwater' people and settlements

Samoa 25, 27, 125, 165

Samoic-Outliers languages 17, 25, **25,** 27, 165

San Cristobal *see* Makira (San Cristobal)

Santa Ana (Owa Raha) 12, 13, 24; archaeology 30–31, 32, **33,** 60, **60, 61,** 61–62, 101; carvings 24; compound fishhooks 20; drift voyaging from Santa Cruz 62; Eastern Triangle culture area 108, 118; languages 18; pottery 31, 61–62, 165; settlement 104, **105,** 105–06, 117, 118

Santa Catalina 13, 104, 106, 108; compound fishhooks 20; languages 18

Santa Cruz (Nendö) 14, 23, 125; archaeology 15, 33; backstrap loom 25; canoes 17; carvings 24; contact with islands outside group 24; dance circles 121, **121;** drift voyaging to Santa Ana 62; exchange of women with Reef Islands 24; intertidal site 65; languages 17, 23, 24; Lapita peoples 14, 64; Lata 23; map **23**; plank-built canoes 21; red-feather money exchange 24, 123; *see also* Reef–Santa Cruz Group

Santa Isabel 12, 13, 100; archaeology 34, 35, **57,** 131; chert 146; compound fishhooks 20; cultural similarity to New Georgia 22, 131; headhunting 22, 136, 137, 138, 166; languages 18, 20, 28; major cultural and linguistic distinction 28; plank-built canoes 21, 22; pottery 35, 57; sculpture 20; settlement patterns 22, 131; subsidence 86; Western Solomons sphere of interaction 131, 136, 138

Savo 18, 64

Scaridae (parrotfish) 39, 41

Scombridae (mackerels and tunas) 39, 41

sculpture 20, 148

sea levels: decline resulting from hydrostatic adjustment 43; drop, towards glacial maximum 42; Pleistocene fluctuations affecting western Melanesia **36;** rising levels in Holocene 42, 43, 44, 45, 46, 164

seabirds 39

seafaring *see* canoe travel and transport

Serranidae (groupers and cods) 39, 41

sharks: armband motifs 118; cult and ceremonial rites 20; fishing 78

shell: adzes 25, 44, 58, 79, 83, 85, 119, 125, 126, 129, 148, 150; chisels or abraders 44, 55, 58, 83, 126; dating 53, 61, 62,

66, 67, 119–20; fishhooks, blanks and lures 50, 52, 62, 64, 80, 83, 84, 85, 102, 106, 129; Kilu Cave shell samples 38, 41; knives 52; money 100–01, 103–04; Nanggu 68; vegetable peelers 125, 129

shell ornaments, location: Buka 55; Guadalcanal 102, 103; Makira 106; Nuatambo Island 56; Reef–Santa Cruz Group 119, 124, 125, 126, **127,** 128, 129; Roviana 58, 135, **136,** 141, 146, 147, 148, 150, 151, 152; Taumako 79, 82; Tikopia 82; Uki Island 110, **114, 115, 116,** 118; Vatuluma Tavuro Cave 50; Western Solomons 29

shell ornaments, type 82, 103, **114,** 119; armbands 58, 62, 83, 102, 103, 106, 110, **115, 116,** 118, 119, 129, 146; bakiha 135, **136,** 146, 150, 161, 162, 167; bareke 151; bracelets 58, 83, 126; discs 29, 79, 102, 125, **127;** motifs from decorated shell armbands 110, **116,** 118; necklaces 110; rings 29, 50, 56, 58, 79, 129, 141, 146, 147, 148, 151, 152, 161; shell-inlay 20, 110; tavi 126, **127**

shell valuables tradition: Central Solomons 50, 62, 104, 105, 117, 118; Eastern Solomons 24, 83, 123; Melanesia 166; Western Solomons 22, 56, 135, 139, 141, 148, 150, 151, 152, 157, 160, 161, 162, 166–67

shellfish 40, 50, 78, 80, 82, 85, 125, 145; see also molluscs

Sheppard, Peter 32, 34–35, 45–46, 58, 59, 61, 62, 67, 68, 72, 82, 83, 86, 87, 88, 104, 136–62

Shortland Islands 13, 90, 131; archaeology 15, 29, 30, 99, **99;** compound fishhooks 20; interaction spheres 92, **92,** 97, 98; languages 20, 92; pottery 30, 35, 55, 56, 97, 98, 99; settlement pattern **99,** 99–100

shrines: association with shell valuables tradition 151, 152, 157, 158, 160, 166; historical references 121; New Georgia Group 138, 147–48, 149, 151, 152–53, 161; Tiola shrine 138, 148, **149;** see also religious shrines; skull shrines

Siakile 136
Sikaiana 16, 25, 88
Sikaiana language 25, 27
Sikeura Tamana Lado boulder, rock art **63**
Sikopo 57, 140
Silao Peninsula 95, 98
Simbo 13, 29, 56; headhunting 136, 139; shrines **91,** 146; trade network 136
Sinapupu Phase, Tikopia 126, 128, **128**
Sirebangara Cave 55
Sivu ceramic style 95, 97
Sivu rockshelter, Bougainville 95
Siwai, Bougainville 96, 98
skinks 39
skull shrines 121, **134,** 135, 139, 147, 148, 151, 161, 166; adjacent cooking hearths or ovens 145–46, 152, 158, 160; coral-rubble 145–46, **146;** dating **160,** 160–61; Roviana barrier islands 149–50, 151, 152; Tetepare 153, 161; Vella Lavella 157–58, **158, 159, 160,** 160–61, 166
Slot, The 12
snails, land 126

snakes 39
social networks: Bismarck Archipelago 44, 87; Eastern Triangle culture area 108, 109, 117–19, **118;** model of connectivity, nearest-neighbour analysis 16, **17,** 20, 130; Northern Solomons 92, **92,** 131; regional 162; relationships between homeland and colony 87–88
Sohano 29, **31,** 42, 54, 95; see also Kilu Cave
Sohano ceramic style, Buka 30, 55, 93–95, **94,** 97, 141
Solomon Islands: cultural and economic interaction 13, 16, 18, 20, 130; cultural diversity 14, 16, 90, 130, 162, 165, 166, 167; cultural geography 16–28, 161; geographic divisions used in the text **13;** major islands **12;** model of connectivity, nearest-neighbour analysis 16, **17,** 20, 130; modern nation state 167; overlapping culture areas **13;** Pleistocene settlement 11, 14, 38–42; Pre-Austronesian (Holocene) expansion and adaptation 14, 31, 44, 45, 50–52; stilt-house tradition 60; see also archaeology; Central Solomons; Eastern Solomons; languages; Lapita peoples; Main Solomons; Northern Solomons; Western Solomons
Solomon Islands National Museum 34, 48, 61, 62, 101, 125, 157, 165, 167
Southeast Asia 23, 25, 36, 43, 119, 132, 163; see also Wallace Line
Southeast Solomon Island Cultural History Project (SESP) 32–33, **33,** 34, 53, 60, 62, 64, 65, 78, 82, 84, 101, 106, 108, 117, 119, 122, 165
Southeast Solomonic languages 18, **18, 19,** 22; and distribution of plank-built canoes 22; Guadalcanal–Nggelic 20, 22; Makira–Malaitan 20, 22
Spanish visitors and settlements 21, 33, 61, 103, 106, 108, 110, 118, 120, 136
Specht, Jim 29, 30, 43, 44, 54, 55, 87, 88, 93, 94, 95, 97, 98
Spondylus shell 83, 102, 119, 126
Spriggs, Matthew 30, 43, 51, 54, 58, 59, 92, 93, 95, 99
St Matthias group see Mussau
Star Harbour Peninsula, Makira 60, 105–06, 108, 117, 118
stilt-house occupation 55, 56, 59–60, 88
stone and coral platforms and mounds 105–06, 108, 141, 144–45
stone, long-distance movement 50, 64, 66, 75–77, **77,** 86–87, 88, 103, 117, 118–19, 122, 126, 145, 146, 147, 164
stone tools: early to mid-Holocene 44, 47, 48, 50; exchanges 117, 118; Kilu Cave 41–42; Lapita peoples 55, 58, 64, 74, 76, 79, 83, 119; Nenumbo site 74; Palandraku Cave 44; Polynesian Outliers, Eastern Solomons 79, 83; Reef–Santa Cruz Group 125; regionalisation process 66, 67; Su'ena site, Uki 109–10, **110, 111–12;** terminal Pleistocene changes 43; Vatuluma Posovi (Poha) Cave 47, 48, 50, 62, 64, 102, 103; Vatuluma Tavuro Cave 50; see also chert and chert artefacts; obsidians and tools; and under adzes
subsidence 45, 56, 65, 86, 132, 140
subsistence practices: early to mid-Holocene forest hunting and gathering 44, 50, 102; early to mid-Holocene harvesting of nuts and tree fruits 44; foraging also

involving movement of species 43; Lapita peoples 77–78, 83; New Georgia 145; Northern Solomons, last 2000 years 98–99, 100; Pleistocene colonisation, adaptation and technology 11, 14, 39–42; Pleistocene forest hunting and gathering 39, 42; reorientation of systems and technologies, terminal Pleistocene 42–43, 164; Su'ena village, Uki 109; *see also* hunter–gatherer populations

Su'ena village, Uki 108–09, **109**, 122; material culture 109–10, **110, 111–16,** 117, 118; subsistence 109

Sunda 36, 37; map **12**

Swadling, P. 104, 105, 106

sweet potato 100, 145

swidden (slash-and-burn) systems 98, 104, 122, 126, 130, 132, 145, 156; forest 122, 132

swordfish 118

Taebangara (Nusa Roviana chief) 150–51

Tahua period, Taumako 126

Taiwan 53

Takasugi, Hiroaki 32

Takuu 16, 25, 27

Talasea, New Britain 43, 52, 55, 76

Talepakemalai, Mussau 59

Tamberamakoto site 46

Tanga 17, 58

taro (*Colocasia esculenta* and *Cyrtosperma*): cooking 78; cultivation 17, 98, 100, 104, 122, 128, 130, 145, 156, 162; Pleistocene harvesting and management 41–42

Taumako 16, 23, 24, 25, 32, 78–82, 88; four-phase sequence 124–26; location of archaeological sites **79**; *see also* Duff (Taumako) Group

Tavatava period, Taumako 124–25; fishhooks from Tavatava Phase sites **81,** 83; plan of Tavatava excavation **80**

tectonic processes 45, 86, **87,** 100, 132

Tedder, James 31, 47, 62

teeth: ornaments 32, 110, 125; perforated shark teeth 44; pig teeth 78, 106

Temotu Province 23, **23,** 103

Temotu subgroup of Oceanic Austronesian languages 24

Teop, North Bougainville 30, 35, 95, 98

Terebra shell 25, 150

Terebralia shell 44

Terrell, John 16, 20, 30, 90, 92, 93, 95, 96, 97, 98

Tetepare 35, 86, **87,** 131, 152, 153, **154,** 161, 166

Themeda grasslands 103

Thomas, Tim 34, 35, 152, 162

Three Sisters 119

Thunnidae 125

Thylogale browni (wallaby) 43

Tikopia 14, 16, 23, 125, 126; archaeology 32, 82–84, **83;** canoe voyages 24; exchange 122, 124; historic phase 24, 129; languages 25; and Micronesia 25; Polynesian genetic profile 27; pottery 65, 76, 77, 85, 126, 128; sequence 126, **128,** 128–29; settlement 88, 126

Tikopian language 25, 78

Tinakula 23, 24, 65, 92

Tiola, shrine dedicated to 138, 148, **149**

Tokelau 165

Tömoto Neo, Reef Islands 64, 120–21

Tongatapu Island 122

tools 44; *see also* adzes; stone tools; and under shell

Torau migration 98

Touo language 136, 152, 166

Toupalado, Vella Lavella **156,** 157

tree crops 17, 42, 43, 44, 98, 103, 130

Tridacna shell 29, 44, 59, 61, 79, 83, 106, 119, 125, 126, 129, 146, 150, 158

Trochus artefacts 48, 50, 62, 64, 68, 80, 83, 102, 106, 121, 125, 129, 150

Tryon-Hackman Line 18, **18,** 20, 22, 164, 165

Tuakamali Phase, Tikopia 128–29

Turbo spp. 39, 50, 119, 129; *T. marmoratus* 41, 80, 83, 85; *T. petholatus* 83, 85; *T. setosus* 109

turtles 78, 80, 83, 85, 125, 126, 128, 148; hawksbill turtle 137–38

turtleshell 22, 28, 57, 126, 138, 166

Tuvalu 27, 165

Ughele language 152

Uki 32, **33,** 60, 101, 105, **108,** 108–09, **109,** 117, 119, 122

Ulawa 12, 13, 100, 117, 118, 164; archaeology 32, **33,** 60, 62, 101; chert 64, 66, 76, 82, 83, 103, 109, 117, 118, 122, 126, 164; compound fishhooks 20; languages 18; plank-built canoe style 22; settlement 103, 106

Uromys endemic murids 50

Utupua 23, 24, 123, 124, 165

Vaeakau–Taumaki language (Pileni) 23–24, 25, 78, 79, 124

Vaghena 56

Vangunu 13, 136

Vanikoro 14, 23, 25, 65; archaeology 32, 33, **33,** 65; exchange 24, 25, 122, 123, 124; languages 24; pottery 65, 76, 77

Vanua Lava 76

Vanuatu 27, 82, 84, 88, 125, 126, 128; chalcedonies 83; Lapita peoples 53, 85, 86, 125; mammals 38; Mangaasi ceramics tradition 65, 76, 77, 85, 126, 128; and Micronesia 25; Vanuatu Island arc 14

varanids 39

Vatuluma Posovi (Poha) Cave 31, 47–48, **48, 51,** 52, 117, 165; Phase 1 (6000 to 4000 cal BP) 48, 50, 101–02; Phase 2 (3000 to 2900 cal BP) 102; Phase 3 (2700 cal BP) 102; Phase 4 (1300 to 1200 cal BP) 102; Phase 5 (700 cal BP to recent) 102; plan of excavations **49;** radiocarbon dates 48, 50, 51, **51,** 62, 164; rock art 62, **63;** stratigraphy of excavations **49**

Vatuluma Tavuro Cave **48,** 50, 51, 62, 117; radiocarbon dates 51

Vella Lavella 13, 22, 154–55; archaeology 29, 34–35, 140, **155,** 155–61, **156**; headhunting and related exchange 35, 154, 157, 167; Mbilua language 136, 155, 166; pottery 57, 58, 140, 156; rock art **63**; settlements 131, 155, 156–57; shrines 157–58, **158, 159, 160,** 160–61, 166; tectonic uplift 86, **87**; trade 136; warfare with Roviana 149, 154
vertebrates: introduced species 11, 43; terrestrial 38, 39, 50; *see also* mammals
violence and raiding associated with trade 137, 138–39, 161, 166, 167
Visale, Guadalcanal **48,** 101, 102, 117
Visale Roman Catholic Mission 103
Vitori 57
volcanic glass 122, 126, 128
volcanism: Bougainville 92, 95, 98–99; distribution of Northern Solomons volcanic ash deposits **91**; Mela Swamp ash deposition 62, 64; New Georgia Group 131, 132; Plio-Pleistocene 45; Reef–Santa Cruz Islands ash deposition 65; Savo Island eruption 64; sources of stone 76; Tinakula eruptions 65
Vonavona Lagoon, New Georgia 46, **140,** 146, 154, 166
Vuru Valley, Guadalcanal 103
Vurugare, New Georgia 147, 148

Waite, Deborah 20, 22
wallaby *(Thylogale browni)* 43
Wallace Line 11, **12**
Wallacea 36
Walter, Richard 34–35, 45–46, 57, 58, 59, 68, 86, 88, 108–09, 110, 136–62
Ward, G.K. 103, 106
warfare 100; New Georgia (Roviana) 131, **134,** 138, 139, 148, 149, 154; war canoes (tomoko) 22, **132,** 135, 138, 139, 150, 161
West Polynesia 24, 25, 28, 53, 167
Western Solomons 12, 13; archaeology 15, 34–35, 42, 45–46, **132,** 135; art styles 22; carvings 20; cultural and economic interactions 14, 130, 131, 135, 136–39, 166; cultural homogeneity 130, 135; differences from Central Solomons 22–23; early to mid-Holocene 45–46; European explorers, whalers and traders 130, 132, 136, 137, 138–39, 166; forests and logging 132, **133**; headhunting complex and socio-political developments 22, 23, 28, 130, 131, 135, 136, 137, 138–39, 161, 162, 167; Holocene uplift 86, **87**; lagoon systems **45,** 50–51, 132, 140; languages 18, 20, 130, 135–36, **137**; Lapita peoples 14, 15, 53–54, 55–60, 86, 94, 103, 140, 164; localised material culture complexes 14, 135; maps **13, 132**; plank-built canoes 21, **132,** 135; pottery 55–60, 94, 97, 128, 140, 141, 164, 165; prehistory distinct from neighbouring regions 13, 135, 166; sculpture 20; settlement 135; *see also* names of individual island groups and islands, particularly New Georgia Group and New Georgia (Roviana)
wharfs 90, 146, 147, 148, 152
Wickler, Stephen 29–30, 38, 39–40, 42, 44, 54–55, 59, 93–95
Woodford, Charles 21, 22
Woodlark Island 60, 141, 165
World War II 29, 147

yams 104, 117, 122, 130
Yen, Doug 32–33, 55, 82–84, 117, 120, 122, 126, 128–29

Zabaiburo shrine, Vella Lavella **159,** 160